madrid

1. Abby /Brittany
2. Callum
3. Elizabeth
4. Emily
5. Ashley S.
6. Nick
7. Andres
8. Ana
9. vassar - July 2nd
10. Ani ?
11. Ashley M. ?
12. Julia ?
13. charles

14. Emily/Abby/Jan
15. Lauren
16. Sean
17. John Blozuski
18. Sam
19. Becca
20. Clark
21. Connor
22. Kendall
23. charlie
24.

NATIONAL GEOGRAPHIC

TRAVELER

madrid

by Annie Bennett
photography by Tino Soriano

National Geographic
Washington, D.C.

CONTENTS

Pages 2–3: Nuestra Señora de la Almudena, Madrid's grandiose cathedral
Page 4: In front of La Fontanilla tavern, on Calle Cuchilleros

TRAVELING WITH EYES OPEN

Alert travelers go with a purpose and leave with a benefit. If you travel responsibly, you can help support wildlife conservation, historic preservation, and cultural enrichment in the places you visit. You can enrich your own travel experience as well.

To be a geo-savvy traveler:

- Recognize that your presence has an impact on the places you visit.

- Spend your time and money in ways that sustain local character. (Besides, it's more interesting that way.)

- Value the destination's natural and cultural heritage.

- Respect the local customs and traditions.

- Express appreciation to local people about things you find interesting and unique to the place: its nature and scenery, music and food, historic villages and buildings.

- Vote with your wallet: Support the people who support the place, patronizing businesses that make an effort to celebrate and protect what's special there. Seek out shops, local restaurants, inns, and tour operators who love their home—who love taking care of it and showing it off. Avoid businesses that detract from the character of the place.

- Enrich yourself, taking home memories and stories to tell, knowing that you have contributed to the preservation and enhancement of the destination.

That is the type of travel now called geotourism, defined as "tourism that sustains or enhances the geographical character of a place—its environment, culture, aesthetics, heritage, and the well-being of its residents." To learn more, visit National Geographic's Center for Sustainable Destinations at *www .nationalgeographic.com/travel/sustainable.*

madrid

ABOUT THE AUTHORS AND PHOTOGRAPHER

Annie Bennett writes about Spanish travel, food, and culture for UK national newspapers including *The Daily Telegraph, The Sunday Telegraph,* and *The Times,* and has won the Spain Travel Writer of the Year award for her articles. She has written the Blue Guides to Madrid and Barcelona, and *Art Shop Eat Barcelona.*

After studying Spanish and German in London, she lived in Madrid for ten years, working as a journalist and translator for Spanish magazines specializing in art, architecture, and design. She has translated books on the Prado museum and Spanish food and wine. Annie divides her time between her home on the Gower coast in South Wales and bases in Madrid and Barcelona.

Tino Soriano, born and raised in Barcelona, Spain, divides his work between photojournalism and travel photography. He has received a first prize from the World Press Photo Foundation as well as awards from UNESCO, Fujifilm, and Fotopres.

Since 1988 Tino has photographed in Spain (Catalonia, Andalucía, Galicia), France, Italy, Sicily, Portugal, Scotland, and South Africa on assignments for National Geographic. His work has appeared in *Geo, Merian, Der Spiegel, Paris Match, La Vanguardia,* and *El País* as well as many other major magazines around the world. He also provided photographs for *National Geographic Traveler: Sicily* and *National Geographic Traveler: Portugal.*

Tino likes to write, and he has published *El Futuro Existe,* a story about children living with cancer. He also regularly lectures and teaches workshops at the University of Barcelona.

Damien Simonis, a travel writer since 1992 and the author of more than 20 guidebooks, wrote the History & Culture chapter. He lives in Barcelona, Spain.

Xander Fraser, who wrote the Travelwise section, is a writer and editor based in Santander, Spain.

Charting Your Trip

Madrid is a great place to recover your zest for life. Most people will want to spend time in at least a couple of its outstanding museums, but even the best of cultural intentions are likely to go astray, as this is a city with very tempting distractions. Do your sightseeing in the mornings, then get into the local rhythm with a long lunch and a walk around one of the city's many fascinating neighborhoods.

However long you have to spend in Madrid, get your bearings as soon as you arrive by heading for the Puerta del Sol, the undisputed center of not just the city but the whole of Spain. It is impossible not to get caught up in the stream of people surging in and out of the metro, swirling around the lottery stalls, and jostling at the newspaper kiosks. Just follow the flow up to the Plaza Mayor and look around until you are wafted back a few centuries. Then drift down into the Austrias quarter, where medieval vestiges alternate with lively tapas bars, traditional restaurants, and quirky shops. Central Madrid is enjoyably walkable, main streets connecting plazas, small streets composing neighborhoods, and the metro is efficient. There are also many taxis.

On your first evening, it is not a bad idea to sign up for a tapas tour with a guide (see sidebar p. 23). As well as going to some of the best bars in town, you learn a lot about local life and of course try some tasty Spanish specialties, too (see p. 23).

NOT TO BE MISSED:

First Things First

Looking at a map, you might think you can visit the major museums in one day because they are so close together on the Paseo del Prado. But think again. If you want to do the big three–Prado, Thyssen-Bornemisza, and Reina Sofía–plus the new CaixaForum, you should allow two, or preferably three, days. Get to the Prado first thing in the morning and spend at least half a day there. Afterward, chill out in the Botanic Gardens alongside, or stroll around Retiro Park. The next day you could go to the Thyssen-Bornemisza

What to Take With You

With airlines charging dearly for any excess baggage, it's wise to pack light. One tactic: Bring a half-empty suitcase you can fill with souvenirs. As for what clothes to bring, casual is all right, but a few nice outfits for dinners out will be welcome—after all, Madrid is a European fashion capital.

Spain has a temperate climate. Warm days yield to cool nights. And it is usually dry, so you shouldn't bother with packing an umbrella—if rain threatens, buy a cheap one in Spain. Make sure to bring all the medicines you absolutely need; for nonemergencies, there are *farmacias* throughout the city.

Appliances will require a plug adapter, which costs less than $10. Spain, as the rest of Western Europe, uses 230-volt outlets, so you may also need a transformer ($15-$30).

Remember to bring your passport! In addition, make photocopies of it and other important documentation (such as health insurance) to carry with you. You can get euros from your bank before leaving, but most people see this as unnecessary—a simple debit card will do fine, and there are ATMs everywhere.

If you're in search of a book for the plane, Ernest Hemingway's *The Sun Also Rises* nicely captures the richness of Spanish life. Madrid has innumerable Internet cafés, and Wi-Fi is almost everywhere, so you might want to include your laptop, despite the added bulk.

museum in the morning, have lunch nearby in a tapas bar in the Plaza de Santa Ana, then visit CaixaForum or the Reina Sofía, which is open until 9 p.m.

Another morning should be spent in the splendid Palacio Real, taking in the opulent grandeur of royal life over the centuries. Have a look at Nuestra Señora de la Almudena next door, and enjoy the panoramic views to the Guadarrama mountains. Afterward, rest your feet while taking in the scene at a café in the elegant Plaza de Oriente before having a look at the treasures of the Encarnación or Descalzas Reales convents nearby.

Outskirts & Out-of-the-Way

If you are in Madrid on a Sunday morning, join the crowds at the Rastro flea market in the colorful Lavapiés neighborhood—but leave your valuables in the hotel—and observe the local custom of stopping off for snacks and drinks in tiny bars along the way. The area is also interesting on a normal weekday, as there are lots of antique stores and traditional shops, and you get an insight into how

The sculpture known as the Dama de Elche is a masterpiece of Iberian art.

Traveling Around

At the center of Spain, Madrid is the nucleus of highways and railroads. So there are several ways to explore the Spanish regions outside the capital. Taking the train is a great way to see the countryside. Discounts are available for seniors, children, and students. If you plan on riding more than a few trains, a Eurail pass is a great option (www.eurail.com). The AVE, Spain's high-speed train, zips across Spain at 186 mph (300 kmh). The Spanish rail system, Renfe, can be reached at www.renfe.es in Spanish or www.raileurope.com in English. A U. S. number for Rail Europe is 800/382-7245 and a Canadian one 800/361-7245.

Renting a car is easy and inexpensive. You do, however, need a driving permit (see p. 236). Buses are also available, and there are eight bus terminals around Madrid. The main one is the Estación Sur de Autobuses (tel 91 468 4200).

people live in downtown Madrid.

If you only have time for one trip out of town, choose between Toledo, where more than 1,000 years of history are compressed in the narrow streets of the hilltop town, and the monastery of El Escorial, with its magnificent architecture and art collections.

With more time to spend in the city, venture beyond the traditional tourist routes and experience how the Madrileños live. For a taste of slick Spanish style, hit the grid of streets that composes the Salamanca district. This is where to find smart boutiques, galleries, and restaurants, and the area is particularly interesting if you are into new Spanish cuisine or contemporary design. On the way, don't miss the Museo Arqueológico Nacional, one of the best museums in the country, with some extraordinary exhibits.

Uptown

Heading uptown, it is worth seeking out the Residencia de Estudiantes, founded a century ago. Federico García Lorca, Salvador Dalí, and Luis Buñuel were just a few of the students who spent time here. An exhibition is usually running. The Sorolla museum is fascinating, too, with works by the Valencian artist displayed in his palatial former home. You may be surprised how many of his paintings, depicting Mediterranean scenes, are familiar from greeting cards.

Safety Tips

The streets of downtown Madrid get pretty crowded, making the pickpockets' job very easy. Using a bit of common sense will reduce your chances of being targeted. Keep your money and valuables close to your body, and only carry what you need. Be particularly vigilant when you're riding public transport and in Internet cafés. Stashing your wallet in your back pocket is an invitation to thieves. Never put your purse down on the floor or sidewalk at a café or restaurant—always keep it on your lap, preferably with the strap looped over your arm if outdoors. It is safer to use the ATMs inside banks, rather than on the street, and try to avoid withdrawing cash at night, particularly if alone.

Madrileños exercise their dogs in Plaza de Santa Ana, the hub of the Literary Quarter.

Special Treats

If you are interested in finding out more about the art scene in Madrid, you might enjoy a walking tour with an expert, perhaps to lesser-known museums or around the trendiest galleries. Or if you are intrigued by Spanish wines after trying a few glasses from different regions over dinner, why not spend an evening at a tasting session? The experience might well inspire you to visit a couple of the vineyards found nearby the city.

For a surprisingly rewarding day out, take the train to Alcalá de Henares, where Cervantes was born. The many monuments include the 16th-century university and an authentic 17th-century theater. Or head for the beautiful town of Segovia, with its golden-stone buildings, Roman aqueduct, and a castle that inspired Walt Disney. Madrileños go to Segovia just to eat roast lamb or suckling pig at one of the renowned restaurants, and you might want to follow their example. ■

Tipping

Spaniards generally leave smaller tips than you would expect and often nothing at all—even though salaries are low. In a bar or café, small change is fine. In a restaurant, leave around €1 per person in an inexpensive place and up to 10 percent somewhere fancier. Tip cab drivers small change (not more than 50 cents) for short hops. For an airport trip, €2 is considered generous. Give bellboys and doormen €1, apart from five-star hotels, where a €5 note is more the norm.

History & Culture

Changing of the Royal Guard
at the Palacio Real
Left: The Cervantes monument
in Plaza de España

Madrid Today

Sitting at the geographical heart of Iberia, Madrid has been Spain's capital only since 1561, when Felipe II decided to situate the court in one place. Perhaps short on history compared with other capitals of Europe, Madrid makes up for it with a forward-looking dynamism and energy. Possibly the busiest nightlife capital on the continent, it is also a magnet for art lovers.

Madrileños relax, eat, drink, and gossip in the old Plaza Mayor.

You'll sense right away Madrid's modern verve, with its wide, bustling boulevards and fashionable shopping quarters. Contemporary high-rises mingle seamlessly with grand turn-of-the-19th-century edifices. Around the tight web of old town lanes unfolds a dynamic metropolis. Next to timeless taverns glitter the bright lights of the latest gourmet restaurants. Immaculately maintained old-time hotels vie for guests with 21st-century showpieces and boutique charmers. The whole city is suffused with a lively unstoppable quality. It would be difficult to get bored in Madrid.

Above all, Madrid is known for its legendary nightlife. Where else are you likely to encounter traffic jams at 5 a.m. on a Sunday? In summer, café terraces, whether along

the Paseo de la Castellana or across the city's main squares, fill to bursting throughout the long, hot evenings until well into the early hours. Everything and everyone seem to blur together in an effusive atmosphere of loudly chattering bonhomie. Madrileños, known as *gatos* (cats) for their urban savvy, parade from one tapas joint to another, from flamenco den to music venue, from historic vermouth bar to all-night club.

Madrid is a powerful art magnet. In its three leading museums, along with countless smaller ones, you'll discover a wealth of masterpieces. The Prado, which has been given a major overhaul, offers a concentration of Spanish masters that is second to none. Among them are such greats as Velázquez, El Greco, José de Ribera, Zurbarán, Murillo, and Goya, just to name a few. The Prado collections encompass thousands of precious works from the Middle Ages to the 19th century. The Thyssen-Bornemisza is a more broad-ranging and eclectic international collection stretching from medieval Italian art to late-20th-century icons such as David Hockney and Francis Bacon. The Museo Nacional Centro de Arte Reina Sofía (Museo Reina Sofía) concentrates on modern and contemporary art, with a heavy Spanish presence but also has works by prestigious international artists. Among the gems is Picasso's powerful antiwar painting "Guernica."

Art and precious artifacts as well can be seen in the stately baroque and Renaissance buildings that line the narrow lanes twisting off Plaza Mayor. The nearby Palacio Real (Royal Palace), filled with magnificent treasures, was long the residence of Spanish monarchs. Even today it remains an official home of the Bourbon dynasty, although it is rarely occupied now. A steady flow of visitors passes through its seemingly endless grand halls, guest rooms, and labyrinthine nooks and crannies.

The hectic pace in Madrid and the danger of over stimulation in its myriad museums may leave you gasping for air. Luckily, the city is blessed with plenty of green spaces and tranquil parks. Just behind the Prado stretches the Parque del Buen Retiro, a grand stretch of sculpted gardens, woods, and artificial lakes where you can paddle about in little rented boats. Also nearby is the splendid Real Jardín Botánico (Royal Botanic Garden), which is educational as well as relaxing.

The Good Times: Football, Festivals, & Bullfighting

Ask many Madrileños their religion, and you might almost expect them to reply football (soccer). The city's team, Real Madrid, one of the best in Europe, is the object of adoration of much of the city's population. (It is also one of the richest teams, which is how it can afford to pepper its ranks with multimillion-euro international stars.) Officially founded in 1902, the *merengues* ("meringues" because of the white stripe on their uniforms) lead the field in Spain, with 29 national championships under their belts since they won their first cup in 1932. In 1998, the world football federation, FIFA, declared Real Madrid to be the best team of all time.

Soccer Lingo

The white strip usually worn by the Real Madrid soccer team has given rise to the nickname *merengues* ("meringues"), applied to both the players and their supporters. Top players are called *galácticos*, owing both to their extraordinary talents and to the exorbitant amounts paid to bring them to the club.

Just as important as football and the fate of Real Madrid, and celebrated with just as much gusto, are Madrid's numerous traditional festivals. In summer especially, heat drives Madrileños into the streets for neighborhood celebrations, where eating, drinking, music, and dancing into the wee hours are the norm.

One of the greatest events is the Fiesta de la Comunidad de Madrid in May, which commemorates the Dos de Mayo uprising against the French in 1808 (see pp. 104–105). The bars in the Malasaña district, particularly around Plaza Dos de Mayo, are especially lively, and a host of cultural events is organized for the following week or two across central Madrid. Also in May, the Fiestas de San Isidro Labrador, the city's patron saint, not only mark the beginning of the month-long bullfighting festival at Plaza de Toros Monumental de Las Ventas (see p. 44) but also inaugurate another packed program of concerts and cultural events. After the Festimad outdoor rock concerts in May, the Gay Pride marches in June, and the packed concert and theater calendar of Veranos de la Villa ("Summers in Town," with performances at venues all over the city), comes the stifling month of August and its madcap local festivities. The Fiestas of San Lorenzo, San Cayetano, and La Virgen de la Paloma, the first two of which take place in Lavapiés, and the third in neighboring La Latina, are the catalyst for eating, drinking, and dancing in the streets until dawn. The remainder of the year's calendar is punctuated by all sorts of events, from the ARCO contemporary art expo and Flamenco Festival in February to spectacular Easter processions.

In Madrid one could be forgiven for surmising that the Catholic faith has long ceased to have a hold over anyone. A visit to the Iglesia de Jesús de Medinaceli, in Plaza de Jesús, on the first Friday of Lent will dispel such impressions. A place of

The splendid Plaza de Toros Monumental de Las Ventas is the best place to see a bullfight.

pilgrimage, it still attracts long snaking queues of the faithful. The quest is to kiss the feet of a wooden sculpture of Christ inside the church. After hearing Mass, pilgrims address three wishes to Jesus, who, tradition claims, will grant one.

The other place you'll find fervent crowds of Madrileños is at the bullfighting ring. Reviled by many foreigners and not a few Spaniards, the bullfight is nonetheless a dramatic expression of a certain theatrical Spanishness. Its pomp and ceremony, *sol y sombra* (sun and shade), the deep sense of drama, tragedy, and fatalism, are all evocative of the *furia española,* the legendary fury of the Spanish troops that once made Spain's enemies tremble.

A City in Ferment

Long the political capital of Spain, Madrid has more recently dethroned Barcelona as the country's prime economic and financial center. Most multinational

In summer especially, heat drives Madrileños into the streets for traditional neighborhood celebrations, where eating, drinking, music, and dancing into the wee hours are the norm.

companies based in Spain have their headquarters in Madrid. Some studies suggest that as much as three-quarters of all international investment in Spain goes into Madrid. At €24,000 ($28,000), Madrileños enjoy the highest average wages in the country.

With a population of nearly 3.2 million, the city seethes with seemingly limitless energy, building new metro lines at breakneck speed. Construction carries on at such a cracking pace that critics warn of a lack of considered planning. The city seems to be ringed by thick flocks of cranes as up to 12 residential suburbs destined to house nearly a million people are created from scratch. The expansion is set to

Plaza Mayor, once the site of executions, has been a hub since its construction in the 17th century.

continue until at least the 2020s, although potential building land within the city limits is rapidly being used up.

The new housing may well be needed. Long a country of emigrants, Spain has become a beacon for vast waves of hopeful immigrants, legal and otherwise. Curiously, official predictions of the city's population growth are fairly modest (3.3 million by 2016), but between 2000 and 2005 more than 350,000 legal immigrants settled in Madrid alone. The number of additional clandestine migrants can only be guessed at. As late as the mid-1990s, visitors from more multicultural cities would often remark that everyone "looks the same" in Madrid. The growing presence of

Moroccan, African, Asian, and South American communities has changed all that forever.

Paradoxes abound. While state-of-the-art apartment blocks are being raised at the extreme edges of the city and many fine old apartment buildings in central Madrid have been lovingly restored, plenty of others remain as reminders of darker times. In some of the traditionally poorer quarters of central Madrid, such as colorful Lavapiés, long-term elderly residents with limited resources live alongside equally hard-pressed newcomers in poky, century-old slum apartments without the comforts of gas, hot running water, or private baths.

While some architects and urban planners criticize the speed and greed of the city's growth, few carp at the city's transportation policy. Since the mid-1990s, the metro system has been expanded and modernized to such an extent that by 2012 it will consist of 143 miles (230 km) of what the town council claims will be the most modern metro in the world. While that is probably a trifle exaggerated, there is no doubting the system is slick. The Barajas airport, too, has entered the 21st century with an inspiring new terminal building designed by Sir Richard Rogers.

With a population of 3.2 million, the city seethes with seemingly limitless energy, building new metro lines at breakneck speed. Construction carries on at . . . a cracking pace.

The building frenzy has touched the heart of the city as well. All three major galleries of the so-called Museum Mile have undergone major transformations. Senior Spanish architect Rafael Moneo (b. 1937) is behind the expansion of the Museo del Prado, by far the most complex and controversial project of the three. Aside from running way over budget and way past deadline, it involved the destruction of what remained of the one-time cloister of the Iglesia de San Jerónimo Real. Jean Nouvel's extension of the Mueso Reina Sofía, opened in 2005, startles observers with its gleaming bright red roof. Meanwhile, at the Museo Thyssen-Bornemisza, two adjacent buildings were acquired and transformed in 2004 to house the eclectic new collection of Carmen Thyssen-Bornemisza (b. 1943).

Top Ten Local Phrases

¿Hola, qué tal?	Hi, how's it going?
Bien, gracias	Fine, thanks
¿Cómo se llama usted/te llamas?	What is your name?
Lo siento, no hablo español	I'm sorry, I don't speak Spanish
¿Habla inglés?	Do you speak English?
Me pone un café/cerveza, por favor	Could I get a coffee/beer, please
Me encanta este plato/ restaurante/sitio	I love this dish/ restaurant/place
Está riquisimo	It's really delicious
¿Cuánto es?	How much is it?
¿Dónde están los servicios?	Where are the rest rooms?

Politics In Madrid

Given all that Madrid can boast about its modernized metro system, it seems extraordinary that there was such a delay in extending the metro line to T4, the futuristic international air terminal at Barajas, designed by Sir Richard Rogers. The Ayuntamiento (city council) and the regional government of the Comunidad de Madrid (the region of which Madrid is capital) wrangled for more than a year before coming to a financial agreement.

Perhaps there is more to this than meets the eye. Esperanza Aguirre (b. 1952), president of the Comunidad de Madrid region since late 2003 and an intimate of the most right-wing forces in the conservative Partido Popular (PP), has never been on good terms with the more moderate (and vastly more popular) mayor, Alberto Ruiz-Gallardón (b. 1958), despite belonging to the same party. The terminal opened to great fanfare in February 2006, winning many awards for its light-filled spaces, undulating bamboo ceilings, and use of natural materials. Just ten months later, however, it was in the news again when a bomb exploded in one of its parking lots, killing two people and causing widespread and expensive damage. The Basque Country's ETA terror group claimed responsibility.

> The average gato has ... an irrepressible desire to enjoy today without worrying overly about tomorrow. That live-for-the-present joie de vivre keeps the restaurants, bars, and clubs filled to bursting.

Local politics is overshadowed by the antics of Spain's national politicians. Long used to assassinations and terrorism from Basque terrorists, Madrid received a brutal introduction to extremist Islamic terrorism when, on the morning of March 11, 2004, bombs were detonated on four commuter trains, killing 190 people and injuring more than 1,800. Carried out three days before national elections, it was the biggest such attack in Spanish history. The outgoing prime minister, José María Aznar (b. 1953) (PP), had, against the will of the majority of Spaniards (judging by demonstrations and polls), supported U.S. President Bush's invasion of Iraq. As a result, Spain sent army units in as part of the coalition occupation force in 2003. The PP's challengers, the left-wing Partido Socialista Obrero Español (PSOE), under José Luis Rodríguez Zapatero (b. 1960), had vowed to pull Spanish troops out of Iraq if elected. The PP's attempts to attribute the bombings to ETA terrorists unleashed the fury of many citizens, whose antiwar demonstrations turned into anti-PP marches. Zapatero won the poll on March 14, 2004, and immediately withdrew the Spanish contingent from Iraq. U.S.-Spain relations have yet to recover fully. Zapatero has been ambitious in several fields, one of the most controversial being the decision to legalize gay marriages in 2005. In March 2008, his party once again won the general election.

As seriously as Madrileños take their politics, in the opinion of most city-dwellers, life is too short to get too worked up about the nation's politicians. The average gato has a healthy disregard for the country's political class, an irrepressible desire to enjoy today without worrying overly about tomorrow, and an innate conviviality. That live-for-the present joie de vivre keeps the restaurants, bars, and clubs filled to bursting. So sidle up to a bar, squeeze in, shout your order for a couple of tapas and a caña (small glass of cold beer), and allow yourself to be swept up in the rush of a truly 24-hour city. ∎

Tibaldi's ceiling frescoes crown the beautiful Royal Library of the monastery at El Escorial.

Food & Drink

Madrid's diners are a fortunate lot. Smack in the heart of a sun-scorched region and lacking an enormous variety of local food products, Madrid does not at first glance look like a promising place for a gourmet parade. Don't worry. Madrid has for centuries acted as a magnet for internal migrants from all over Spain, and they have brought their cuisines with them.

It is still traditional to buy bread daily at bakeries where the loaves are made in the back.

Nowhere else in Spain can you so easily sample the whole range of Spain's cuisines, from simple Castilian soups and game dishes to the refined surf-and-turf meals of Catalunya. Disciples of Catalan super-chef Ferran Adrià and his Basque counterpart Juan Mari Arzak have long since created niches for themselves in the city. They bring to Madrid's foodies the most inventive of what has been dubbed *nueva cocina española* (Spanish new cuisine).

Madrid's own culinary tradition is meager and largely assimilated into that of Castile. A standard Castilian first course is *sopa a la castel-lana*, a thin broth with an egg. Meat was long

a luxury for most and so *callos* (tripe) became a favorite. Perhaps the best known of the city's dishes is *cocido madrileño*, a kind of hot pot into which just about anything at hand is thrown in.

Castilian dishes revolve around meat. A favorite is *cochinillo*, spit-roasted suckling pig, a speciality in Segovia and some taverns in Chinchón. Game dishes and partridge are also common. Farther west, Extremadura is known above all for its top-class *jamón de bellota*, cured ham from free-range pigs fed on acorns.

From the northwest coast of Galicia comes an amazing variety of seafood. Long among the country's poorer regions, Galicia exported two items: seafood and its inhabitants, many of whom wound up in Madrid and opened restaurants. *Pulpo a la gallega* is boiled octopus chopped into bite-size, melt-in-the-mouth pieces and served in olive oil with sliced potatoes and paprika. A delicacy, because of their rarity, are the twisted, gnarled *percebes* (goose barnacles). Indeed, Madrileños have a special weakness for *pescados* (fish) and *mariscos* (shellfish). Despite being an inland city, its inhabitants are some of the greatest consumers of seafood in all of Europe.

The mountain territories of Asturias, Aragón, and Catalunya have brought steaming stews to the winter table—dishes such as Asturian *fabada* (pork and beans) or Catalan (from Catalunya) *escudella* (a more general meat, sausage, and vegetable stew). Catalan cuisine is considered, along with the Basque, the best in the country. It uses seafood and meat, a rich palette of fresh products, and sauces. If anything, Basque cuisine is more refined still. From Catalunya and the coastal region of Valencia comes a series of mouth-watering rice and noodle dishes, from the world-renowned *paella* (a rice, saffron, and seafood stew) to the less well-known Catalan *fideuà*, basically a noodle version (without saffron) of *paella*.

Tapas, small saucers with bite-size snacks, originate in the southern region of Andalucía. In most traditional Madrid bars you will be offered a simple *tapa* of at least a few olives with your glass of wine or *caña*. More elaborate tapas will generally cost you a few euros apiece. Bigger servings are called *raciones*. Popular tapas include *boquerones* (white anchovies, best served in *vinagre*, vinegar) or *pincho moruno* (skewered pork). The Basque versions, elegant canapés on slices of baguette, are known as *pintxos* and best sampled with the Basque white wine, Txacoli, or alcoholic cider from Asturias.

Among the best wine-producing regions are Rioja (especially reds) in the north of Spain, the Penedès area outside Barcelona (whites and *cava*, which is champagne-style bubbly), Galician Albariño (whites), and Ribera del Duero (reds), the vineyards spread out along the Río Duero. Excellent wines are now being produced in the Madrid region as well. Valdepeñas, in southern Castilla-La Mancha, was long the national supplier of cheap table wine, but its vintners have made huge strides in producing higher quality tipples recently. From Andalucía comes *jerez* (sherry), a fortified wine ranging from bone dry to sickly sweet.

EXPERIENCE: Take a Tapas Tour

Venturing into a tapas bar in Madrid for the first time can be a daunting experience. There are rows of mouthwatering dishes on the bar, but what are they? And how do you go about ordering something? Even if you speak some Spanish, how do you attract the waiter's attention, and make yourself understood in the din? How do you get the check? All these questions and a lot more are answered during a tapas tour around the old town with **Adventurous Appetites** (tel 63 933 1073, www.adventurousappe tites.com). You join a small group and pay an initial fee for the tour, which covers tapas and drinks in the first bar, then pay for whatever you order after that.

You might start out in a traditional bar specializing in the food of Asturias in northern Spain, and try Cabrales blue cheese and chorizo sausages cooked in cider. At the next stop, you could try a red wine from Ribera del Duero, accompanied by wild mushrooms and, for the brave, the Madrid specialty of tripe in a paprika sauce. After that, it is on to a seafood bar for shrimp sizzling in olive oil, accompanied by a crisp white wine from the Rueda region. By the end, you are all set to embark on your own tapas crawl the next evening—and will have learned a lot about Madrid's history along the way, too.

History of Madrid

Imagine the surprise (and glee) of the ruling families of Madrid when, in 1561, King Felipe II of Spain, master of an empire stretching from the Andes to the Netherlands, chose this insignificant, grubby plains town to establish the Spanish monarchy's first permanent capital. Madrid's chroniclers soon began a little rewriting of history to buff up the town's image.

From Roman Villas to Muslim Frontier Fort

Even when Madrid was founded, glorifying the present was difficult, as the provincial backwater was no Rome, London, or Paris. Giving a sheen to the past was easier, even if the scholarship was dubious. The fact that the Muslims established Madrid was quietly ignored. Then a suitably noble story was concocted about Madrid having started life as the Roman town of Mantua.

Evidence for the existence of such a settlement is noticeable by its complete absence, but the old adage about not letting the facts get in the way of a good story prevailed. Excavations have revealed that the Río Manzanares, nowadays little more than a dribble as it passes around the west and south of central Madrid, attracted a sparse and probably nomadic rural population as long ago as Neolithic times.

Even when Madrid was founded, glorifying the present was difficult, as the provincial backwater was no Rome .... Giving a sheen to the past was easier, even if the scholarship was dubious.

Under the Romans (who first invaded Spain during the Punic Wars in 218 B.C.), farming families lived in villas scattered about the countryside. Nothing, however, sustains the fond idea that the Romans built a town here.

In the fifth century A.D. the Roman Empire wobbled and the Visigoths invaded from France, but things down on the Roman farms around the Manzanares barely changed. The Visigoths were few in number and the Hispano-Roman population they came to rule remained largely in control of their own administrative and financial affairs, serving the Visigoths much as they had done Rome.

It was a rather different story when a zealous Muslim force under Tariq Ibn Zayid (?–720) landed on the south coast of Spain near what is today the town of Algeciras in 711. In less than a century since the death of the prophet Muhammad in Arabia in 632, Muslim Arab legions had moved across North Africa. In Spain, Tariq and his motivated men, mostly Berbers under the command of a handful of Arabs, found the Visigoth kingdom divided and weak. They swept across the peninsula and into Frankish territory (modern France) to Poitiers, where Christian forces finally repulsed them in 732.

By the ninth century, the Muslims had been pushed back to a natural defensive line that followed the course of the Río Duero and Río Ebro from the Atlantic coast of Portugal across to the Mediterranean just south of Barcelona.

Although in its early centuries Al-Andalus, as Muslim Spain was known, was largely

Before Madrid became the capital in 1561, the city of Toledo (right) was home to the Spanish court.

united and ruled from Córdoba, infighting was not uncommon, especially close to the front lines. Such internecine squabbling encouraged incursions by Christian forces from the north. To better ward off such attacks, the Muslims established a series of forts, of which Magerit (or Mayrit) was one, across the unstable frontier territory known as the Middle March, whose capital was Toledo.

The fort (al-qasr in Arabic, from which derives the Spanish word for palace or fortress, alcázar) was founded in 854 by Muhammad I, Emir of Córdoba (r. 852–886), on the site of the present Palacio Real. It occupied a strategic rise that dominated key routes south to Toledo over the Sierra de Guadarrama (Guadarrama Mountains).

Ferdinand and Isabella see Christopher Columbus off in 1492, in an illustration by Victor A. Searles.

The fortress was the forerunner of the Alcázar that for centuries would host the kings of Spain when their traveling courts stayed in Madrid.

The Caliphate of Córdoba collapsed into a series of bickering kingdoms, the *taifas*, in 1031. Magerit fell into the orbit of the Toledo *taifa*, but the latter's rulers clearly felt exposed and abandoned the city (and Magerit) to Castile's King Alfonso VI (r. 1065–1109) about 1085.

From Provincial Backwater to Imperial Capital

Throughout the centuries of the Reconquista (the "Reconquest" by Christian armies of Spain from the Muslims), the conquering kings of Castile, León, Navarra, and Aragón had a policy of repopulating newly won territories, and so Christian newcomers quickly arrived in the fort town of Magerit.

A handful of these new families (the Vargas and Luzón clans in particular) soon had a stranglehold on municipal power. Madrid, as the town came to be mispronounced, had now lost all strategic significance and early on was largely neglected by its roaming Christian monarchs, who preferred to set up their mobile court in more important cities.

The newly Christianized town lived a moment of anxiety when a raiding Muslim army drew up before the fortress walls in 1109 and unsuccessfully besieged the town, in what has been known ever since as the Campo del Moro (Field of the Moor).

Madrid, like other medieval Christian towns in Spain, developed a feudal system of government, known in this instance as the Comunidad de Villa y Tierra. In simple terms, the peasants of the *tierra* (land) slaved away to supply the *villa* (own).

Increasingly towns were governed according to charters granted by the king. Madrid received its charter, or *fuero*, in 1202. Until then it had been considered a subsidiary of Toledo. The fuero put the town under the more direct control of the king, allowing the latter to intervene (theoretically at least) to curb abuses of power by local barons.

The 14th century brought catastrophe to Madrid and the rest of the country in the form of the plague. The most infamous wave came in 1348, during the epidemic of Black Death that swept across Europe. Chronicles also recount that, in the following century, the city was brought low by terrible years of drought in the 1430s.

The unification of Christian Spain under the Reyes Católicos (Catholic Monarchs), Ferdinand and Isabella (r. 1479–1516), beginning in 1474, finally brought stability to Madrid. The rulers completed the Reconquista with the defeat of Granada in 1492. That same year, Christopher Columbus set off on a voyage that would change the course of history. The lands he discovered in the Caribbean and also in South America would in the following decades be opened up by Spanish freebooters whose caravels were soon plying the Atlantic back to Spain laden with gold, silver, and all manner of exotic foods (from potatoes to tomatoes to cocoa).

By 1550, when the heir of the Catholic Monarchs, King Carlos I (r. 1516–1556), came for a stay in the Alcázar of Madrid, it is estimated the city had a population of 12,000 to 15,000. The warrior king had also inherited the Habsburg throne in Austria in 1519. Thereafter he became better known as Carlos V, Holy Roman Emperor (and indeed he barely spoke Spanish), ruling over an empire that stretched from Austria to America. Spain was at the height of its power, although Carlos's interminable wars with France, rebel Dutch provinces, and Turkey were exhausting the Spanish treasury despite the flow of American gold.

> **Carlos's son Felipe II soon decided that it was inappropriate for the king of Spain to have an itinerant court. The question was, which city would he choose to make his permanent capital?**

Carlos's son Felipe II (r. 1556–1598) soon decided that it was inappropriate for the king of Spain to have an itinerant court. The question was, which city would he choose to make his permanent capital? Valladolid, Toledo, Segovia—all were cities with cachet.

Why Felipe finally selected Madrid, a middle-ranking town, in 1561 has been the subject of much speculation. Some reasons seem clear. Toledo was at first glance the most obvious candidate, but, as the seat of the Catholic Church in Spain, it represented a rival power base. Noble families had vested interests in many other cities. Madrid, insignificant as it was, presented no such potential threats, and Felipe probably still recalled the 1520 revolt of many nobles and cities against his father.

Much as it surprised nearly everyone (and somewhat frightened the town's masters, who could foresee short-term supply problems when the court and its entourage descended upon the ill-prepared town), the choice clearly made sense to Felipe II and his successors. Only his son, Felipe III (r. 1598–1621), would tire of Madrid sufficiently to move the court to Valladolid in 1601, a move that lasted a mere five years.

Felipe II inherited the Spanish half of the imperial possessions, including the rebellious Dutch provinces, the American colonies, and considerable territories in Italy. In 1581 Felipe II became king of Portugal, too. At the same time, although it was not evident to many, Spain was slowly dropping from its apogee. The failure of the Spanish Armada to subdue England in 1588, the constant waring in the Protestant Dutch provinces, and revolts from largely Muslim territories in the south all sapped the country's strength.

Capital of the Austrias

Bad as the news often was from far afield, in Madrid the impending decline in Spanish power could not yet be felt. Felipe II built his imposing monastery-palace complex at San Lorenzo de El Escorial, just outside the city. The court attracted nobles, courtesans, artists, and writers from all corners of the country. The Siglo de Oro (Golden Century or Golden Age) (ca 1492–1681) of Spanish painting and letters blossomed. American precious metals continued to pour into the royal coffers.

Although Felipe II was too distracted by his wars and progress on San Lorenzo de El Escorial to lavish much attention on the expansion and embellishment of his capital, Madrid seethed with activity. Even today the core of the city is known as Los Austrias, synonymous with the grandeur of Spain under the descendants of the Habsburg emperor Carlos V. In reality, most of the city did not look the imperial part, retaining rather the air of a small town. But when Felipe II died in 1598, the population had rocketed to about 60,000. By the 1650s it had risen to 150,000.

If Felipe II had been something of an austere control freak, his successors clearly were not cut from the same cloth. Felipe III and Felipe IV both preferred to hand over the daily grind of rule to advisers such as Count-Duke Olivares.

While Olivares attempted to introduce measures to shore up a weakening internal economy (the Castilian countryside in particular had been allowed to decline), the city experienced a building boom. The Palacio del Buen Retiro was completed in 1630 and became the preferred royal residence (the Casón del Buen Retiro and adjoining buildings are all that remain today). Churches and convents were raised and noble mansions built.

The growth of the city went virtually uncontrolled. By the mid-17th century it extended from Campo del Moro in the west to the Paseo de los Recoletos in the east, and from the present-day Ronda de Toledo in the south to Calle de Sagasta in the north. The only planned space was Plaza Mayor, home to the city's main markets. Its size and good order made it ideal for bullfighting and autos-da-fé, acts of the Inquisition.

Since Madrid's designation as capital in 1561, people had flocked to the city from all over the country in search of opportunities. Tradesmen, desperate country people prepared to do anything for a crust, and hopeful artists and writers were joined by a stream of *hidalgos (hijos de algo:* "sons of something"), a peculiarly Spanish category of

> **The Palacio del Buen Retiro was completed in 1630 and became the preferred royal residence. . . . Churches and convents were raised and noble mansions built.**

generally impoverished also-rans in this tightly hierarchical society. The hidalgos, scions of well-educated families but with little or no noble blood, considered themselves a cut well above the plebs. As such, they preferred not to work at any manual trade but to try their luck at landing some modest sinecure in the burgeoning court administration. Some made it, but many did not and joined the growing ranks of Madrid's poor.

The arrival of the court in 1561 meant the eclipse of municipal power. The Consejo de Madrid, the town council, although given to spending copious sums on grand parades and festivals, was rapidly subordinated to the absolute power of the royal house. Only in the 17th century did the Consejo work up the courage to request funding for the creation of a city hall. Royal approval came in 1621, but the Casa de la Villa (until recently the Ayuntamiento) was not completed until the end of the century.

The Spanish Succession & Slide into Decay

The death of Carlos II (r. 1665–1700) without an heir in 1700 unleashed the War of the Spanish Succession (1702–1714). France supported Felipe V (1700–1746), the Bourbon-family grandson of France's Louis XIV and María Teresa (a daughter of Felipe IV). His lineage was hard to dispute, but in 1702 hostilities broke out between, on the one hand, France and Spain and, on the other, an alliance uniting Austria, England, Holland, Portugal, some German states, and the House of Savoy behind Archduke Charles, an Austrian pretender to the throne.

Felipe V won, but at a cost. Spain was exhausted and lost considerable territory (the island of Menorca, for instance, became a British territory). Felipe V's victory served primarily to accelerate the country's decline on the European stage. An absolutist, Felipe V accelerated the process of centralizing power in the hands of the king and his bureaucracy in Madrid, abolishing numerous autonomous charters and local governments.

Plaza Mayor

Its size and good order made it ideal for bullfighting, public executions, and autos-da-fé, the public execution of supposed heretics. Madrid's first auto-da-fé occurred there in 1632 in the presence of the king and queen.

In Madrid, the medieval Alcázar burned to the ground in 1734. This rather suited Felipe V, who found the gloomy old residence depressing. In its place he ordered the construction of a new Palacio Real (Royal Palace). It was completed 30 years later, in time for one of Spain's most savvy monarchs, Carlos III (r. 1759–1788), to enjoy it. But Madrid needed more than a nice new palace. Known, with good reason, as the *pocilga de Europa* (the pigsty of Europe), Madrid was crying out for serious urban improvement.

Called the *rey-alcalde* (king-mayor) because of the exceptional interest he took in the improvement of his city, Carlos had streets widened and paved, sewers and street lighting improved, and crime reduced. A central post office was established at the Puerta del Sol (the building is still there today). Carlos ordered the creation of the Real Jardín Botánico and encouraged beautification projects such as the laying out of the tree-lined Paseo del Prado. It was at this time that the neoclassic Palacio de Villanueva, today home to the Museo del Prado, was built to house a science academy.

On the wider national front, Carlos III began a program of road construction in a country that until then had been notable for its difficult travel. Trade between Spanish ports and the Latin American colonies was liberalized, and small-scale industry, such as textiles in Catalunya, began to take off.

The original Palacio Real burned to the ground in 1734. The new one was built entirely of stone.

Napoleon & the War of Independence

Although Spain had significant problems, the long and sensible rule of Carlos III had at least given the country some sense of stability. Things were to go badly awry in the 20 years after his death.

Only one year into the reign of Carlos IV (r. 1788–1808), all Europe was rocked by the violence of the French Revolution (1789–1799), which set itself against monarchical rule. Under Carlos IV, Spain at first sided with Revolutionary France's most implacable enemy, Great Britain. Carlos's minister, Manuel Godoy, then decided to switch sides. Spain paid a terrible price for this changed alliance in 1805 when the bulk of its navy was sunk in the Battle of Trafalgar, in which Admiral Horatio Nelson routed the Franco-Spanish armada off the south coast of Spain.

Three years later, Napoleon (r. 1852–1870) persuaded Godoy to allow French troops to pass through Spain to launch an assault on Portugal, allied with Great Britain. The first French troops arrived in early 1808, and by March they were in Madrid. As it became clear the French presence was turning into an occupation, Madrid rose in popular revolt on May 2 (see pp. 204–205). Carlos IV and Godoy had already fled. The city folk had little chance and were routed by the end of the day. Francisco Goya immortalized the events of that day, and the executions of rebels on the morrow, in paintings that hang in the Museo del Prado.

By July, Joseph Bonaparte (1768–1844), Napoleon's brother, was installed as king in Madrid. Across the country resistance fighters began to harry French troops, but it was not until the Duke of Wellington (1769–1852) marched into Spain with a combined British-Portuguese force that the Peninsular War (known as the Guerra de la Independencia, or the War of Independence, in Spain) got under way in earnest. The French were ousted in 1814.

Joseph Bonaparte's stay in Madrid was not all bad. The hardships of war hit the city hard, and in 1812, 30,000 Madrileños died of hunger. In a bid to improve living conditions in the city, numerous churches and convents were demolished, and the area that is now the Plaza de Oriente was cleared of its warren of streets and ramshackle housing. Cemeteries were moved to the outskirts. Resented at the time, these moves were later accepted by most Spanish observers as necessary improvements.

The Age of Coups

With the French gone, Fernando VII (r. 1814–1833) returned to Madrid as king. He soon showed that he was an absolutist of the old school and shut down publication of the many political and satirical pamphlets that briefly flourished in the capital after 1814. He would in no way countenance the idea of a parliamentary system of government. Rigidly rooted in the past though he was, he did open up parts of the Parque del Buen Retiro, hitherto the private domain of the royal family and intimates, to the general public. He was also behind the formation of a public art gallery in the Palacio de Villanueva. In October 1816, the first stagecoach line from Madrid to Barcelona via Valencia opened.

Overall, however, these were disastrous times for Spain. After the calamities of the Napoleonic wars, many of Spain's restless American colonies gained their independence, particularly after Spanish forces were defeated in Peru in 1824.

Fernando left his three-year-old daughter Isabel II (r. 1833–1868) behind as heir, and thus began the long regency of her mother, María Cristina (r. 1833–1840) . Fernando's brother, Carlos, refused to accept the accession of a woman to the throne and sparked off the Carlist Wars, which would sputter on through much of the 19th century, mostly in the north.

To fight the Carlists, María Cristina and then Isabel II turned to liberal figures in the army and politics for support. From the 1840s until Isabel was obliged to abdicate and flee the country in 1868, *pronunciamientos* (military coups), riots, and counter-coups followed one another with monotonous regularity.

Madrid had barely developed since Joseph Bonaparte set in motion his plans for urban change, plans thwarted with the return to the throne of the Bourbons in 1814. In 1836, however, the government ordered the *desamortización* (disentailment) of Church property. The Church would lose 1,600 properties in Madrid in the following four decades, fueling a speculative boom. It also favored the rise of an entrepreneurial class in a city still dominated by a nobility that disdained work of any kind.

> **In the 1920s especially, Madrid was the center of the country's intellectual life, attracting the likes of poet Federico García Lorca and painter Salvador Dalí.**

The city's first railway line, between Madrid and Aranjuez, opened in 1851 and was followed seven years later by the Canal de Isabel II, which still supplies the city with water from the Guadarrama Mountains. Other public works included the opening of the Teatro Real (Royal Theater), the Biblioteca Nacional (National Library), and the Congreso de los Diputados (lower house of parliament). Much-needed plans to extend the city commenced in the 1860s, when work on an *ensanche* (extension) began around Calle de Serrano.

The flight of Isabel II to France led to still more instability. In the course of seven years, Madrid was run by an interim government, an Italian king, a series of republican governments, and, finally, after yet another coup, Isabel's son, Alfonso XII (r. 1875–1885). He was succeeded by Alfonso XIII (r. 1886–1931).

A New Century & the Republic

It would be an exaggeration to claim the early decades of the 20th century were ones of peaceful progress in Madrid, but progress was nonetheless felt. After the final colonial catastrophe of 1898—when Spain lost Cuba, Puerto Rico, and the Philippines, to an infinitely more powerful United States—it was almost as though the country could now concentrate on matters closer to home.

In 1891, the country's national bank, the Banco de España, opened its headquarters in Madrid. Seven years later, the first city tramlines were electrified. In 1910, work on the Gran Vía started and, in 1919, the first underground metro line was running. In 1934, the grand Las Ventas bullring opened. Internal immigration doubled the population to one million by 1930. In the 1920s especially, Madrid was the center of the country's intellectual life, attracting the likes of poet Federico García Lorca and painter Salvador Dalí.

Madrid was a hive of activity, but the almost frenetic pace of development could not disguise the deepening political crisis in Spain, fueled by serious problems at home and abroad. Remaining neutral in World War I had at first brought prosperity to Spain as it freely traded with all sides in the conflict. Boom was shortly followed by bust, however, and a pointless colonial war in northern Morocco in the 1920s proved disastrous.

In 1923, Gen. Miguel Primo de Rivera installed himself as dictator, but he was removed by the king in 1930. The following year, a coalition of republicans and socialists won municipal elections around the country and proclaimed a republic. The king fled, but the left-wing government soon developed divisions and in 1933 was replaced by a right-wing government. Two years later, the left-wing Frente Popular (Popular Front) defeated the right-wing Frente Nacional (National Front) at national elections in February.

By this time, Madrid and other major cities were racked by spreading political violence in the streets, in what seemed an almost inevitable descent into war.

Civil War

Seeing the danger, the Frente Popular government removed suspect generals (including Gen. Francisco Franco Bahamonde, sent to the Canary Islands) from the capital. It was to no avail. In July 1936, Franco fomented military insurrection in Spain's North African enclaves. Garrisons on the mainland followed suit. What followed was three years of carnage and hardship that tore the country apart.

Madrid itself was under siege by November, about the time volunteer soldiers of the International Brigades began to arrive in the capital. Franco's forces pulled up in the Casa de Campo, and over the following years his Nationalist troops would penetrate into the university and Argüelles districts of the city, but no farther. Artillery duels centered on key spots (such as Las Vistillas) became part of everyday life for Madrid's populace. Still, people continued to go about their business as best they could, catching the metro, going to the cinema, and just getting by.

The government fled early on to Valencia and Barcelona. Madrid itself did not surrender until March 28, 1939, long after much of the rest of the country (including Barcelona) had fallen. Three days later, the war was over.

María Cristina de Borbón acted as regent until her daughter took the throne as Queen Isabel II.

From Franco to Democracy

For years after 1939, Madrileños breathed the air of repression and reprisals. Of course, not all of them were unhappy at the outcome of the war. The middle classes generally welcomed Franco's victory, and many of those who had suffered under the republicans now turned informer. Summary trials and executions went on well into the 1940s, but figures are hard to come by. By one account, in 1939, 200 to 250 executions were being carried out daily. Many of the 200,000 death sentences said to have been passed by 1944 were commuted to terms in prisons and labor camps. One trade union leader estimated that two million Spaniards went to prison or to labor camps in the three years after the war. Many were set to work on the Valle de los Caídos, a Fascist monument to the war dead outside Madrid.

After the initial euphoria experienced by some citizens, the city settled into the difficult period of the 1940s and 1950s, the Años de Hambre (Years of Hunger). Although Spain remained neutral in World War II, the regime was shunned by all the main powers after 1945. Only in 1953, when the United States decided that Spanish military bases would be handy in the Cold War, did Washington come to Madrid with aid from the Marshall Plan. Two years later, Spain had a seat at the United Nations.

Throughout the 1950s, starving peasants streamed into Madrid from the country's poorest regions. By 1960 it is estimated that 600,000 had arrived, creating massive *chabolas*, shanty towns without running water or electricity, on the city's edge.

Marshall aid and foreign investment began to breathe life into Madrid. America's Chrysler automobile manufacturer was the capital's top employer in the 1960s. A construction boom took off, and many of the towers and office blocks started going up.

Growing prosperity did not dampen political opposition to Franco's regime. Protests at many of the universities became more open, and clandestine trade unions began to organize themselves as well. In 1973, the Basque separatist terrorist group Euskadi Ta Askatasuna (ETA; Basque Homeland and Freedom) assassinated Adm. Carrero Blanco (r. 1973), Franco's prime minister and designated successor, in the streets of Madrid. The following year Franco fell ill, and he died on November 20, 1975. No one quite knew what would happen next.

Franco had wanted the royal Juan Carlos to assume power and rule in a manner consistent with Franco's policies, but the young king liberalized the government instead (see sidebar this page) and fashioned a parliamentary democracy.

A year later Felipe González's PSOE won the national elections. He remained in power until 1996, when the right-wing Partido Popular (PP) under José María Aznar picked up the baton. The González years were ones of rapid growth in Spain, though many problems remained unresolved. Under the charismatic native of Seville, Spain joined the NATO defense alliance and the European Economic Community (now the European Union). The country quickly became the EU's biggest net beneficiary of cohesion funds, which were aimed at bringing the country and its infrastructure into line with the EU's core members. Combined with the profits from being one of the biggest tourist destinations in the world, these programs have helped turn the country around. But unemployment remained high, and embarrassing corruption scandals blackened the name of the PSOE.

Under Aznar, conservative economic policy helped ease unemployment and improve productivity, but by the time his party lost power in 2004 (see p. 20), alarm bells were sounding. Investment in research and development has been low and inflation higher than in most EU countries. Spanish wages run below the EU average.

In Madrid, the charismatic Marxist Enrique Tierno Galván was elected mayor in 1979 in the city's first free elections after Franco's death. He governed a city in ferment until 1986. These were the years of the *movida*, that sudden burst of nocturnal madness that shook Madrid out of its Francoist slumber. The city partied.

Juan Carlos

Franco, who died in 1975, had groomed the Bourbon prince Juan Carlos to take over in his image as Spain's head of state after his death. But the newly crowned King Juan Carlos I had other plans. As Spanish trade unions and socialist and communist parties emerged from hiding, the king asked the moderate Francoist Adolfo Suárez to form a government and pass a series of reforms leading to the creation of a parliamentary democracy. By 1978 a new, federal-style constitution, with the king as head of state, was in place.

Gen. Francisco Franco, who ruled as a dictatorship from 1939 to 1975, gives the Nationalist salute.

Things slowed a little under Galván's Socialist successor, Juan Barranco, who was ousted after a censure motion in 1989. Conservative José María Álvarez del Manzano took over in 1991. By then the downside of the previous excesses was making itself felt, with an explosion in the number of heroin addicts in the capital. The arrival of AIDS in the 1980s, spread in part by needle-sharing addicts, added a further note of danger.

In May 2003, the PP's Alberto Ruiz-Gallardón, until then president of the Comunidad de Madrid regional government, was elected mayor.. Six months later, his party colleague Esperanza Aguirre became the first-ever female president of a Spanish region when she took over in Madrid. ■

The Arts

Spain and its capital present several conundrums. Their most glorious moments in painting came at times of decline and confusion. Architecturally, Madrid developed late, and expanded fitfully—a pleasing old center remains alongside an explosion of later building. The city also has a busy music scene, ranging from flamenco bars to grand classical spectacles.

Architecture

No more than a small provincial town until suddenly catapulted to the status of capital in the latter half of the 16th century, Madrid preserves virtually nothing of architectural interest from its early years. A pleasing concentration of historic buildings in Madrid's center does bear witness to the following two centuries. The grand boulevards and haughty edifices that most distinguish the city center are largely a product of the 19th and early 20th centuries, when Madrid got a blast of belle époque and, later, art deco beauty treatment.

From Muslim Fort to the Renaissance: Of the original Muslim frontline fort that encircled Madrid, only a modest stretch of defensive wall below the Catedral de Nuestra Señora de la Almudena remains today. The bell towers of two modest churches in the Old Town, the Iglesia de San Pedro El Viejo and Iglesia de San Nicolás de los Servitas, are reminders of the Mudejar style of building. The Mudejares were Muslims who remained behind in territory conquered by the Christians. Common across much of central and southern Spain, where Catholic forces gradually ejected the Muslims, Mudejar architecture is marked by the use of brick and stylized decoration.

> The grand boulevards and haughty edifices . . . are largely a product of the 19th and 20th centuries, when Madrid got a blast of belle époque.

About the only reminders of the Gothic period in Madrid are the delightful Capilla del Obispo, a chapel in the central Iglesia de San Andrés, and the late-Gothic Casa de los Lujanes on Plaza de la Villa.

One of Spain's great Renaissance architects was Juan de Herrera (1530–1597). His robust, austere take on the era's style is exemplified by his work on San Lorenzo de El Escorial, Felipe II's mighty palace-monastery-pantheon outside Madrid.

Madrid Baroque & the 18th Century: Herrera's influence on construction in Madrid itself was more indirect. Juan Gómez de Mora (1586–1648) and his uncle Francisco de Mora (1560–1610) worked in a hybrid style clearly reminiscent of Herrera and known as *barroco madrileño*. The former produced the Ayuntamiento, city prisons (one is now the Ministry of Foreign Affairs on Plaza de la Santa Cruz, another the Casa de la Villa), and the Convento de la Encarnación. The latter

The twin towers of the Iglesia de San Isidro, also known as La Colegiata, rise above Calle Toledo in the heart of old Madrid.

The Bernabéu soccer stadium, home to Real Madrid, is a signature structure of modern Madrid.

worked on the Palacio de Úceda (now the Capitanía General on Calle Mayor). The colorful Real Casa de la Panadería on Plaza Mayor also dates from this period.

More clearly baroque, although hardly florid, are the Basílica de San Isidro, built in the 1660s, and the entrance to the Museo Municipal.

Ventura Rodríguez (1717–1785), who designed the Palacio de Liria and laid out the Campo del Moro gardens, competed for attention with the Italian Francesco Sabatini (1722–1797), who also worked on the Palacio Real and raised the Puerta de Alcalá. The other dominating figure of the 18th century was Juan de Villanueva (1739–1811), who designed the building we know today as the Museo del Prado.

The Belle Époque: The second half of the 19th century brought a building boom to Madrid. Boulevards like the Paseo de la Castellana and the residential district of Salamanca took form. The pace picked up at the end of the century. Spearheaded by Antonio Palacios (1874–1945), a bevy of architects joined forces to coat the capital in the glow of grandeur it still exudes today. This was the age of looking back to look forward. Palacios's gargantuan Palacio de Comunicaciones was (and remains) an extreme example of neo-Gothic.

By the early 20th century, designers felt freer than ever to indulge their whims, creating such art deco gems as the Edificio Grassy (1917) and Edificio Metrópolis (1911). The Gran Vía is laced with many such fanciful caprices.

Modern Times: The Franco years did little to make Madrid a cheerier place. The Edificio de España in its eponymous square is an Iberian Fascist amalgam of New York skyscraper and Soviet dourness. Most modern development during and since Franco's day has taken place along the Paseo de la Castellana. With the exception of the inward-leaning Torres Kio on Plaza de Castilla, completed in 1998, little in the way of eye-catching construction has yet taken hold in Madrid.

In the early 21st century, the city is passing through an unprecedented spurt of urban expansion. A drive around the city's ring roads reveals whole medium-rise suburbs popping up out of nowhere, the horizon lined with cranes. Landmark buildings are in the offing as well. Richard Rogers's terminal at Barajas airport is an original, undulating design. Henry Cobb has built an exciting glass tower, the Torre Espacio, at the northern end of the Paseo de la Castellana. And Spaniard Rafael Moneo, who designed the clever restoration of the old Atocha train station building and its conversion into a tropical garden (1992), is the creative mind behind the remodeling and modern extension of the Museo del Prado.

Painting & Sculpture

The Old Masters of Spain, led by Velázquez, shed their radiant light in the gloom of Spain's accelerating political and economic decline in the 17th century. The capital and the court were as one, and it was largely from the latter that artistic patronage came. A couple of centuries later, the titan of early 19th-century Spanish art, Francisco de Goya, would also benefit from its largesse. Civil war and the Franco years forced several Madrid artists into exile. Times have changed, and Madrid not only is the country's greatest single repository of paintings but also hosts what has become one of Europe's top annual contemporary art fests, ARCO (see feature pp. 190–191).

Old Masters of the Golden Age: Felipe II's decision to make his permanent capital in Madrid in 1561 had perhaps only one serious artistic consequence. Cretan-born Domenikos Theotokopoulos (1541–1614), better known to us today as El Greco, settled in the city of Toledo, which was thought to be a prime candidate for the country's capital. From this, the seat of the Church in Spain, he tried and failed to awaken interest in the king for his ethereal figures. As it became clear that the choice of Madrid was irreversible, Toledo lost importance and El Greco's personal fortunes also slid.

> **The star of what came to be known as the apogee of fine arts in Spain was Diego Rodríguez de Silva y Velázquez, a man with extraordinary talent, a taste for glory, and a way with the powerful.**

The star of what came to be known as the apogee of fine arts in Spain was Diego Rodríguez de Silva y Velázquez (1599–1660), a man with extraordinary talent, a taste for glory, and a way with the powerful. Born a year after Felipe II's death, he moved from Seville to Madrid as court painter under Felipe's successors. He was born at the right time, for Felipe had shown a penchant for Italian painters that might otherwise have left Velázquez languishing in Seville as El Greco did in Toledo.

We are fortunate that this was not so. Velázquez may have been vain (during all his life at court in Madrid, one of his biggest preoccupations was to receive a knighthood), but he was also good, and some of his grandest works now hang proudly in the Museo del Prado. Easily the best known is the enormous canvas "The Maids of Honor" ("Las Meninas," circa 1656). The painting repays close observation, for it is not merely a portrait of King Felipe IV's little daughter, the Infanta Margarita, and friends. To the left is the painter himself, painting a portrait of ... whom? The clue is in the mirror at the back of the room, in which we see the king and his queen. Velázquez has captured several ideas and moments at once, including the cheeky detail of including on his vest the much desired Cross of the Order of Santiago—a decoration that the painter openly coveted but was not awarded until toward the end of his life.

In the Prado hang various of his master-pieces. Among the most powerful are his "Christ Crucified," in which he captures the pain of Christ's death, and "The Surrender of Breda," depicting the yielding of the Dutch town of Breda to Spanish forces after a ten-month siege in 1625.

A contemporary and friend of Velázquez, the painter Francisco de Zurbarán (1598–1664) cut his teeth in Seville, but he too came to Madrid (circa 1634–1635) to carry out commissions for the court and convents in the capital. He returned to Seville with the title of Royal Artist. He is known above all for his chiaroscuro portraits of saints and monks, in which light and shadow play a key role. Some can be seen in the Prado and the Real Academia de Bellas Artes de San Fernando. He returned to Madrid toward the end of his life, where he died in relative poverty.

Although neither had much contact with Madrid, two further masters of the period, many of whose works also hang in the Prado, require mention. José (Jusep) de Ribera (1591–1652) and Bartolomé Esteban Murillo (1618–1682) are signal artists. Ribera lived in the Spanish-controlled city of Naples (the Italians know him as Lo Spagnoletto, "the little Spaniard") and was a disciple of the Caravaggio school of chiaroscuro painting.

Murillo, like Velázquez born in Seville, carried out the bulk of his work in his native city, although he did visit Madrid to acquaint himself with the royal collections. His was a breezy, colorful style. Religious scenes dominate his paintings, as was typical in the period, but Murillo is also known for portraits of young children, often poor, in the streets.

The Madrid School: Lesser-known artists, collectively known as the Madrid school, were also busy at work in the capital. The Ricci brothers, Fray Juan (1600–1681) and Francisco (1614–1685), were active in a variety of convents and churches around Castile.

More important, and the last artist of stature to emerge in the baroque context of the Madrid school, was Claudio Coello (1642–1693). Born in the capital of Portuguese

---

EXPERIENCE: Art Class

Visiting Madrid can usher up the urge to paint and draw, or otherwise be artistic. Here are some places in the city to take classes in the arts.

2 Taller De Grabado *(Calle Ponciano 1, tel 91 542 0320, Mon.–Fri. 5–8:30 p.m.)* Classes in etching.

Artepolis *(Calle Olivar 1, tel 91 539 0843)* Classes in dance from different lands, drama, drawing, photography, singing, and more.

Estudio Albahaca *(Calle San Dimas 7, tel 91 522 5510, www.estudioalbahaca. com, Mon.–Fri. 10 a.m.–7 p.m.)* Classes in papier-mâché, puppeteering, and scene-making.

Estudio De Arte *(Toledo 40 Primera Izquierda, www.estudio13.com)* Classes in clay sculpting drawing, painting, print-making, and restoration.

Taller Rita Luna *(C/Fuentes 10 bajo Dcha., www.ritaluna.com)* Classes in etching, drawing, and painting.

parents, he studied with Francisco Ricci. Some of his works are on display in the Prado, but the most important, the enormous "The Sacred Form," hangs in El Escorial. The panoramic portrait shows King Carlos II and his court worshipping the Eucharist, thus symbolizing the role of the monarch as guarantor of Catholic order in Spain.

Goya: Towering above the remainder of Spain's 19th-century artists, Francisco José de Goya y Lucientes (1746–1828) came to Madrid from a small town in Aragón to work in the royal tapestry factory as a designer. By 1799 he had become court painter to King Carlos III, seven years after becoming deaf.

Goya was wild at heart. In the course of his long career his style changed continually, crashing through artistic conventions with divine indifference. He carried out religious and court portraits, but increasingly did so with a ruthless realism. Said to have had a long affair with the Duchess of Alba, it is thought that his paintings "The Clothed

The intriguing "Las Meninas," or "The Maids of Honor," painted by Diego Velázquez in 1656, is one of the most renowned artworks in the world.

Maja" and "The Nude Maja" are portraits of the duchess. The scandal attached to the latter was such that it was long hidden from view.

What is most extraordinary about his works is their sheer variety, both in method and subject matter. Profoundly affected by the events of his time (above all, the War of Independence), he executed several series of engravings, for instance, "The Disasters of War." In these images the cruelty of war is portrayed without quarter. In another series, "Bullfighting," it appears the artist was repelled by the violence and cruelty of the activity.

Goya's best-known paintings refer to the Madrid uprising against occupation by

Juan Gris was a master of the cubist still life, as shown by "The Mandolin" (1921).

Napoléon's troops. "The Second of May" and "The Third of May" depict scenes, respectively, of the uprising and the execution of rebels the day after.

Surely the most bizarre of the artist's works were his *pinturas negras*—"black paintings"—murals he painted in his house west of the Río Manzanares after the War of Independence. These nightmarish images include one of the god Saturn devouring his own children.

Goya was far ahead of his time, providing inspiration for future generations of European painters, especially the French Impressionists.

The 20th Century: Goya was a hard act to follow. Closing the 19th century in Madrid were Valencia-born Joaquín Sorolla (1863–1923), best known for his sunny beach scenes, which can be viewed in the gallery housed in his former home in Madrid. Local boy José Gutiérrez Solana (1886–1945), some of whose works can be seen in the Museo Reina Sofía, depicts in dark tones and avant-garde fashion scenes and people of his city, largely influenced by the tragic events of the Spanish Civil War.

At about the same time, Madrid's Juan Gris (1887–1927) came to the fore as one of the most important of the cubist painters, along with his friend Pablo Picasso (1881–1973).

The so-called Vallecas (a Madrid suburb) school produced the likes of Benjamín Palencia (1894–1980) and Toledo-born sculptor Alberto Sánchez (1895–1962). The latter was one of the leading modern sculptors of Spain. He worked in stone, plaster, wood, and metal, and his themes, with lean human figures, are shared in the canvases of Palencia. Sánchez preferred exile in the Soviet Union to life in Franco's Spain, and much of his opus was destroyed. Works by both artists are on display in the Museo Reina Sofía. Another exile was Eduardo Arroyo (b. 1937), whose paintings lean to pop art lightness laden with social critique.

Literature

The center of contemporary Spanish publishing is now in Barcelona, but Madrid has long acted as a magnet for great Spanish writers. For centuries they were attracted by the royal court and its patronage. Later, they came simply because the capital was the place to be for people of letters.

Generations of writers in Madrid and beyond have tended to look back in awe to the Siglo de Oro (Golden Age) of Spanish writing, when Spain had already edged away from the zenith of its power but the all-powerful court, finally established in one place, attracted writing talent from around the country to Madrid.

The same era saw the birth of one of Spain's great poets, Luis de Góngora (1561–1627). Drama also had its stars, particularly the playwright Lope de Vega (1562–1635), whose house can still be visited in Madrid's old city center. Of the estimated 800 plays he wrote, some 300 have survived to this day. The ladies' man Don Juan was a character in the play *El Burlador de Sevilla (The Seducer of Seville)* by Lope de Vega's colleague, Tirso de Molina. At the tail end of the Golden Century also emerged another eternal great of the Spanish stage, Pedro Calderón de la Barca (1600–1681).

Born some two centuries later in the Canary Islands and often referred to as Spain's Balzac, Benito Pérez Galdós (1843–1920) lived most of his adult life in the capital. There he published one of the greatest novels of early 20th-century European literature, *Fortunata y Jacinta*, a fascinating exploration of life in 19th-century bourgeois Madrid.

Galdós lived in Madrid at a time of political and literary ferment. He watched as younger writers, led by the likes of the philosopher-essayist José Ortega y Gasset, founded the Generation of '98 movement in the wake of defeat at the hands of the United States and loss of most of its remaining colonies in 1898.

The trials of the Franco years in the capital have fascinated writers down the decades. Nobel Prize winner Camilo José Cela (1916–2002) explored the wounds of the city in the wake of the Civil War in his 1950s *La Colmena (The Beehive)*. While not overtly critical of the regime, it painted a bleak picture of the lives of Madrileños in the 1940s.

Like Cela, Francisco Umbral (1935–2007) was a winner of the prestigious national

Cervantes

For many, the European novel sprang from the mind of a turbulent man born just outside Madrid in Alcalá de Henares. Miguel de Cervantes Saavedra (1547–1616) had nothing if not an interesting life. Soldier of fortune, prisoner in the hands of the Moors, public functionary, accused at one time of murder, Cervantes finally settled in Madrid where, to make a little money, he started writing a short story. "El Ingenioso Hidalgo Don Quijote de la Mancha" ("Don Quixote"), the tale of the wanderings of a ruined knight and his faithful sidekick, Sancho Panza, wound up being a rather longer story than Cervantes had intended—the forerunner of the modern novel.

Bullfighting

A buzz fills the arena on a brilliant mid-May afternoon. Since lunchtime, spectators have been converging on the world's greatest *corrida* (bullfight) stadium. They come from all over Madrid and across Spain to witness the finest exponents of this ancient blood sport. It is a spectacle of life and death, a dance of bravery and blood. It is not for the squeamish.

The picador on horseback aims to tire and weaken the bull before the matador moves in for the kill.

Madrid's Plaza de Toros Monumental de Las Ventas (capacity 25,000; see pp. 192–193) is a mighty setting. Built in 1931, it exudes a mix of classical grandeur and Moorish mystique. To triumph here is the ultimate dream of the *torero* (bullfighter)

The Tradition.

Toreros seek fame and fortune through physical prowess and bravura. They all aspire to become a *matador* (killer) and reach the top by fighting at Las Ventas.

The *lidia,* as bullfighting is also known, dates from ancient Roman times and, although associated mostly with Spain, is also practiced in Portugal, southern France, and Latin America.

The one-month season of daily fights that begins at Las Ventas with the Fiestas de San Isidro Labrador (Madrid's patron saint) in mid-May is the acme of the season, but the corrida is a part of town festivals up and down the country. In bigger cities, fights can be a regular weekend fixture.

Evening Spectacle

The ritual typically begins around 6 p.m. As a rule, three matadors with their *cuadrillas* (teams of toreros) present themselves to fight six bulls from different breeders (each matador and team takes on two bulls). *Toros bravos* (fighting bulls) are bred for this day. Each encounter takes about 20 minutes. The fight is cruel and the bull is bound to lose—but no one should doubt the dangers involved. Matadors frequently wind up in the hospital with horrific wounds, although few have been killed.

A complex ritual accompanies the fight. The bull is released from a dark corral into the ring, full of rage and confused after being penned up for a long period. Toreros dash about with heavy rose and yellow percale capes, testing the bull's energy and willingness to fight before the matador appears.

The matador then takes on the bull in single combat with a smaller red cape. The "art" of his fight lies in the daring and finesse of his *faenas* (moves). Particularly good maneuvers move the knowledgable crowd to scream *Olé!* in encouragement.

The End Approaches

The matador is followed by *picadores,* mounted on horseback, who fight off the bull while it charges at the horses. Next come the *banderilleros,* who rush headlong at the bull to lodge short, harpoonlike instruments (*banderillas*) in its withers. All this serves to wear down and goad the bull for the return of the matador, whose bravado is now fully tested. When he judges the bull can give no more, he steadies himself before his victim with his sword to execute the *estocada* (kill).

If the matador performs well, he is awarded one or even two of the bull's ears, and sometimes its tail. The matador's dream is to exit Las Ventas by its Moorish Puerta de Madrid—an honor reserved only for the most daring, artistic victories in the grandest bullring in the world.

EXPERIENCE: See a Bullfight with an Aficionado

Going to a bullfight is undoubtedly one of the great experiences in Spain, although of course it does not appeal to everyone. A good *corrida* is a wonderful spectacle, with an electric atmosphere, but may well be totally baffling to the uninitiated. As you watch, the crowd suddenly roars or sighs in unison at the slightest movement from the matador. You might be left wishing you had read up a bit more about the whole thing before buying a ticket, or maybe fantasizing that you had a friend in Madrid who happened to be a huge bullfighting fan. Help is fortunately at hand in the form of Tom Kallene, a Swedish writer, broadcaster, and television producer who has lived in Madrid for nearly 20 years and is a regular pundit on bullfighting programs on the national radio networks.

Passionate about bullfighting and a mine of information, he will accompany you to a *corrida,* talk you through every stage of the proceedings, and provide you with all sorts of insider information, too. You leave the bullring having learned a lot about Spanish culture and feeling part of the whole experience, rather than just looking on from the outside. Book Tom Kallene's services through Madrid & Beyond (*Calle Bailén 19, 1 Izqda, tel 91 758 0063, www.madridandbeyond.com*), a specialist agency that can also organize trips to bull breeding ranches.

literary prize, the Premio Cervantes. A prolific writer and journalist, Umbral penned several novels set in Madrid, most importantly the *Trilogía de Madrid,* a journey through the life and times of Madrid into the Franco years.

Almudena Grandes (b. 1960) is one of the most successful Madrid-born authors of the moment. Her numerous novels range across a variety of settings but generally turn on complex human relationships. The protagonists are frequently Madrileños, and in her latest novel, *El Corazón Helado* (2007), she traces the history of the Civil War and its devastating effects on Spanish society in the second half of the 20th century.

Many other contemporary writers, whether local or not, frequently set their novels in Madrid. Juan Eduardo Zúñiga (b. 1929) examines the city's resistance to Franco during the Civil War in his acclaimed novel *Capital de la Gloria,* while Andalucía's Antonio Muñoz Molina (b. 1956) chose Madrid as the scene for such novels as *El Dueño del Secreto (The Master of the Secret).*

Flamenco

It rumbles from the depths of the Spanish soul, crying out with universal sorrow and passion. For many, flamenco (be it the music, song, or dance of that name) is the quintessence of Spain. In fact, it derives from the country's *gitano* (Gypsy) community, and its original home lies in Andalucía. But Madrid, as a city of

immigrants, has long been a second home for that southern heat.

The origins of flamenco remain obscure. It is thought to have its roots in the 15th century, when Gypsies arrived in southern Spain from India via Egypt and eastern Europe. The Muslims were still in control of Granada and parts (but by no means all) of Andalucía at this time, and the immigrants soon picked up elements of Arab and Berber music.

Flamenco song evolved over the centuries into different styles, ranging from the anguished *siguiriyas* and *soleás* common in Seville to the more toe-tapping *bulerías* of Jerez de la Frontera, as well as *boleros, fandangos, alegrías, farrucas,* and more.

At the base of it all is *cante hondo* (deep

Concert, Theater, & Opera Tickets

The Fnac store in central Madrid (Calle Preciados 28, 91 596 6100, www.fnac.es) handles tickets for all sorts of concerts and events and is therefore useful if you have just arrived and do not have access to a computer. As well as the agencies listed in the Entertainment section, if you know basic Spanish you could check out the Atrápalo website (www.atrapalo.com), which offers discounted tickets, often last minute, for a wide variety of cultural events and activities.

The story of Carmen, the tragic beauty from Seville, is told by the Ballet de Madrid.

song), the throaty, anguished singing that often talks of grief, loss, and injustice. Flamenco guitar (performed by a *tocaor*), initially probably no more than accompaniment to the singing, evolved into its own virtuoso musical genre, as did the powerful dancing of the *bailaores.*

What was long a largely ignored folk music began to attract wider attention in the 19th century. In Madrid, Gypsies lived around Calle de Toledo, and Andalucían taverns on that road frequently hosted flamenco performers. The genre subsequently had its ups and downs in Madrid, but from the 1950s, the spread of *tablaos* (flamenco bars) kept it alive in the capital. A few, like the Corral de la Morería and Café de Chinitas, are active today.

Flamenco Today: Since the 1980s, flamenco has undergone a revolution, and opinions on its current merits are sharply divided. The proudest of the purists, Gypsies, affirm that non-Gypsies can't really acquire *duende,* that indefinable quality that allows the flamenco singer or musician to work his or her magic on the audience. Such claims are probably twaddle, but the traditionalists view dimly the tendency among the younger generation (Gypsy or otherwise) to mix genres (producing fusion, flamenco rock, and even flamenco hip-hop). Yet it is this very openness to fresh influences that has brought flamenco artists a whole new worldwide audience.

Of the more traditionally inclined performers, the Carmona family (also known as Los Habichuela) are probably the best known, especially Juan (b. 1933) and Pepe (b. 1944), along with the Montoya family.

Universally acclaimed as the greatest of the younger generation of singers was El Camarón de la Isla (1950–1992), a friend of Paco de Lucía (b. 1947) and probably the best-known exponent of flamenco guitar beyond Spain. From much the same generation are the cantaores Enrique Morente (b. 1942) and Carmen Linares (b. 1951). A younger guitarist who has duende in spades is Vicente Amigo (b. 1967).

Of the contemporary bailaores, those with the greatest international profile are the fiery, highly theatrical Joaquín Cortés (b. 1969) and the more classical Antonio Canales (b. 1961). Also to be watched are Belén López (b. 1987), Belén Maya (b. 1966), Eva la Yerbabuena (b. 1973), and Antonio El Pipa (b. 1971).

The New Wave: Nuevo Flamenco may attract opprobrium from the purists, but since the 1980s the groups that dare to innovate have won over a young and otherwise mostly uninterested audience for flamenco in Spain. Two groups that fall squarely into this camp of flamenco rock (also called Gypsy rock) are Ketama and Pata Negra. To the youngest generation, however, even these groups are beginning to look a little stale. This explains the growing success of singers such as Raquel Riquelme, a non-Gypsy *(paya)* whose music has been described as "paya punk."

Other musicians have gone in the direction of fusion. Radio Tarifa is a group that experiments with a mix of flamenco, medieval European, and North African sounds. Juan

The Spanish National Orchestra at the Auditorio Nacional, Madrid's main venue for classical music.

EXPERIENCE: A Night at the Zarzuela

Zarzuela is Madrid's version of light opera and is performed regularly during a season stretching from November to July, or at other times of the year during festivals. Catch it at the **Teatro de la Zarzuela** *(Teatro de la Zarzuela, Calle Jovellanos 4, tel 91 524 5400, www. teatrodelazarzuela.mcu.es)*, which is a beautiful 19th-century building, or where festivals take place. If you get the chance, take in an outdoor performance during the Veranos de la Villa events in July and August, which is a particularly memorable experience on a hot summer night.

Unlike mainstream opera, there is never any snobbery attached to zarzuela, a form of singing and drama that has enjoyed great popularity since the 19th century, although it first emerged in the early theaters of the 17th century, with works written by the great playwrights of the day, Lope de Vega and Calderón de la Barca. The most well-known zarzuela composers include Ruperto Chapí, Federico de Chueca, and Francisco Asenjo Barbieri, and the works are usually set in the working-class neighborhoods of downtown Madrid.

Like the city itself, zarzuela is all about raucous fun with lots of jokes and local humor. The members of the audience usually know all the words to the songs and merrily sing along with the performers, which may come as a shock if you are used to the more formal atmosphere in other opera houses.

Peña Lebrijano (b. 1941), or El Lebrijano, plays more traditional flamenco, accompanied by the mellifluous music of traditional Moroccan orchestras. Aside from the tablaos, which tend to be touristy, there is a smattering of more genuine flamenco bars in the Lavapiés and La Latina areas of central Madrid. Frequent concerts are held on principal stages like the Centro Cultural de la Villa.

Music

In 1997, the Teatro Real, Madrid's grand opera house on Plaza de Oriente, opened ... again. A site with a long history of mishaps and hiccups, it had been shut for restoration for nine years. Now Madrileños have a premier location with the latest technological innovations for seeing top-quality opera.

Madrileños might like hearing opera and classical music, but Madrid has produced little world-class talent, with the mighty exception of the gentle tenor Plácido Domingo (b. 1934). This world-renowned singer was born in Madrid, then grew up in Mexico with his family of zarzuela performers.

Zarzuela, a uniquely Madrid creation, is a cross between musical, light opera, and spoken theater. It emerged in the 17th century as home entertainment for King Felipe IV, taking its name from the palace (official home to the royal family today) in which it was regularly performed. After all but dying out in the 18th century, zarzuela returned to Madrid as popular entertainment in the 19th century. Playwright Calderón de la Barca wrote many of the original scripts, in those days usually of a mythological nature.

Madrid has been a serious party town since the days of the *movida* in the 1970s and 1980s but for most night owls neither opera nor zarzuela cuts the mustard. The intense nocturnal scene spawns countless rock, pop, hip-hop, and other groups.

One of the icons of Madrid soft pop remains Antonio Vega (b. 1957), who went solo after his 1980s group, Nacha Pop, went belly up. Local rock legends include Rosendo Mercado and the band Seguridad Social. The latter has produced more than a dozen albums since it emerged in the early 1980s.

A new young talent to keep an eye on is Belén Arjona, Madrid born and compared by some with Canada's rock-and-roll wild child, Avril Lavigne.

Cinema

Franco had died only seven years earlier and the *movida* was still in full swing. The passing of the Generalísimo had lifted the lid on the city's creative spirit. Enrique Tierno Galván, Marxist philosopher and Socialist mayor who once told Madrileños to "get stoned and watch out," was still at the municipal helm in 1982 when a landmark film, *La Colmena (The Beehive),* premiered on the city's screens.

Based on the masterpiece novel by Camilo José Cela, Mario Camus's (b. 1935) film is set in 1940s Madrid. It depicts the trials and tribulations of characters struggling in the gray days of Franco's post-Civil War capital, following them around its listless cafés, police stations, and dark apartments. Such a picture would have been unthinkable only a few years earlier, and in some ways symbolizes the birth of modern Spanish cinema.

More than 20 years later, Spanish film-making is more prolific than ever and sparkling with inventiveness and originality.

At the same time as *La Colmena* came out, a joyously outrageous young phone company employee from the south of Castilla-La Mancha, Pedro Almodóvar (b. 1949), was also trying his hand at moviemaking. He had arrived in Madrid in the late 1960s, and, in the wake of the dictator's death, Almodóvar and his cohorts spearheaded the movida in wickedly stylish fashion. Partying aside, he whipped off a series of uneven films, all based on zanily complex stories in deeply manic Madrid.

> **Partying aside, Almodóvar whipped off a series of uneven films, all based on zanily complex stories in deeply manic Madrid.**

His first seriously successful picture did not come until 1988, with *Mujeres al Borde de un Ataque de Nervios (Women on the Edge of a Nervous Breakdown).* A typically Almodóvarian web of hysterical relationships sweeps across Madrid. In passing, some of his favorite actors come to the fore, including Carmen Maura, Antonio Banderas, and Rossy de Palma.

An astonishing concentration of screen talent, especially actresses, comes from or at least lives in Madrid. Local icon of stage and screen Victoria Abril has down the years been another of Almodóvar's favorites, starring in the likes of *¡Átame! (Tie Me Up! Tie Me Down!;* 1990). Others include Ana Belén, Maribel Verdú, and Penélope Cruz, the latter making her name in Hollywood after appearing in such films as Fernando Trueba's Oscar-winning *Belle Époque* (1992). Trueba co-wrote that film with Madrid-based Rafael Azcona, one of the country's most important screenwriters.

By the time Almodóvar's Oscar-winning *Todo Sobre Mi Madre (All About My Mother;* 1999) reached international screens, he and several of his Madrid colleagues had made the leap to international fame. Following the international success of *Volver* in 2006, which was filmed in Madrid and La Mancha, Almodóvar once again used Madrid as the setting for his latest picture, *Los Abrazos Rotos* (2009). Javier Bardem (b. 1969), who appeared in several of Almodóvar's movies, won an Oscar in 2007 for his menacing role in the Coen brothers' *No Country for Old Men.* ■

Timeless hub of historic Madrid, and symbol of the importance
of the city in the 17th century

Plaza Mayor &
Old Town

Traditional embroidered shawls

Plaza Mayor & Old Town

The old town is known as "Madrid de los Austrias," meaning "Habsburg Madrid," but this title is in fact misleading as this area has been inhabited since the Moors established the first settlement in the ninth century. The reign of the Habsburg monarchs lasted from 1516 to 1700, during which time Madrid became the capital of Spain and the hub of an empire following the discovery of the Americas.

Murals brighten Plaza de la Puerta Cerrada, once the site of a gate in the city walls.

17th century was the most important urban development of the Habsburg period. The area provided a public space for all sorts of ceremonies and entertainment. Today it is an imposing setting for enjoying a cup of coffee at one of its many cafés, but it is no longer the heart of the city.

South of these two squares is an evocative area of tiny squares and winding streets, where, although little remains from medieval times, you can still trace the course of the old city walls. Plaza de la Paja is now a pleasant spot for an evening drink under the trees; 900 years ago it was a bustling market square. Over the course of the next four centuries, some of the most important events in Madrid's history took place there. Muslims and Christians alike have deep roots in the neighborhood, and the area boasts some of

Although this was a buoyant period in Spain's history, the architecture of the era reflects the relatively austere tastes of the Habsburg monarchs, characterized by elegant redbrick buildings with slate roofs, turrets, and pinnacles. Exploring this area gives visitors an insight into how Madrid developed from its origins as a Moorish stronghold to become a powerful player on the world stage.

Plaza de la Villa, the administrative center of the growing town, was the most important square in Madrid for 500 years following the Christian reconquest in the 11th century. The City Hall was situated there in a magnificent Habsburg building until 2007, when it moved to larger premises in the palatial post office in Plaza de Cibeles.

The construction of Plaza Mayor in the

NOT TO BE MISSED:

Spending some time at a café in the Plaza Mayor 54–55

The Habsburg Casa de la Villa 57–58

Walking through the elegant Basílica Pontificia de San Miguel 58

Iglesia de San Nicolás de los Servitas, Madrid's oldest church 58–59

Dinner at a traditional tavern on Calle Cava Baja 61

A drink in Plaza de la Paja 62–63

The dome of the Basílica de San Francisco el Grande 66

Gazing up in the baroque Iglesia de San Isidro el Real 67

the city's most interesting older churches.

Some of the apartment blocks date from the 17th century, although most have now been sumptuously restored and constitute some of the most coveted real estate in the city. The two-story buildings are the oldest, with red pan-tiled roofs and tiny attic windows. All around this area there are traditional taverns, pavement cafés, and quite a few designer bars, making it one of the most enjoyable parts of Madrid to while away a few hours whether by day or by night. ∎

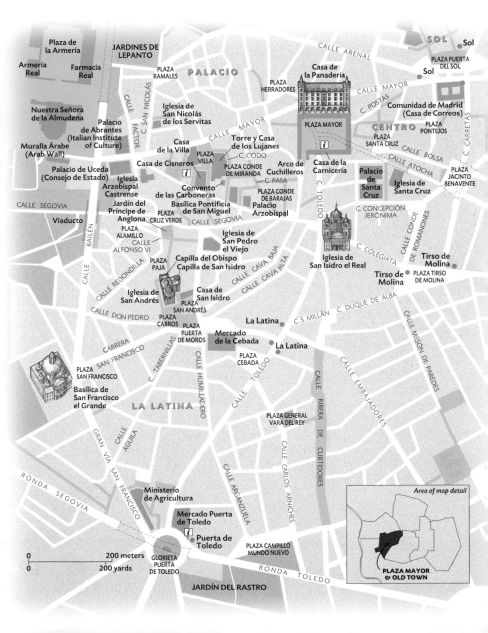

Plaza Mayor

Built nearly 400 years ago, Plaza Mayor is still a spectacular space. Enclosed by redbrick buildings, with the slate roofs, spires, and dormer windows typical of the architecture of the Habsburg dynasty, this elegant square is now full of pavement cafés, with traditional shops and tapas bars under the porticoed arcades. At night, it is used for concerts, performances, and fireworks displays, and on Sunday mornings it holds a stamp and coin market.

People soak up the sun year-round at the outdoor cafés of historic Plaza Mayor.

Plaza Mayor

🅰 Map p. 53

🚇 Metro: Sol

Visitor Information

✉ Madrid Tourist Center, Plaza Mayor 27

☎ 91 588 1636

www.esmadrid.com

For several centuries before the square was built, the area served as a marketplace outside the city walls. In view of the rapid expansion that took place in the decades after Madrid became the capital in 1561, it was decided to develop the space into a public square that could be used for official events.

Construction began in 1617 and was completed just two years later. Designed by Juan Gómez de Mora, the great architect of the Habsburg period, the sqaure is surrounded by buildings that provided accommodation for about 3,000 people—a population density that was unusual in those days and became the source of many local jokes about people living on top of one another.

As well as official ceremonies, the square was used for such varied activities as bullfights, jousting, and theatrical performances

INSIDER TIP:

Plaza Mayor in Madrid is the most beautiful square in Spain and is best just before Christmas with its special market.

—PATXI HERAS &
MARTA INFANTE

National Geographic field researchers

by the top playwrights of the time. Crowds also gathered to witness more sinister events, such as the grim trials of faith, known as autos-da-fé, which were held there by the Spanish Inquisition.

Walking into the square, you are inevitably drawn to the extraordinary frescoes adorning the building on the north side.

the balcony overlooking the square. Only the doorway remains of the original structure. It is now occupied by the Madrid City Council, and the main **tourist center** is on the ground floor. The principal building on the opposite side of the square is the **Casa de la Carnicería,** where butchers used to sell their meat.

The appearance of the square today dates back to the end of the 18th century, when a fire caused severe damage. The architect of the Prado Museum, Juan de Villanueva, remodeled the space by making the buildings more uniform and adding the entrance arches. These changes made the square a much more enclosed space than it had previously been, which some Madrileños blame for its decline in popularity. The

Ordering Coffee Just How You Like It

If you simply ask for *un café,* in most bars you will get an espresso, also known as *café solo. Café con leche* is an espresso with about double the quantity of hot milk. A *cortado* is an espresso with a dash of hot milk, like an Italian *macchiato.* An *americano* is an espresso topped up with hot water. To get more or less milk or coffee, specify *largo* or *corto de leche/café.* Most bars offer decaf espresso. Ask for a *descafeinado de máquina.* If you prefer instant coffee, ask for a Nescafé, which is usually served as a sachet with a cup of hot milk. If you want hot water instead, say *con agua.* You can ask separately for *un poco de leche fria/caliente* (a little cold/hot milk).

This is the **Casa de la Panadería,** which existed on this site before the square was built and for centuries was the headquarters of the bakers' guild. The frescoes, featuring the signs of the zodiac and allegories of temperature and time, were created in 1992 by Carlos Franco. The royal family had apartments in the building and used to watch events from

statue of Felipe III by Giovanni de Bologna and Pietro Tacca was created in 1616 but not installed here until the mid-19th century.

Nowadays, the square is more popular with tourists than locals, and the bars and restaurants have tailored their menus to cater to the largely foreign clientele. Check the prices before ordering and count your change carefully. ∎

EXPERIENCE: Flamenco & Other Dance Classes

Although flamenco is the traditional dance of Andalucía in southern Spain, it is very popular in Madrid, where there is a substantial Andalusian community. In fact, Madrid is widely regarded as the capital of flamenco, owing to the concentration of great dancers who are based here.

There are some excellent dance schools where you can take a class or two and at least get a basic idea of this most complex of dance forms, which will also enhance your enjoyment if you go to see a flamenco show. And there is no need to feel embarrassed about your lack of expertise; just make sure to sign up for

A flamenco dancer

a beginner's class and get ready to twirl your hands and stamp your feet.

Just being in the studio, part of the clattering din, is an experience unlike anything you are likely to have had before. The simple commands of "toe, heel, stamp" may sound straightforward enough, but you will really need to concentrate as the pace picks up. After an hour, you leave exhausted but exhilarated, and determined to track down a class when you get back home.

Centro de Danza Karen Taft *(Calle Libertad 15, tel 91 532 1373, www.karentaft .com)* Founded 60 years ago by the renowned Danish dancer Karen Taft, many famous names— including Penelope Cruz—have taken classes at this popular school in the funky Chueca neighborhood. As well as flamenco and *sevillanas*, the program includes tap, jazz, salsa, ballroom, and Caribbean dancing, with English-speaking teachers.

Estudios Amor de Dios *(Calle Santa Isabel 5, tel 91 360 0434, www.amorde dios.com)* Many of the great flamenco dancers have stamped their feet at Amor de Dios, which is the most renowned studio in Spain and is famous all over the world. You do not have to be an expert to take a class, however, as there are great programs for beginners, too.

Fundación Conservatorio Flamenco Casa Patas *(Calle Cañizares 10, tel 91 429 8471, www.casapatas. com)* Although best known as a flamenco venue and restaurant, Casa Patas also runs a cultural foundation that offers a program of dance, singing, and music classes. Intensive flamenco courses, usually lasting five days, are held periodically at reasonable prices, and you can also join classes on a one-time basis. This is a great place to hang out for anyone interested in flamenco.

El Horno *(Calle Esgrima 11, tel 91 527 5701, www.centroel horno.com)* There are nearly a hundred different classes offered at these friendly studios near Plaza de Tirso de Molina. Payment is by a voucher system, which works best if you are in Madrid for at least a week. It enables you to spend all day at the center if you wish and attend whatever classes take your fancy. There is a range of flamenco classes, as well as tango, *capoeira* (Afro-Brazilian dance), tap, Bollywood, ballroom, belly dancing, and dozens more.

Although El Horno is popular with professional dancers who come here to rehearse, most people frequent the place simply to enjoy themselves and do a little toning up. El Horno has a laid-back vibe; everyone is welcome and a lot of the instructors speak English.

Plaza de la Villa & Around

Plaza de la Villa, which today exudes a quiet dignity, was the most important square in Madrid until Plaza Mayor was built. The buildings framing it on three sides were built between the 15th and 17th centuries. In medieval times, the city council used to meet in the San Salvador church, situated at the top of the square until it was demolished in the 19th century.

The oldest building now is the **Torre y Casa de los Lujanes,** on the left as you look down from Calle Mayor; it dates from the end of the 15th century. The facade features bands of flint and mortar alternating with brick, a typical style of the time for aristocratic residences. While the arch on the right was built by Mudejar craftsmen, the main portal on the left dates only from the 1920s, when it was rebuilt in Castilian Gothic style by Luis Bellido. The various coats of arms are original, however, and belong to the prestigious Lujanes family.

The statue in the middle of the square is of Admiral Ivaro de Bazán, who triumphed at the Battle of Lepanto, fought between Christians and Ottomans off the coast of Greece in 1571. Author Miguel de Cervantes took part in the fighting and was wounded, losing the use of his left arm.

Taking up the other side of the square is the **Casa de la Villa,** formerly the City Hall, one of the signature buildings of Habsburg Madrid. Designed by Juan Gómez de Mora in the 1640s, the building was not completed until 1693 due to a shortage of funds. This was because mayors in Madrid did not have royal support, making it much more difficult to finance construction. In the late 18th

Slate pinnacles crown the austere Casa de la Villa, the civic center of Madrid from the 17th century until 2007.

century, Juan de Villanueva added the colonnaded loggia, which gives onto Calle Mayor.

Inside Casa de la Villa you will find 18th-century tapestries from the Royal Tapestry Factory and a late 16th-century silver monstrance that is carried through the neighboring streets for the

Plaza de la Villa
- Map p. 53
- Metro: Sol

Casa de la Villa

✉ Plaza de la
Villa 5

☎ 91 588 1000

🕐 Free guided
tours on Mon. at
5 p.m.

Corpus Christi processions. In the Assembly Room, where the councilors meet, there are 18th-century ceiling frescoes by Antonio Palomino (1655–1726).

The **Casa de Cisneros** (*Plaza de la Villa 4, tel 91 588 2906/7*), which takes up the bottom of the square, was built in 1537 as the residence of Benito Jiménez de Cisneros, the nephew of Cardinal Cisneros. It is linked to Casa de la Villa via a gallery and inside has a staircase decorated with tiles from Talavera, added after the Civil War. It is in the Plateresque style, which is the term used to describe the use of filigree decoration, similar to the work of silversmiths, popular with Spanish Renaissance architects in the 16th century. This facade, which was remodeled by Luis Bellido in the early 20th century, is now the main entrance, but originally this was the rear of the building.

Baroque Beauty

Next to the Casa de Cisneros is the elegant **Basílica Pontificia de San Miguel** (*Calle San Justo 4, tel 91 548 4011*), a truly baroque church with a concave facade that was designed by the Italian architect Giacomo Bonavia in 1739–1745. It was built for Prince Don Luis—the youngest son of Felipe V and Isabella Farnese—who was Archbishop of Toledo at the time, even though he was still a child. The church was originally dedicated to the child saints Justo and Pastor, who were martyred in Alcalá de Henares, east of Madrid, in the time of the Roman emperor Diocletian. Carvings of these

saints appear in a circular relief over the doorway. It is now run by the Opus Dei organization, and there is a highly realistic statue of the group's founder, José María Escrivá de Balaguer, in the second chapel on the left.

INSIDER TIP:

Breakfast like a Spaniard, standing up at a counter eating pastries and sipping *café con leche*.

—DEAN SNOW
National Geographic field researcher

Next to the church is the **Palacio Arzobispal** (Archbishop's Palace), built at the same time. Turn left up Calle de la Pasa and walk through Plaza Conde de Barajas to Plaza Conde de Miranda. On the left is the **Convento de las Carboneras** (*tel 91 548 3701, closed Sun.*), which was founded in the 17th century and belongs to the Spanish Hieronymite order. If you ring the bell marked *monjas* (nuns), you can buy cakes through a *turno*, a rotating drum that allows the cloistered nuns to deal with the outside world without being seen.

Leaving the square along the narrow Calle del Codo—the name means "elbow," reflecting the shape—by the convent brings you back to Plaza de la Villa. If you turn left out of the square along Calle Mayor and turn immediately right up Calle San Nicolás, you come to the **Iglesia de San Nicolás de**

los Servitas *(Plaza de San Nicolás, tel 91 559 4064)*. Begun in the 12th century, this is the oldest church in Madrid, although it has been altered and restored over the years. It is thought that a mosque once stood on this site. Built by Arab craftsmen, the bell tower with its horseshoe arches resembles a minaret. The presbytery features 15th-century Gothic vaulting, framed by the pointed horseshoe arch of the nave. Juan de Herrera, the architect of El Escorial (see pp. 228–231), was buried inside.

Tragic History

Returning to Calle Mayor, you will see a bronze angel across the way that commemorates the bomb, hidden in a bouquet of flowers, that was thrown on May 31, 1906, at the wedding procession of Alfonso XIII and Victoria Eugénie of Battenberg. The new queen of Spain was the granddaughter of Britain's Queen Victoria and the grandmother of the current King Juan Carlos. The two monarchs were not injured, but 23 other people died, and the bride's gown was stained red with blood.

Behind the monument is the **Iglesia Arzobispal Castrense** *(Calle del Sacramento 11, tel 91 547 3624)*, started in the 17th century and completed in the mid-1740s by Bartolomé Hurtado for the powerful Duke of Úceda, whose palace is next door. Originally it was part of a convent that was demolished in 1970. The frescoes on the ceiling vaults were painted in 1744 by the González Velázquez brothers, who worked on several other Madrid churches during that time. It is now the church of the Spanish armed forces in the capital. ■

The San Isidro Festival

A lot of festivals these days seem to be staged for tourists, but that cannot be said of San Isidro, which celebrates the patron saint of Madrid. Although visitors are very welcome to enjoy the festival, the activities are really aimed at locals. The main day is May 15, but there are related events for a couple of weeks either side of this date, with processions, concerts, theatrical performances, dances, and children's activities, mostly held at open-air venues, as well as a fortnight of bullfights featuring the most prestigious matadors in the country.

The most popular venue is the **Pradera de San Isidro,** now a park on the hill on the far side of the Río Manzanares river. It was here that San Isidro worked in the fields at the end of the 11th century,

performing some of the miracles attributed to him. Now, you can line up to drink from a fountain reputed to be on the spot where he made water spring from the ground on a hot day to quench the thirst of the landowner.

People also gather in the **Plaza Mayor,** the **Plaza de la Paja,** and the surrounding streets, with special Masses in Iglesia de San Isidro el Real church, which houses the remains of the saint. Women wear long, tight dresses and fringed silk shawls, with carnations in their hair. The men wear checked vests and caps, narrow black trousers, and neckerchiefs. The **Plaza de Vistillas,** where bands play *pasodobles* and other traditional dances, is perhaps the most atmospheric spot to get into the swing, particularly as night falls.

A Walk Around Habsburg Madrid

This walk takes you through the lanes of the oldest part of the city, known as "Madrid de los Austrias," or Habsburg Madrid. Only a few buildings survive from the period, but the medieval atmosphere still permeates the streets, particularly at dusk.

A couple snatch a kiss outside Taberna de San Isidro in Plaza de la Puerta Cerrada.

Leave **Plaza Mayor ❶** (see pp. 54–55) through the arch in the northwest corner, along the passageway called Calle Ciudad Rodrigo. The Bar Valle del Tiétar, on the left at No. 5 with a typical red wooden frontage, was a notorious criminal den in the 19th century. The **Mercado de San Miguel ❷** *(Plaza de San Miguel, tel 91 548 1214, closed Sat. p.m & Sun., Metro: Sol, La Latina)*, constructed in 1916, is the last ironwork-built market in Madrid. The structure has been restored, but these days Madrileños increasingly favor supermarkets over traditional markets.

Turn immediately left on Calle Cava San Miguel, originally a ditch outside the city wall. The 17th-century houses get taller down the hill, forming the wall of Plaza Mayor. Now it is lined with tapas bars, known as *mesones*, each one specializing in a particular dish.

The street becomes **Calle Cuchilleros**, named after the knife- and swordmakers who

NOT TO BE MISSED:

Plaza Mayor • Calle Cuchilleros
• Plaza de la Paja

used to be based along it. **Casa Botín** at No. 17 is the oldest and best known restaurant in Madrid (see p. 242). You reach **Plaza de Puerta Cerrada ❸**, where one of the city gates used to stand. Murals were painted onto the buildings in the 1980s.

Turn right down the steep **Calle Segovia,** a stream in medieval times, flowing to the Río Manzanares. Paleolithic, Roman, and Visigothic remains have been found nearby. The imposing concrete bridge up ahead is known as the **Viaducto** and was built in the 1930s. The leaning Mudejar tower of **Iglesia de San Pedro el Viejo ❹** (see p. 63) rises up on the left.

On the right is the sloping **Plaza de la Cruz Verde,** which got its name from a green wooden cross that once stood there. These crosses had a sinister significance, as they marked the spots where the Inquisition held trials of faith and carried out executions. These days, café tables sit peacefully under the trees.

Opposite the square, turn right along Calle Alamillo, which leads to the tiny, triangular **Plaza de Alamillo ❺.** This plaza is where the Arab law courts were situated and served as the center of the Moorish quarter after the Christian conquest.

Turn up Calle Alfonso VI, which leads to **Plaza de la Paja,** with the Iglesia de San Andrés at the top (see p. 63). Walking just beyond San Andrés you emerge into a large open space with pavement cafés. This part is called **Plaza de los Carros ❻,** but each side has a

different name. This was the site of another city gate, the **Puerta de Moros,** where wine merchants used to arrive from the vineyards of La Mancha. Turn off the square into **Calle Cava Baja ❼,** which, like Calle Cava San Miguel, was originally a ditch around the city wall. The many bars and restaurants lining the street today are vestiges of the medieval inns that provided accommodation for the wine merchants.

Cava Baja leads back to Plaza de la Puerta Cerrada. Cross the road and cut up Calle Latoneros to Calle Toledo, then walk back up through the arch to Plaza Mayor.

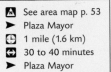

🅰	See area map p. 53
►	Plaza Mayor
🕐	1 mile (1.6 km)
↔	30 to 40 minutes
►	Plaza Mayor

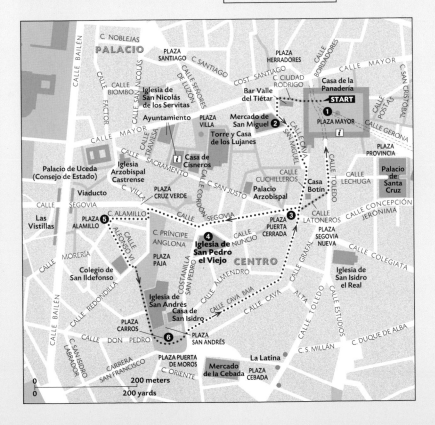

Plaza de la Paja & Around

Plaza de la Paja is a laid-back urban space now, but in the Middle Ages it was the busiest spot in town. It was the most important marketplace in Muslim Madrid, and, for centuries afterward under Christian rule, it was flanked by grand residences where the most important families lived. Farmers who worked in the nearby fields were obliged to donate a tenth of their crop to the Iglesia de San Andrés, which became a powerful economic institution.

The Capilla de San Isidro was even more ornate before it was severely damaged in the Civil War.

Plaza de la Paja
Map p. 53
Metro: La Latina

At the beginning of the 12th century, a young man named Isidro worked as a laborer for Iván de Vargas, a nobleman who lived in the square and owned land on the other side of the river. Deeply religious, Isidro did all he could to help the sick, children, animals, and people down on their luck. More than 400 miracles were attributed to him, and he is now the patron saint of Madrid.

When Ferdinand and Isabella, the future Catholic Monarchs, came to Madrid to claim their right to the throne at the end of the 15th century, they stayed at a palace in the square, where No. 14 is now. At the bottom of the square you can take a break in the **Jardín del Príncipe de Anglona.** This small garden was laid out in 1920 adjoining the Palacio de Anglona, a grand residence that

INSIDER TIP:

South of Plaza de Oriente, take your siesta among rose pergolas, acacia, and plane trees in the beautiful little 18th-century Jardín del Príncipe de Anglona.

—CHRISTOPHER SOMERVILLE
National Geographic author

is now apartments. Just off the square beyond the palace is the **Iglesia de San Pedro el Viejo** *(Calle Nuncio 14, tel 91 365 1284),* which was built in the mid-14th century on the site of a mosque and has a leaning tower with loophole windows built by Arab craftsmen. The church was largely rebuilt in the 17th century, but it still has 15th-century Gothic vaulting and a Renaissance door from 1525.

The **Iglesia de San Andrés** *(tel 91 365 4871),* at the top of Plaza de la Paja, was one of the first to be built following the Christian Reconquest, in the heart of what was then the Moorish quarter. The church was mostly destroyed by fire in the Civil War. The facade facing Plaza de la Paja belongs to a separate private chapel called the **Capilla del Obispo,** one of the finest late-Gothic structures in Madrid. This was built in 1520 by the Vargas family to provide a grand setting for the tomb of San Isidro. The chapel is undergoing a lengthy renovation process and is not scheduled to open to the public in the near future.

The octagonal dome rising up behind it belongs to the recently restored **Capilla de San Isidro,** built alongside San Andrés in the 17th century using stone from an old Arab wall. The remains of San Andrés are now incorporated into the rear section of this structure. The Capilla de San Isidro was also built to house the tomb of San Isidro, but in the late 18th century the tomb was transferred to the nearby Iglesia de San Isidro el Real (see p. 67).

On the other side of the church, on Plaza de San Andrés, is the interesting **Museo de los Orígenes,** on a site where Isidro is believed to have lived, and, indeed, died. Exhibits chart the saint's life and also deal with the development of Madrid from prehistory to the 17th century. ■

Museo de los Orígenes

✉ Plaza de San Andrés 2

☎ 91 366 7415

🕐 Closed Sat. p.m., Sun. p.m., & Mon.

 Metro: La Latina, Tirso de Molina

www.munimadrid .es/museosanisidro

Mealtimes— & Odd Hours Options

It is unusual in Madrid to have lunch before 2 p.m., or dinner before 10 p.m., but there are ways around this. Lots of cafés serve food all day, and tapas bars are particularly good for eating around 8 p.m. Usually you can grab a table and order a series of dishes, thus enjoying a sit-down meal if that's how you feel more comfortable. If you want to eat at around 6 p.m., look for a *cafetería*, which is a large bar with tables that usually serves full meals at all times.

Traditional Taverns

The fashion for bars and cafeterias meant that Madrid lost dozens of its traditional taverns in the second half of the 20th century. In recent years, however, the Madrileños have realized that the taverns are an important part of their heritage and those that have survived are firmly back in vogue.

Colorful taverns such as Venta el Buscón are having a revival in Madrid.

Taverns are closely connected to the history of Madrid because they started to appear soon after the Christian Reconquest in 1085. Muleteers stoked the tradition by bringing wine from the Valdepeñas vineyards in La Mancha to the city gate at Puerta de Moros in the heart of the old town. By the 14th century, there were about 40 bars, a figure that rose sixfold by the 17th century, during the reign of fun-loving Felipe IV.

Classic taverns have wooden frontages painted a deep red or brown, a tradition dating to the 19th century. Signs are either hand-painted or engraved on glass. In the 1920s, the facades began to be decorated more ornately with hand-painted tiles. Inside, the taverns typically have a marble or carved wooden bar with a long shallow trough at one end made of tin or zinc. A tap is left running all the time to keep everything cool and clean, and flasks of wine sit chilling in the pool of water in the trough.

Totally authentic, **La Taberna de Antonio Sánchez** (*Calle Mesón de Paredes 13, tel 91 539 7826, closed Sun. p.m.*) was founded in 1830 and has always been run by ex-bullfighters, as borne out by the paintings and photographs adorning the paneled walls—not to mention the enormous bull's head. Customers sit at marble tables to drink draft vermouth and eat tasty canapés. The restaurant at the back specializes in braised bull's tail and blood sausage, as well as *torrijas*, a delicious dessert made from bread soaked in milk, sugar, and cinnamon.

Cervantes Lived Here

Believed to the oldest surviving tavern in the city, **Casa Alberto** (*Calle Huertas 18, tel 91 429 9356, closed Sun. p.m. & Mon.*) opened in 1827. A couple of centuries earlier, Cervantes lived in a house on this site, where he wrote the second part of *Don Quixote*. These days, a range of traditional tapas is displayed on the onyx counter, with more substantial meals served in the tavern's restaurant.

Casa Labra (*Calle Tetuán 12, tel 91 531 0081*) has a typical brown wooden frontage with an acid-engraved glass sign, a skill that sadly is dying out. Founded in 1860, it was a favorite haunt of Ernest Hemingway's, as well as of the bullfighters Antonio Ordóñez and Luis Miguel Domínguín. In 1879, the Spanish Socialist Workers' Party was founded in a back room by Pablo Iglesias. Everything but the counter is original, and people flock here from the surrounding shopping streets for exquisite cod in batter, croquettes, and excellent draft beer.

With its mosaic tiles from 1908, **La Taberna de la Dolores** (*Plaza de Jesús 4, tel 91 429 2243*) is easy to spot. There were tiles inside too until the 1960s, when the owner thought them old-fashioned and tore them out. The draft beer is renowned as the best in Madrid, as it is still pulled by the traditional method of leaving it to settle, then putting a head on it before serving.

EXPERIENCE: Cocido Madrileño

The signature dish in Madrid is not paella or gazpacho, but a hearty stew called *cocido madrileño*, made with chickpeas, ham, beef, chorizo sausage, cabbage, leeks, noodles, and quite a few other things besides.

Surprisingly, it is difficult to find a really good cocido madrileño, but for an authentic Madrid experience it is well worth making a trek to one of the places recommended here. Although all of the ingredients are cooked together, the stew is usually served in two stages. First you eat the broth, and then the chickpeas, vegetables, meat, and sausages are served on separate platters for everyone to help themselves. Until the late 1950s, cocido was the staple meal in Madrid, eaten nearly every day, but it is now reserved for special occasions in most households.

La Bola (*La Bola 5, tel 91 547 6930*) The cocido is served in blackened earthenware pots in this pretty restaurant, founded in 1870, near the Royal Palace.
Lhardy (*Carrera de San Jerónimo 8, tel 91 521 3385*) Reputed to serve the best cocido in Madrid, Lhardy has barely changed since the late 19th century.
Taberna de la Daniela (*Calle General Pardiñas 21, tel 91 575 2329*) This is a lovely tiled restaurant in the Salamanca district where the cocido is prepared to perfection. In addition, Taberna de la Daniela is off the tourist beat.
Taberna Malacatín (*Calle Ruda 5, tel 91 365 5241*) Such is the popularity of this traditional tavern, you need to book at least a day ahead ... and order your cocido at the same time.

Basílica de San Francisco el Grande

San Francisco was Madrid's unofficial cathedral until the Almudena was completed in 1994, and many still consider it to be the most important church in the city. After decades in the doldrums, it is gradually being restored. A work by Goya is just one of its artistic treasures.

Basílica de San Francisco el Grande

 Map p. 53

☎ 91 365 3800

🕒 Closed Sat. p.m., Sun., & Mon.

💲 $

🚇 Metro: La Latina, Puerta de Toledo

According to legend, St. Francis of Assisi founded a monastery on this site in 1217, making it one of the earliest such buildings in Madrid. In 1760, Carlos III decided a grander structure was required and had the original buildings demolished.

The inexperienced architect Brother Francisco Cabezas drew up big plans for the new cathedral, which included a dome 183 feet (56 m) high with a diameter of 108 feet (33 m), making it one of the world's biggest. The design posed problems, which the leading architects of the time—Francesco Sabatini, Ventura Rodríguez, and Diego de Villanueva—helped to overcome, amid much acrimony. The monks had to leave following the disentailment of the monasteries in 1836. The structure later served as an army barracks and a national pantheon.

The cathedral's main altar was restored in 2005 and features paintings depicting the life of St. Francis by Manuel Domínguez and Alejandro Ferrant. The Goya painting, dating from 1782–1783, is in the first chapel on the left as you enter the church; it shows St. Bernardino of Siena preaching a sermon. Goya painted himself into the picture on the right, wearing a yellow jacket. The artist was only 37 years old at the time and had not yet been appointed court painter. The church also contains paintings by Francisco de Zurbarán, Alonso Cano, and Francisco Pacheco, who was Velázquez's father-in-law.

On the right of the main entrance is the **Capilla del Cristo de los Dolores de la Venerable Orden Tercera.** Built in the 17th century, the chapel features a baldachin containing a sculpture of Christ. ■

The huge dome of the Basílica de San Francisco el Grande

Iglesia de San Isidro el Real

One of the most important churches in Madrid, San Isidro acted as the city's cathedral for a century, until Nuestra Señora de la Almudena (see pp. 78–79) opened in 1994. Built in 1664, it was originally the church of the Colegio Imperial de la Compañía de Jesús, a Jesuit school funded by Empress María of Habsburg. The royal patronage attracted some famous names, including writers Lope de Vega, Calderón de la Barca, and Francisco de Quevedo.

The baroque structure with twin towers and a slate dome was designed by Pedro Sánchez and Francisco Bautista, who was inspired by Il Gesù in Rome. After the Jesuits were expelled from Spain in 1767 by Carlos III, Ventura Rodríguez revamped the interior in neoclassic style. The remains of San Isidro and his wife, Santa María de la Cabeza, were transferred here from the nearby Capilla de San Isidro in 1789 (see p. 63).

In the reign of Fernando VII, the church returned to the Jesuits, but tragedy struck in 1834 when rumors spread through the city that the priests were responsible for poisoning the water in fountains around Madrid. An angry mob burst into the church and killed 14 priests. The building was badly damaged in 1938 during the Civil War and had to be largely rebuilt. There is still a school

Festivalgoers at San Isidro venerate Madrid's patron saint.

alongside, the Instituto San Isidro, which retains its original baroque granite courtyard.

The main altar, built in the 18th century by Ventura Rodríguez, contains the tombs of the saint and his wife. On the left of the main altar, an oval chapel holds figures of the two saints. The three chapels on the right have figures of the Virgen de los Reyes, the Virgen de la Esperanza Macarena, and Jesús del Gran Poder, images that are revered by Madrid's Andalusian community. ∎

INSIDER TIP:

I love sitting on a rooftop terrace in La Latina on a Sunday afternoon with a sweet red vermouth.

—LAURA MARTIN
National Geographic Glimpse
contributor

Iglesia de San Isidro el Real

- 🅰 Map p. 53
- ✉ Calle Toledo 37–39
- ☎ 91 369 2037
- 🚇 Metro: La Latina

More Places to Visit in Plaza Mayor & Old Town

Iglesia de Santa Cruz

The neo-Gothic church with a distinctive neo-Mudejar tower was designed in 1878 by the Marquis of Cubas (1826–1899), although it was not completed until 1902. It contains a rich collection of religious paintings, sculptures, and monstrances from local convents that were demolished in the 19th century. During Holy Week the church leads the Procession of Silence held on Good Friday.  Map p. 53 ☒ Calle de Atocha 6 ☎ 91 369 1239 🚇 Metro: Sol, Tirso de Molina

Palacio de Abrantes

Now the Italian Institute of Culture and formerly the Italian Embassy (1888–1939),

Palacio de Abrantes, now the Italian Institute of Culture, dates back to the 17th century.

the palace was built in 1652 and restored from 1842 onward when it was owned by the Duke of Abrantes. During the Civil War, the building was occupied by the Italian battalions of the International Brigades. Fragments of the 12th-century Iglesia de Santa María and the 9th-century Arab wall are visible alongside it. Map p. 53 ☒ Calle Mayor 86 ☎ 91 547 5205 🚇 Metro: Ópera

Palacio de Santa Cruz

With its redbrick facade and slate turrets, this palace is a fine example of Habsburg baroque architecture. Designed by Cristóbal de Aguilera, it is now the Ministry of Foreign Affairs. Originally built as a prison between 1629 and 1643 it later housed law courts and the Overseas Ministry. The stone portal features the coat of arms of Felipe IV, sculpted by Antonio Herrera Barnuevo. George Borrow (1803–1881), the British writer, linguist, and salesman for the Bible Society, spent three weeks in the prison in 1838, accused of promoting heretic beliefs, but he was treated as an honored guest rather than a prisoner. Other famous inmates included the colorful bandit Luis Candelas and the playwright Lope de Vega. Map p. 53 ☒ Plaza Provincia 1 ☎ 91 379 9550 🚇 Metro: Sol, Tirso de Molina

Palacio de Úceda

Built in the early 17th century for the Duke of Úceda, the favorite of Felipe III, the palace set a design precedent for some of the most important civil buildings of the period, including the Casa de la Villa (see pp. 57–58). It no longer looks so imposing as its two towers were destroyed by fire in the 18th century. The palace currently houses the Council of State and is also the army's military headquarters. Map p. 53 ☒ Calle Mayor 79 ☎ 91 516 6262 🚇 Metro: Ópera

Where opulent buildings bear witness to the French and Italian influences of the 18th and 19th centuries

Palacio Real
& Around

A young Madrileño in traditional dress

Palacio Real & Around

The Palacio Real (Royal Palace) stands on the edge of a promontory in the west of the city. This excellent vantage point, with views across the plains to the Guadarrama mountains, was the reason the Moors chose this site for their citadel in the ninth century.

The palace began its existence as part of a string of fortresses that spanned the countryside to protect the important city of Toledo to the south. After the Christian Reconquest at the end of the 11th century, the new rulers occupied the fortress, known as the Alcázar, and established their first churches nearby, often converting existing mosques.

After Felipe II made Madrid his capital in 1561, religious orders flocked to the city and convents sprang up all over town. One of the most important, the Descalzas Reales, was founded by his sister, and its amazing treasures are now open to the public. Fifty years later, Felipe III's wife set up a less extravagant but equally fascinating convent, the

Encarnación, close to the Palacio Real.

In the 17th century, the royal family was still living in the ramshackle structure left over from the Muslims. A devastating fire in the 18th century gave monarch Felipe V the opportunity to build a much more fitting residence, which he indeed began. It was, however, not completed until 1764, when his son, Carlos III, was on the throne. Future Bourbon monarchs added to the palace's decoration and extensive collections

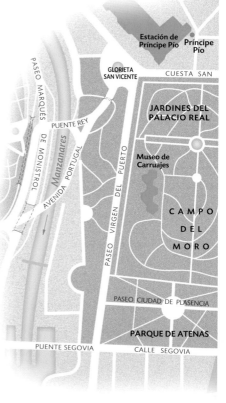

NOT TO BE MISSED:

to create the lavish residence seen today.

Madrileños are still getting used to the Almudena cathedral next to the palace. It was completed in the 1990s after more than a century of delays and setbacks. Local resistance to the new church was softened to some extent by the widespread delight arising from the royal wedding in 2004 between Prince Felipe, heir to the Spanish crown, and Letizia Ortiz, a former television journalist. The couple had their first public kiss on the Palacio Real's balcony overlooking grand Plaza de Oriente.

The construction of the opera house on the opposite side of the square strengthened the stylish character of the area, where the handsome apartment buildings are now some of the most coveted addresses in the city. Sit at a café and soak up the elegant atmosphere in this area, a world away from the medieval streets of the nearby Plaza Mayor. ■

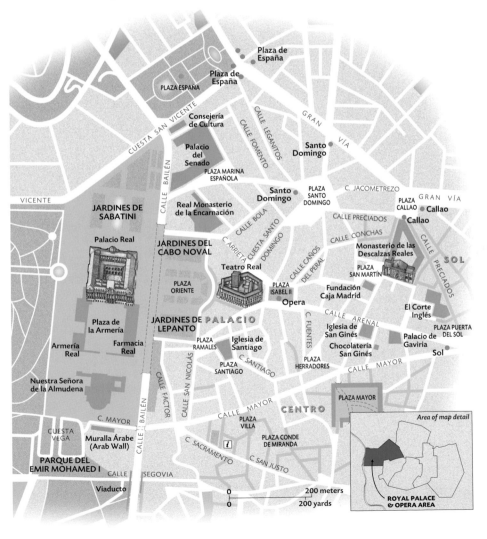

Palacio Real & Gardens

The present Spanish royal family projects a relatively modest, low-key image, but their fore-bears in the 18th and 19th centuries loved to flaunt their importance and wealth. Their residence, the Palacio Real (Royal Palace), is a dizzying ensemble of ornately decorated rooms. It was the main royal residence until 1931, when Alfonso XIII, the grandfather of King Juan Carlos, abdicated and went into exile. Today, the Palacio Real is used for state ceremonies.

The Palacio Real's strategic site affords panoramic views across the city to the Guadarrama Mountains.

Palacio Real

- 🅰 Map pp. 70–71
- ✉ Calle Bailén
- ☎ 91 454 8800
- 🕐 Closed Sun. p.m. & for official ceremonies
- 💲 $$. Free on Wed. for EU citizens. Optional guided tours in English.
- 🚇 Metro: Ópera

www.patrimonionaci onal.es/preal/preal .htm

The elegant Palacio Real rises on on the site of a ninth-century former Moorish fortress, which became a royal residence after Felipe II moved the court to Madrid in 1561. After much of the building was destroyed by fire in 1734, the Bourbon Felipe V ordered the construction of a new palace. The expansive design was influenced by the tastes he had acquired while growing up at Versailles in France, as well as by the opin-ions of his forceful Italian wife, Isabella Farnese.

The original architect was the Italian Filippo Juvarra, who planned a palace twice the size of Versailles. However, he died before his ideas got any further than the drawing board, and his plans were then modified by Giovanni Battista Sacchetti, with contribu-tions by Ventura Rodríguez and Francesco Sabatini. To reduce the risk of further fires, the palace was built using limestone from

Colmenar and granite from the Guadarrama mountains northwest of Madrid.

Visiting the Palace

To enter the palace, you walk across the vast parade ground, where the Changing of the Royal Guard takes place at noon on the first Wednesday of each month, except in July, August, and September. The visit starts in a hall where a statue of King Carlos III as a Roman general stands at the foot of a grand staircase made from Toledo marble. The surprisingly shallow steps were designed so that ladies could go upstairs in their restrictive clothing or be carried in sedan chairs.

The ceiling above the staircase is covered with frescoes by Corrado Giaquinto (1703–1765). The staircase leads up to the **Hall of the Halberdiers,** which was used by the royal guards and is decorated with tapestries. The ceiling was painted by Giovanni Battista Tiepolo (1696–1770). Bronze sculptures symbolizing the planets and Roman busts in the **Hall of Columns** were saved from the 1734 fire. The dictator General Franco lay in state there after his death in 1975.

The ceiling of the lavishly decorated **Throne Room,** also painted by Tiepolo, is an allegorical representation of the power of the Spanish monarchy. The decor dates from the original monarchs. The room also contains mirrors, Venetian chandeliers, and several ornate clocks. The two thrones, made in 1977 for King Juan Carlos and Queen Sofía, feature their portraits in miniature. Spanish monarchs are not crowned, only proclaimed, so the king and queen do not wear crowns when sitting on their thrones.

The **King's Rooms** were occupied by Carlos III when he moved into the palace in 1764. The antechamber contains four portraits by Goya of Carlos IV and Queen María Luisa of Parma, which are the highlight of all the paintings on display in the palace. Carlos III used to get dressed, aided by his courtiers, in the rococo **Gasparini Room,** which is named after the Italian decorator responsible

The Spanish Inquisition

Lasting three and a half centuries and resulting in the torture and death of thousands of people, the Spanish Inquisition has certainly left an impact on Spain. But on the local level, the grand inquisition often began and ended with a petty allegation, often made by a grudge-holding neighbor against someone else in the village.

In 1635, a man was tried because he ate bacon on a day he was supposed to abstain from eating meat. In 1530, a man was brought before the Inquisition for having drunkenly urinated on a wall outside a church.

In an interesting case from 1581, two men, afraid their wives would denounce them, turned themselves in for telling their spouses that sex wasn't a sin (it was viewed as such at the time). Luckily, most of these heretics received no more than a slap on the wrist.

for the embroidered silk walls, swirling marble mosaic floor, and ornately stuccoed ceiling. The blue walls in the **Bedroom**, where the king died in 1788, are decorated with lions, castles, and fleurs-de-lis, the symbols of the Spanish monarchy.

The **Porcelain Room,** which was used for smoking, is decorated with china panels on the theme of Bacchus, god of wine. Tapestries adorn the walls of the adjoining **Yellow Room,** where the ladies would eat chocolates, sitting on marquetry chairs, while the men puffed away next door.

The **Banqueting Hall** takes opulence to new heights with Flemish silk tapestries, Chinese and French vases, and gilded stucco on the walls. It was created in 1879 in the reign of Alfonso XII from a series of smaller rooms. A row of 25 chandeliers illuminates the table, which seats 144 and is used for entertaining foreign heads of state. Diners can gaze up at the ceiling painting of Christopher Columbus announcing his discovery of the New World to Ferdinand and Isabella. The slightly larger dining chairs are used by the king and queen.

The next series of rooms is used to exhibit some of the palace's extensive collections. The first room was used as a cinema by Alfonso XIII. These days, an orchestra occasionally plays in the room to entertain guests in the Banqueting Hall. Although much of the royal silver was melted down by Joseph Bonaparte, the **Silver Room**

Gasparini Room

Plaza de Armas

Armería Real

Visitor Center

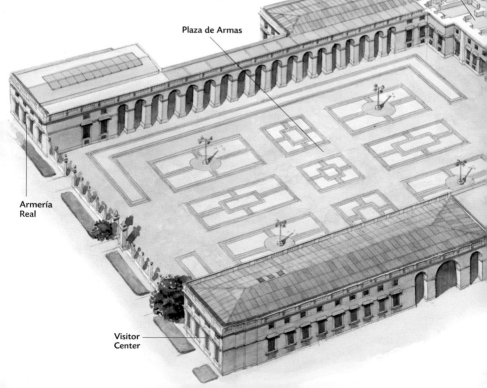

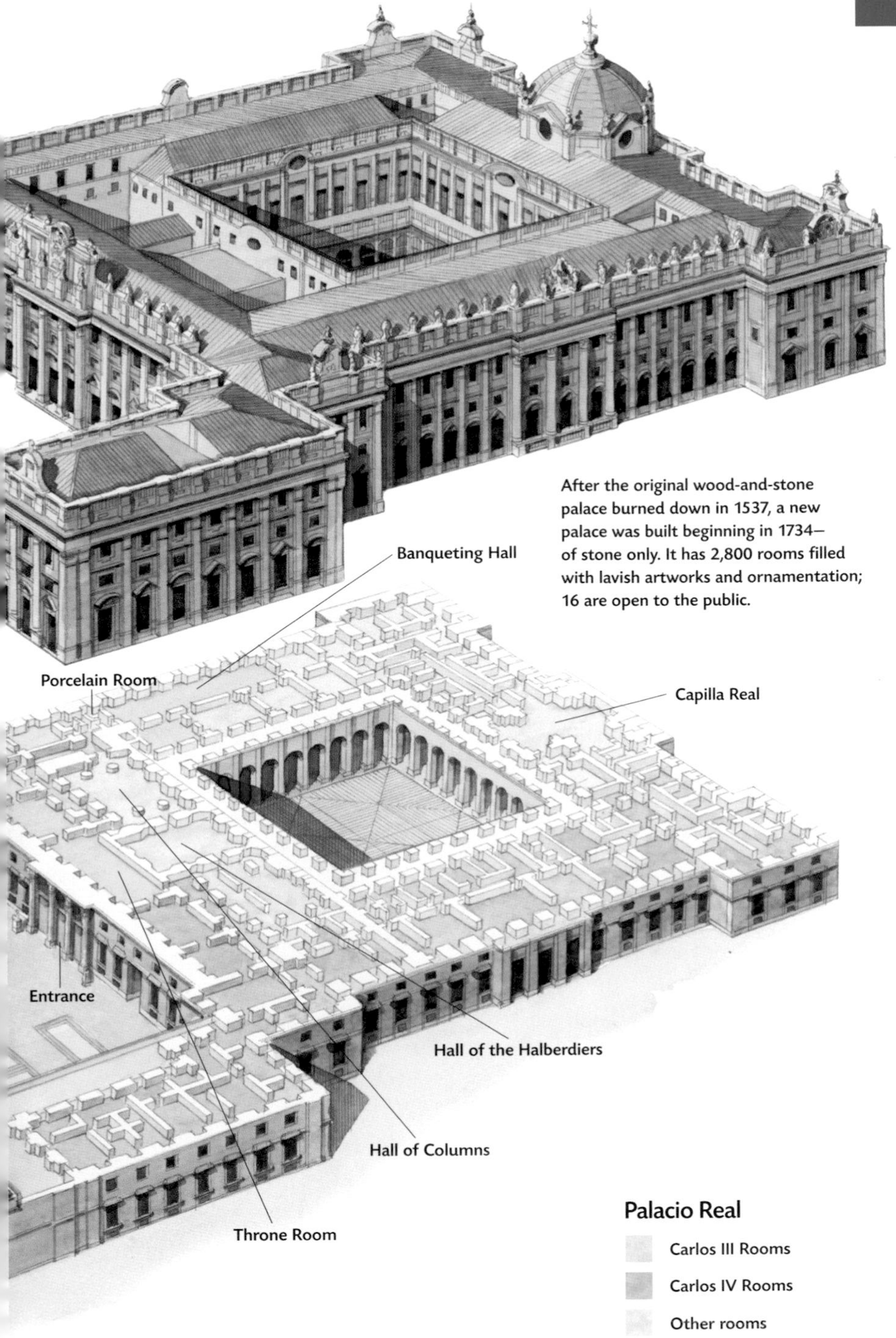

Banqueting Hall

After the original wood-and-stone palace burned down in 1537, a new palace was built beginning in 1734—of stone only. It has 2,800 rooms filled with lavish artworks and ornamentation; 16 are open to the public.

Porcelain Room

Capilla Real

Entrance

Hall of the Halberdiers

Hall of Columns

Throne Room

Palacio Real

Carlos III Rooms

Carlos IV Rooms

Other rooms

EXPERIENCE: Sangria on a Hot Day

Sangria comes from the Spanish word for blood (sangre), and it powers many a Spanish and Spanish-lover's heart. Madrileños and visitors to their fair city find few better ways to mellow out from the bright Iberian sun than enjoying a jarra (pitcher) of the local drink with friends and some pleasant conversation. You can find sangria at almost any bar; **Las Cuevas De Sesamo** (Calle Principe 7) and **Stop Madrid** (Calle Hortaleza 11) are favorites.

To make your own sangria, the following classic recipe makes four to six servings:

Begin with a lemon, orange, and apple. Cut the lemon and orange into 1/4-inch slices, and the apple into chunks. Toss the fruit into a pitcher, then add anywhere between 1/4 and 1/2 cup of sugar. Pour in a bottle of dry red wine plus a shot of brandy.

Refrigerate the solution for at least an hour, giving it time both to chill and to mix the flavors. Before serving, mix in 2 cups of soda water. Serve over ice, and don't forget to eat the fruit. A rioja makes the best base, but sangria made with white wine is just as good.

There are many variations on the classic. One of the best is spicy sangria, made the same way but substitute rum for the brandy and add a teaspoon of hot sauce.

contains some interesting exhibits, including a punch bowl brought to the palace by Alfonso XIII's English wife Victoria Eugénie. The queen wanted to introduce the custom of drinking punch, but the Spanish resisted her efforts and chose to stick with sangria.

Felipe V commissioned Antonio Stradivari (1644–1737) to make a cello, a viola, and two violins, which now form the most valuable collection of Stradivari's instruments in the world and are on display in the **Stradivarius Room.** They are still played occasionally at concerts in the Hall of Columns. The **Ceramics Room** contains chinaware made by the East India Company, Meissen, and Sèvres.

After emerging into the gallery around the inner courtyard, you enter the **Capilla Real** (Royal Chapel), designed in neoclassic style by Ventura Rodríguez. Black marble columns surround the single nave; frescoes on the dome

INSIDER TIP:

Spend a couple of hours bar-hopping in the neighborhood around Cava San Miguel. Each bar specializes in a different tapa.

—STEVEN RAICHLEN
National Geographic Traveler magazine writer

are by Corrado Giaquinto.

The final series of rooms made up the collected apartments of Queen María Luisa of Parma. Alfonso XII remodeled part of this section to create a walnut-paneled billiard room and a smoking room in Japanese style. The final room is a rococo study with marble marquetry and embroidered silk wall panels.

Much more remains to be seen when you return to the outside courtyard. On the right is the **Armería Real** (Royal Armory), which was founded by Felipe II and displays armor worn by kings and princes over the centuries, as well as shields, helmets, and swords.

On the other side of the outside courtyard is the **Farmacia Real** (Royal Pharmacy), founded in 1594. It contains a reconstruction of a distillery and an alchemy laboratory modeled on ones at El Escorial. Exhibits include ceramic jars from Talavera and copper stills. Huge books record treatments for the royal family, and leather trunks contain pharmacy kits the family used when traveling. Next door is a visitors' center with a café and a good bookshop on the top floor.

The Gardens

You cannot currently reach the gardens from this end of the palace. Leaving the complex, turn left and walk the length of the building to reach the **Jardines de Sabatini.** Although these landscaped gardens were not created until the royal stables were demolished in the 1930s, the designs were drawn up in the 18th century. From this angle, you get a good view of the chapel's dome and can appreciate the way the palace is built into the hillside.

To get to the main palace gardens, known as the **Campo del Moro,** you have to cross the Sabatini Gardens, then walk down Cuesta de San Vicente and turn left along Paseo de la Virgen del Puerto to reach the entrance. The name, which means "Field of the Moor," arose from the encampment held there by besieging Arab soldiers in 1109, 24 years after

Alfonso VI and his Christian army had taken over Madrid.

Until the gardens were created in the late 1800s, the palace stood on a steep escarpment. The sloping hillside was devised by the architect Narciso Pascual y Colomer (1801–1870) and features avenues flanked by magnolias, chestnuts, acacias, cedars, and bamboos. The impressive lawn leading down from the palace was added in the 1960s. The 16th-century Triton fountain was originally found in the palace gardens in Aranjuez (see p. 220). ■

Visitors climb the grand staircase to visit the state rooms.

Nuestra Señora de la Almudena & Around

Madrid did not have its own cathedral until Pope John Paul II consecrated this structure in 1993. It took more than a century to build, proceeding in several phases with long periods of inactivity. Every time construction resumed, the new architects altered the plans to suit changing architectural tastes. To describe the end result as "eclectic" is putting it mildly.

The Almudena cathedral fits neatly alongside the Palacio Real on the edge of the old town.

Nuestra Señora de la Almudena

- Map pp. 70–71
- Calle Bailén 10
- 91 542 2200
- Cathedral: free. Temporary exhibitions: $
- Metro: Ópera

Construction began during the period of economic buoyancy that followed the restoration of the monarchy in the late 19th century. The cathedral started out as a neo-Gothic structure with a large neo-Romanesque crypt, designed by the Marquis of Cubas. Although the crypt was completed in 1911, the main cathedral was only partly built. Further development was hindered by political upheaval, financial restraints, and the Civil War. In the 1940s, Fernando Chueca Goitia and Carlos Sidro

came up with a design that encased the crypt and what had been built of the main structure in a neoclassic shell.

The name "Almudena" is of Arabic origin and refers to the grain store situated on the edge of the Muslim enclave. According to legend, a figure

INSIDER TIP:

Stay at an inn over-looking the Plaza de Oriente. Wake up to a view of the Palacio Real and music from accordion players.

—ELLIANA SPIEGEL
National Geographic contributor

of the Madonna was hidden in the wall in the eighth century by Visigothic settlers to protect it from the invading Moors. After the Reconquest, the figure miracu-lously reappeared, flanked by burning candles, thereby lending some weight to Madrid's tenuous Christian heritage.

The most elegant element of the cathedral is the slate dome, which sits on an octagonal drum over the Latin-cross transept. Light floods into the side naves through upper rose windows. As you enter, look for the figure of St. John the Baptist by 18th-century French sculptor Robert Michel (1720–1786). In the chapel opposite is an exceptional "Christ Tied to the Column," which was sculpted by Giacomo Colombo in the 17th century.

Don't miss the **crypt,** which is arguably of greater interest than the cathedral itself. You can reach it either by the main door on Cuesta de la Vega or via a stone stair just inside the cathedral entrance. It features scores of neo-Romanesque capitals, intricately adorned with plants, castles, and animals, illuminated by the multi-colored light of the stained-glass windows. The chapels contain the tombs of important 19th-century families. Presiding over the presby-tery behind the high altar is a copy of the figure of the Madonna of the Almudena.

Crossing the Cuesta de la Vega, you can also see a small section of the ninth-century **Arab wall,** which now forms part of the open space known as the Parque del Emir Mohamed I. There is now excavation work underway on the slope behind the Cathedral to find more vestiges of the ancient wall, which in the future will become part of a museum. ■

Arab wall

Map pp. 70–71
Parque del Emir Mohamed I, Cuesta de la Vega
Metro: Ópera

Housing Story

In the 16th century, a bylaw was introduced to ease the housing shortage arising from Madrid's having been named the nation's capital. People in homes of more than one story were forced to pro-vide accommodation for courtiers and the nobility. Many Madrileños were annoyed. To get around the bylaw, they built houses with only one story facing the street but rising higher at the back.

Plaza de Oriente

This vast, semicircular space was conceived during the brief reign of Joseph Bonaparte (1808–1813) as king of Spain. It was the most important of the many urban changes he started, but the square was not completed until the second half of the 19th century. The mansard roofs and stuccoed facades reflect the French influence at that time. Unlike the popular, practical Plaza Mayor, Plaza de Oriente was always intended to be a ceremonial plaza.

Visitors cool off by the fountains in Plaza de Oriente.

Work began in 1811 and drastically altered the area, destroying several churches as well as the library of the Palacio Real. When Fernando VII returned as king in 1814, he was eager to continue the project, commissioning new plans that would include a grand opera house. The square remained a mass of rubble for 30 years, however, until the architect Narciso Pascual y Colomer was put in charge of the project in 1842.

Colomer came up with the idea of installing the bronze equestrian **statue of Felipe IV** in the square as its centerpiece. The monument had been made in 1639 for the gardens of the Buen Retiro palace, which by the mid-19th century had become the Parque del Retiro. The figure of the king, modeled by Juan Martínez Montañés, was based on a portrait by Velázquez. Pietro Tacca designed the rearing horse with the help of the great Italian scientist Galileo Galilei, who figured out that the horse needed to be hollow at the front and solid at the back to stop it from falling over.

The **stone statues** around the landscaped gardens were originally intended for the parapet of the Palacio Real. They represent Roman emperors, Visigoth kings, and Christian monarchs. Carlos III vetoed the idea of placing them on the palace, claiming that they would be too heavy and might crash down. It is more probable, however, that the figures simply did not comply with his neoclassic tastes.

The square underwent large-scale restoration at the end of the 20th century. Most of the traffic was routed into tunnels, allowing the square to become pedestrian-friendly and much more pleasant.

Teatro Real

The curving east side of the square is presided over by the gray bulk of the Teatro Real. Madrid's opera house has had a checkered history, to say the least. Although this structure dates from 1850, there have been makeshift theaters on the site since the early 18th century. In medieval times, several streams flowed down from the adjacent hills to form a lake here. Bathhouses and washtubs were later built to take advantage of this abundance of water.

The lake, which is still underneath the site, caused construction problems from the outset. The project was always running out of money, too, and in 1826 a special tax was levied on cork trees in Spain to raise funds to carry out the work. Designed by Antonio

Verdi attended the premiere of *La Forza del Destino,* and in 1916–1917 Diaghilev's Ballets Russes performed there.

The water problems persisted, however, causing problems over the years. During the Civil War, a gunpowder store exploded inside, producing extensive damage. The building reopened as a concert hall in the 1960s, closed again in 1988 when the Auditorio Nacional opened across town, and opened again after remodeling in 1997.

The building rises up nine stories, with a further six stories below ground. It has a spectacular

Teatro Real
- Map pp. 70–71
- Plaza de Oriente
- 91 516 0600
- Closed Mon.
- Guided tours: $

www.teatro-real.com

EXPERIENCE: Olive Oil Tasting

Apple, banana, artichoke, grass, and cucumber are just a few of the flavors you might taste when sampling a range of olive oils. Spain is the largest producer of olive oil in the world, and its oils have undergone something of a renaissance in the last two decades, with an increasing number winning international awards.

Many different varieties of olive are grown around the country, which together with the soil and climate conditions affect the color and flavor of the oil. In Andalusia, the most important variety is picual, which produces fruity oils with a hint of fig leaf and a woody aroma. In

Catalunya, the fragrant oils made from the tiny arbequina olives taste of tomato and almonds.

A powerhouse of Mediterranean exuberance, Alicia Ríos *(tel 91 417 5448, www.alicia-rios.com)* is an official taster for organizations in Spain and throughout the world. A few hours in her company awakens your senses to all sorts of aromas, colors, and tastes, and is a highly entertaining experience, too. As well as learning the correct way to taste oils and which qualities to look out for, you are treated to a lively account of the history of olive oil and how it is used in Spanish cuisine.

López Aguado (1764–1831), the theater was completed in 1850 and was opened by Isabel II on her 20th birthday with a performance of Donizetti's *La Favorita.*

The opera house soon became the hub of cultural and social life. It had a ballroom, now a restaurant, where people would dance after the performances. In 1863,

interior. The stage covers an area of approximately 15,400 square feet (1,390 sq m), and there is room for an audience of 1,740. Galleries around the theater on the second floor are decorated with paintings, tapestries, and mirrors. The restaurant has a midnight blue ceiling studded with stars. ■

Chocolate & Churros

One of Madrid's great traditions entails forgetting all about calories for an hour or so. Dipping churro fritters into thick hot chocolate is an experience everyone should have while visiting the city. You can have churros for breakfast, in the late afternoon, or at the end of a long night out. They are also an essential part of local festivals, when they are sold from street stands.

Ladies restore their energy with hot chocolate and churros at a local festival.

The fritters are made from a dense, smooth batter of flour, water, and salt. The mixture is piped through a container, emerging as long, ridged strips, which are dropped into huge vats of boiling oil. Once fried, the strips are drained, cut into short lengths, and sometimes dipped in sugar. In Madrid, the two ends of the churros are typically pressed together to form a loop, although sometimes they are served simply in strips. They must be eaten straightaway, otherwise they become chewy and indigestible.

The Spanish have been drinking hot chocolate since the conquistadors brought cocoa beans back from the Americas in the 16th century. Be prepared for a different taste

and texture when you try a cup at a *chocolatería*, as the specialty cafés are called. Spanish hot chocolate is made by melting slabs of bitter dark chocolate with milk, cornstarch, and sugar. It is usually so wonderfully thick that you can stand the churros up in it, and not as sweet as you might expect.

Madrileños love going out to bars for breakfast, often as a break from the office at around 11. This is a good time to try churros, as the turnover of customers means the pastries will almost certainly be freshly made. Not all bars make their own, however, as there are little shops around town, called *churrerías,* that specialize in churros and potato chips. You can buy some to eat as you go if you are short of time.

After a day's sightseeing, you may well be tempted to pop into a café for a break, and this is when you will see people having their *merienda*, the Spanish version of afternoon tea. Coffee or hot chocolate is often accompanied by a plate of churros. This is a great way to restore your energy levels, as dinner is unlikely to be before 10.

Time for Chocolate

Perhaps the most typical time to consume churros, however, is between 4 and 7 in the morning. Unlikely as it may seem, this is the busiest time for chocolaterías, as starving revelers emerge from dancing the night away in the city's clubs.

The best known place in Madrid for chocolate and churros is undoubtedly the Chocolatería San Ginés (*Pasadizo de San Ginés 5, tel 91 365 6546*), which has been in business since 1894. Before dawn, waiters in black bow ties and green vests attend exhausted nightclubbers seated at marble tables, and throughout the day they serve office workers, families, and shoppers.

INSIDER TIP:

Don't miss sharing in the local indulgence of savoring rich hot chocolate and churros. Eat the churros on the premises; once they cool they lose their appeal.

—ELLIANA SPIEGEL
National Geographic contributor

This is one tradition that shows no sign of dying out. In fact, it has moved easily into the 21st century by keeping up with these fast-food times. The Maestro Churrero (*Plaza Jacinto Benavente 2, tel 91 369 2406*) was founded more than a century ago as a street stand on the Paseo del Prado, but these days it is a franchise where the baseball-capped waiters have handheld devices that send your order straight to the kitchen. It's fast, but it is certainly not junk, as the cooks use natural ingredients and everything is fresh. You can order traditional churros or versions that are coated in chocolate or filled with custard or strawberry cream.

EXPERIENCE: La Vida Dulce

The churro is far from the only sweet in town. Some Spanish desserts are closely related to French pastries, such as *crema catalana,* the precursor of *crème brûlée.* Others carry the honey and almond hallmark of Arabic desserts. But most, like *brazo de gitano,* are uniquely Spanish. This cream-filled spongy roll translates as "gypsy's arm."

Antigua Pasteleria del Pozo (*Calle del Pozo 8, tel 91 522 3894*) is the oldest pastry shop in Madrid, dating from 1830. *Turrones* are the specialty here. These nougat-esque concoctions are based on honey and almonds.

La Mallorquina (*Puerta del Sol 8, tel 91 521 1201*) is a local favorite. Another granddaddy of a shop, this *pasteleria* (pastry store) has been putting dentists' children through school since 1894. La Mallorquina has remained a hometown favorite for all these decades by providing more for less. Most of the pastries here cost around one euro. But be warned—the low price is a double-edged sword. Just because you can afford ten doesn't mean you should eat ten.

The ornate **El Riojano** (*Calle Mayor 10, tel 91 366 44 82*) has been selling first-rate pastries from behind its polished wood facade since 1855. It was founded by a pastry chef who launched his career at the Palacio Real. On top of 30 types of cake, 400 types of cookies, and 60 types of pastries, the chefs here find time to make their own chocolate.

Real Monasterio de la Encarnación

Just nine nuns still live in a closed order in this Augustinian convent, which was founded in 1611 by Margarita de Austria, the wife of Felipe III. Though next to the Palacio Real, the convent is situated in a quiet corner just off Plaza de Oriente. It contains paintings and sculptures by important Spanish artists, many of which were created specifically for the convent.

The spirit of the 17th century lives on at the Real Monasterio de la Encarnación.

A deeply religious lady, Queen Margarita wanted a convent close to the Alcázar, the fortress that preceded the current palace. Sadly, she died in childbirth soon after it was built, at the age of 26.

The convent was designed by Juan Gómez de Mora and Fray Alberto de la Madre de Dios, who created a beautifully proportioned structure within brick and rubblework walls. A covered wooden bridge linked it to the Alcázar, so that the queen could move easily between the two buildings. It was originally a much bigger structure, with a huge vegetable garden at the back, much of which was built on in the 19th century. The courtyard in the front became a popular meeting place where people would get the latest royal gossip.

Visiting the Convent

You have to follow a one-hour guided tour, which begins in a hallway containing one of the most interesting paintings in the convent. Created by Peter van der Meulen, it depicts the ceremony that took place in 1615 on the Bidasoa River between Spain and France. The Habsburg Princess Ana was being sent to France to marry Louis XIII, whose sister, Princess Isabel of Bourbon, crossed into Spain to marry the future Felipe IV.

The tour continues through rooms containing **paintings** by Vicente Carducho, José de Ribera, Corrado Giaquinto, Antonio Pereda, and Juan Carreño de Miranda. The elegant, simple **cloister,** which is undergoing a long restoration process, was influenced by Juan de Herrera's designs at the monastery of El Escorial (see pp. 228–231).

In the **upper antechoir** there are two superb wooden sculptures of Christ by Gregorio Hernández. The rooms still have some of the original furniture and decoration from the 17th century, including hand-painted tiles from Talavera. The antechoir contains tiny figures in polychrome wax of St. Anthony of Padua and St. Teresa of Jesús.

Perhaps the most intriguing exhibit in the convent is to be found in the reliquary room, which has a coffered ceiling and walls lined with mahogany cases containing about 700 relics. A tiny vial is said to contain the blood of Pantaleón, the doctor saint, who lived in the fourth century in Turkey. Every year, on the saint's day, July 27, the thick substance mysteriously liquefies. If it does not happen, it is a sign of impending doom.

Divine Traces

Relics, from the Latin word *reliquiae* for remains, are revered because they lend tangibility to religious belief. The Catholic and Buddhist faiths have traditionally been most active in relic devotion. But as to be expected, not all relics are authentic. Many times, uncovered bones were attributed to martyrs merely because they were discovered near churches. In his 1543 treatise on relics, John Calvin quipped that there are enough pieces of the true cross to build a ship. Nevertheless, if the function of these bits of wood and bone is to make people believe, they have succeeded.

Real Monasterio de la Encarnación

- Map p. 71
- Plaza de la Encarnación 1
- 91 454 8800
- Closed Fri. p.m., Sun. p.m., & Mon.
- $. Free Wed. for EU citizens.
- Metro: Ópera

patrimonionacional. es/encarna/encarna. htm

Ventura Rodríguez designed the neoclassical Latin-cross church in 1767 after the original structure burned. One of Madrid's most beautiful churches, it is decorated with marble from various parts of Spain and has ceiling frescoes by the González Velázquez brothers and Francisco Bayeu, Goya's brother-in-law. ■

Monasterio de las Descalzas Reales

Every day, thousands of people flock to El Corte Inglés department store on Calle Preciados in the heart of the city. Most of them are unaware that hidden away behind the store is a building containing artistic treasures of far greater value than anything in Spain's favorite shop. Formerly a powerhouse of the Habsburg empire, the Descalzas Reales is now one of Madrid's most fascinating museums.

The Monasterio de las Descalzas Reales's reliquary contains treasures from around the world.

The building was originally a palace, built for the Emperor Carlos V's treasurer, Alonso Gutiérrez. The emperor and his wife, Isabel of Portugal, also lived here for a period, and their daughter, Juana of Austria, was born here in 1535. In 1557, Juana, who was Felipe II's sister, decided to found a convent in the palace, which was converted to its new use by Antonio Sillero and Juan Bautista de Toledo. The structure was restored in the 18th century by Diego de Villanueva.

In 1582, Felipe's other sister, the Empress María of Austria, came from Prague to live in the convent, where she had also been born. This prestigious patronage meant that the convent always had close ties with royalty and the aristocracy. Over the years it received a number of lavish donations, many of which are on display today. These include Flemish tapestries and paintings by El Greco, Zurbarán, Velázquez, Goya, Titian, and Rubens.

The convent is still home to 22 nuns belonging to the closed Franciscan order of the Poor Clares, who live in complete privacy in part of the building, while visitors follow a 50-minute guided tour around the public areas.

INSIDER TIP:

To avoid being lost in Madrid, keep La Puerta del Sol as your reference point. Many consider it the center of the city.

—CHRISTEL CHERQAOUI
National Geographic Books

Visiting the Convent

The **grand staircase** survives from the original palace, but the frescoes were added at the end of the 17th century by artists including Claudio Coello and Francisco Ricci. The portrait of the family of Felipe IV, on a trompe l'oeil balcony, is attributed to Antonio Pereda.

In the **upper cloister,** look for the "Guardian Angel" by Luisa Roldán (1656–1704), the panel of the "Madonna and Child" by Bernardino Luini (circa 1480–1532), and a particularly stunning recumbent Christ by Gaspar Becerra. One of the more ornate chapels is dedicated to the Virgen de Guadalajara, with unusual portraits painted on mirrors.

Upstairs, what was once a dormitory is now the **tapestry room.** You'll see a portrait of the Infanta Isabel Clara Eugenia, Felipe II's daughter, who bought the tapestries for the convent. Made in Brussels, the hangings depict "The Triumph of the Eucharist," based on cartoons by Rubens.

The choir, which the nuns use every day, contains the marble **tombs** of Empress María and her daughter Margarita. There is also an astoundingly realistic Madonna by Pedro de Mena (1628–1688), as well as a portrait of St. Teresa.

A series of rooms overlooking the nuns' vegetable garden contain paintings including a "Ship of Fools," attributed to Brueghel the Elder, and others by Isenbrandt and Rubens.

One of the most intriguing paintings in the convent is "The Journey of Empress María from Prague to Madrid," which depicts a procession of young orphan girls with masked faces who were accompanying the empress to the convent.

The interior **church** was altered in the mid-18th century when Diego de Villanueva introduced neoclassic decoration. It contains the tomb of Juana of Austria with a marble statue of the princess by sculptor Pompeo Leoni. ■

Monasterio de las Descalzas Reales

- Map p. 71
- Plaza de las Descalzas Reales 1
- 91 454 8800
- Closed Fri. p.m., Sun. p.m., & Mon.
- $
- Metro: Callao, Ópera, Sol

www.patrimonionacional.es/descreal/descreal.htm

More Places to Visit Around the Palacio Real

Fundación Caja Madrid

The cultural foundation of the Madrid savings bank has a permanent collection of contemporary art and stages temporary art and photography exhibitions in an elegantly restored late 19th-century building. The foundation also sponsors shows in other venues, organizes concerts, and funds the restoration of historic buildings. ⚠ Map pp. 70–71 ✉ Plaza de San Martín 1 ☎ 91 379 2050 🚇 Metro: Ópera, Sol

Iglesia de San Ginés

Although built in 1645, there has been a church on this site since the 12th century. Playwrights Lope de Vega and Francisco de Quevedo attended the church in the 17th century. It was largely rebuilt after a fire in 1824, and in 1872 the entrance was moved to Calle Arenal. The Capilla del Santísimo Cristo contains "The Expulsion of the Merchants from the Temple" by El Greco. ⚠ Map pp. 70–71 ✉ Calle Arenal 13 ☎ 91 366 4875 🚇 Metro: Ópera, Sol

Iglesia de Santiago

This simple neoclassic church was built in 1811, replacing a Romanesque structure demolished to create space for Plaza de Oriente. Dedicated to the Order of St. James, the church contains a painting of "St. James the Moor Slayer" by Francisco Ricci and works by other 17th-century artists. ⚠ Map pp. 70–71 ✉ Plaza de Santiago 24 ☎ 91 548 0824 🚇 Metro: Ópera

Palacio de Gaviria

Built by the Marquis of Gaviria in 1851, this is one of the few grand buildings remaining from the reign of Isabel II. One of the great social venues of the 19th century, the palace saw many glamorous events in the ornate ballroom. The palace is now a nightclub, but it still retains some of its rich decoration. ⚠ Map pp. 70–71 ✉ Calle Arenal 9 ☎ 91 526 6069 🚇 Metro: Ópera, Sol

Palacio del Senado

Built in 1581 as a convent school, this Renaissance structure became the Senate—the upper house of the Spanish Parliament—when the two-chamber system began in 1834. The Senate now uses a new debating chamber added to the rear of the building in 1991. ⚠ Map pp. 70–71 ✉ Plaza de la Marina Española 8 ☎ 91 538 1000 🕐 Guided tours by appt. 🚇 Metro: Plaza de España, Ópera

Residents of the Ópera area attend Mass at their local church, the Iglesia de Santiago.

Brash, noisy, and always busy, with grand buildings on Calle Alcalá and the Gran Vía

Downtown Madrid

Caryatids adorn one of the palatial bank buildings on Calle Alcalá.

Downtown Madrid

The Puerta del Sol has been an important gathering place through most of Madrid's history. The heart of the commercial center, it is also the point from which all distances in Spain are measured. While the majestic avenues of Calle Alcalá and Gran Vía have a big-city feel, the narrow streets to the north have a more intimate character.

Crowds stream along the Gran Vía at all hours of the day and night.

With ten streets leading off the square and one of the busiest metro stations in Madrid, the Puerta del Sol is always packed with people and traffic. Unlike Plaza Mayor (see pp. 54–55), however, this is not a place for sitting at pavement cafés and watching the world go by. It seems as if everyone is rushing to somewhere else.

Calle Alcalá, which leaves the square to the east, has changed character over the centuries. In medieval times, this section was the beginning of the ceremonial royal route to Alcalá de Henares (see p. 222). After many of the religious buildings flanking it were demolished in the 19th century, it became the heart of café society, the place to see and be seen.

The lively atmosphere of those days was, however, gradually diluted as the banking sector moved in at the turn of the 20th century. This led to the appearance of some signature buildings, illustrative of the way Madrid was booming as a financial center. Their foreign influences show Madrid's eagerness to project itself as a modern European city. This trend was continued along the Gran Vía, which did not exist at all until the first half of the 20th century and changed the face of central Madrid.

The areas north of the Gran Vía have a much longer history, with parts dating back to the 15th century. Most of what's there today

was built in the late 19th century, and is made up of elegant brick apartments with wrought-iron balconies. At ground level, these neighborhoods are changing radically. Chueca has become the center of gay life in Madrid, leading to the emergence of dozens of bars, restaurants, and boutiques.

Neighboring Malasaña, always a bohemian quarter, is becoming more gentrified but still exudes its own particular charm. ■

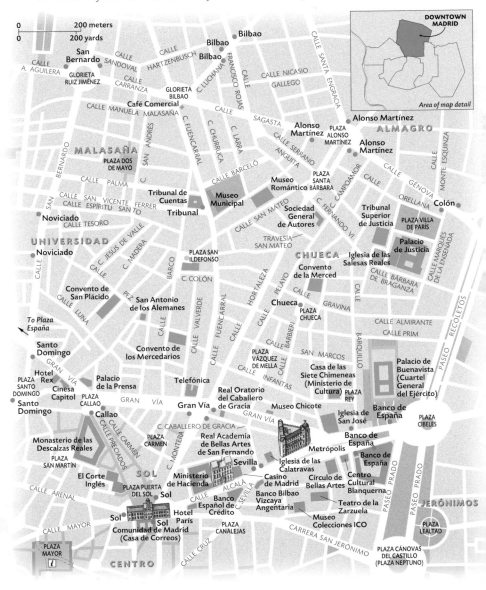

Puerta del Sol

The Puerta del Sol took on its present appearance in the mid-19th century, when society was becoming less influenced by the church and more interested in shopping and entertainment. Convents bordering the square were demolished and replaced by residential and commercial buildings, which form a semi-elliptical shape. The pedestrian areas have been extended recently, but the sheer density of people makes it difficult to negotiate at peak times.

The Puerta del Sol is the central point not only for Madrid, but for the whole of Spain.

Puerta del Sol
🅼 Map p. 91
🚇 Metro: Sol

The name Puerta del Sol—Gate of the Sun—originated when the east gate of the 15th-century city wall stood where the Hotel París is now. Known simply as Sol, the gate was a social hub in the 17th and 18th centuries, when people used to meet on the steps of the San Felipe church (where

McDonald's is now). Long before the invention of celebrity magazines, people came here to exchange gossip. Until a century ago, there was a café on nearly every corner, where intellectuals would gather to discuss the issues of the day.

The square is dominated by the redbrick and stone **Casa de**

Correos, which was designed by Jacques Marquet in 1768 as the central post office. The facade is crowned by a baroque pediment featuring the coat of arms of Carlos III, in whose reign it was built. The clock tower was added in 1866. The clock, Spain's official timepiece, is one of Madrid's most famous landmarks.

INSIDER TIP:

At Puerta del Sol, look for the statue of the bear pawing the arbutus tree, a symbol of Madrid and an icon on public vehicles.

—DEAN SNOW
National Geographic field researcher

A Sinister Turn

In the mid-19th century, the building housed the Ministry of the Interior; then, during the dictatorship of General Franco, from 1939 to 1975, it became the headquarters of the sinister security police. Many people were tortured or killed in the cells below the building. It is now home to the regional government, the Comunidad de Madrid, and used for ceremonial purposes.

In front of the building, look for the semicircular paving stone known as *Kilómetro Cero,* Kilometer Zero, which is considered to be the center of Spain. Distances to every town in Spain are measured from here. On May 2, 1808, this was also one of the main scenes of the uprising against Napoleon's army (see pp. 204–205), which is commemorated on a plaque to the left of the main door.

Madrid's Jumping Bear

The equestrian statue of Carlos III on the north side of the square was not installed until 1997, but it manages to look as if it has been there for centuries. Just beyond it, at the entrance to Calle del Carmen, is one of Madrid's best known symbols: a bronze statue of a bear jumping up at an arbutus tree, also known as wild strawberry. The bear is female and represents the fertility of the land around Madrid, while the tree represents the aristocracy, who traditionally owned everything above ground level.

The pedestrian streets north of the statue are packed with shops, dominated by the several buildings occupied by different sections of the El Corte Inglés department store. ∎

New Year Fortune

On New Year's Eve, thousands of people gather in the Puerta del Sol to take part in the tradition of eating a grape with each chime of the clock. In theory, this will bring good fortune in the coming year. Once the feat has been accomplished, bottles of sparkling cava wine are opened and shared among the crowd.

Calle Alcalá

Originally part of a drovers' track used to drive herds from Extremadura to the north of Spain, Calle Alcalá acquired grand mansions and convents in the 17th and 18th centuries. In the early 20th century, the street became Madrid's financial center, resulting in the construction of the impressive buildings seen today. Although the business area has now shifted to Paseo de la Castellana, many banks still keep their headquarters here.

The grandiose Metrópolis building dramatically heralds the beginning of the Gran Vía.

The first imposing building is the **Ministerio de Hacienda** (the Treasury) on the left at No. 5. Built as the Customs House in 1769, it was designed by Francesco Sabatini, who was inspired by Rome's Palazzo Farnese. Nearby is the **Real Academia de Bellas Artes de San Fernando** (see pp. 96–97), the Fine Arts Academy.

The opulent **Casino de Madrid** at No. 15 *(tel 91 521 8700)* is a private gentlemen's club. Although not open to the public, you can see inside to the opulent hallway and staircase. You do not have to be a member to eat at the superb restaurant (see p. 246) on the top floor, which has a Michelin star.

The first major commercial building on the street, the **Banco Español de Crédito,** is the triangular structure on the right on the corner of Calle Sevilla. It was designed by Catalan architect José Grases Riera in the 1880s. Look for the stone elephant heads that support the balcony.

The **Banco Bilbao Vizcaya Argentaria,** which curves around the facing corner of Calle Sevilla, was designed by Richard Bastida at the beginning of the 20th century. Look up at the two chariots, each drawn by four horses, which seem to be galloping off the roof.

EXPERIENCE: Renting a Vacation Apartment

Short-term apartment rental is becoming increasingly popular in Madrid, particularly with people who have visited several times or who want to spend longer than a few days here. It can also be much more economical than a hotel, and it gives you a chance to get into the swing of the city.

There is no shortage of agencies offering holiday apartments, some of which rent out their own properties, while others act as intermediaries between owners and visitors. Check exactly what is included in the price (utilities, cleaning, towels, etc.) and bear in mind that postings sometimes omit to mention the less desirable aspects of a property. A trendy neighborhood, for example, may be noisy or unsafe at night. Older properties, while charming, often do not have elevators. If you book directly with an apartment's owners, they often provide a wealth of local information that will enhance your stay.

One of the big pluses of staying in an apartment is being able to buy groceries at the wonderful markets and delicatessens in central Madrid, enabling you to try specialties such as Iberian ham and artisan cheeses, as well as fine Spanish wines, at a fraction of the price charged at a bar or restaurant.

Reputable agencies include **Madrid Apart** *(tel 91 125 0110, www.MadridApart.com)*; **Friendly Rentals** *(tel 93 268 8051, www.friendlyrentals.com)*; **Chic Rentals** *(www.chicrentals.com)*; **Way To Stay** *(tel 93 802 1535, www.waytostay.com)*; and **Houses and Days** *(tel 91 393 2768, www.housesanddays.com)*. Another option is the Madrid holiday rentals section of the Loquo website *(www.loquo.com)*, which advertises properties by both agencies and individuals.

Looming up on the left is the slate dome of the **Iglesia de las Calatravas** *(Calle Alcalá 25, tel 91 521 8035)*. Built in the 17th century as part of a convent, the church's facade was altered to reflect Milanese Renaissance influences in the mid-19th century—a change that detracts from the baroque style of the church itself. Inside there is a magnificent altarpiece by José Benito de Churriguera (1665–1725).

The junction of Calle Alcalá and the Gran Vía is marked by one of Madrid's signature buildings: the **Metrópolis** *(Calle Alcalá 39)*. Designed by French architects Jules and Raymond Février between 1907 and 1910, the elaborate facade features Corinthian columns, sculptures, and a slate dome crowned with a bronze figure of Winged Victory. It looks spectacular lit up at night.

The large eclectic structure opposite the Metrópolis is the **Círculo de Bellas Artes,** or Fine Arts Circle. Designed by Antonio Palacios in 1919–1920, it looks like different buildings stacked on top of each other. Several exhibitions usually run concurrently at this lively cultural center, along with films, plays, and concerts. The large café on the first floor is known as the *pecera,* or goldfish bowl, owing to its panoramic windows; it is a popular spot with writers and artists. ■

Calle Alcalá

- Map p. 91
- Metro: Sevilla, Sol

Círculo de Bellas Artes

- Map p. 91
- Calle Alcalá 42
- 91 360 5400
- Exhibitions closed Sun. p.m. & Mon.
- $
- Metro: Banco de España, Sevilla

www.circulobellasartes.com

Real Academia de Bellas Artes de San Fernando

It is a shame that so few people visit the museum of the Royal Fine Arts Academy as it contains some first-class artworks. It is worth going in just to see the 13 Goya paintings, not to mention those by Picasso, El Greco, Zurbarán, Van Dyck, and Rubens. The fine 18th-century building also contains important collections of drawings, prints, and engravings.

An artist hard at work at the Real Academia de Bellas Artes de San Fernando

Real Academia de Bellas Artes de San Fernando

- Map p. 91
- Calle Alcalá 13
- 91 524 0864
- Closed p.m. Mon. & Sun.
- $
- Metro: Sevilla, Sol

rabasf.insde.es

The building was designed in the 1720s by José Benito de Churriguera as a private residence and altered in 1775 in neoclassical style to house the Royal Fine Arts Academy. The Academy, which taught painting, sculpture, and architecture until 1967, was founded in 1752 during the reign of Fernando V and originally housed in the Palacio Real. It began collecting works by Spanish and foreign artists who were working in Madrid at the time, and later received valuable private legacies. New members also have to donate a piece of their work when they are admitted.

The collections now comprise more than a thousand works from the 16th to 21st centuries. Two series of Goya etchings are occasionally on display as part of the National Chalcography Collection.

Room 6 contains a series of five portraits of Mercedarian monks by Francisco de Zurbarán,

along with his masterful "Vision of the Blessed Alonso Rodríguez."

Rooms 11–14 deal with 17th-century Spanish artists and include flower paintings by Juan de Arellano (1614–1671) and "Christ Collecting his Vestments" by Alonso Cano (1601–1667). José de Ribera is well represented with several portraits of saints, including a "Penitent St. Jerome."

Room 17 contains several works by Bartolomé Esteban Murillo, including "La Magdalena," which reflects the tendency in the Counter Reformation to depict madonnas in a gentler, more realistic way. Murillo, who was from Seville, contributed to many churches and convents in Andalucía.

One of the Academy's most famous paintings is "Spring" (circa 1563) by Giuseppe Arcimboldo (1527–1583), which is in **Room 19.** This intriguing canvas shows a man in profile, made up entirely of flowers and plants. An allegory of imperial power, it was presented to Emperor Maximilian II by the artist in 1569 and is one of a series depicting the four seasons.

The Goya (1746–1828) paintings are displayed in **Rooms 20 and 21** and include two small self-portraits. One was painted in 1793–95 and is a full-length portrayal of the artist at work. The other was painted 20 years later and shows the artist looking resigned to his fate as he approached the age of 70.

The six portraits include one of Juan de Villanueva, the architect of the Prado, and a sensitive depiction of the writer Leandro Fernández de Moratín. "The Burial of the Sardine" (1813–1814) shows a ritual from the Madrid carnival that still exists today, but at another level it refers to the French occupation of the city.

The next floor deals mainly with 18th- and 19th-century work by Spanish and Italian artists. **Room 22** contains Tiepolo's "Head of an Oriental Elder." The top floor has works by Joaquín Sorolla, the 19th-century Valencian painter, as well as an excellent collection by 20th-century artists including Zóbel and Tàpies. **Room 56** contains etchings, sculptures, and lithographies by Picasso and paintings by Juan Gris. ∎

Places Open on Mondays

Although lots of museums close on Mondays, these worthy destinations are open for business:
Museo Reina Sofía (pp. 154–158) For Picasso's "Guernica" and top contemporary art
Palacio Real (pp. 72–77) See the opulent grandeur of the Royal Palace
CaixaForum (p. 154) Major temporary art exhibits and cultural activities
Real Academia de Bellas Artes de San Fernando (pp. 96–97) For paintings by Goya and other leading Spanish artists
Museo Lázaro Galdiano (p. 185) Fabulous art in a palatial home

Gran Vía

The Gran Vía sweeps through the center of Madrid, heavy with traffic at all hours. The avenue was conceived more than a century ago to connect the new residential districts of Salamanca and Argüelles. It is still a crucial link between the east and west sides of the city.

The cacaphonic Gran Vía cuts through central Madrid.

A showcase for 20th-century architecture, with strong French and American influences, the Gran Vía was developed in three stages and took 50 years to build.

The first stretch, which was built between 1910 and 1917, runs from Calle Alcalá to the junction with Montera, Hortaleza, and Fuencarral. The ornate buildings with art nouveau decoration reflect the buoyant economic situation at the time. The Grassy Jeweler at the foot of the street on the left sets a suitably grand precedent with its colonnaded cream facade. Downstairs there is a **museum** of clocks and watches, some dating back to the 16th century *(tel 91 532 1007, closed Sun.)*.

One of Madrid's great institutions is on the right at No. 12. The **Museo Chicote** cocktail bar *(tel 91 532 6737, closed Sun.)* still has its original art deco interior from the 1930s. A haunt of Ernest Hemingway, Orson Welles, and Salvador Dalí—to name but a few—these days the bar is a chic place for a late-night drink.

On the left at No. 17, you see the curving rear facade of the **Real Oratorio del Caballero de Gracia** *(entrance on parallel Calle Caballero de Gracia at No. 5, tel 91*

INSIDER TIP:

The streets around Sol are bathed in a beautiful golden light as the fading sun heads for the horizon —a must for any photographer.

—MATT TAYLOR
National Geographic Channel editor

532 6937). Recently restored, the church was designed by Juan de Villanueva at the end of the 18th century and is one of the best examples of neoclassic architecture in Madrid. The narrow nave is flanked by a Corinthian colonnade; there is a stunning baroque

Theater Posters

Movies showing along the Gran Vía are advertised by hand-painted posters rather than official promotional material. Decades ago, the artists' union cannily got the theaters to agree to long-term contracts. Madrileños now regard these interesting posters as part of their city's artistic heritage.

Gran Vía
Map p. 91
Metro: Banco de España, Callao, Gran Via

figure of Christ from the mid-17th century by Juan Sánchez Barba.

The second stage of the street, built in the 1920s, is changing character as movie theaters are turned into shops. The massive **Telefónica** building, which is 290 feet (88 m) tall, was designed between 1926 and 1929 by the American architect Louis S. Weeks and was the first skyscraper in Madrid. The Fundación Telefónica holds temporary exhibitions on the first floor, and there is a permanent telecommunications display on the second floor *(tel 91 522 6645, closed Sat. p.m., Sun. p.m., & Mon.)*. This section ends at Plaza de Callao, named after the naval battle off Callao in Peru in 1866.

The third stretch of the Gran Vía, which runs to Plaza de España, was developed from the 1930s to the 1950s. It is heralded by the spectacular art deco **Cines Capitol** *(No. 41)*, a theater designed by Luis Martínez Feduchi and Vicente Eced in the 1930s. Opposite is the towering redbrick **Palacio de la Prensa** at No. 46, designed by Pedro Muguruza in 1926. ∎

Pedro Almodóvar's Madrid

Pedro Almodóvar, Spain's most renowned moviemaker, has been depicting Madrid in his films since his career began a quarter of a century ago. He has used several well-known landmarks as backdrops, but also likes to portray the sorts of neighborhoods that do not usually feature in the itineraries of people visiting the city for just a few days. You might recognize some of Almodóvar's locations as you explore Madrid.

Volver (2006) is based in La Mancha, where Almodóvar was born, but he also filmed in **Vallecas,** a blue-collar neighborhood in the south of Madrid. Although removed from the city's core, the area has broad open spaces and is host to bold ideas. Almodóvar also set part of the film in **Cuatro Caminos,** an area that has changed character over recent years owing to the influx of foreign workers. Almodóvar concentrated on the streets in the north of the district, which has become known as "The Little Caribbean" owing to the proliferation of shops, restaurants, and businesses catering to the needs of the new community.

Revealing New Madrid

Almodóvar has always been eager to show new developments in the city. *Kika* (1993) featured scenes at the new terminal at **Atocha train station.** Built for Spain's AVE high-speed train to Seville, the new terminal had just started operating at the time. The picture itself is based in an apartment near the Paseo de la Castellana, Madrid's north-south axis, and includes views of the **Torre Picasso,** Madrid's tallest building.

In *Live Flesh* (1997), starring Javier Bardem, Almodóvar swung his cameras on the **Torres Kio,** the odd-looking leaning twin towers at the top of the Paseo de la Castellana. At that time, the area beyond the modern towers was rough ground, revealing more than a few run-down houses. Now, however, the neighborhood is a burgeoning business district of high-rise buildings, extending the city to the north.

Depicting the Familiar

Labyrinth of Passions (1982), Almodóvar's second film, starts with the lead actors, Imanol Arias and Cecilia Roth, wandering through the crowded streets of the **Rastro market** on a Sunday morning. They have breakfast at La Bobia, a legendary café on Calle San Millán. The café, now an ice-cream parlor called **Wooster,** has shed its notorious reputation, but you can still sit at the pavement tables just as the characters do in the movie.

Hardly changed at all is the café of the **Círculo de Bellas Artes** (see p. 95), where Victoria Abril and Peter Coyote sit at a window table in *Kika*. In *High Heels* (1991), the lead characters go to a drag show at **Villa Rosa,** a famous flamenco bar with ornately decorated tiles on **Plaza de Santa Ana.** Also easily recognizable is the **Cine Doré,** Madrid's national film theater, featured in *Talk to Her* (2002), which won an Oscar for best original script.

Not Forgetting Fashion

In *High Heels,* Marisa Paredes lives in a basement apartment in **Plaza de Alamillo,** on the corner of Calle Alfonso VI in the heart of Habsburg Madrid. This neighborhood also features in *The Flower of My Secret* (1995), which again stars Marisa Paredes. In that film she is seen trying to take off her boots while sitting on the edge of a fountain in the **Puerta de Moros,** by the church of San Andrés.

Paredes also strolls late at night with the actor Juan Echanove through **Plaza Mayor,** which looks even more dramatic without the usual crowds.

The Oscar-nominated *Women on the Verge of a Nervous Breakdown* (1988) is based in an even

Madrid's viaduct over Calle Segovia, where Assumpta Serna awaited her fate in *Matador*

grander penthouse apartment in the upscale quarter of **Los Jerónimos,** between the Parque del Retiro and the Prado.

Perhaps the most dramatic location, how-ever, is the **Viaducto,** spanning Calle Segovia, which appears in *Matador* (1986). Assumpta Serna, her black and yellow satin cape billowing in the breeze, stands on the bridge and awaits her fate as she gazes out at the mountains in the distance. In his 2009 movie, *Los Abrazos Rotos,* Almodóvar returns to this area to shoot on the **Calle Bailén.**

North of the Gran Vía

The areas just off the Gran Vía give a fascinating insight into how people live in downtown Madrid. While the atmosphere at street level is commercial, look up and you see rows of balconies adorned by flowerpots and shaded by green wooden blinds. These traditional neighborhoods of Chueca and Malasaña are becoming increasingly fashionable, with boutiques and bars fast replacing the small workshops occupied by carpenters, upholsterers, and electricians.

The dense mesh of streets in the Malasaña quarter lace north of the Gran Vía.

North of the Gran Vía

⚠ Map p. 91

🚇 Metro: Banco de España, Chueca, Gran Vía

Iglesia de las Salesas Reales

⚠ Map p. 91

✉ Calle General Castaños 2

☎ 91 319 4811

🚇 Metro: Alonso Martínez, Colon

By far the oldest building is the **Casa de las Siete Chimeneas** (House of the Seven Chimneys), built in 1577 on Plaza del Rey in Chueca. It has been restored and is now part of the head office of the Ministry of Culture. A young woman who died there is rumored to haunt the building, appearing occasionally on the roof in a white dress. In the early 17th century, the ill-fated future Charles I of England stayed in the house when he came to Madrid to meet Princess María,

the sister of Felipe II, with a view to marrying her.

Calle del Barquillo leads north from Plaza del Rey and is lined with stores specializing in music equipment. Originally, this street was part of the royal route up to the majestic **Iglesia de las Salesas Reales.** Also known as Santa Bárbara, this church was built in the mid-18th century as part of a convent intended as a retreat for the Portuguese wife of Fernando VI, Bárbara de Braganza. It was designed by French architect

François Carlier, whose plans were modified after his death by Francisco Moradillo.

The lavish late-baroque interior contains the **tombs** of Fernando VI and Bárbara de Braganza, which were designed by Francesco Sabatini and sculpted by Francisco Gutiérrez. **Statues** of San Fernando and Santa Bárbara adorn the high altar, which is flanked by green marble columns. The convent was rebuilt following a fire in 1915 and now houses the Supreme Court.

The street in front of the church is also named after Bárbara de Braganza. One block west it becomes Calle Fernando VI. At the end on the left is the extraordinary building housing the **Sociedad de Autores** *(Calle Fernando VI 4, tel 91 349 9550)*, the Society of Authors, an organization that deals with the copyrights of authors and artists. Designed by José Graces Riera in 1902 as a private residence, it is the best example of art nouveau in Madrid. Influenced more by the architecture of Hector Guimard

than the modernisme of eastern Spain's Catalunya, the building's stone plants seem to trickle down the caramel walls, which are encircled by twisted green railings. Around the corner on Calle Pelayo, you get a glimpse of the exotic garden behind the building.

Museo Romántico

Take the first right off Calle Pelayo into Travesía San Mateo, which leads to Calle San Mateo. The unusual Museo Romántico is housed in the late 18th-century mansion that was the home of the Marquis of Vega-Inclán (1858–1942). This eccentric aristocrat collected not only art but also musical instruments, fans, and chinaware. An avid promoter of Spanish tourism, he was the man behind the reconstruction of El Greco's house in Toledo and the Santa Cruz quarter in Seville. He later came up with the idea of turning disused historic buildings into hotels, which gave birth to the highly successful Parador chain.

The marquis was a leading exponent of the Romantic move- ment, which lasted approximately from the 1820s to the 1870s, during the reign of Isabel II. Artists and writers, influenced by liberal politics, began to throw off the constraints of academicism to explore free expression in their work. Visiting this museum gives an insight into this fertile period of Spanish culture.

The displays begin on the first floor with exhibits charting the many achievements of the marquis. You then enter into the mind-boggling world

Museo Romántico

- Map p. 91
- Calle San Mateo 13
- 91 448 0163 or 91 448 1045
- Reopening late 2009
- $. Free Sun.
- Metro: Alonso Martínez, Tribunal

http:// museoromantico. mcu.es

Caped Crusaders

The Italian Marquis of Squillace caused a mutiny in 1766 when he banned long capes and wide- brimmed hats, claiming that thieves were wearing them to conceal what they had stolen. Madrileños refused to give in and rioted at several places in the city center, including Plaza del Rey in Chueca.

EXPERIENCE: Shopping & People-watching

If you are in Madrid on a Friday or Saturday evening, don't miss a stroll up Calle Fuencarral, a narrow artery leading north from the Gran Vía. Check out the haircuts, hemlines, and heels as the crowds of hip young and not so young Madrileños swarm down the sidewalk, dipping in and out of funky boutiques.

On the border of Chueca, Madrid's gay neighborhood, the street's place on the coolhunters' map began with the avant-garde fashion and music outlets in the Mercado de Fuencarral mall *(Calle Fuencarral 45, tel 91 521 4152)*, but really took off when brands like Camper, Mac, Muji, and Mango started moving in,

taking over traditional shops and changing the vibe from a polluted artery to Madrid's trendiest shopping street. Now that every available space houses a new store, café, or bar, the surrounding streets are becoming gentrified too, bringing a new glamour to downtown.

For a snapshot of what makes Madrid tick, and to get a flavor of the infectious, spontaneous vitality of the people, just join the throng. To make sure you don't miss the best shops, galleries, or bars, book a tour of the area with an insider guide from Made for Spain *(Calle Antonio Flores 4, 1 D, tel 91 448 7275, www.madefor spain.com)*.

Museo de la Historia

- Map p. 91
- Calle Fuencarral 78
- 91 701 1863
- Closed Sat. p.m., Sun. p.m., & Mon.
- Metro: Bilbao, Tribunal

of his collections on the main floor upstairs. A highlight is "St. Gregory the Great," a painting by Goya of There are portraits by leading 19th-century artists including Leonardo Alenza and José and Federico de Madrazo, and scenes from everyday life—a style known as *costumbrista*—by Valeriano Bécquer and Eugenio Lucas. One room is devoted to the writer Mariano José de Larra (1809–1837), who shot himself after a lover abandoned him.

Museo de la Historia

Around the corner, the Museo de la Historia has also been undergoing refurbishment, but it is at least partially open during the alterations. The building, designed in the early 18th century by Pedro de Ribera, has an elaborate **baroque portal,** a characteristic feature of his style. Originally a poorhouse, the building also housed workshops where the political activist Pablo

Iglesias trained as a printer.

Even if you are short of time, be sure to pop into the museum to see the extraordinary wooden **scale model of Madrid.** Measuring 17 feet by 11.5 feet (5.2 x 3.5 m), it was made in 1830 by León Gil de Palacio, a few years before the disentailment of religious property led to the disappearance of many churches, convents, and monasteries. It shows how different Madrid looked before the development of the mid-19th century.

During refurbishment, only a limited selection of the museum's rich art collection is on display. When it is fully open again (not until at least 2011), exhibits will chart Madrid's history from Paleolithic to Roman times, before showing how the town grew during the Muslim period and after the Christian Reconquest.

Malasaña District

Calle Fuencarral marks the

boundary between Chueca and the district of Malasaña (see also pp. 106–107). The area is named after Manuela Malasaña, a heroine of the uprising against the French army on May 2, 1808 (see pp. 204–205), which took place nearby. A 17-year-old seamstress, Manuela attacked the French soldiers who tried to detain her, using her sewing scissors as a weapon. The soldiers shot her dead on the spot.

This area has been a nightlife hub since the 1960s, when artists and musicians moved in, attracted by low rents in what was then a run-down district. By day it is peaceful, but at night the atmosphere changes drastically when the many bars and clubs open up.

One of Madrid's most surprising churches is hidden in this neighborhood. **Iglesia San Antonio de los Alemanes** was built between 1624 and 1633 by Pedro Sánchez, a leading church architect of the time. The elliptical interior is covered with **frescoes** related to the life of St. Anthony of Padua, a Franciscan monk who died in Padua, Italy. The frescoes were painted by leading artists of the day, including Francisco Ricci and Juan Carreño de Miranda. ∎

Historic Soup Kitchen

At the beginning of the 18th century, a brotherhood set up a refuge next to the Iglesia San Antonio de los Alemanes. Every night the monks would take to the streets with baskets of bread and boiled eggs to hand out to the many vagrants in the area. The tradition has continued into the 21st century with a soup kitchen that still feeds dozens of people every day.

Iglesia de San Antonio de los Alemanes

- Map p. 91
- Calle Puebla 22
- 91 522 3774
- Metro: Gran Vía, Callao

Frescoes richly decorate the baroque church of San Antonio de los Alemanes.

A Walk Around Chueca & Malasaña

This walk takes you around the rapidly changing areas north of the Gran Vía. While not rich in monuments, these traditional neighborhoods have taken on a new lease on life and now have the most avant-garde boutiques and bars in Madrid. Early evening is a good time to explore these areas, particularly on weekends when the streets are thronged with people.

Children play in the shady Plaza Dos de Mayo, the heart of the Malasaña district.

From the Gran Vía metro station, walk up Calle Hortaleza, a busy shopping street. The mesh of streets to the right is the Chueca district, now well known as one of the liveliest gay quarters in Europe. The success of the area has led to its becoming much more mainstream, and it is now popular with a young, trendy crowd.

Turn right down Calle Augusto Figueroa, which is lined with shops selling designer shoes at discount prices. Turn left down Calle Barbieri, which leads into **Plaza de Chueca ❶**, a square that epitomizes the changes taking place in the area. The pavement cafés are popular on summer nights, while the **Taberna de Ángel Sierra** *(Calle Gravina 11, tel 91 531 0126),* on the far side of the square, is a great traditional tavern

NOT TO BE MISSED:

Plaza de Chueca • Calle Almirante
• Iglesia de las Salesas Reales

with a zinc bar, tiled walls, and good tapas. The apartment buildings around the square, most dating back about a hundred years, have been spruced up, turning this formerly scruffy space into an attractive focal point.

Walk down Calle Gravina, which after crossing Calle Barquillo becomes **Calle Almirante,** renowned for its boutiques. Turn left up Calle Conde de Xiquena, where the elaborate doorways show the wealth of this area at the end of

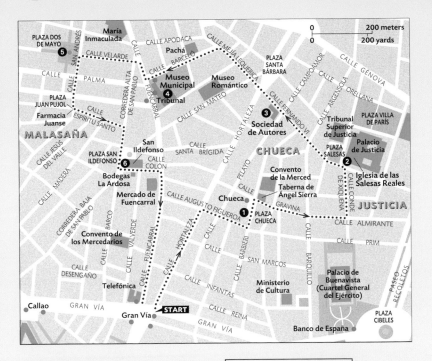

Map labels:
- PLAZA DOS DE MAYO ⑤
- María Inmaculada
- CALLE VELARDE
- CALLE APODACA
- CALLE BARCELÓ
- Pachá
- CALLE MEJÍA LEQUERICA
- PLAZA SANTA BÁRBARA
- CALLE GÉNOVA
- CALLE SAN ANDRÉS
- CALLE
- CALLE PALMA
- CORREDERA ALTA DE SAN PABLO
- Museo Municipal ④
- FUENCARRAL
- Museo Romántico
- CALLE SAN MATEO
- CALLE CAMPOAMOR
- CALLE ARGENSOLA
- CALLE ORELLANA
- PLAZA JUAN PUJOL
- Farmacia Juanse
- CALLE ESPÍRITU SANTO
- Tribunal
- CALLE FERNANDO VI
- Sociedad de Autores ③
- CALLE HORTALEZA
- Tribunal Superior de Justicia
- PLAZA VILLA DE PARÍS
- MALASAÑA
- CALLE JESÚS DEL VALLE
- San Ildefonso
- CALLE SANTA BRÍGIDA
- CHUECA
- PLAZA SALESAS
- Palacio de Justicia ②
- PLAZA SAN ILDEFONSO ⑥
- CALLE COLÓN
- PELAYO
- Iglesia de las Salesas Reales
- Bodegas La Ardosa
- CALLE MADERA
- CALLE CONDE DE XIQUENA
- JUSTICIA
- Mercado de Fuencarral
- CALLE AUGUSTO FIGUEROA
- Convento de la Merced
- CALLE
- Taberna de Ángel Sierra
- Chueca
- GRAVINA
- CALLE ALMIRANTE
- CORREDERA BAJA DE SAN PABLO
- Convento de los Mercedarios
- CALLE BARCO
- CALLE VALVERDE
- CALLE FUENCARRAL
- CALLE HORTALEZA
- CALLE
- PLAZA CHUECA ①
- CALLE BARBIERI
- SAN MARCOS
- CALLE BARQUILLO
- CALLE PRIM
- CALLE DESENGAÑO
- Telefónica
- CALLE INFANTAS
- Ministerio de Cultura
- Palacio de Buenavista (Cuartel General del Ejército)
- PASEO RECOLETOS
- Callao
- GRAN VÍA
- Gran Vía
- START
- CALLE REINA
- GRAN VÍA
- Banco de España
- PLAZA CIBELES

Scale:
- 0 — 200 meters
- 0 — 200 yards

the 19th century. At the end of the street is the magnificent **Iglesia de las Salesas Reales** ② (see pp. 102–103).

Turn left along Calle Fernando VI, with the **Sociedad de Autores** ③ (see p. 103) at the end on the left. Continue straight along Calle Mejía Lequerica, then turn left onto Calle Barceló. On the right at No. 11 is the curving facade of **Pachá** (tel 91 447 0128), one of Madrid's most famous nightclubs. Built in the 1930s as a cinema, the building remains a good example of functionalist architecture. The **Museo de la Historia** ④ (see pp. 104–105), on the left, is well worth a look.

Crossing Calle Fuencarral takes you into Malasaña, where the gay scene disappears, replaced by a New Age atmosphere. Walk down Calle Velarde to the **Plaza Dos de Mayo** ⑤, which is named after the uprising against the French beginning here on May 2, 1808 (see pp. 204–205).

Leave the square by walking south down Calle San Andrés, which leads to **Plaza de Juan Pujol**. Don't miss the **Farmacia Juanse** (Juanse

	See area map p. 91
►	Gran Vía metro station
⏲	3 miles (5 km)
⏱	2 hours
►	Gran Vía metro station

Pharmacy) on the corner on the right; hand-painted tiles on the facade depict a variety of ailments. Turn left along Calle Espíritu Santo, which gets its name from the Cross of the Holy Spirit that was installed here in the 17th century to commemorate the fact that several brothels were struck by lightning.

Turn right at the end into Corredera Alta de San Pablo, which leads to **Plaza de San Ildefonso** ⑥, dominated by its 19th-century church. Turn left into Calle Colón, where there is a tiled bar at No. 13, **Bodegas La Ardosa** (tel 91 521 4979), renowned for its draught beer and tapas. Turn right down Calle Fuencarral, one of the trendiest places to shop in Madrid (see pp. 104). Carry on down the street to return to the Gran Vía metro station.

More Places to Visit in Downtown Madrid

Centro Cultural Blanquerna

This new center promotes the culture of the Catalunya region in northeast Spain. Although it specializes in Catalan authors, the center also provides a good range of fiction, art, and travel books in both Spanish and English. The space downstairs is used for exhibitions, talks, concerts, and other events. www.gencat .es/blanquerna ⚠ Map p. 91 ✉ Calle Alcalá 44 ☎ 91 524 1890 🕐 Closed Sat. & Sun. 🚇 Metro: Banco de España

Convento de San Plácido

Built in the mid-17th century by Fray Lorenzo San Nicolás, this convent was soon immersed in a scandal involving the novices, their confessor, members of the aristocracy, and even the king, Felipe IV. The rich decoration in the church is at least partly the result of donations aimed at silencing the rumors and includes an amazingly realistic "Recumbent Christ" by Gregorio Fernández. A Velázquez painting, "Christ on the Cross," painted for the convent on the orders of Felipe IV, is now in the Prado Museum, replaced in this collection by a copy. The convent's dome is decorated with frescoes by Francisco Ricci, and the painting of the Annunciation on the high altar is by Claudio Coello. ⚠ Map p. 91 ✉ Calle San Roque 9 ☎ 91 531 7999 🕐 Closed Sat. a.m. & Sun. 🚇 Metro: Gran Vía

Iglesia de San José

Designed by Pedro de Ribera in 1730, the baroque church is now slotted between grand commercial buildings. It originally adjoined a Carmelite convent, which was demolished following the disentailment of religious property in 1836. Iglesia de San José contains one of the most impressive collections of religious artwork in the city, including famous 18th-century sculptures by Robert Michel and Juan Pascual de Mena. The ornately decorated Capilla de Santa Teresa features an exquisitely frescoed dome. A plaque commemorates the wedding of Simón Bolívar (1783–1830), the great Venezuelan general, to María Teresa Rodríguez del Toro y Alaysa, the daughter of a Spanish nobleman. The ceremony took place in the church in 1802. ⚠ Map p. 91 ✉ Calle Alcalá 43 ☎ 91 522 6784 🚇 Metro: Banco de España

Museo Colecciones ICO

This interesting exhibition space is run by the cultural foundation of the state credit organization, the Instituto de Crédito Oficial. The permanent collection contains works by leading Spanish contemporary artists including José María Sicilia, Jaume Plensa, and Miquel Barceló. Works by Pablo Picasso are displayed in the Vollard Suite. In addition, there is usually at least one temporary exhibition running, featuring Spanish and international artists. Family oriented workshops are offered every Saturday. www.ico.es ⚠ Map p. 91 ✉ Calle Zorrilla 3 ☎ 91 420 0717, free cellphone 900 121 121 🕐 Closed Sun. p.m. & Mon. Free guided tours on Tues. & Thurs. at 11:30 a.m., 5:30 p.m., & 6:30 p.m. 🚇 Metro: Banco de España

Teatro María Guerrero

Designed in 1885 by Agustín Ortiz de Villajos, the theater is named after the renowned actress who for many years owned the building and performed there regularly. Originally it was called the Teatro Princesa, after the daughter of Alfonso XII, which is why the letters T and P feature entwined in stone on the neo-Greek facade. One of the best examples of 19th-century cast-iron architecture in Madrid, the theater has a neo-Mudejar interior with intricate red and gold decoration. It is now home to the Centro Dramático Nacional, which specializes in contemporary theater, particularly the work of Spanish playwrights. www.mcu.es ⚠ Map p. 91 ✉ Calle Tamayo y Baus ☎ 91 310 2949 🚇 Metro: Colón

Packed with cafés, bars, and restaurants, an entertainment hub for hundreds of years

Around Plaza de Santa Ana

A ceramic portrait of the 17th-century writer Francisco de Quevedo

Around Plaza de Santa Ana

The triangle of streets east of the Puerta del Sol is usually known as the Barrio de las Letras, the Literary Quarter. Bordered by Carrera de San Jerónimo, Paseo del Prado, Calle Atocha, and Calle de la Cruz, the area got its name from the concentration of poets, playwrights, journalists, and novelists who flocked to the area after Madrid's first makeshift theaters were established at the end of the 16th century.

Known as *corrales*, the first two courtyard theaters were the Príncipe, where the Teatro Español now stands on Plaza de Santa Ana, and the Cruz, on the street of the same name. The 17th century was the golden age of Spanish theater, and plays by leading writers of the time—Lope de Vega, Pedro Calderón de la Barca, Tirso de Molina—are staged to this day both in Spain and abroad.

Madrid's population rose sharply after Felipe II made the city the capital in 1561. Many of these people were unemployed and kept themselves amused by spending their time at the corrales, which were open from noon until 10 p.m. Most stood throughout the performances and were anything but a passive audience. Only the clergy and aristocracy sat down, either at the front or in private compartments around the sides.

There was an enormous number of plays, which led to dozens of workshops being set up to print them. Bookshops opened, too, along with taverns to cater to the thousands of people who thronged to the area every day. The 19th century saw the emergence of literary cafés, where the literati would meet to discuss literature, art, and current affairs (see pp. 118–119).

Though the Teatro Español remains Madrid's most prestigious theater, the Santa Ana area is now better known for its exciting nightlife. Popular

NOT TO BE MISSED:

The tapas bars in and around Plaza de Santa Ana 112–113

A beer in the Cervecería Alemana, a Hemingway haunt 113

A drink in the Casa Alberto tavern, on the site where Cervantes once lived 115

The quaint home of playwright Lope de Vega 116

The grand Ateneo club 117

A performance at La Corrala 120–121

The Rastro market on Sunday mornings 120–121

An arthouse movie at the Filmoteca Española 122

with locals and visitors of all ages, this is a good place to try a few tapas bars.

Corrales also appeared south of Santa Ana, in the area known as Lavapiés, where courtyards still exist behind the 19th-century facades. One of Madrid's most traditional neighborhoods, it features in the work of many golden age writers. In recent years, an influx of people from Africa, Latin America, and the Far East has given the area a new lease on life. On Sunday mornings, a huge flea market, the Rastro, attracts thousands of visitors in search of bargains. ■

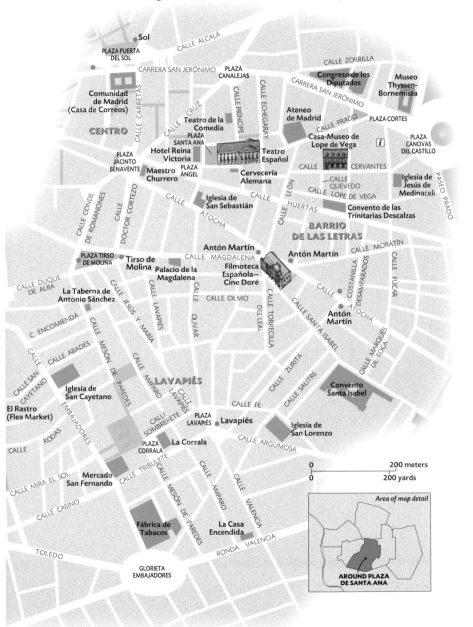

Plaza de Santa Ana

Plaza de Santa Ana gets its name from the convent that stood here until the 19th century. This large, open space is now a popular meeting place with lots of cafés and tapas bars. The square is dominated by the Teatro Español, which has developed over the centuries from a courtyard playhouse into a grand edifice.

With its tapas bars and cafés, Plaza de Santa Ana is a popular meeting place.

Now known as the Corral del Príncipe, the grand old theater was originally founded by a charity to generate income for a hospital on nearby Calle Toledo. The theater was highly successful, although the authorities had to introduce tight controls to stop unruly crowds from gaining entry without paying.

The open, wooden playhouse was replaced in 1745 by a covered Italian-style theater, which was rebuilt by Juan de Villanueva following a devastating fire at the beginning of the 19th century. After the square was created by the demolition of the old convent, the new owners added a neoclassic facade, featuring oversized medallions with busts of many famous playwrights. The interior of the building was rebuilt after another fire in 1975, and the theater now stages both classical and more contemporary plays under the directorship of Mario Gas.

A likeness of poet and playwright Federico García Lorca (1898–1936) stands in front of the theater. The large marble statue at the other end of the building depicts playwright Pedro Calderón de la Barca, one of the best known golden age dramatists; several scenes from four of his plays surround the base.

The most famous of the many

bars on the square is **Cervecería Alemana** at No. 6 *(tel 91 429 7033),* which was founded in 1904 and has changed very little over the years. The bar was a favorite haunt of famous bull-

INSIDER TIP:

Stay into the early hours for flamenco musicians at Candela bar, a shady joint near the Antón Martín metro. When flamenco erupts it's spontaneous, memorable, and very late indeed.

—CHRISTOPHER SOMERVILLE
National Geographic author

fighters; Ernest Hemingway and his circle of drinkers were also regulars here.

The bullfighters, including Manolete (1917–1947) and Luis Miguel Dominguín (1926–1996), favored the **Hotel Reina Victoria** (now the Me Madrid; see p. 248), with its gleaming cream facade and distinctive corner beacon at the top of the square. Built in 1919, it has been remodeled and is now a chic designer hotel.

Just off the square, to the left of the hotel, is the **Iglesia de San Sebastián.** The original structure, from the 16th century, was destroyed in the Civil War. In the 17th century, the church became the base for the charitable organizations that had set

up the two courtyard playhouses. Funds from these organizations helped actors and writers cover basic expenses and medical care.

Writer Lope de Vega was buried in the church's crypt, and although his remains were eventually lost, he is commemorated by a monument inside. Many other famous writers, including Ramón del Valle-Inclán, Bécquer, Larra, and Zorrilla, were married in this church.

Through a glass screen in the church, visitors can see the neoclassic **Chapel of Our Lady of Bethlehem,** originally designed by Ventura Rodríguez in the 18th

---

Patrons' Revenge

Back in the 17th century, if the audience did not like either the play or a particular actor, they would shout, throw rotten fruit, and bang kitchen utensils to make their feelings known. Their unequivocal reaction could close down a play after just one performance, with disastrous consequences for the actors and writers. Spectators sometimes became so immersed in the play that they believed it was real, and would jump onto the stage to attack the actors with knives and other weapons.

---

century and meticulously reconstructed by the Architects' Guild. Leading architects, including Juan de Villanueva, are buried there, as is Ventura Rodríguez himself. ∎

Iglesia de San Sebastián
- ✉ Calle Atocha 39
- ☎ 91 429 1361
- Ⓜ Metro: Antón Martín

Plaza de Santa Ana

- Ⓜ Map pp. 110–111
- Ⓜ Metro: Antón Martín, Sol

Teatro Español
- ✉ Calle Príncipe 25
- ☎ 91 360 1484
- Ⓜ Metro: Antón Martín, Sevilla

Candela
- ✉ Calle del Olmo 2
- ☎ 91 467 3382
- Ⓜ Metro: Antón Martín, Lavapiés, Tirso de Molina

A Walk in the Barrio de las Letras

This walk is more about atmosphere than sights. As you stroll through the narrow streets, let your imagination take you back to the 17th century, when the area was the seedbed of cultural life in Madrid.

Bars and restaurants with literary associations line the lanes around Plaza de Santa Ana.

From the **Puerta del Sol ❶**, walk along Carrera de San Jerónimo and turn right up Calle Victoria. One of Spain's most renowned authors, Benito Pérez Galdós, set his first novel, *La Fontana de Oro,* in a café of the same name on this corner. Although the café disappeared long ago, the novel is commemorated by a marble plaque a little farther along outside a bar that now uses the name.

Bearing right up Calle de la Cruz, on the left at No. 23 is **Capas Seseña** *(tel 91 531 6840),* which sells traditional capes. You come almost immediately to a small square. Facing you is a large mural of this street as it is now, featuring Felipe IV in the bottom right-hand corner. The Corral de la Cruz, one of Madrid's first theaters, began in a courtyard here in the 16th century.

Turn left down Calle de Álvarez Gato, a lane with a series of distorting mirrors on the left, the originals of which featured in Valle-Inclán's play *Bohemian Lights* (1924). At the end on the right,

NOT TO BE MISSED:

Plaza de Santa Ana • Teatro Español • Casa-Museo de Lope de Vega

hand-painted tiles of Spanish cities decorate **Villa Rosa** *(tel 91 521 3689),* a flamenco club that dates back to 1919.

Turn right into **Plaza de Santa Ana ❷**, with the **Teatro Español** at the far end. Walk diagonally across the square and turn right into Calle Príncipe. On the first corner on the right, you reach the **Palacio de Santoña,** which was designed in 1734. It features ornate baroque doorways designed by Pedro de Ribera and that face on Calle Príncipe. It is not usually open to the public, but the Madrid Tourist Center *(tel 91 588 1636)* organizes tours of the lavish interior.

In 1614, Cervantes lived across the street, where the **Casa Alberto** tavern (see pp. 64–65) is now. Turn left down Calle Huertas, one of the busiest streets for nightlife and where quotes by authors including Galdós and Cervantes are set into the sidewalk.

The austere neoclassic building on the corner with Calle León was designed by Juan de Villanueva in 1788 and houses the **Real Academia de la Historia** (Royal Academy of History) ❸. It was originally used by monks from the monastery at El Escorial (see pp. 228–231), who printed their prayer books here.

Turn right up Calle León—whose name derives from a lion kept in a cage here in the 17th century—then left down the broad Calle Atocha. At No. 87 you come to the **Sociedad Cervantina** ❹ (tel 91 420 3437), which promotes the work of Cervantes. As shown by a plaque, this was the site of the printing press that published the first part of Don Quixote in 1605.

Turn left up Costanilla de los Desamparados and take the third left back up Calle Huertas, then walk up the hill on the right, Costanilla Trinitarias. The wall running the entire block on the left belongs to the **Convento de las Trinitarias Descalzas** ❺ (see p. 117). Turning left up Calle Lope de Vega, you can appreciate the size of the convent. Cut down Calle Quevedo to Calle Cervantes, where the **Casa-Museo de Lope de Vega** ❻ is situated (see p. 116), and turn left back to Calle León. A plaque on the corner marks the place where Cervantes lived. Turn right down to Calle Prado, then left to arrive back at Plaza de Santa Ana.

- ⓜ See area map pp. 110–111
- ▶ Puerta del Sol
- ⏱ 1.4 miles (2.25 km)
- ↔ 45 minutes
- ▶ Plaza de Santa Ana

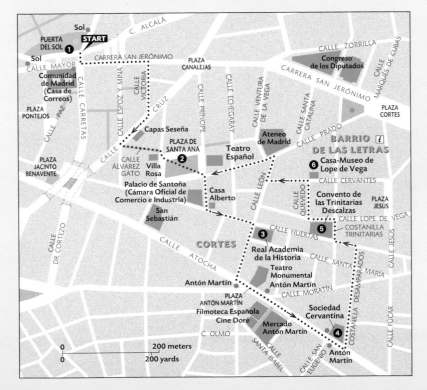

Calle Cervantes & Around

Many streets in this area are named after literary figures who lived (or were buried!) in the neighborhood. The street now called Calle Cervantes was home to both Cervantes and playwright Lope de Vega, but only the latter's home survives. The parallel Calle Lope de Vega is also associated with Cervantes, as he was originally buried there. Calle Quevedo, which links the two streets, was home to the poet and satirist Francisco de Quevedo (1580–1645).

Intellectuals have been meeting in the imposing library of the Ateneo club for more than a century.

Calle Cervantes

🅰 Map pp. 110–111

🚇 Metro: Antón Martín, Sevilla

Although largely rebuilt, the **Casa-Museo de Lope de Vega** is a traditional 17th-century house and is worth visiting to see how professional people lived in the area at that time. One of Spain's most renowned playwrights, Félix Lope de Vega lived in this house from 1610 until his death in 1635 at the

age of 73. He was married twice, had three lovers, and fathered at least 14 children. In the course of his tumultuous life, he wrote about 1,500 plays, as well as poetry and novels.

The house has two main floors, set around a peaceful courtyard garden, with orange, lemon, fig, and cypress trees. In

Lope de Vega's time, half was used as a vegetable garden to provide food for the family.

The furniture and decoration are authentic from the 17th century, although most of the pieces on display did not belong to the writer. In the study, the desk is near the window as Lope de Vega worked very long hours and needed optimal use of the natural light. Two paintings in this room

Nonsmoking Regulations

Although smoking in the workplace has been banned since 2006, regulations allow smoking in bars and restaurants with an area of less than 120 square yards (100 sq m), if the owner so chooses. Larger places have to provide a separate smoking area. The reality is that you can still smoke in at least 90 percent of bars and restaurants, and there is no social stigma involved. Higher-category hotels offer smoke-free rooms. Smoking is not allowed in shops, public transport, airports, cinemas, or theaters.

belonged to him, one depicting his own children, Carlitos and Lope Félix. Lope de Vega decided to become a priest at the age of 51, and the house contains a small chapel dedicated to San Isidro, patron saint of Madrid (see p. 63).

Chess was a very popular game in Lope de Vega's lifetime, and a room on the top floor contains a chessboard. There was no bathroom available; inhabitants simply used pitchers and bowls and threw the waste out of the window at night.

Lope de Vega and a well-known actress named Micaela de Luján had five children together, one of whom became Mother Superior of the nearby **Convento de las Trinitarias Descalzas** (*Calle Lope de Vega 18*). There are now just 21 nuns living in a closed order at the convent, which is not open to the public. Inside the church entrance on the left, a hatch with a revolving drum allows the nuns to communicate with the outside world without being seen. To the left of the presbytery in the church, a stone tablet commemorates the fact that Cervantes is buried here. On the anniversary of his death, April 23, the church holds a special Mass in his memory.

Calle Prado, one block north of Calle Cervantes, is lined with antique bookshops. One of the great intellectual institutions of the 19th century, the **Ateneo de Madrid** is still going strong at No. 21. Founded in 1835 by a group of liberal thinkers, the organization was dedicated to reforming the educational system. Its activities often met opposition from the government or the Church, and over the years it was shut down several times. Designed in 1884 by Enrique Fort, the building comprises a lecture theater, large library, and club room. It is a private club, but visitors are welcome to look around; the café is open to the public. ∎

Casa-Museo de Lope de Vega
- ✉ Calle Cervantes 11
- ☎ 91 429 9216
- 🕐 Closed p.m., Sun., & Mon.
- 💲 $. Free Sat. a.m.
- Ⓜ Metro: Antón Martín, Sevilla

www.rae.es

Ateneo de Madrid
- ✉ Calle Prado 21
- ☎ 91 429 1750
- Ⓜ Metro: Antón Martín, Sevilla

Traditional Cafés

Sitting at marble tables in cavernous cafés has been a favorite pastime for Madrileños for nearly two centuries. Although the city lost most of its original cafés to rapid development in the second half of the 20th century, the tradition has returned with dozens of newer watering spots. In these cafés, people can sit for hours, drinking coffee, engaging in intellectual debate, or simply passing along the latest gossip.

For nearly 200 years, Madrileños have relaxed, discussed, and worked at the city's many cafés. Some are old, some are new, but all offer a prime spot to watch the world go by.

Madrid's café society began during the repressive regime of Fernando VII in the early 19th century, when intellectuals used to gather to debate ways to reform the political and cultural situation. These gatherings gave rise to the term *tertulia,* meaning an informal discussion group. Tertulias usually had a special area of interest—such as politics, literature, poetry, bullfighting, or science—with each group favoring a specific café for its meetings.

Discussion Time

One of the most renowned early tertulias included the impressive group of politicians and writers that went on to found the Ateneo club (see p. 117), which flourishes to this day. Led by Ramón de Mesoneros

Romanos (1803–1882), a writer and city councilor who chronicled life in Madrid, this group was known as El Parnasillo and met in the Café del Príncipe, now called the **Café del Español** *(Calle Príncipe 25, tel 91 420 1755)*, alongside the Teatro Español (see p. 112).

INSIDER TIP:

For great views of the old town, go to the rooftop café in the Universidad de Educación a Distancia, on Calle Tribulete in the Lavapiés neighborhood.

—ANNIE BENNETT
National Geographic author

The present café opened in the late 1990s, but the traditional decor is based on descriptions by Mesoneros Romanos and the writer Benito Pérez Galdós. Among the group's other colorful members was the satirist Mariano José de Larra. In his article "El Café," written in the year 1932, Larra proclaimed, "I don't know if it is my natural curiosity ... that makes me take a seat at corner tables four times a day to eavesdrop on other people's conversations, which later keep me entertained when I am back home ... when I laugh like a lunatic at all the lunatics I have overheard."

Literary Heyday

By the end of the 19th century, cafés had proliferated all over downtown Madrid, particularly around the Puerta del Sol, Calle Alcalá, and Plaza de Santa Ana. One of the most famous was the Café del Pombo just off the Puerta del Sol. A famous tertulia group used to meet in the basement— dubbed "the Sacred Crypt"—and was led by Ramón Gómez de la Serna (1888–1963), who specialized in writing about Madrid. This group was depicted by expressionist artist José Gutiérrez Solana in his painting "La Tertulia del Café del Pombo," which hangs in the Reina Sofía (see pp. 154–159).

After the Civil War, many of the leading exponents of café society went into exile, and a number of cafés were turned into banks and shops. Two great institutions do, however, survive to this day: the **Café Comercial** *(Glorieta de Bilbao 7, tel 91 521 5655)* and the **Café Gijón** *(Paseo de Recoletos 21, tel 91 521 5425)*.

The Comercial opened in 1887 and has been packed with a mixture of politicians, poets, intellectuals, and office workers ever since. Originally the café featured musical performances on a stage, which sadly no longer exists. The decor has remained essentially unchanged since 1953, when the café's marble tables were installed.

The Gijón has been going since 1888 and tertulia groups still meet there, particularly at the coveted window tables. Regulars over the years have included writers Valle-Inclán, García Lorca, and Nobel Prize–winner Camilo José Cela, whose novel *The Hive* was based on the characters who frequented the Gijón in the 1940s.

Sandwich or *Bocadillo?* Clearing up the Confusion

Order a "sandwich" in a Spanish bar, and in most places you'll get a toasted sandwich in white sliced bread, with a cheese and ham filling (known as a *mixto*) unless otherwise specified. If you want the chunky, French-style local bread, ask for a *bocadillo*. Hot or cold fillings are usually available, the most typical being tortilla omelette, calamares, chorizo sausage, salami, ham, or cheese. Some bars offer *montaditos*, which are canapés on thick slices of local bread, with interesting hot and cold toppings including blue cheese, crab, prawns, anchovies, and blood sausage. Take-out sandwich shops are now popping up in central Madrid, which also offer a better range of juices and smoothies than bars.

Lavapiés & the Rastro

The streets sloping down from Plaza de Santa Ana form the neighborhood of Lavapiés, traditionally known as the *barrios bajos*, or low districts. Now the most racially mixed part of the city, its character is changing fast. Over the centuries, Lavapiés has provided a wealth of material for writers and artists. Lope de Vega, Cervantes, and Tirso de Molina wrote about the area in the 17th century, followed by Ramón de la Cruz and Galdós.

You never know what treasures you might discover while browsing the Rastro flea market.

Lavapiés & the Rastro

📍 Map pp. 110–111

Ⓜ️ Metro: La Latina, Lavapiés, Tirso de Molina

Many paintings by Goya were inspired by events he witnessed in this area. If possible, explore Lavapiés on a Sunday morning, when the Rastro flea market is in full swing.

Plaza de Lavapiés was the heart of the Jewish quarter in medieval Madrid. The synagogue stood near the square on the corner of Calle de la Fé and Calle de Salitre, where the 19th-century **Iglesia de San Lorenzo** is now.

After the Catholic Monarchs expelled the Jews in 1492, this area was occupied by *conversos*, Jews who had converted to Christianity. The conversos traditionally named their first son Manuel, which led to the area also becoming known as the Barrio de los Manolos. Over the years, the term Manolo has come to mean a streetwise Madrid character who features in many plays and novels.

Near the square, on the corner of Calle Sombrerete and Calle Mesón de Paredes, is **La Corrala**, a 19th-century galleried building open on one side to reveal a courtyard. In summer, concerts and theatrical performances are sometimes held here, featuring people dressed in traditional costume as Manolos and Manolas.

One block west, on Calle Embajadores, is the area's most important church, the **Iglesia de San Cayetano.** The church was rebuilt in the 1960s after most of the original structure, from the late 17th and early 18th centuries, was destroyed in the fighting of the Civil War.

The Rastro

The Rastro market takes place between Calle Embajadores and Calle Toledo, with Ribera de Curtidores as the main street. The term *rastro* has unpleasant origins, as it refers to the trail of blood left on the streets from the two abattoirs that used to exist in the area. Those are long gone, replaced by stands selling clothes, bags, books, and all manner of secondhand junk. Be careful here: Theft is rife in the crowded streets.

Start from Plaza de Cascorro, then turn to the right into Plaza General Vara del Rey, where stands sell rustic furniture. Head down the hill to the stands of old records and books at the bottom, then cut through to Ribera de Curtidores and back up the hill. ∎

Iglesia de San Cayetano

☒ Calle Embajadores 15

☎ 91 527 0790

🚇 Metro: Lavapiés, Tirso de Molina

Rastro flea market

☒ Ribera de Curtidores

🕐 Sundays until 3 p.m.

🚇 Metro: La Latina

EXPERIENCE: Learning Spanish

Sign up for a Spanish course these days and you can expect to learn how to flirt, argue, and curse as well as conjugate irregular verbs. Lessons are no longer a passive affair of endless exercises, but an interactive experience where you are constantly practicing what you have learned. You can combine your classes with all sorts of activities, too, such as flamenco dancing, guitar lessons, cooking, or wine tasting.

While most courses last a term, there are plenty of one-week or one-month options available, often involving 20 or 30 hours of lessons a week, so you make fast progress. The day usually begins with grammar lessons, followed by more informal conversation sessions with an emphasis on communication and expression rather than getting everything right the first time.

Be sure to enroll at one of the more dynamic schools with fun teaching methods and a wide range of cultural and recreational activities. These are a few of the best:

Ailmadrid *(Calle Doctor Esquerdo 33 1-2, tel 91 725 6350, www.ailmadrid.com);* **Don Quijote** *(Calle Duque de Liria 6, tel 923 277 200, www.donquijote.org);* **Elemadrid** *(Calle Serrano 4, tel 91 432 4540, www. elemadrid.com);* **Enforex** *(Calle Alberto Aguilera 26, tel 91 594 3776, www.enforex.com);* and **Instituto Cervantes** *(Calle Alcalá 49, tel 91 436 7600, www.cervantes.es).*

More Places to Visit Around Plaza de Santa Ana

La Casa Encendida

Run by José Guirao, a former director of the Museo Reina Sofía near Paseo del Prado, this is an exciting cultural center located in a neo-Mudejar building. The varied program includes exhibitions, concerts, and performances, as well as workshops and courses. Activities often have an ecological angle, and there is also a fair-trade shop. www.lacasaencendida.es ⚒ Map pp. 110–111 ✉ Ronda de Valencia 2 ☎ 902 430 322 🚇 Metro: Atocha, Embajadores, Lavapiés

Filmoteca Española–Cine Doré

This beautiful art nouveau cinema was built in 1923 and is now owned by the Filmoteca Española, the national film archive, which programs showings in its three theaters. In summer, movies are also shown on the roof terrace. There is a good bookshop and café. www.mcu.es/cine ⚒ Map pp. 110–111

The 18th-century Palacio de la Magdalena now houses the National Film Institute.

✉ Calle Santa Isabel 3 ☎ 91 369 2118 🕐 Closed Mon. 🚇 Metro: Antón Martín

Iglesia de Jesús de Medinaceli

Although this structure was built only in 1920, it stands on the site of a monastery founded in the early 17th century. The church was popular with theater people, who always came to Mass on Sundays. It contains a 16th-century figure of Jesus of Nazareth that is believed to have miraculous qualities, having been rescued by Trinitarian monks from the Moors in North Africa in the 17th century. On the first Friday of every month, people stand in line to kiss the feet of the statue in the hope it will bring them good fortune. www.archimadrid.es/jesusmedinaceli ⚒ Map pp. 110–111 ✉ Plaza Jesús 2 ☎ 91 429 6893 🚇 Metro: Antón Martín

Palacio de la Magdalena

Recently restored, the building was designed by Pedro de Ribera in 1731 and has an elaborate baroque doorway. It was built as the residence of the Marquis of Perales, who was governor of Madrid at the time of the 1808 uprising against the French (see pp. 204–205). It is now the headquarters of the National Film Institute, which organizes a program of exhibitions. ⚒ Map p. 111 ✉ Calle Magdalena 10 ☎ 91 467 2600 🕐 Closed Sun. & Mon. 🚇 Metro: Antón Martín, Tirso de Molina

Teatro de la Comedia

The theater, home to the Compañia Nacional de Teatro Clásico, has seen the debut of many classical productions. The building was constructed in 1874 and underwent major renovations in 1915 and 2002. It is located very near to **Teatro de Pavón** (Calle Embajadores 9). ⚒ Map pp. 110–111 ✉ Calle Principe 14 ☎ 91 528 2819 🚇 Metro: La Latina

Madrid's museum mile, with an astounding assemblage of some of the world's greatest art

Paseo del Prado

The figure of Carlos IV decorates a balcony on the Paseo del Prado.

Paseo del Prado

Madrid's three greatest art museums are all located on or near the Paseo del Prado, a boulevard designed for leisure and learning during the reign of Carlos III in the 18th century. Now it is becoming known as the Paseo del Arte, or Art Walk, and being developed as a grand promenade. The Prado, Thyssen-Bornemisza, and Reina Sofía museums contain some of the most famous artworks in the world.

Visitors inspect Goya's painting, "The Nude Maja," rumored to depict the Duchess of Alba.

All three museums have undergone expansion in recent years to provide more space for their prestigious collections. The most far-reaching changes are still taking place at the Prado, where work is under way on neighboring buildings that will eventually create a huge complex across the hill above the Paseo del Prado. CaixaForum, an arts venue that opened in 2008, usually has three temporary exhibitions running as well as a range of cultural activities.

Visiting the Prado is a stimulating but often overwhelming experience. You could easily spend several days contemplating its treasures, but if you have only a few hours, it really pays to decide which areas interest you most and visit those first. You also need at least three hours for the Thyssen-Bornemisza, where the displays span eight centuries of art history, with

masterpieces from every period. The Reina Sofía is a vast museum of contemporary art, with two or three major temporary exhibitions usually running at any given time. Again, you are likely to spend a minimum of three hours looking at the displays, and possibly another couple of hours in the excellent restaurant and bookshop.

The Paseo itself is also going to be altered to make it more pedestrian-friendly. A development plan devised by Portuguese architect Álvaro Siza restricts traffic to the west side of the street, with ramps and walkways improving access to the museums.

These changes will create a 21st-century version of the original concept for the Paseo del Prado. During the Enlightenment, this stretch was the most fashionable social area in the city. That situation is likely to be repeated when it is once again the preserve of pedestrians rather than cars. ∎

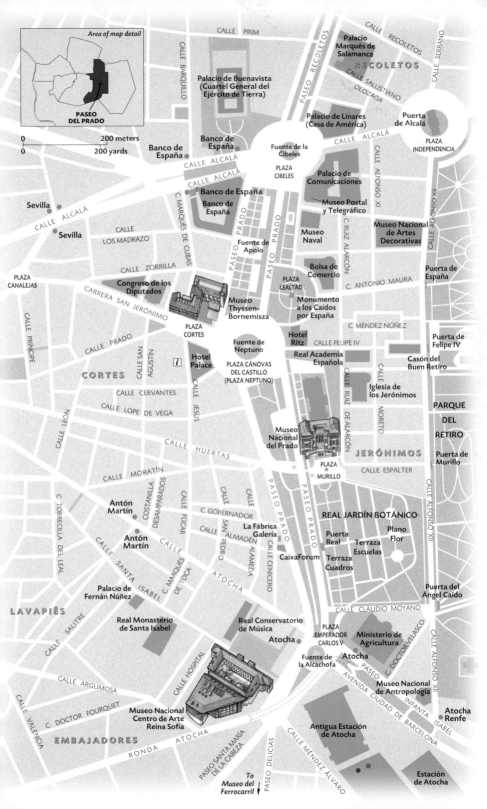

Museo Nacional del Prado

The Prado is one of the greatest museums in the world, with an awe-inspiring wealth of masterpieces. Although best known for its collections of works by Velázquez, Goya, and other Spanish masters, it also has superlative displays of Italian and Flemish paintings. No matter how determined you are to follow a planned route, you will be constantly distracted by the breathtaking artworks that assail your senses as you stroll through the galleries.

An artist replicates "La Vendimia," one of Francisco de Goya's tapestry designs.

Museo Nacional del Prado

- 🅐 Map p. 125
- ✉ Paseo del Prado
- ☎ 902 10 7077
- 🕐 Closed Mon.
- 💲 $$. Free after 6 p.m. Tues.– Sat., after 5 p.m. Sun.
- 🚇 Metro: Atocha, Banco de España, Atocha

www.museodel prado.es

The Prado has always suffered from a severe lack of space, and it displays only about 10 percent of its holdings. This problem has been at least partially addressed by the construction of an extension at the rear of the building. Designed by Rafael Moneo, it opened in 2007. Neighboring buildings are being remodeled as well to provide more exhibition rooms.

One of the most important neoclassical buildings in Spain, the Prado was designed as a natural history museum in 1785 by Juan de Villanueva (1739–1811). This museum was intended to be the focal point of Carlos III's ambitious plan for the development of Paseo del Prado. Progress on the grand project slowed, however, following Carlos III's death in 1788 and came to a total halt during the War of Independence (1808–1814), when the building was used as a barracks by French soldiers.

The possibility of creating a public museum to display the royal collections of art had first been suggested by German painter Anton Raphael Mengs in 1775, but the idea did not come to fruition until the reign of Fernando VII. The Prado museum finally opened on November 19, 1819, with about 1,500 paintings on display.

The Prado's works were acquired by different monarchs over the centuries in accordance with their personal tastes and the political circumstances of their reigns, rather than with any intention to create a coherent collection. Carlos V and his son Felipe II were both keen on Venetian artists, particularly Titian. Felipe II was an astute art lover whose taste was influenced by his Flemish aunt. He built up an extensive art collection at El Escorial (see pp. 228–231), a substantial part of which is now in the Prado, including several superb paintings by Hieronymus Bosch.

The more conservative Felipe III favored Peter Paul Rubens (1577–1640), while Felipe IV chose Diego de Velázquez (1599–1660) as court painter. Goya worked for both Carlos III and Carlos IV.

In 1872, the Prado acquired approximately 3,000 works that had been requisitioned as a result of the disentailment of religious property. In addition, the Francisco Cambó bequest in 1941 brought an important collection of Italian and Spanish primitive art to the museum.

Visiting the Prado

You can buy tickets and enter the Prado at the main entrance in the middle or at the downstairs door at the north end. The upstairs entrance at the north end gives direct access to temporary

Bosch's Vision

Notions of beauty and the sublime aside, some works of art simply inspire confusion and discomfort. Hieronymus Bosch's "The Garden of Earthly Delights" falls into this category. Painted by an intensely religious man, the triptych is an allegory for the fall of man. Apparently, damnation involves aliens riding giant birds. The painting foreshadows the 20th century via Freudian dream analysis, surrealism, and the Grateful Dead.

exhibitions. Rooms are often closed for restoration or used to house temporary exhibitions, particularly the section at the north end of the first floor. Pick up a floor plan as you go in to check on the current arrangements.

Bear in mind that there is only one restaurant in the Prado, and it consequently gets very busy at peak times. The restaurant is located in the new extension at the rear of the building and frankly leaves a lot to be desired. You are not allowed to take bottles of water or other drinks into the museum. Backpacks of any size must be checked into the cloakroom, but bags of any other shape are okay.

Romanesque & Early Spanish Art: Starting from the Puerta de Goya at the north end of the ground floor, stop in at **Room 51c** off the

rotunda. The room contains 12th-century hunting scenes from the Mozarabic church of San Baudelio de Berlanga in Soria and Romanesque murals from the Santa Cruz chapel in Maderuelo in Segovia. In **Room 50,** don't miss the superb "St. Dominic of Silos Enthroned as Abbot" by Bartolomé Bermejo (circa 1405–1498), a masterpiece of Aragonese painting.

Early Italian Painting: As you enter the long **Room 49,** look to your left to see the three panels by Sandro Botticelli (circa 1445–1510), portraying "The Story of Nastagio degli Onesti" (1483) from Boccaccio's *Decameron*. The fourth and final panel is in the Watney Collection in the United States. Opposite is the delicately painted "Annunciation" (circa 1435) by Fra Angelico (circa 1400–1455), which was transferred here from the Monasterio de las Descalzas Reales (see pp. 86–87). The series of paintings by Raphael (1483–1520) chart his evolution as an artist. The most striking

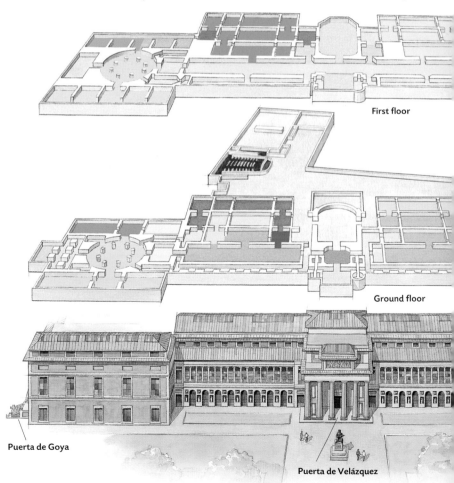

First floor

Ground floor

Puerta de Goya

Puerta de Velázquez

is "Portrait of a Cardinal" (circa 1510), with the cardinal in a brilliant red robe.

15th- & 16th-century Spanish Painting:

Pedro de Berruguete (circa 1450–1504) is credited with moving Hispano-Flemish art forward by introducing Renaissance elements, as illustrated by the fascinating "Auto-da-fé presided over by St. Dominic" (circa 1490) in **Room 57b.** "The Last Supper" by Juan de Juanes (circa 1523–1579) in **Room 56** was painted for the

Paintings from Romanesque chapels around Spain have been transferred to the Prado to avoid deterioration.

altar of a church in Valencia and is considered to be one of the artist's best works.

Early Flemish & German Art:

Room 58 houses the exceptionally vivid "Descent from the Cross" by Rogier van der Weyden (1400–1464), which Felipe II inherited from his aunt, María of Hungary. The faces in the painting are brilliantly executed, and the composition leads the eye to

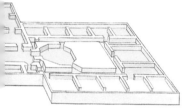

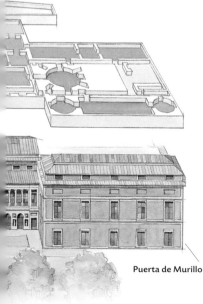

Puerta de Murillo

Italian paintings

Spanish paintings

Flemish paintings

Dutch paintings

French paintings

Sculpture

Drawing & Exhibition Halls

German paintings

New Areas

Other

the figures of Christ and Mary, whose robe was painted in lapis lazuli. Also in this room is "The Virgin and Child" (circa 1460) by Petrus Christus. In **Room 58a** is

"Christ in the Garden of Olives" by El Greco features the flowing figures and soft tones that are typical of his style.

Hans Memling's triptych "Adoration of the Magi" (circa 1470).

There are always crowds in **Room 56a,** which is dominated by the intriguing paintings of satirist Hieronymus Bosch (circa 1450–1516), whose passions ranged from the bawdy to the mystical. "The Garden of Earthly Delights" (circa 1505) depicts "Earthly Paradise" on the left and

"Hell" on the right. "The Haywain" (circa 1510) was inspired by a Flemish proverb: "The world is like a haywain from which everyone takes whatever they can." Joachim Patinir's dreamlike landscape "Crossing the Styx" (circa 1515) portrays the Greek myth of Charon taking the dead to Hell.

Room 55 is devoted to Anthonis Mor (circa 1519-1576), who was court painter to Felipe II. Previously he worked in Flanders for Carlos V, for whom he painted the portrait of "Mary Tudor" (1554). The painting was intended to impress Felipe II, who was considering marriage to Mary at the time. She subsequently became his second wife. Mor's "Pejerón, Jester of the Count of Benavente and the Duke of Alba" is believed to be the earliest pictorial representation of a jester.

The Prado's limited holdings of German art are exhibited in **Room 55b,** which contains four masterpieces by Albrecht Dürer (1471-1528), including his magnificent "Self-portrait" (1498) and the panels of "Adam" and "Eve" (1507), which were all brought to Spain by Felipe IV.

Venetian School: Crossing the central concourse, you move into the south wing, where the next set of rooms is devoted to 16th-century Italian art. In the long **Room 75** is "Christ Washing the Disciples' Feet," also known as "El Lavatorio," by Jacopo Tintoretto (1518–1594), which is a masterpiece of perspective. Take a good look at it while standing to the right of the painting, letting your gaze wander from the figure of Christ across the canvas to the triumphal arch on the left. This painting was one of the many works acquired by Felipe IV from the collections of Charles I of England.

The painters of the Venetian school surpassed all other Renaissance artists with their masterful blending of color and light. Titian worked extensively for both Carlos V and Felipe II and is represented in Room 75 by "Adam and Eve" and "Salomé." Titian painted his "Self-Portrait" late in life, when he was 80 years old. His fame during his lifetime rivaled that of Michelangelo, and it is said that Carlos V once did him the honor of picking up a paintbrush he had dropped. One of his most famous works, "Charles V at Mühlberg" (1548), is displayed on the first floor in **Room 11**. This brilliantly executed equestrian painting was commissioned to commemorate the emperor's victory over the

Protestants in the 1547 battle. Carlos V is not depicted in a triumphant way, however, but rather with a reflective, resigned expression.

El Greco: Rooms 9a–10a on the first floor are devoted to El Greco (1541–1614), starting with early works and moving into his Spanish period, when his figures lengthened and he became obsessed with the division between Heaven and Earth. Born in Crete, El Greco (Domenikos Theotokopoulos) spent the last four decades of his life in Toledo, where many of his best works are to be found (see pp. 214–217). "The Nobleman with his Hand on his Breast" (circa 1578), which was restored in the 1990s, depicts a knight of the realm making a solemn promise and has become an iconic image of 16th-century Spain. "The Resurrection," which was painted

EXPERIENCE: Visiting Museums with an Art Historian

Whether you are a total novice or a bit of a scholar where art is concerned, you will get a lot more out of Madrid's magnificent museums and galleries in the company of an art historian, contemporary art expert, curator, or professor. You might be short of time and want to make sure you see the key works in the Prado or Thyssen-Bornemisza museums, or perhaps feel you need some help to understand the conceptual art in the Reina Sofía. In a few hours, an expert can give you insight into the works of such celebrated artists as Velázquez, Goya, Picasso, Miró, or Dalí, tailored to your

interests and level of knowledge. You could also do an entertaining gallery tour with a consultant who will explain the kind of art each place deals with, while also telling you which established or emerging artists to look out for, and even offering advice and helping you buy artworks if you so wish.

You can book a tour with an expert through the services of either of the following companies: **Made for Spain** (*Calle Antonio Flores 4, 1 D, tel 91 448 7275, www .madeforspain.com*) or **Madrid & Beyond** (*Calle Bailén 19, 1 Izqda, tel 91 758 0063, www.madridandbeyond.com*).

two decades later, features his trademark elongated figures and free brush strokes. (See pp. 38–42 for further discussion on Spanish painters.)

Goya: The Prado's superlative collection of works by Francisco de Goya is usually displayed at the southern end of the museum, on the ground, first, and second floors. It is a good idea to concentrate on viewing these paintings before continuing through the rest of the exhibits.

Goya was court painter to

INSIDER TIP:

Spend an hour in the Prado looking at Velázquez's "Las Meninas" and listen to viewers' interpretations as they pass by: "He's looking in a mirror," "He's doing a self-portrait," etc. Then decide for yourself.

—BARBARA ASCHER
National Geographic Traveler magazine writer

Carlos IV and painted many portraits of members of the royal family, often depicting them in a less than flattering way. One of his best known works is "The Family of Charles IV" (1800), in which the king looks melancholic, while the sharp-eyed Queen María Luisa is center stage, in charge of proceedings. The queen had 24 pregnancies but bore only 14 children, 7 of whom survived. In a nod to Velázquez, Goya included himself on the left of the painting. His "Self-Portrait" (1815) is a very honest work, with no airs and graces, painted when he was 69 years old.

Two of Goya's most powerful paintings, "The Second of May, 1808, in Madrid: the Charge of the Mamelukes," and "The Third of May in Madrid: the Executions at Príncipe Pío" (both 1814), depict scenes from the Madrileños' desperate and ultimately unsuccessful efforts to free their city from French occupation (see pp. 204–205). These works have universal resonance, however, brutally conveying the unequivocal message of the absurdity and futility of war.

In the last decade of his life, during a period of deep depression caused by the deaths of his wife and son and by his own illness, Goya produced the perplexing "Black Paintings." Originally painted on the walls of his house by the Río Manzanares River, these disturbing works were later transferred to canvas and donated to the Prado in 1881. "Dog Half-submerged" seems extraordinarily modern today, with its composition of a dog's head against textured space.

Two canvases that always attract attention are "The Nude Maja" and "The Clothed Maja," which are often said to depict the Duchess of Alba, who was a close friend of Goya's. This attribution may not be true, but the strange position of the heads lends weight to the belief that they may have been added later, obscuring the real identity of the sitter.

Goya worked at the Real Fábrica de Tápices (see p. 172) for almost 20 years, producing a series of designs for tapestries that often depicted local festivals or portrayed the everyday folk of Madrid. "The Parasol" (1777) shows a young man shading a girl with a parasol, through which light filters down onto her face and clothes.

17th-century Spanish Painting:

The fabulous holdings of Spanish art from the 17th century are displayed on the first floor. If not occupied by a temporary exhibition, the long hall on this floor may also display works from this rich period. The many highlights include "The Holy Family of the Little Bird" by Bartolomé Esteban Murillo from Seville, which is representative of his gentle, sympathetic style. His depiction of children and religious figures in domestic settings helped people to identify with the subject matter and earned him enormous popularity both during his lifetime and in the following centuries.

Works by José de Ribera, known as "El Españoleto," include four paintings of hermit saints, including "The Magdalen" (or "Saint Thais"), the sitter for which is believed to have been the artist's daughter. Also look for the ethereal light in "Christ Embracing Saint Bernard" by Francisco Ribalta (1565–1628). Ribalta was a key figure in Spanish baroque painting who trained in Madrid but worked mainly in Valencia.

Velázquez: The center of the first floor is devoted to Diego de Velázquez in **Rooms 12, 14–16, and 18.** The Prado has his best paintings, and the greatest of them all, "Las Meninas" ("The Maids of Honor" or "The Family of Felipe IV"), dominates the oval Room 12. Created circa 1656, it depicts a scene in Velázquez's studio in the Alcázar, when he was painting a portrait of Felipe IV and his second wife, Mariana of Austria, who are reflected in the mirror at the back. Velázquez himself observes you from where he stands beside his easel, while the Infanta Margarita, attended by her maids and two dwarves, stares out of the canvas. José Nieto, a court chamberlain, oversees proceedings from the staircase leading down

Goya's self-portraits depict his changing appearance over the years. This one dates from 1815, when he was 69 years old.

to the studio. If you are lucky enough to visit the Prado when the museum is not too crowded, spend some time looking at this remarkable painting from different angles, and new elements will jump out at you every few seconds.

"The Triumph of Bacchus," more commonly known as "The Topers" (circa 1629), depicts the mythological tale of Bacchus, but in Velázquez's version the god of wine is being worshipped by a group of decidedly unsavory-looking characters, such as might have been regular drinkers in the taverns of Madrid. "The Spin-

is being remodeled to become part of the Prado (see p. 136). When the work is completed, the painting may be hung once again in its original location. It depicts the well-known occasion in 1625 when the Spanish had triumphed over the Dutch at the Siege of Breda. The victor, Ambrosio Spinola, is shown humbly receiving the key to the town from Justin of Nassau, acknowledging the courage of his adversary.

The Prado exhibits only a few works by Francisco de Zurbarán, but all are masterpieces, displayed in **Rooms 18** and **18a**. These include the sublime "Still Life with

Visions of War

Modern war photography arose during the Spanish Civil War. Taking advantage of technological advances in camera speed and portability, photographers loaded film into their 35mm Leicas and followed the sound of guns. In 1936, Robert Capa launched his career in Spain—war photography is practically synonymous with his photograph "The

Falling Soldier," which freezes the moment of a loyalist soldier falling backward from a bullet. Long before this was Goya's "The Disasters of War." His series of 82 etchings, produced between 1810 and 1820, served the same function as modern war photography: to vividly portray war's horrors in hopes of bringing about peace.

ners," also known as "The Fable of Arachne," which was painted almost 30 years later in 1657, also uses ordinary people to portray a mythological subject. Look at the light falling on Arachne's neck and white blouse. Velázquez has managed to make the wheel seem as if it is spinning furiously, making the spokes disappear.

"The Surrender of Breda" (1634–1635), popularly known as "The Lances," was painted for the Hall of Realms of the Palacio del Buen Retiro, a building that

Four Vessels," an astoundingly realistic depiction of jars and pots of different materials and textures in shades of cream and brown. Also in this section is the exquisite "Still Life with Game, Fruit and Vegetables" by Juan Sánchez Cotán, one of the most well-known Spanish still life paintings.

17th-century Flemish & Dutch Art: The north wing of the first floor is largely devoted to the Flemish school in **Rooms 7a–11,** with one work by the Dutch master Rembrandt (1606–1669) in **Room 7.** His renowned "Artemisa" (1634) shows the portly queen of Pergamon receiving the ashes of her husband. The sitter was probably Rembrandt's wife, Saskia. Look for the shadowy figure in the background.

The Prado has about a hundred works by Peter Paul Rubens, but only a small selection is on display in **Rooms 8–11.** His masterpiece, "The Three Graces" (circa 1635), in **Room 9** features the faces of his two wives and depicts companions of Venus who represent the sensual enjoyment of life. Rubens kept this painting in his own collection during his life; after his death it was acquired by Felipe IV.

Room 10b contains a number of portraits by Anthony Van Dyck (1599–1641), including "Sir Endymion Porter and Van Dyck" (circa 1635), in which the artist painted himself standing next to the nobleman.

French Painting: The Prado's displays of French art are found in **Rooms 2–4** at the north end of the first floor and **Room 86** on the second floor. Nicolas Poussin (1594–1665) is represented by several works, some of which were bought to decorate the Palacio del Buen Retiro. These include his painting "Parnassus," which depicts the god Apollo surrounded by the nine muses.

Among the sublime landscapes by Claude Lorrain (1600–1682) is "Embarkation of St. Paula Romana at Ostia," in

which the saint is setting off for the Holy Land on a misty early morning. Observe how the light seems to permeate the canvas from the back of the painting.

"The Three Graces" by Rubens is a highlight of the Prado's Flemish and Dutch holdings.

The Dauphin's Treasure:

The basement contains part of the collection of gems, crystal, and vessels that originally belonged to the Grand Dauphin Louis, the son of Louis XIV of France. The Grand Dauphin was the father of Felipe V of Spain, who inherited the treasure in

Iglesia de los Jerónimos
- ✉ Calle Moreto 4
- ☎ 91 420 3578
- Ⓜ Metro: Atocha, Banco de España

Casón del Buen Retiro
- ✉ Calle Alfonso XII 28
- ☎ 91 330 2800
- Ⓜ Metro: Atocha, Banco de España

1712. One of the highlights of his collection is an onyx saltcellar decorated with a gold mermaid. There are crystal objects, goblets, and dishes adorned with diamonds, rubies, emeralds, and other jewels.

The New Prado

The new section of the Prado, the Jerónimos building, contains the café and restaurant, an auditorium, and two exhibition spaces that are used for temporary shows and selections from the outstanding 19th-century collections of Spanish art.

The extension links the Prado building to the **Iglesia de los Jerónimos,** the 16th-century cloisters, which have been restored and remodeled as an exhibition area, with a spectacular entrance designed by leading Spanish sculptress Cristina Iglesias.

The church is a vestige of the monastery that was set up here in the 15th century for a community of Hieronymite monks. Carlos V also used to stay at the monastery, a custom continued by successive monarchs, who extended and embellished the accommodation here. This residence became known as the Buen Retiro, as it was a place for quite contemplation and prayer.

In the reign of Felipe IV, it was decided that something grander was required, which led to the construction of the Palacio del Buen Retiro, an immense complex that occupied most of the space between what is now the Parque del Retiro and the Paseo del Prado. Most of the palace was demolished in the late 19th cen-

tury, but the sections that remain are now set to become part of the Museo Nacional del Prado.

The **Casón del Buen Retiro,** which was originally the ballroom of the palace, will eventually be a study and research center for the museum. It was designed in the mid-17th century by Alfonso de Carbonell and embellished in 1695 with a vaulted ceiling, on which Luca Giordano painted "The Triumph of the Order of the Golden Fleece." Until the remodeling work is completed, the ballroom is periodically open to the public and well worth a look.

INSIDER TIP:

Consider spending a whole day at the Prado. Don't miss Bosch's "The Garden of Earthly Delights."

—TIM MOUSSEAU
National Geographic field researcher

The surviving section of the main palace, a red-brick building with slate turrets, will provide further exhibition space and administrative areas for the Prado. Velázquez painted his masterpiece, "The Surrender of Breda," for the Hall of Realms in the palace, and his equestrian portraits of several monarchs were originally displayed here. All these works are now in the main building of the Prado, but plans are to bring them back here when the remodeling is finished. ∎

Along the Paseo del Prado

The northern half of the Paseo del Prado, between Plaza de Neptuno and Plaza de Cibeles, was conceived as a leisure area. The southern section, from Plaza de Neptuno to Atocha, was devoted to science, medicine, and learning, flanked by the natural history museum (now the Prado), the Real Jardín Botánico, and the San Carlos hospital (now the Museo Reina Sofía).

Back in the 18th century, this stretch was the eastern edge of the city and the closest most ordinary Madrileños got to the countryside. Known as the Salón del Prado, the promenade was designed by engineer José de Hermosilla and architect Ventura Rodríguez, under the supervision of the Conde de Aranda, Carlos III's senior minister. Hermosilla was responsible for landscaping the area, while Ventura Rodríguez was in charge of decorating the boulevard. The layout is typical of the baroque urban style prevalent at the time. It is thought that the arrangement of the fountains (see pp. 142–143) may have been inspired by Piazza Navona in Rome, as Hermosilla had studied there.

Just north of the Prado museum is the junction officially known as Plaza Cánovas del Castillo, after a leading politician who was assassinated in 1897. The square is marked by the Neptune fountain and in fact is more commonly known as **Plaza de Neptuno.**

The southwest corner of the square is occupied by the grand Parisian-style building of the **Palace Hotel** (see p. 249), which was opened in 1912 by Alfonso XIII and has a white stuccoed facade decorated with

Inside the venerable Palace Hotel, a monument of elegance

Palace Hotel

✉ Plaza de las Cortes 7

☎ 91 360 8000

🚇 Metro: Banco de España

www.starwood hotels.com

garlands. Designed by Belgian architect Léon Monnoyer, the hotel features a spectacular circular lobby, La Rotonda, and a beautiful stained glass dome, La Cupola. The hotel has always been popular with politicians,

cast from cannon in 1866. The main door is used only for the State Opening of Parliament, a ceremony presided over by King Juan Carlos. The ceiling of the semi-elliptical debating chamber, which was painted by Carlos

Book-lovers spend hours browsing the stands of used books on the Paseo del Prado.

Congreso de los Diputados

✉ Plaza de las Cortes

☎ 91 390 6000

🕐 Guided tours Sat. a.m., except Aug. & special events

🚇 Metro: Banco de España, Sevilla

www.congreso.es

bullfighters, actors, writers, and artists. Guests over the decades have included Hemingway, Picasso, Dalí, and Madonna.

Just north of the hotel is the triangular **Plaza de las Cortes,** with a 19th-century statue of Miguel de Cervantes by Antonio Solá. On the opposite side of the square is the **Congreso de los Diputados,** which houses the Spanish Parliament, known as Las Cortes. Standing on the site of a monastery, the building was designed by Narciso Pascual y Colomer and constructed between 1843 and 1850. The bronze lions on the steps were

Luis de Ribera, depicts Isabel II flanked by prominent figures in Spain's history, including Columbus, Cervantes, and Velázquez. An undulating glass extension was built alongside the building in 1990 by the architectural studio of Clos, Rubert de Ventós y Parcerisa.

As you return to the Paseo del Prado, on the left is the **Museo Thyssen-Bornemisza** (see pp. 146–151). Crossing the boulevard, you arrive at the semicircular **Plaza de la Lealtad.** In the center of the square is the **Monumento a los Caídos por España,** a cenotaph with a granite

INSIDER TIP:
Join elegant Madrile-
ños for afternoon tea
in the lobby of the
Hotel Ritz. Sit as long
as you like.

—BARBARA ASCHER
National Geographic Traveler
magazine writer

obelisk that commemorates those
who lost their lives in the battle
against the invading French troops
on May 2 and 3, 1808 (see pp.
204–205). Some of the worst
fighting actually took place on
this spot. Completed in 1840,
the monument was designed by
Isidro González Velázquez. It now
also serves as the Tomb of the
Unknown Soldier.

On the southeast corner is
the sumptuous **Hotel Ritz** (see

p. 249), which was designed in
1908 by the French architect
Charles Mewes, architect of the
Ritz hotels in Paris and London.
Until then, the Hotel Paris in
the Puerta del Sol had been the
most fashionable place to stay in
Madrid. The luxurious carpets in
the Hotel Ritz were handmade
at the Real Fábrica de Tápices
(see p. 172), which sends expert
craftsmen to repair them when
necessary. During the Civil War,
the hotel was used as a hospital.
The bar is a soothing place for a
drink after a day in the museums,
and the terrace is a popular meeting place in summer.

The north side of Plaza de
la Lealtad is dominated by the
neoclassic facade of the **Bolsa
de Comercio** (Stock Exchange),
which was designed by Enrique
María Repullés y Vargas and built
between 1884 and 1893. The

Hotel Ritz
✉ Plaza de la
Lealtad 5
☎ 91 701 6767
Ⓜ Metro: Banco de
España
www.ritzmadrid.com

**Bolsa de
Comercio**
✉ Plaza de la
Lealtad 1
☎ 91 589 2264
Ⓜ Metro: Banco de
España
**www.bolsamadrid
.es/ing/portada.htm**

EXPERIENCE: Moorish Hammam *&* Urban Day Spas

A day in Madrid's museums can leave you exhausted, but the city has a wide range
of urban spas where you can relax and recharge your batteries for the next day's
cultural activities.

One of the most
interesting places is the
Medina Mayrit *(Calle
Atocha 14, tel 90 233 3334,
www.medinamayrit.com),*
which is right in the center
near the Plaza Mayor. This
is a surprisingly authentic
re-creation of an Arab
baths, with mosaic walls,
stone floors, and a
Moorish tea room. There
are three pools of
different temperatures, as
well as a steam room, and

you can also have a
massage if you wish.
Numbers are strictly
limited and it is very
popular, so you do need to
call ahead.
Masqueagua *(Calle
Manuel Cortina 5, tel 91
445 5331, www.masquea
gua.com),* near the Bilbao
metro stop, is ideal for a
quick pick-me-up. You can
pop in for a 90-minute
wallow in the pools of the
thermal circuit, followed

by a 10-minute massage.
Manicures, facials, and
other beauty treatments
are also available, and
you'll emerge totally
energized.
Put your spare time
at Madrid Barajas airport
to good use at one of
the two **Elysium Spas**
in Terminal 4 *(tel 91 746
6280).* These oases of
comfort offer treatments,
hairstyling, massages, and
showers.

Museo Naval

✉ Paseo del Prado 5

☎ 91 523 8789

🕐 Closed Mon., & Tues.–Sun. p.m. Guided tours 11 a.m. Sat. & Sun.

🚇 Metro: Banco de España

www.museonaval madrid.com

building looks enormous from the front, but the site is triangular, with surprisingly little space behind the facade. The trading floor features an arcaded gallery and an iron and stained-glass vaulted roof.

Museo Naval

As you walk north up the Paseo del Prado, on the right you'll see the Museo Naval, which specializes in Spain's seafaring history.

In **Room 1**, which deals with the reign of the Catholic Monarchs at the end of the 15th century, you will find documents written by Christopher Columbus

INSIDER TIP:

To quench your thirst after a long day of sightseeing, ask for a *tinto de verano.* **This light mixture of red wine and bubbly soda is enjoyed by many locals and is guaranteed to make you feel more Spanish.**

—MATT TAYLOR
National Geographic Channel editor

on his arrival in Santo Domingo. **Room 5** contains the bronze cannon that were used in the Siege of Gibraltar (1780–1783), and **Room 7** charts the events of the Battle of Trafalgar in 1805. A model of one of the ships that took part in the battle, the *Santa Ana,* is in the **Central Patio. Room 8** contains nautical instruments, including

compasses and sextants. Also in this room is a model of the submarine designed by Isaac Peral (1851–1895) in 1888.

Room 16 is devoted to General Franco and King Juan Carlos. Exhibits include the curiously small uniform that Franco wore as commander-in-chief of the armed forces and a model of the aircraft carrier *Príncipe de Asturias,* which is the flagship of the Spanish fleet.

The highlights of the museum are found in **Room 17,** which deals with Spain's principal voyages of discovery from the 15th to the 18th centuries. The museum's most important exhibit is a parchment map that was the first document to show the New World. It was drawn in 1500 by Juan de la Cosa in El Puerto de Santa María near Cádiz, probably for the Catholic Monarchs. It shows places discovered by Columbus in 1492, 1493, and 1498. The Mediterranean is depicted fairly accurately, and Africa shows the latest Portuguese discoveries. The Asian continent and its archipelagos, however, are incomplete and only vaguely drawn.

Also in this room are two globes made by Italian monk and cartographer Vincenzo Coronelli (1650–1718) in the late 17th century and an astronomical pendulum made in the 18th century by English clockmaker John Ellicott (1706–1772).

Room 18 is devoted to the nautical sciences and contains an interesting collection of navigational quadrants and astrolabes from the sailing times of 16th to the 19th centuries. ∎

EXPERIENCE: Cooking & Tasting Local Cuisine

Although a lot of Spanish dishes look relatively simple, there are in fact quite a few tricks and techniques involved in making them properly. If you want to try and re-create the tortilla omelette, gazpacho, or paella you had for lunch, you might enjoy spending a morning with an expert who will share with you the know-how passed down through the generations.

Paella, the archetypal Spanish dish

Classes are available at cooking schools or in private homes by both professional chefs and knowledgeable foodies, and you can expect to learn about the local produce and seasonal ingredients that form the basis for all Spanish dishes. You need to understand the basics of the most traditional recipes before moving onto the surprising tastes and textures of new Spanish cuisine. Most classes last half a day, and often start with a trip to the market to buy ingredients. The group usually cooks together in an informal way, rather than working individually. The session ends with everyone digging in to the dishes that have been prepared.

Alambique

(Plaza de la Encarnación 2, tel 91 559 7858, www.alambique.com)* This kitchen store and cooking school just off the Plaza de Oriente has a wide range of classes and courses, often led by well-known chefs. Although most are given in Spanish, some classes and events are given by American, British, or Australian chefs who are either working in Madrid or visiting the city. Classes range from traditional Spanish dishes to tapas, using artisan cheeses, cooking with different olive oils, making *turrón nougat,* or how to cut Iberian ham. Private classes in English can be arranged on request.

Cellar Tours

(Calle Infantas 27, 3 Derecha, tel 91 521 3939, www.cellartours.com) For an upscale cooking experience, put yourself in the hands of Pilar Latorre, a gourmet chef and teacher. You start off with her on a walking tour of some of Madrid's best specialty food stores, during which she talks you through the most traditional and delicious Spanish ingredients. You then proceed to her home to learn how to prepare a series of sophisticated dishes using fresh, seasonal produce. You also get to taste some interesting Spanish wines and are given a recipe book to take home with you. Pilar LaTorre's is a private rather than a group activity, tailored to individual preferences and priced accordingly.

A Taste of Spain

(c/o Viajes Solymar, Calle Saturnino Calleja 6, tel 856 079626, www.atasteofspain.com)* Learn to cook traditional Spanish dishes from a professional cooking instructor in her own home. These are private events, so book with one or more friends. You will spend a morning preparing two main courses and a dessert, which you then dine on for lunch with a bottle of Rioja. Alternatively, go for the *nueva cocina* option. For this, you spend half a day learning how to make a few of the signature dishes of Spain's top chefs, including Ferrán Adriá, Juan Mari Arzak, and Carme Ruscalleda.

The Paseo's Fountains

Eight *fuentes* (fountains) adorn the Paseo del Prado, all part of the original plan to develop the boulevard as an area of leisure in the late 18th century. The scheme was instigated by Carlos III, who was astonished by the lack of sophistication in Madrid when he arrived from Naples to take the throne.

The "Fuente de la Cibeles" represents the fertile land around the city.

Ventura Rodríguez, the king's favorite architect, devised the overall concept for the fountains, which were made by leading sculptors of the day. The fountains are linked by a broad promenade that soon became popular with Madrileños as a place to see and be seen.

Fuente de la Cibeles

The splendid Fuente de la Cibeles, crowned by the figure of Cybele, goddess of nature,

punctuates the Paseo del Prado's north end; she is riding in a chariot drawn by two lions. One of Madrid's most important symbols, the monument symbolizes the fertility of the surrounding land. The fountain was made in the late 18th century by Francisco Gutiérrez and Robert Michel, but the cherubs were added at the end of the 19th century.

Originally Cybele faced south down the boulevard, but she was moved in 1891 to look toward the Puerta del Sol. As part of the Prado-

Recoletos development plan, the fountain will be moved again. It is a place of pilgrimage for supporters of the Real Madrid soccer team; they congregate there after important wins and jump in the fountain.

Fuente de Apolo

Halfway down the center of the Paseo you reach the Fuente de Apolo, almost concealed among the trees, with a circular pool on each side of the central spray. The figure of Apollo, god of beauty and the arts, was sculpted by Manuel Álvarez and Alfonso Giraldo Bergaz. Four figures representing the seasons surround Apollo. Completed in 1802, the fountain has been restored several times as the porous stone used to make it, from Redueña east of Madrid, erodes easily.

Fuente de Neptuno

The Paseo del Prado is divided in two by Plaza de Cánovas del Castillo, more usually known as Plaza de Neptuno because of its Fuente de Neptuno. Sculpted in marble by Juan Pascual de Mena, José Arias, and José Rodríguez between 1780 and 1786, it is a tribute to Spain's colonies and the Navy. Neptune, god of the sea, stands on a horse-drawn chariot shaped like a shell, holding a trident.

Plaza de Murillo

At the south end of the Prado Museum is Plaza de Murillo, where there are four fountains of nymphs and water gods playing with dolphins. They were made between 1777 and 1782 of Colmenar stone by Robert Michel, Francisco Gutiérrez, Narciso Aldeb, José Rodríguez, and Alfonso Giraldo Bergaz. The fountains are a bit lost in their current location between the Prado and the Real Jardín Botánico, but should regain importance when they are moved as part of the remodeling.

Fuente de la Alcochofa

The end of the Paseo del Prado is marked by the Fuente de la Alcochofa (Artichoke fountain) in the Glorieta de Atocha. This is a replica; the original piece was moved to the Parque del Retiro (see pp. 164–167) in 1880. It was sculpted in 1781 by Alfonso Giraldo Bergaz and Antonio Primo. Water flows from the bronze artichoke at the top of the fountain, which is supported by four cherubs. The artichoke is an allegory of the way wisdom must be discovered by gradually peeling away the outer layers. It also represents life and health, as it is situated between the Museo Reina Sofía, originally a hospital, and the Royal Botanic Garden.

The Fuente de la Alcochofa is a symbol of the many layers of wisdom.

Plaza de Cibeles

Plaza de Cibeles is the place where Madrid's north-south and east-west thoroughfares meet. Because the plaza is a major traffic hub, it is currently difficult for pedestrians to get a decent view of the grand buildings surrounding it, let alone approach anywhere near the grand fountain of the goddess Cybele (see pp. 142–143) in the center. But improvements are gradually being made that enable pedestrians to maneuver the plaza more comfortably.

Plaza de Cibeles is dominated by the majestic Palacio de Comunicaciones, the city's main post office.

Plaza de Cibeles

Map p. 125

The southwest corner is occupied by the enormous **Banco de España,** the facades of which stretch down the Paseo del Prado and up Calle Alcalá. Founded in the mid-19th century, the bank moved to this landmark site, in what was then the new commercial district, in 1891. The trading floor, added in 1929–1930, was inspired by Roman baths. The ornate corner section facing Plaza de Cibeles was originally the main entrance and is decorated with sculptures by Jerónimo Suñol. The bank, which unfortunately is not currently open to the public, has a formidable art collection, including works by Goya and Zurbarán as well as leading contemporary artists.

In contrast to the forbidding Banco de España, the **Palacio** de **Comunicaciones** on the southeast corner is an exuberant example of the architecture of Antonio Palacios, who designed many of the signature buildings in this area. Curving around the crossroads, the ornate white structure looks like a cathedral, but it was actually built to be the city's main post office at the beginning of the 20th century. It operated as such for nearly a hundred years, and it is now slated to become the City Hall, which will move its headquarters from the present site in Plaza de la Villa (see p. 56). Although this is regarded as the architect's masterpiece, the Palacio was one of his first buildings, designed with his partners Julián and Joaquín

part of the **Casa de América** cultural center, which stages exhibitions and other activities, usually related to Latin America, in the section at the rear.

Designed by Carlos Colubi and Adolphe Ombrecht, the neo-baroque palace has a lavish interior. The layout inside is unusual, as the marquis found out from his dying father that his wife was actually his half-sister. At which point the marquis then devised the residence as two separate apartments so that the couple could live in the same house but not as man and wife. The palace was closed up for many years, during which time there were quite a few reported sightings of ghosts.

Casa de América (Palacio de Linares)

✉ Entrance at Paseo de Recoletos 2

☎ 91 595 4800

🕐 Closed Sun. p.m. & Mon. Guided tours Sat.& Sun. a.m.

🚇 Metro: Banco de España

www.casamerica.es

Join the Soccer Revelry

For a spectacle, check out the Plaza de Cibeles when the soccer team Real Madrid plays. The fans of the club, dubbed Madridistas, lay claim to the Fuente de la Cibeles, making it the epicenter of post-match festivities. The overall mood depends on how the team fared, but it's a sight to see either way.

Madridistas celebrate after almost all matches, but don't miss the revelry that follows a match with rival FC Barcelona

or after a big championship. These come often. Real Madrid has won 9 Euro Cups, two UEFA Cups, 17 Spanish Cups, and 31 La Liga Cups.

However, the best place to cheer with Madridistas is at the Bernabéu Stadium. Here games are attended mostly by season-ticket holders, of which there are almost 70,000. To become a season ticket holder, you must be a club member. Sign up at www.realmadrid.com.

Otamendi. The three successfully combined Spanish style with new ideas from Chicago, New York, and Paris.

The **Palacio de Linares**, on the other side of Calle Alcalá on the northeast corner, was built as a private residence for the Marquis of Linares in the second half of the 19th century. It is now

An even grander palace is set back on landscaped grounds on the corner between the Paseo de Recoletos and Calle Alcalá. Currently housing the General Army headquarters, the **Palacio de Buenavista** (closed to the public) was built for the Duke of Alba by Juan Pedro Arnal in the late 18th century. ∎

Museo Thyssen-Bornemisza

The displays at this outstanding museum represent the best of Western art from the past 800 years. Begun in the 1920s by Baron Heinrich Thyssen-Bornemisza and consolidated by his son, Hans Heinrich, the collection is considered one of the best in the world. Galleries in a new wing contain the Carmen Thyssen-Bornemisza Collection, which specializes in landscape painting.

The museum showcases an outstanding collection of Derick Baegert's 15th-century works.

The artworks were originally kept at the family home, Villa Favorita, in Lugano, Switzerland, but after expanding the collection with hundreds of modern paintings, Baron Hans Heinrich Thyssen-Bornemisza looked for a venue where they could be put on public view.

Several countries vied for the prestigious collection, but the baron decided on the Palacio de Villahermosa in Madrid, a grand 18th-century neoclassic mansion on the Paseo del Prado. After the building was remodeled by Rafael Moneo, the collection was installed in

1992. Since the baron's death in 2002, the museum has been overseen by his widow.

Visiting the Museum

The displays comprise about a thousand exhibits, the majority of which are paintings, but the museum also contains sculptures, tapestries, and decorative objects. Displays are exhibited chronologically on three floors, starting on the second floor and working down to the ground floor. The museum has a pricey café and restaurant and a good store on the ground floor.

Early Art: Starting on the second floor, work your way counterclockwise. **Room 1** contains Italian primitives, among them "Christ and the Samaritan Woman" by Duccio di Buoninsegna (1278–1319), the only artist known to have signed his work at this time.

Room 3 displays early Flemish art. Be careful not to miss the tiny panel by Petrus Christus from Bruges called "Our Lady of the Dry Tree" (circa 1465), which is one of the highlights of the museum. It portrays a story from the Old Testament about the Virgin Mary bringing new life to the chosen people. Also in this room is "The Annunciation," a diptych by Jan van Eyck, which looks like carved stone, and the intricate "Enthroned Madonna" by Rogier van der Weyden.

In **Room 4,** look for "The Resurrected Christ" by Milanese artist Bramantino, a seminal work of the Italian Quattrocento.

Room 5 contains some

exceptional Renaissance portraits. One of the best known works in the museum is Domenico Ghirlandaio's "Portrait of Giovanna Tornabuoni" (1488), a representation of perfection. The Latin epigram on the portrait is from the first-century Roman poet Martial and says "Art, if only you could portray character and moral qualities, there would not be a more beautiful painting in the world." Hans Holbein the Younger's masterly "King Henry VIII," which depicts the English monarch looking coolly regal, is one of the most valuable paintings

Museo Thyssen-Bornemisza
- Map p. 125
- Palacio de Villahermosa, Paseo del Prado 8
- 91 369 0151
- Closed Mon.
- $$
- Metro: Banco de España

www.museothyssen.org

Tips for Visiting Museums

Security has understandably been tightened at the major museums, so expect to put your things through an X-ray machine. You may have to leave bottles of water and other drinks in the cloakroom, as well as large bags, umbrellas, and anything cumbersome that you might accidentally bash into an artwork. Even tiny backpacks are not allowed at some museums, so it is worth taking a plastic bag to decant your essential stuff into. Bear in mind that air-conditioned interiors are often quite cool, so you might want to take along a jacket or sweater. You might well spend all day in the Prado, so wearing comfortable, cushioned shoes will mean you can concentrate on the art, not your feet.

in the collection. There is also a delightful portrait of Catherine of Aragón, Henry's first wife, by Juan de Flandes.

16th-century German & Italian Art: You now enter the long **Room 6,** the Villahermosa Gallery, which displays "Portrait of a Young Man" by Raphael. Rooms 7–12 run alongside. The highlight in **Room 7** is Vittore Carpaccio's "Young Knight in a Landscape" (1510), which is thought to be one of the earliest full-length portraits.

The German paintings in **Room 8** include "Jesus among the Doctors" (1506) by Albrecht Dürer, which portrays Christ as a young man surrounded by inquisitive old men and draws the eye to the hands at the center. There are also several works by Derick Baegert (circa 1440–1515), including Christ carrying the cross.

In **Room 9,** the "Reclining Nymph" by Lucas Cranach the Elder (1472–1553) has a superbly painted transparent veil. Artists of the Venetian school, including Titian, Tintoretto, and Bassano, are displayed in **Rooms 11 and 12.** Titian's "St. Jerome in the Wilderness" (circa 1575) was painted at the end of his life. El Greco appears here because he began his working career in Italy. An early Caravaggio canvas, "St. Catherine of Alexandria" (circa 1597), shows Flemish influences.

17th- & 18th-century Baroque: Rooms 13–18 contain early baroque works, including "San Sebastián" and "La Piedad" by Bernini (1598–1680). Francisco de Zurbarán's "Santa Casilda" (circa 1630) depicts the saint as a serious young woman, set against the artist's trademark dark background. There are also splendid views of Venice by Canaletto (1697–1768) and Francesco Guardi (1712–1793).

The final section on this floor, **Rooms 19, 20, and 21,** contain Flemish and Dutch paintings, including superlative works by Van Dyck, Brueghel the Elder, and Rubens, especially his "Toilet of Venus." Don't miss Rembrandt's penetrating "Self-Portrait" displayed in **Room 21.**

The portrait of King Henry VIII by Hans Holbein the Younger, dating from 1536, depicts the monarch in a confident mood.

EXPERIENCE: Themed Guided Walks

You may not have time to spend hours reading up on Madrid before you visit, but there are shortcuts available to ease you into the city. Whatever your particular interest, there is likely to be a specialized walk led by an expert in that field. The Madrid tourist board runs a wide program of walks at a very reasonable cost, which last a couple of hours and take you into parts of the city that you would be unlikely to discover on your own. First Class Madrid, for example, gains you access to some of the grandest 18th- and 19th-century palaces in the city, while Aristocratic Madrid is a tour around the elegant private mansions of the Almagro neighborhood. Anyone interested in literature will enjoy the Galdós walk, which traces a route around the places mentioned in the books of the writer considered to be the Spanish equivalent of Charles Dickens. Or perhaps you will like Madrid de las Letras, where the secrets of the streets around Plaza de Santa Ana are revealed and you are transported back to the 16th and 17th centuries, when the great authors Cervantes, Quevedo, and Lope de Vega lived in the area. Alternatively, a tour around Madrid's traditional shops, which are still doing a roaring trade, takes you back to an age before malls and chainstores.

These and other tours can be had through the city's tourist bureau program called **Discover Madrid** (*Centro de Turismo de Madrid, Plaza Mayor 27, tel 91 588 2906 www.esmadrid.com, $*).

17th-century Dutch & Flemish Painting: Down on the first floor, the first section, **Rooms 22–27**, contains some elegantly composed scenes of daily life, interiors, and landscapes by artists including Frans Hals and Pieter de Hooch. The still lifes presented in **Room 27** include an intriguing work by Willem Claesz Heda (circa 1593–circa 1680), which shows a magnificent array of silverware and glass beside a half-eaten pie.

19th-century American & European Painting: **Rooms 29 and 30** contain landscapes by artists of the Hudson River school. There are several seascapes by Fitz Lane and Martin Johnson Heade, pioneers of the Luminist school.

Room 31 marks an abrupt change of style to European Romanticism, with a wall of Goya, Géricault, and Delacroix, followed by Courbet and Constable. The Impressionists are in **Rooms 32 and 33**. Highlights include Manet's "Woman in Riding Habit" (1882) and two exquisite pastels on paper by Edgar Degas: "Swaying Dancer" and "At the Milliner's." Vincent van Gogh's "Les Vessenots" (1890), in thick impasto, was painted shortly before he committed suicide.

Modernism: The modern art collection begins in **Room 34** with André Derain (1880–1954) and the other fauves ("wild beasts"), so-called because they seemed to break all the rules. **Rooms 35–40** display the museum's superlative collection of German expressionists. The Dresden-based

group known as Die Brücke is represented by Emil Nolde, Karl Schmidt-Rottluff, and Ernst Ludwig Kirchner. The Blaue Reiter artists emerged from the magazine of the same name, founded in 1912 in Munich. There are works here by several of its members, including Franz Marc (1880–1916) and Wassily Kandinsky (1866–1944). The last room on this floor contains more objective and realistic works, including "Metropolis" by Georg Grosz (1893–1959) and "Hugo Erfurth with a Dog" by Otto Dix (1891–1969).

INSIDER TIP:

I know it's a heresy, but if I could visit only one museum in Madrid, it would be the Museo Thyssen-Bornemisza.

—LITO TEJADA-FLORES
*National Geographic Traveler
magazine writer*

On the ground floor, **Rooms 41–44** are devoted to the experimental avant-gardes, with examples of cubism, futurism, dadaism, and surrealism. There are works by Braque, Léger, and Juan Gris; Picasso is represented by "Man with a Clarinet" and "Head of a Man." Geometrical abstraction is represented by Moholy-Nagy, El Lissitsky, Schwitters, and Mondrian. The United States rules in **Room 46,** with abstract expressionism by Rothko, O'Keeffe, and De Kooning.

The final section, **Rooms 47 and 48,** rounds things off with surrealism, figurative tradition, and pop art, with works by artists including Dalí, David Hockney, Francis Bacon, Edward Hopper, R.B. Kitaj, James Rosenquist, and Yves Tanguy.

Carmen Thyssen-Bornemisza Collection

Two buildings adjoining the Palacio de Villahermosa were remodeled to house the collection of the baroness, which includes about 200 works. The displays are arranged over two floors, which are accessed from the second floor of the main building. The ground floor of the area is used for temporary exhibitions. This collection was begun in the 1980s and ranges from 17th-century Dutch painting to examples of 20th-century avant-garde.

Rooms A and B contain early Flemish and Italian art. "The Judgment of Solomon" by Lucas Jordán shows the influence of Caravaggio. There is an exquisite "Christ on the Cross" by Van Dyck, and Brueghel the Elder is represented by "The Garden of Eden." **Room C** is a long gallery that charts the development of landscape painting over four centuries. Look for Constable's "The Lock," which is one of the masterpieces of the collection. There is an interesting section devoted to the 18th-century vogue for architectural urban views, as well as superb works by Corot and van Gogh.

There is more 18th-century work in **Room D,** with examples of the rococo influences on French and Italian art, illustrated by the paintings of Boucher, Fragonard, and Piazzetta.

The North American 19th-century landscapes in **Rooms E and F** include work by such luminaries of the genre as Martin Johnson Heade, Sandford Robinson Gifford, and Frederic Edwin Church. **Room G** exhibits work by artists from the Barbizon school in France and the Hague school in Holland, both of which introduced a more naturalistic approach to landscape paintings. Artists include Courbet, Corot, Rousseau, and Boudin. **Room H** deals with early Impressionism, featuring work by Degas, Monet, Pissarro, Renoir, and Sisley.

The displays continue downstairs on the first floor in **Room I,** which is devoted to Auguste Rodin (1840–1917). The marble sculptures here were commissioned by August Thyssen in 1905 and are considered to be among the best examples of Rodin's work. Other pieces from this group are distributed throughout the exhibition rooms. This space is unusual in that it is an original room from the Palacio de Goyeneche, one of the two buildings that were converted to create this new part of the museum.

Room J shows how American art was influenced by European Impressionism in the last two decades of the 19th century, with works by Sargent, Metcalf, and Frieseke. The exhibits of late Impressionism in **Room K** include several masterpieces. Look for Monet's "Charing Cross Bridge" and Gauguin's "Orchard below Bihorel

The Carmen Thyssen-Bornemisza Collection is displayed in an extension to the museum's original building.

Church." More works by Gauguin can be found in **Room L,** including the superb "Allées et Venues, Martinique" and "Mata Mua." Also in this room are paintings by Bonnard and Vuillard. **Room M** moves onto Post-Impressionism, illustrated by Maximilien Luce, Nolde, and Munch.

German expressionism is well represented in **Room N,** with excellent paintings by Pechstein, Kandinsky, and Kirchner. Don't miss Erich Heckel's sublime "The House at Dangast." The emergence of fauvism in the beginning of the 20th century is addressed in **Room O,** with works including "The Midi Canal" by Matisse and "Seascape, L'Éstaque" by Braque. **Room P** is devoted to cubism, illustrated by Picasso's "The Harvesters" (1907), "Seated Woman" by Juan Gris, and "Still Life with Bananas" by Raoul Dufy. ∎

Real Jardín Botánico

The Real Jardín Botánico, or Royal Botanic Garden, was founded in 1755 by Fernando VI on the banks of the Rio Manzanares. It was transferred here by Carlos III in 1781 as part of his plans to create a science hub along the lower part of the Paseo del Prado. The garden contains more than 30,000 plant species from all over the world and is a soothing place to stroll after a morning in the Prado.

A neoclassical entrance gate leads to the three levels of the Real Jardín Botánico.

Real Jardín Botánico

- Map p. 125
- Plaza de Murillo 2
- 91 420 3017
- $
- Metro: Atocha

www.rjb.csic.es

The design of the garden was begun by Francesco Sabatini, who died before completing the project. It was continued by Juan de Villanueva with the collaboration of the botanist Casimiro Gómez Ortega. Their aim was to create a research center for cultivating the species brought to Spain by the botanic expeditions of the 18th century.

As you go in, take a look at the elegant neoclassical entrance gate,

the **Puerta de Murillo,** which was designed by Villanueva in 1789 and is flanked by two sets of Doric columns. The garden is arranged across three levels, with a pavilion at the top where temporary exhibitions are held.

The lower level is called the **Terraza de los Cuadros** and is divided into 16 beds. In **Bed C3** there is a beautiful pomegranate tree that is thought to be 200 years old. At 23 feet (7 m), it is much taller than these trees normally grow. The pomegranate was brought to Spain by the Arabs, who planted it in the Nasrid kingdom of Granada, which took its name from the tree.

Beds C5 and C6 contain medicinal plants, which have been cultivated here since the garden was founded and are given out free to the public. Originally, these plants were grown to provide supplies for the neighboring Hospital General de San Carlos, which is now the Museo Reina Sofía museum.

INSIDER TIP:

For a cool spot in summer, stroll through the Real Jardín Botánico, the first botanical garden in Spain. It was opened by King Carlos III and retains its original neoclassical design.

—PATXI HERAS &
MARTA INFANTE
National Geographic field researchers

Between **Beds C7 and C10,** which hold old varieties of roses, the Paseo de Carlos III leads down to the **Puerta Real,** a granite entrance arch that was designed by Sabatini and commemorates Carlos III. **Bed C12** contains a small selection of the one thousand species of plants that grow only in Spain. Many of these species are found in very few areas of the country and are in

danger of extinction. **Bed 13** is laid out as a market garden with plants that are traditionally grown for food. Many of them were brought back from the botanic expeditions to the New World.

The second level is the **Terraza de las Escuelas Botánicas,** which contains plants and trees from different botanical schools. One of the most distinctive examples is an elm known as "Pantalones" because its trunk is divided into two branches that resemble a pair of pants. The tree is 200 years old and 112 feet (34 m) high with a diameter of 8 feet (2.4 m). There are several sequoias as well, which are evergreens that can grow taller than 100 feet (30 m) and live for several thousand years.

The next level, the **Terraza del Plano de la Flor,** was remodeled in the mid-19th century. It is arranged around an oval pond with a bust of the pioneering Swedish botanist Karl von Linné (1707–1778), who devised the binomial nomenclature used to classify plant species. The pond is surrounded by beautiful trees, including a hundred-year-old Canarian palm.

Behind it is a neoclassical **pavilion** designed by Villanueva in 1781. This was originally intended as a hothouse for the cultivation of the most delicate species brought from America. The central space, added in 1794, houses a lecture theater named after Antonio José Cavanilles, one of the many renowned botanists who taught there. Restored in the 1980s, it is now used for temporary exhibitions. ■

Museo Reina Sofía

This vast museum (known officially as the Museo Nacional Centro de Arte Reina Sofía) is undergoing a far-reaching expansion program aimed at strengthening its position in the contemporary art world. Its collections of Spanish 20th-century art include works by Salvador Dalí, Joan Miró, Jorge de Oteiza, and Antoni Tàpies, but the undisputed highlight of the museum is Picasso's masterpiece "Guernica," which draws visitors from around the world.

Picasso's "Guernica," which protests Franco's atrocities against the population in a Basque village

Museo Reina Sofía

- 🗺 Map p. 125
- ✉ Calle Santa Isabel 52
- ☎ 91 774 1000
- 🕐 Closed Sun. p.m. & Tues.
- 💲 $. Free Sat p.m. & Sun. a.m.
- 🚇 Metro: Atocha

www. museoreinasofia.es

The museum's international collections include works by artists of the caliber of Julian Schnabel, Donald Judd, Gerhard Richter, and Anish Kapoor. At least three temporary shows are usually running, and the museum also sponsors interesting cultural activities and concerts.

The Reina Sofía occupies the former Hospital General de San Carlos, the monumental bulk of which is reminiscent of the monastery at El Escorial (see pp. 228–231). Although it was designed by José de Hermosilla in the mid-1700s, much of the construction was overseen by Francesco Sabatini in the reign of Carlos III. The hospital remained open until 1965, but then deteriorated so badly there was talk of demolition. Owing to its historical interest, however, it was decided to renovate and remodel it as a home for the Spanish collection of contemporary art. The Museo Reina Sofía opened in 1986.

In 2005, a spectacular extension designed by renowned French architect Jean Nouvel added two new spaces for temporary exhibitions, as well as a library, research center, bookstore, and two auditoriums. Together these areas form a triangle around a central atrium under a red metal roof. There is also a café and restaurant run by Sergi Arola, one of the best and most innovative chefs in Spain.

The museum plans to remodel the original building so that the collection can be displayed on four floors. Under director Manuel Borja-Villel, who took up the post in 2008, the museum is to be extended a further 5,380 square yards (4,500 sq m). The work is expected to be completed in 2010. Levels 2 and 4 will be rearranged, and level 3 will be used for the permanent collection, too. The art will be displayed chronologically, charting the developments of the 20th century as exemplified by such Spanish masters as Piacsso, Miró, Dalí, Juan Gris, Solana, and Sorolla. The increased exhibition space will also allow new display areas for some of the museum's extensive holdings of video art, photography, and design.

Visiting the Museum

The permanent collection is currently exhibited on two floors, with about 500 works on display. The visit begins on **Floor 2,** which you can reach via a glass elevator.

At the turn of the 20th century in Spain, artists were particularly active in the Basque country and Catalunya. Work by leading artists from these two regions is exhibited in **Room 1.** Artists include Ignacio Zuloaga, Francisco Iturrino, Hermenegildo Anglada-Camarasa, Santiago Rusiñol, and María Blanchard.

Madrid produced the more experimental Solana, found in **Room 2.** Solana was a key figure in the *tertulia* discussion groups

Early Film

A straight razor, a cloud gliding across a full moon, a beautiful woman's face, and then a calf's eye. In 1928, this rapid succession launched *An Andalusian Dog,* and, with it, the modern cinema. The 16-minute short was a collaboration between Salvador Dalí and Luis Buñuel. The film progresses via "dream logic," a Freudian version of the free-association trumpeted by the surrealists. Not surprisingly, the film was not a blockbuster.

that formed an essential part of Madrid café society early in the 20th century (see pp. 118–119). The members of one of the most influential groups are portrayed in "The Gathering at the Café Pombo" (1920), which features writer Ramón Gómez de la Serna and Solana himself.

Room 3 takes you through constructivism and cubism. Keep an eye out for the striking colors of Robert and Sonia Delauney, who visited Spain during World War I, as well as the geometrical forms of Joaquín Torres García (1874–1949). The cubist artist Juan Gris, who was born in Madrid and lived in Paris, is represented by a series of superb works including a portrait of his wife, "Josette" (1916), and "The Guitar in Front of the Sea" (1925), painted at the end of his life. The twisting bronze and iron sculptures of Pablo Gargallo, including "The Great Prophet" (1933), are displayed in **Room 4** at the end of this wing.

Picasso: Rooms 5 and 6 are devoted to Pablo Picasso, the most influential artist of the 20th century. You are con-

fronted by the shocking canvas of "Guernica" (1937), revealed in all its tortured, monochromatic splendor. Painted in less than two months for the Spanish Pavilion at the 1937 Paris World's Fair, it was a protest against the bombing of the Basque town of Gernika-Lumo by German aircraft on the orders of General Franco during Spain's Civil War. There was worldwide outrage when photographs of the attack appeared in newspapers, and the images affected Picasso so deeply that he was driven to produce the painting that would become a universal symbol of the brutality of war.

A long-term plan for this room involves showing other exhibits related to the Spanish Pavilion alongside the mural to help visitors understand its original

Schoolchildren learn about the bold colors and abstract shapes used by the Catalan artist Joan Miró in his "Mujer, párajo y estrella" (1970).

There are always a few important temporary art exhibits in the city, so ask at your hotel or buy a local paper to see what's going on.

—GINNY DELGADO
National Geographic contributor

context. These elements include the model for the Pavilion, a copy of Alexander Calder's sculpture "Mercury Fountain," and the screening of films shown during the Paris World Fair.

Surrealists: Development in Salvador Dalí's art is traced in **Rooms 9 and 10,** where works by the archsurrealist include "Cenicitas" (1928) and "The Great Masturbator" (1929), which was painted in the year he filmed the seminal movie *Un Chien Andalou* with Luis Buñuel. His "Portrait of Joella" (1933) is an oil and plaster sculpture that he made with the collaboration of Man Ray. Room 10 also features the pioneering surrealist filmmaker Luis Buñuel (1900–1983). You can see screenings of his films, which are regarded as some of the most important creative works of 20th-century Spain.

Joan Miró features among other artists in **Rooms 11 and 12,** from his early work in the 1920s to the second half of the 20th century, including "Man with a Pipe" (1925) and the sculpture "The Lovers II" (1932–33). His work is set along-side paintings by Kandinsky, Jean Arp, and Tàpies.

Postwar: Take the elevator to **Floor 4.** The exuberant canvases of José Guerrero from Granada contrast with the geometric iron sculptures of Basque artist Jorge de Oteiza in **Rooms 13–16,** which compare Spanish and international artistic trends in the 1950s.

The brilliant French artist Yves Klein (1928–1962) is well represented in **Room 18,** while his Italian counterpart Lucio Fontana (1899–1968), the master of slashed, perforated, monochrome canvases, has good coverage in **Room 19.**

The energetic brushstrokes of Antonio Saura (1930–1998) are prominent in **Room 22,** while **Room 25** features Pablo Palazuelo's outstanding steel sculptures. The leading figures of the Arte Povera movement, including Mario Merz and Jannis Kounellis, are represented in **Room 26.**

Lost "Guernica"

Soon after Picasso finished "Guernica" in 1937, it toured the world, attracting attention to Spain's Civil War. After Franco's victory, Picasso lent the painting to the Museum of Modern Art in New York, saying the painting could not hang in Spain until the country had reverted to a republic. It came home in 1981, six years after Franco's death.

The work of Spain's greatest living artist, Antoni Tàpies (born 1923), is displayed in **Rooms 27 and 28.** His fusion of sculpture and painting is well illustrated by the superb "Superposition of Grey Material" (1961), an excellent example of his trademark matèrica technique of layering different textures, often using clay, earth and sand.

Don't miss the stunning steel, iron and alabaster sculptures of Basque artist Eduardo Chillida (1924–2002), one of the leading creative figures of the 20th century, in **Rooms 34–35.**

Room 36 contains some superlative American minimalist art from the 1960s and '70s, with work by internationally renowned figures such as Ellsworth Kelly, Barnett Newman, Bruce Nauman, and Donald Judd, who is represented by a group of open-sided cubes.

The final section of this floor, **Rooms 37 to 39,** contains a wide range of Spanish and international art from the last two decades of the 20th century, including work by Miquel Barceló, Ferrán García Sevilla, José Manuel Broto, José María Sicilia, Juan Uslé, Cristina Iglesias, Ross Bleckner, and Georg Baselitz. Particularly powerful is one of the museum's newest acquisitions, Juan Muñoz's bronze and steel installation "I Saw It in Verona" (1991).

Temporary exhibits feature Spanish and international artists of all mediums. The museum also organizes special exhibitions throughout the city. ■

EXPERIENCE: Getting to the Heart of Art

Imagine standing in front of the "Guernica" and having a distinguished expert describe its hidden and themes—how every single line and shape is meaningful. Did you know, for example, that Picasso included a hidden image of a skull in the middle of the painting, symbolizing death?

Every Tuesday between 7 and 8 p.m., the Museo Reina Sofía offers the public an excellent opportunity to delve behind the scenes of its artwork. Recent courses have included Luis Gordillo, dialogues with Miró, and, of course, Guernica.

Each course entails two lessons, held a week apart. For more information, contact the museum *(tel 91-774-1000, ext. 2034, www.museoreinasofia.es, e-mail: formacion.mncars@mcu.es).* The cost is €18 per course.

Another fabulous learning opportunity that the museum offers is its "Meet the Artist" series. Contemporary artists showing their work at the museum are invited to discuss their careers and provide insight into their work and into the specific exhibition being displayed. Contact the museum for further information.

Another way to get to better know the artwork is through the museum's free, 90-minute guided tours of its permanent collection. Different tour itineraries are offered, including "From Abstraction to the Current Day" and "Guernica: History of a Painting."

CaixaForum

Designed by renowned Swiss architects Herzog & De Meuron, CaixaForum opened in 2008, alongside the Prado, Thyssen-Bornemisza, and Reina Sofía museums. The center is run by the Fundació La Caixa, part of Catalunya's largest savings bank, and is used for temporary exhibitions, including selections from La Caixa's prestigious art collection. There is also a cultural program, including concerts, literary events, and activities for children and families.

People flock to the new CaixaForum with its huge vertical wall of patterned plants.

Originally an electrical power plant, built in the 19th century, this was one of very few industrial structures surviving in downtown Madrid. The architects describe it as an "urban magnet," and it certainly has a mesmerizing effect. The spectacular building has been encased in a galvanized steel structure and seems to float above the ground since the building rests on supports at street level. As you approach, your eyes are drawn to the extraordinary "vertical garden" that has been created on one of the exterior walls, comprising 15,000 plants of more than 250 varieties.

There are seven storeys altogether, with two floors of exhibition space, an underground auditorium, lecture theaters and a rooftop café, all linked by a helicoidal white concrete staircase.

With free admission at all times, long opening hours, and a wide range of exhibitions and events running at any given time, this dynamic organization has successfully moved the museum concept into the 21st century. ■

CaixaForum

Map p. 125

Paseo del Prado 36

91 330 7300

Metro: Atocha

www.laCaixa.es /ObraSocial

More Places to Visit Around the Paseo del Prado

La Fábrica Galería

Top international artists such as Sol LeWitt exhibit at this lively space, which also runs a program of cultural activities and art events, including dance, theater, and other performances once a month on Monday nights. It specializes in photographic shows and video installations and is one of the main venues during the PhotoEspaña festival in June and July. La Fábrica also publishes art books and magazines. www.lafabricagaleria.com ⚠ Map p. 125 ✉ Calle Alameda 9 ☎ 91 360 1325 🕐 Closed Sun. & Mon. Ⓜ Metro: Atocha

INSIDER TIP:

Madrid's tap water is wonderful and safe to drink, so it's fine to ask for a pitcher of tap water instead of buying expensive bottled water

—GINNY DELGADO
National Geographic contributor

Museo del Ferrocarril

The Estación de las Delicias, an elegant late 19th-century ironwork railroad station, has been converted to house a railway museum. A good place to take children, it features exhibits including steam engines, model railways, and station clocks. Displays illustrate all the different elements that make up a railroad network and how they work. www.museodelferrocarril.org ⚠ Map p. 125 ✉ Paseo de las Delicias 61 ☎ 902 228 822 🕐 Closed Mon. & Aug. 💲 $. Free Sat. Ⓜ Metro: Delicias

Museo Postal y Telegráfico

The museum charts the development of postal services beginning in the 13th century, when mail was delivered by messengers on horseback, to the creation of a railroad

mail system in the second half of the 19th century. Displays include Spain's first postage stamp, produced in 1850, along with machines and materials used to make stamps. The extensive stamp collections feature many first-day issues from all over the world, and 19th-century examples from Cuba, the Philippines, and Puerto Rico. One section deals with the history of telecommunications, including a model of the Hispasat satellite. www.correos.es ⚠ Map p. 125 ✉ Calle Montalbán ☎ 91 396 2679 🕐 Closed Sat. p.m. & Sun. Ⓜ Metro: Banco de España.

Palacio de Fernán Núñez

This sumptuous mansion was built in the mid-19th century for the Duke and Duchess of Fernán Núñez and is now occupied by Renfe, the Spanish railway network. Although used as a stronghold by republicans in the Civil War, the palace is incredibly well preserved with a series of lavish reception rooms decorated with antiques and handmade carpets from the Real Fábrica de Tápices (see p. 172). The most extraordinary space is the rococo ballroom, with gold-plated walls, plush yellow silk seating, and elaborate chandeliers. ⚠ Map p. 125 ✉ Calle Santa Isabel 44 ☎ Tours: 91 527 1812 Ⓜ Metro: Antón Martín, Atocha

Real Monasterio de Santa Isabel

Felipe II founded this enormous Augustinian convent at the end of the 16th century. It later came under the patronage of Queen Margarita de Austria, wife of Felipe III, who established the Real Monasterio de la Encarnación (see pp. 84–85). The church, which is open only during services, was designed by Gómez de Mora. The convent contains a collection of artistic treasures, but these are not currently on public display. www.patrimonionacional.es ⚠ Map p. 125 ✉ Calle Santa Isabel 48 ☎ 91 527 3183 Ⓜ Metro: Antón Martín, Atocha

Once the grounds of a palace, now the city's most popular space—
a place to jog, skate, or simply sit at one of the many cafés

Parque del Retiro & Around

A granite artichoke, peeled open to reveal its heart, tops the Fuente de la Alcachofa in Parque del Retiro.

Parque del Retiro
& Around

In a city as densely packed as Madrid, the Parque del Retiro (Retiro Park) provides an essential breathing space. After the cultural onslaught of the museums along the Paseo del Prado, a stroll around the lake is a great way to clear your head. If you feel like even more artistic stimulation, however, there are usually two or three exhibitions running in the park itself.

The park was originally the gardens of the Palacio del Buen Retiro, built in the 17th century for Felipe IV. In modern times, only one wing and the ballroom of the once expansive palace remain on the hill behind the Prado, where they are extensions of the museum.

The palace gardens were first opened to the

INSIDER TIP:

How about a free guitar concert? The sidewalk strummers in the Jardines del Buen Retiro do it gratis– and they're hot stuff.

—CHRISTOPHER SOMERVILLE
National Geographic author

public in the mid-18th century, although at that time strict rules governed who could enter—to prevent the riffraff from concealing their identities and sneaking in, lace mantilla headscarves were forbidden for women, while men could not wear capes or hats.

These days, you can do more or less anything in the park, which means that the quieter areas are perhaps best avoided. It is generally very safe, however.

For two weeks in June, the road running through two sides of the park is transformed with the installation of hundreds of stands for the city's annual international book fair. Visitors to the fair come not only to buy books but also to attend talks by leading writers and publishers.

The residential area of Los Jerónimos, which occupies the hill west of the park, was also part of the Buen Retiro palace. It is now one of the most prestigious neighborhoods in the city. The Museo Nacional de Artes Decorativas (National Museum of Decorative Arts) is housed here and contains fascinating displays of furniture and ceramics.

Like the Paseo del Prado, the area south of the park will be transformed into a friendly pedestrian area in the next decade as part of the plan to turn this part of Madrid into a cultural hub. A little off the beaten track, a visit to the Real Fábrica de Tápices (Royal Tapestry Factory) is like stepping back a couple of centuries and well worth the short walk to get there. ∎

NOT TO BE MISSED:

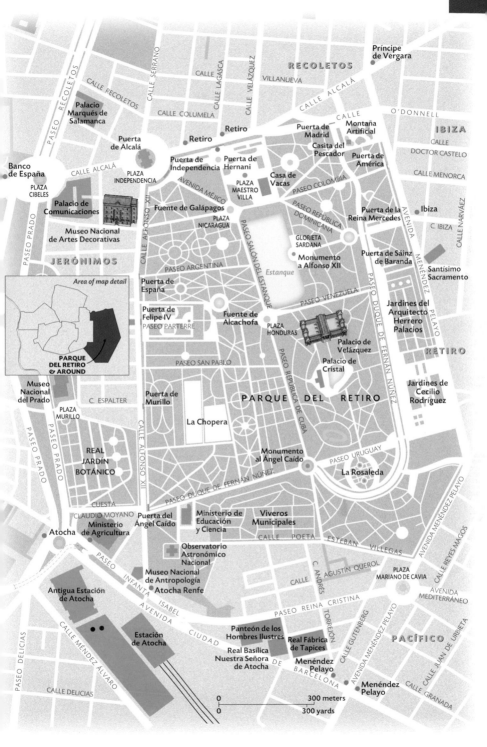

RECOLETOS

Príncipe de Vergara

CALLE VILLANUEVA

CALLE RECOLETOS

PASEO RECOLETOS

CALLE SERRANO

CALLE

CALLE LAGASCA

CALLE VELÁZQUEZ

CALLE ALCALÁ

O'DONNELL

IBIZA

CALLE DOCTOR CASTELO

CALLE MENORCA

Palacio Marqués de Salamanca

CALLE COLUMELA

Retiro

Retiro

Puerta de Madrid

Montaña Artificial

Puerta de Alcalá

Puerta de Independencia

Puerta de Hernani

Casita del Pescado

Puerta de América

Banco de España

CALLE ALCALÁ

PLAZA INDEPENDENCIA

AVENIDA MÉJICO

Casa de Vacas

PASEO COLOMBIA

PASEO REPÚBLICA DOMINICANA

Puerta de la Reina Mercedes

Ibiza

C. IBIZA

CALLE NARVÁEZ

PLAZA CIBELES

Palacio de Comunicaciones

Fuente de Galápagos

PLAZA MAESTRO VILLA

PLAZA NICARAGUA

GLORIETA SARDANA

Puerta de Sáinz de Baranda

Santísimo Sacramento

PASEO PRADO

Museo Nacional de Artes Decorativas

CALLE ALFONSO XII

PASEO ARGENTINA

PASEO SALÓN DEL ESTANQUE

Estanque

Monumento a Alfonso XII

PASEO VENEZUELA

PASEO DUQUE DE FERNÁN NÚÑEZ

PASEO PELAYO

RETIRO

JERÓNIMOS

Puerta de España

Jardines del Arquitecto Herrero Palacios

Area of map detail

Puerta de Felipe IV
PASEO PARTERRE

Fuente de Alcachofa

PLAZA HONDURAS

Palacio de Velázquez

Palacio de Cristal

Jardines de Cecilio Rodríguez

PARQUE DEL RETIRO & AROUND

Museo Nacional del Prado

C. ESPALTER

Puerta de Murillo

La Chopera

PASEO SAN PABLO

PARQUE DEL RETIRO

PASEO REPÚBLICA DE CUBA

PLAZA MURILLO

PASEO PRADO

REAL JARDÍN BOTÁNICO

CALLE ALFONSO XII

Monumento al Ángel Caído

PASEO URUGUAY

La Rosaleda

PASEO DUQUE DE FERNÁN NÚÑEZ

CUESTA

CLAUDIO MOYANO

Puerta del Ángel Caído

Ministerio de Educación y Ciencia

Viveros Municipales

AVENIDA MENÉNDEZ PELAYO

CALLE REYES MAGOS

Atocha

Ministerio de Agricultura

Observatorio Astronómico Nacional

CALLE POETA ESTEBAN VILLEGAS

CALLE GUTENBERG

Antigua Estación de Atocha

PASEO INFANTA ISABEL

Museo Nacional de Antropología

Atocha Renfe

C. ANDRÉS AGUSTÍN QUEROL

PLAZA MARIANO DE CAVIA

AVENIDA MEDITERRÁNEO

CALLE DELICIAS

Estación de Atocha

AVENIDA CIUDAD DE BARCELONA

PASEO REINA CRISTINA

TORREÓN

PACÍFICO

CALLE MÉNDEZ ÁLVARO

Panteón de los Hombres Ilustres

Real Fábrica de Tapices

Menéndez Pelayo

CALLE JUAN DE URBIETA

PASEO DELICIAS

Real Basílica Nuestra Señora de Atocha

Menéndez Pelayo

CALLE GRANADA

CALLE DELICIAS

0   300 meters
0   300 yards

Parque del Retiro

A visit to Parque del Retiro takes in history, architecture, botany, and usually some art, too. And plenty of activities. Some people practice tai chi or play chess under the trees, while others strum guitars or play drums. On weekends, Madrid's various foreign communities, particularly Latin Americans, congregate in different parts of the park for picnics, while Catalans choose a place to perform their traditional dance.

Light floods into the Palacio de Cristal, which was once a hothouse and is now an exhibition space.

Parque del Retiro
- Map p. 163
- 91 588 6318
- Metro: Ibiza, Retiro

All these activities seem mild compared with the extravagant events that took place here when the Palacio del Buen Retiro palace opened in 1635. The park, which was then the palace gardens, hosted fireworks displays, jousting tournaments, and concerts. Plays by Calderón de la Barca, Lope de Vega, and other leading figures of the golden age were performed on a floating stage on the lake.

The gardens were developed during a dramatic downturn in Spain's fortunes, when the country was floundering economically after a period of great prosperity following the discovery of America. Felipe IV was so de-

lighted with his new palace and its grounds, however, that he lost touch with what has happening to his empire—which was exactly what his adviser, the Count-Duke of Olivares, had intended when he ordered the construction of the complex.

The rectangular space covers 292 acres (118 ha) and is planted with 15,000 trees. Although it has changed greatly over the centuries, mostly as a result of wartime damage, the layout is more or less the same and some original features have survived.

Visiting the Park

The most popular entrance is at the northwest corner, by the Puerta de Alcalá (see p. 168). The main path, the Avenida de Méjico, leads diagonally up to the **Fuente de Galápagos,** a fountain adorned with turtles, frogs, and dolphins. Designed by Francisco Javier de Mariátegui in 1831, the fountain was commissioned by Fernando VII to celebrate his daughter Isabel's first birthday.

Immediately south of the fountain is the huge rectangular **Éstanque** (lake), which was dug out when the palace gardens were created in the 17th century. It was used not only for theatrical performances but also for elaborately staged mock battles. In 2003, a new boathouse and moorings were built. The lake is dominated by the **Monument to Alfonso XII,** which was designed by José Grases Riera and completed in 1922. The bronze equestrian statue of the king by Mariano Benlliure is flanked by a semicircular colonnade.

The promenade along the lake, known as the **Salón del Éstanque,** is usually lined with buskers, mime artists, tarot readers, and puppeteers. On the right is the path known popularly as the Paseo de las Estatuas, but officially as **Paseo de la Argentina.** It is flanked by 18th-century statues intended for the Palacio Real.

The end of the Salón del Éstanque, on the lake's southwest corner, is marked by the **Fuente de la Alcachofa,** designed by Ventura Rodríguez in the 18th

Fallen Angel

Madrid claims to have the only statue in the world to celebrate the devil. Serenely situated in the Parque del Retiro, the Monumento el Angel Caído (Monument to the Fallen Angel) was created in 1878 by Ricardo Bellver and depicts Lucifer's descent into Hell. The winged bronze figure crowns a fountain surrounded by gargoyles of monsters.

century. The Artichoke Fountain will return to its original location at the end of the Paseo del Prado, where there is now a replica, during the development over the next decade.

If you turn right here, toward the city center, you come to the **Parterre,** which was inspired by Versailles. It was created in the 18th century during the reign of Felipe V as part of an

Palacio de Velázquez

☎ 91 573 6245
🕐 Closed Tues.
🚇 Metro: Ibiza, Retiro

www.museoreinaso fia.es

unfulfilled plan to build a new palace. Although the garden has been replanted several times, it contains some of its original trees, including a Mexican cypress more than 400 years old and believed to have been brought to Spain by conquistador Hernán Cortés (1485–1547).

From the Artichoke Fountain, the Paseo de la República de Cuba heads south. In the area to the left are two pavilions, both designed by Ricardo Velázquez Bosco in the 1880s. The **Palacio de Velázquez,** a palace that features colored bricks, enameled tiles, and arches, was built for a mining exhibition in 1883. It is used for various shows.

Palacio de Cristal & South

A short distance to the south, the Palacio de Cristal is an elegant glass-and-iron structure inspired by London's Crystal Palace and the Palm House at Kew Gardens. It was built in 1887 to exhibit plants and flowers from the Philippines. The pavilion overlooks a lake where black swans glide through the water. Both buildings are now

INSIDER TIP:

Spend a sunny afternoon at Parque del Retiro. There are many points of interest for the active, or, if you prefer, secluded places for a picnic or nap.

—ELLIANA SPIEGEL
National Geographic contributor

EXPERIENCE: Staying with a Spanish Family

Jump straight into the local way of life by staying in a private home with a Spanish family. If you want to improve your language skills, avoid feeling like an outsider, or are just curious to find out how people live in Madrid, this is a rewarding option that puts you straight on the insider track.

Accommodation agencies and language schools can fix up the arrangement most suitable for you, depending on how involved with the family you want to be. You might just want to use the family's home as a bed & breakfast, having some contact with your hosts but doing your own thing the rest of the time and having a measure of independence for coming and going. You could also choose to have some or all of your meals at home, or you may prefer to really throw yourself into family life, going grocery shopping and

spending weekends in the country. Of course, the more you immerse yourself, the more you will learn about both the language and the culture. Another advantage is that you are likely to be staying in a residential area near the center, but away from the tourist areas, so you get more of a feel for normal neighborhood life. If you prefer, you can specify that you want to stay in a home without children or that you would like to be the only guest, as some families with large homes rent out more than one room.

Reputable agencies include **Madrid Sal y Ven** (*Calle Cochabamba 17, tel 91 457 4779, www.salyven.net*); **Accom Madrid** (*Calle Rodríguez San Pedro 2, 6th fl., www .accommadrid.com*); and **AIL Student Accommodation Madrid** (*Calle Doctor Esquerdo 33 1-2, tel 91 725 4193, www .student-accommodation-madrid.com*).

The steps in front of the Monument to Alfonso XII by the lake are perfect for enjoying the sunshine.

used as exhibition spaces under the auspices of the Museo Reina Sofía (see pp. 154–159).

South of the pavilions, along the Paseo de Uruguay, is the elliptical **Rosaleda,** a rose garden designed by Cecilio Rodríguez in 1915. The rose bushes came from the most famous gardens in Europe, but the Rosaleda had to be replanted in the 1940s after being destroyed in the Civil War.

This part of the park used to be occupied by the Royal Porcelain Factory, which Carlos III had built in 1760. Porcelain produced there is on display in the Palacio Real (see pp. 72–77) and in the palace in Aranjuez (see p. 220). The building was demolished after being damaged during the War of Independence.

The **Jardínes de Cecilio Rodríguez,** on the park's east side, commemorate the gardener who made such a great contribution here and in the Parque del Oeste (see pp. 202–203). Classical music concerts are occasionally held here in the summer.

Paseo del Duque

The broad Paseo del Duque de Fernán Núñez heads north alongside the gardens. Near the end of the road there is a little pavilion on the right in the middle of a pond, the **Casita del Pescador,** which is now an information center. Behind it is a hill known as the **Artificial Mountain,** built in the 1820s for Fernando VII. Water pumped around the structure flows down the hill like a mountain stream. The ruins nearby are the remains of a 13th-century Romanesque church brought from Ávila.

Turning back toward the lake along the Paseo de Colombia, you will see the **Casa de Vacas** on the right. This exhibition building originally housed cows, kept to provide fresh milk for visitors. ■

Palacio de Cristal

☎ 91 574 6614

🕐 Closed Tues.

Ⓜ Metro: Ibiza, Retiro

www.museoreinaso fia.es

Puerta de Alcalá

One of Madrid's most important symbols, the Puerta de Alcalá is a grandiose triumphal arch built to commemorate the first 20 years of the reign of Carlos III. The monument was the point of entry to the city for visitors from Barcelona and France, and it was also close to the Palacio del Buen Retiro.

The Puerta de Alcalá has been a Madrid landmark for more than two centuries.

Puerta de Alcalá
- Map p. 163
- Metro: Retiro

The arch stands in the center of **Plaza de la Independencia,** a circular crossroad between the grand avenues of Alcalá, Alfonso XII, and Serrano surrounded by elegant 19th-century apartment buildings. Nowadays traffic roars around the arch.

The neoclassical granite monument, 70 feet (21 m) high, was designed by Francesco Sabatini, the favorite architect of Carlos III, and completed in 1779. It com-

prises three semicircular **arches.** The central one is larger than the other two, as it was originally used by royal entourages, while the others were for carriages.

Above the arches are **reliefs** featuring horns of plenty, a reference to the good times during the reign of Carlos III. The entablature and attic are decorated with Italianate baroque **sculptures** by Robert Michel and Francisco Gutiérrez in white Colmenar stone. If you manage to get close to the monument, look up at the capitals on the Ionic columns on the outer side, which are decorated with bat heads.

INSIDER TIP:

Don't even think of pulling on your party shoes until 10 p.m.—the Madrileños certainly won't.

—CHRISTOPHER SOMERVILLE
National Geographic author

Calle Alcalá formed part of the authorized route for the seasonal migration of sheep across Spain, an event that took place every year for centuries. To this day, if sheep farmers want to stage a protest, they consider it their right to drive their flocks through the gate to Plaza de Cibeles. ■

Museo Nacional de Artes Decorativas

The National Museum of Decorative Arts contains extensive collections of furniture, ceramics, textiles, jewelry, and Oriental art. The exhibits are displayed over five floors in a palatial late 19th-century residence, which is interesting in its own right. Some of the exhibits appear in rooms that re-create how Spanish aristocratic families lived in different centuries.

If you are on your way to the Parque del Retiro, it is worth stopping here to see the reconstruction of an 18th-century **Valencian kitchen,** which is decorated with about 1,500 hand-painted tiles. Unfortunately, the kitchen is on the museum's top floor, which is sometimes closed owing to staff shortages. Call ahead to check.

The kitchen was transferred to the museum from a mansion in Valencia. In the 18th century, it became traditional on Spain's east coast to cover surfaces with tiles depicting popular themes. In this kitchen we see the servants preparing hot chocolate, pies, and cakes for the lady of the house. The tiles display typical foods such as sausages, onions, and salt cod.

On the ground floor, don't miss the collection of **20th-century design.** Several rooms on the second floor have coffered wooden ceilings, including a 15th-century example brought from León. Displays include Flemish tapestries and Spanish carpets from the 16th century, when Spain's carpet industry was the most important in Europe. The museum has an excellent collection of furniture, including elaborate *bargueño* cabinets from the 16th and 17th centuries.

The **ceramic collection,** on the third floor, comprises more than 4,000 items, the oldest of which is an 11th-century vat from Toledo. The displays include examples from all the major Spanish centers of ceramic production. The great European producers—Meissen, Sèvres, and Capodimonte—are also well represented. Glass displays include Greco-Punic, Roman, and Visigothic pieces and more recent exhibits from Limoges and La Granja.

The collection of **Oriental art,** begun by Carlos III, includes ceramics, costumes, musical instruments, and paintings from the Ming (1368–1644) and Qing (1644–1912) dynasties. ■

Museo Nacional de Artes Decorativas

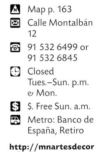

- Map p. 163
- Calle Montalbán 12
- 91 532 6499 or 91 532 6845
- Closed Tues.–Sun. p.m. & Mon.
- $. Free Sun. a.m.
- Metro: Banco de España, Retiro

http://mnartesdecor ativas.mcu.es

Details of 18th-century life are revealed on tiles of a Valencia kitchen in the Museo Nacional de Artes Decorativas.

South of Parque del Retiro

The area south of the Parque del Retiro is part of the far-reaching development plan for the Paseo del Prado (see pp. 137–140). The pedestrian-friendly layout will make the museums and other points of interest much more accessible. The area between the park and Atocha Station is set to become a hub of science-related museums and attractions. While this will be a massive improvement, it is well worth making the effort to visit this area now.

South of Parque del Retiro

Map p. 163

The development should restore the neoclassic **Observatorio Astronómico Nacional** to a position of prominence. Located just off the southwest corner of the Parque del Retiro, this superb building stands on the highest point in the area, with panoramic views across the city. Designed by Juan de Villanueva in 1790 and restored by Narciso Pascual y Colomer in 1845, it was part of Carlos III's Paseo del Prado scheme (see p. 124). Its cruciform structure features a central hall with a rotunda surrounded by Ionic columns. Work is under way on a museum of astronomy, which will not open until at least 2010.

The **Cuesta de Claudio Moyano,** which leads down the side of the Real Jardín Botánico (see pp. 152–153) from Calle Alfonso XII to the Paseo del Prado, is lined with wooden kiosks selling new, secondhand, and antique books. As part of the development, the hill has been pedestrianized and the kiosks will eventually be moved from the side to the center. On the other side of the hill is the rear of the **Ministerio de Agricultura,** built in the 1890s as the Ministry of Development. Designed by Ricardo Velázquez Bosco, it features his trademark elements of tiles and colored bricks.

Next to the ministry, with a grand neoclassic entrance, is the **Museo Nacional de Antropología,** designed by the Marquis of Cubas in the late

Each level of the Museo Nacional de Antropología deals with a different part of the world.

19th century. The museum was founded by the scientist Pedro González Velasco to exhibit his collections from distant cultures. The displays include mummies of Guanches, the original inhabitants of the Canary Islands, and finds from expeditions to Equatorial Guinea undertaken by Spanish explorers in the late 19th and early 20th centuries. A section devoted to North Africa displays objects from the Tuareg and Berber cultures. The American collections include Inuit sculptures and sculptures from Peru.

The round redbrick structure opposite is the new part of **Estación de Atocha**, Atocha Station, designed by Rafael Moneo and

century. It is now a hothouse with palm trees and tropical plants taking the place of platforms. Travelers relax here while waiting for trains, a world away from the station noise.

A five-minute walk along the Paseo de la Infanta Isabel, which becomes the Paseo de Reina Cristina, brings you to the **Panteón de los Hombres Ilustres**. Designed at the end of the 19th century by Fernando Arbós y Tremanti, the pantheon was intended to be a cemetery for important figures in Madrid's history. As the city has been so lax over the centuries with the remains of its most illustrious citizens, many of the most obvious candidates,

Observatorio Astronómico Nacional

✉ Calle Alfonso XII 3

☎ 91 527 0107

🕐 Guided visits Fri.

Ⓜ Metro: Atocha Renfe

www.oan.es

Museo Nacional de Antropología

✉ Calle Alfonso XII 68

☎ 91 530 6418

🕐 Closed Sun. p.m. & Mon.

💲 $

Ⓜ Metro: Atocha, Atocha Renfe

http://mnantropologia.mcu.es

A Tragic History

Although the area around Atocha will be remembered for the infamous bombings of March 2004, it is also home to an earlier terrorist attack. The power vacuum after Franco's death in 1975, although resulting in Spain's democratic transition, was a period of social unrest. On January 24, 1977, members of the neo-fascist group Alianza Apostolica Anticomunista stormed an office building at 55 Calle de Atocha. They were looking for Joaquín Navarro, the leftist head of a

large labor union. Failing to find him, they lined up eight labor lawyers in the hallway and opened fire, killing four and wounding the others. There were another three deaths involved in the attack. This tragic violence galvanized support for the Communist Party, which was legalized shortly thereafter and helped steer Spanish politics away from the far right. To memorialize the massacre, director Juan Antonio Bardem made the film *Seven Days in January*.

---

completed in 1992. On March 11, 2004, a devastating terrorist attack killed 192 people arriving at the station on commuter trains. A monument to the victims, bearing their names, commemorates the tragic event.

The original section of the station was designed by Alberto del Palacio at the end of the 19th

including Velázquez and Cervantes, could not be found. You can, however, see the elaborate tombs of several 19th-century politicians, sculpted by leading artists of the time, including Mariano Benlliure and Agustin Querol.

Next to the pantheon is the **Real Basílica de Nuestra Señora de Atocha**, an uninspiring

Panteón de los Hombres Ilustres

✉ Calle Julián Gayarre 3

☎ 91 454 8800

🕐 Closed Sun. p.m.

Ⓜ Metro: Atocha Renfe, Menéndez Pelayo

Real Fábrica de Tápices

✉ Calle Fuenterrabia 2

☎ 91 434 0550

🕐 Closed Sat., Sun., Mon.–Fri. p.m. & Aug.

💲 $. Guided tour

🚇 Metro: Menéndez Pelayo, Atocha Renfe

www.realfabricade tapices.com

neo-baroque structure that was built after the Civil War when the original church was destroyed. This is the site of one of Madrid's oldest and most important legends, which describes how the figure of Our Lady of Atocha healed and protected a nobleman's family during the Moorish invasion. Many Madrileños are more devoted to Our Lady of Atocha than they are to the Almudena (see pp. 78–79).

Around the corner is the fascinating **Real Fábrica de Tápices** (Royal Tapestry Factory). Founded by Felipe V at the beginning of the 18th century, the factory has been in this building since 1889. Francisco de Goya worked at the original factory, where he

produced preparatory paintings and sketches for tapestries, often depicting popular festivals and scenes from everyday life. Known as cartoons, many of these are now in the Prado Museum.

Today, weavers make tapestries on 18th-century looms that would have been familiar to Goya. About 75 people work there now, compared with 250 in its 18th-century heyday, when Bourbon monarchs provided plenty of business. Every royal residence in Spain is decorated with tapestries and carpets made then. The factory is now a foundation where students train in this intricate craft. It takes three to four months to make a square yard of the costly tapestry. ■

EXPERIENCE: Jamón—How to Get the Best

Magenta Iberian ham, marbled with glistening dots of fat, is perhaps Spain's greatest delicacy. The best quality—*jamón ibérico de bellota*—is produced from black Iberian pigs that have been partially fed on acorns and comes from Jabugo, Guijuelo, Teruel, Los Pedroches, or Extremadura. Jamón ibérico is made from the same breed of pig, though the animal is not fed on acorns.

These special hams are buried in salt for one to two weeks, then rinsed and kept for up to two months, before being hung up to dry and finally stored in cellars for up to two years. The cheaper Serrano ham comes from white-coated breeds of pigs, which are not necessarily Spanish.

Here is where to sample the best jamón:

Gold Gourmet (*Calle José Ortega y Gasset 85-87, tel 91 402 0363, www.gold*

gourmet.es) Gold Gourmet is a delicatessen with an excellent range of hams and a knowledgeable staff.

Mesón Cinco Jotas (*Calle Arenal 6, tel 91 522 7848, www.mesoncincojotas.com*) This upscale chain of bars serves the best Jabugo ham made by Sánchez Romero Carvajal, who is one of the most prestigious producers.

El Miajón de los Castúos (*Calle Serrano 220, tel 91 411 6647*) El Miajón de

los Castúos is a bar and delicatessen that specializes in the produce of Extremadura, with fabulous ham, cheese, salads and other tapas. Watch your ham being cut perfectly by Ovidio Matamoros.

Museo del Jamón (*Calle Alcalá 155, tel 91 431 7296, www.museodeljamon.es*) The "ham museum" is in fact a bar and delicatessen, with multiple branches. It stocks many hams, as well as other charcuterie and cheeses.

A grand boulevard flanked by flagship buildings and neighborhoods that chart the city's architectural development over the last century

La Castellana & Salamanca

A marble sculpture commemorates Spain's 1978 Constitution.

La Castellana & Salamanca

Running north from Plaza de Colón to Plaza Castilla, the Paseo de la Castellana is one of the most prestigious commercial streets in the city. Although streaming with traffic at all hours, the central boulevard showcases the modern city. To the east of the Paseo de la Castellana is the upscale area of Salamanca.

Madrid's smartest boutiques are sprinkled throughout the Salamanca district.

The Salamanca district was developed between 1860 and 1920 by the maverick Marquis of Salamanca and comprises a grid of tree-lined broad streets flanked by stylish apartments and shops. Madrid's bullring, Plaza de Toros de las Ventas, is located on the area's eastern fringe. It is worth visiting even if you do not want to see a bullfight. An interesting museum and good guided tours help give an insight into this most ingrained of Spanish traditions.

Other museums in this part of town include the Museo Arqueológico Nacional, which explores ancient civilizations as well as Spanish history; the Museo Nacional de Ciencias Naturales (the Museum of Natural Sciences); the Museo Lázaro Galdiano, with its excellent art collections; and the Museo Sorolla, displaying paintings of a Valencian artist in his own house. ■

The Paseo de la Castellana is divided into three distinct sections. The first, which covers about half a mile (0.8 km) from Plaza de Cibeles to Plaza de Colón, is known as the Paseo de Recoletos and dates from the second half of the 19th century. The second stretch of 2 miles (3.2 km) ends at Plaza San Juan de la Cruz and was developed between the late 19th century and the Civil War. The third section, up to Plaza Castilla, was built mainly in the second half of the 20th century. A fourth stage beyond Plaza de Castilla is currently taking shape.

As it extends northward, therefore, the street is like a museum of modern architecture, with a chronological progression of styles. Signature high-rise buildings mark it as Madrid's business and financial hub.

NOT TO BE MISSED:

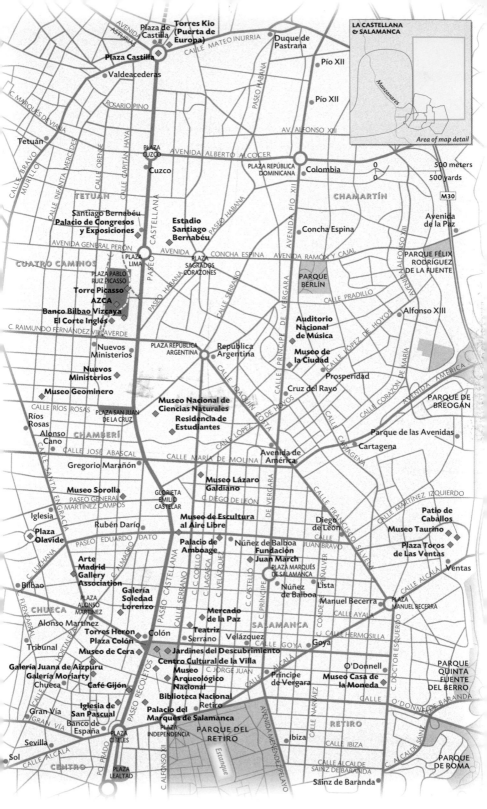

LA CASTELLANA & SALAMANCA

Manzanares

Area of map detail

Asturias

Plaza de Castilla

Torres Kio (Puerta de Europa)

CALLE MATEO INURRIA

Duque de Pastrana

Plaza Castilla

Valdeacederas

ROSARIO PINO

Pío XII

Pío XII

PASEO HABANA

AV. ALFONSO XIII

C. MARQUÉS DE VIANA

CALLE INFANTA MERCEDES

CALLE MURILLO

CALLE BRAVO

Tetuán

PLAZA CUZCO

AVENIDA ALBERTO ALCOCER

Cuzco

PLAZA REPÚBLICA DOMINICANA

Colombia

500 meters

500 yards

M30

TETUÁN

CALLE ORENSE

CALLE CAPITÁN HAYA

CASTELLANA

CHAMARTÍN

Avenida de la Paz

Santiago Bernabéu
Palacio de Congresos y Exposiciones

AVENIDA GENERAL PERÓN

Estadio Santiago Bernabéu

PASEO HABANA

Concha Espina

AVENIDA ALFONSO XIII

PARQUE FÉLIX RODRÍGUEZ DE LA FUENTE

CUATRO CAMINOS

PLAZA LIMA

AVENIDA

PLAZA SAGRADOS CORAZONES

CONCHA ESPINA

AVENIDA RAMÓN Y CAJAL

PARQUE BERLÍN

Alfonso XIII

PLAZA PABLO RUIZ PICASSO

Torre Picasso

AZCA

Banco Bilbao Vizcaya
El Corte Inglés

C. RAIMUNDO FERNÁNDEZ VILLAVERDE

PASEO HABANA

CALLE SERRANO

CALLE PRADILLO

Auditorio Nacional de Música

CALLE PRÍNCIPE DE VERGARA

CALLE LÓPEZ DE HOYOS

CALLE CORAZÓN DE MARÍA

AVENIDA AMÉRICA

PARQUE DE BREOGÁN

Nuevos Ministerios

PLAZA REPÚBLICA ARGENTINA

República Argentina

Museo de la Ciudad

Nuevos Ministerios

Museo Geominero

CALLE RÍOS ROSAS

Ríos Rosas

Alonso Cano

PLAZA SAN JUAN DE LA CRUZ

CALLE JOSÉ ABASCAL

CHAMBERÍ

Prosperidad

Cruz del Rayo

Museo Nacional de Ciencias Naturales

Residencia de Estudiantes

CALLE LÓPEZ

CALLE JOAQUÍN COSTA

CALLE MARÍA DE MOLINA

Avenida de América

Parque de las Avenidas

Cartagena

CALLE CARTAGENA

CALLE FRANCISCO SILVELA

CALLE MARTÍNEZ IZQUIERDO

CALLE SANTA ENGRACIA

Gregorio Marañón

Museo Sorolla

PASEO GENERAL MARTÍNEZ CAMPOS

GLORIETA EMILIO CASTELAR

Museo Lázaro Galdiano

G. DIEGO DE LEÓN

CALLE DE VERGARA

Diego de León

Patio de Caballos

Museo Taurino

Iglesia

Plaza Olavide

Rubén Darío

PASEO EDUARDO DATO

Museo de Escultura al Aire Libre

Palacio de Amboage

Núñez de Balboa

JUAN BRAVO

Plaza Toros de Las Ventas

Ventas

Arte Madrid Gallery Association

PLAZA ALONSO MARTÍNEZ

Galería Soledad Lorenzo

CALLE COELLO

CALLE LAGASCA

CALLE VELÁZQUEZ

Fundación Juan March

PLAZA MARQUÉS DE SALAMANCA

CALLE CASTELLÓ

CALLE PRÍNCIPE

CALLE GENERAL PARDIÑAS

Núñez de Balboa

Lista

Manuel Becerra

PLAZA MANUEL BECERRA

CALLE ALCALÁ

Bilbao

C. LUCHANA

FUENCARRAL

CHUECA

Alonso Martínez

HORTALEZA

Torres Heron
Plaza Colón

Museo de Cera

PASEO CASTELLANA

PASEO SERRANO

Colón

Mercado de la Paz

Teatriz
Serrano

Velázquez

CALLE GOYA

Goya

SALAMANCA

CALLE HERMOSILLA

CALLE AYALA

C. CONDE PEÑALVER

Tribunal

Galería Juana de Aizpuru
Galería Moriarty

Chueca

Café Gijón

PASEO RECOLETOS

Jardines del Descubrimiento

Centro Cultural de la Villa

Museo Arqueológico Nacional

C. JORGE JUAN

Príncipe de Vergara

O'Donnell

Museo Casa de la Moneda

C. DOCTOR ESQUERDO

PARQUE QUINTA FUENTE DEL BERRO

Gran Vía

GRAN VÍA

Iglesia de San Pascual

Banco de España

Biblioteca Nacional

Palacio del Marqués de Salamanca

PLAZA CIBELES

Retiro

PLAZA INDEPENDENCIA

C. ALFONSO XII

PARQUE DEL RETIRO

AVENIDA MENÉNDEZ PELAYO

CALLE NARVÁEZ

CALLE ALCALÁ

O'DONNELL

C. ALCALDE SÁINZ

PARQUE DE ROMA

Sevilla

Sol

PO. PRADO

PLAZA LEALTAD

CENTRO

Estanque

Ibiza

CALLE IBIZA

CALLE ALCALDE SÁINZ DE BARANDA

RETIRO

Sáinz de Baranda

Paseo de los Recoletos

For Madrileños, the Paseo de Recoletos is inextricably associated with the beloved custom of sitting at outdoor cafés, a tradition that began more than a century ago. The name "Recoletos" comes from an Augustinian Recollect monastery that was located on the right of the street until the mid-19th century.

Creating new waxwork figures at the Museo de Cera

Paseo de los Recoletos

🅜 Map p. 175

Palacio del Marqués de Salamanca

- ✉ Sala de Exposiciones BBVA, Paseo de Recoletos 10
- ☎ 91 374 5400
- 🕐 Exhibitions: Closed Sun. p.m.
- Ⓜ Metro: Banco de España

Iglesia de San Pascual

- ✉ Paseo de Recoletos 11
- ☎ 91 521 2705
- Ⓜ Metro: Banco de España

After the monastery was demolished, the land was snapped up by the Marquis of Salamanca (1811–1883), a larger-than-life character who built himself a sumptuous residence on the site. The palace is now the headquarters of the **Banco Bilbao Vizcaya Argentaria,** which holds art exhibitions in the courtyard on the first floor. If the building is open, it is worth going in just to have a look at the interior, particularly the grand staircase to the right of the entrance.

Almost hidden on the left of the Paseo is the rebuilt **Iglesia de San Pascual,** a vestige of the convent that stood there until the 19th century. To the right of the altar there is a figure of Santa Clara. It is revered by people working in show business, who often pop into the church to ask her to help find their next job.

A little farther up is the **Café Gijón** (*Paseo de Recoletos 21, tel 91 521 5425*), founded in 1888 and one of the few remaining traditional cafés in Madrid (see pp. 118–119). With its marble tables and velvet banquettes, this is a good place to spot famous actors and writers. Its outdoor tables are ideal for people-watching. At the end of the Paseo on the left is the **Museo de Cera** (*Paseo de Recoletos 41, tel 91 319 2649, $$$*), a wax museum where exhibits range from Cervantes to Bart Simpson. ∎

Plaza de Colón

Things are on the move in Plaza de Colón, as a major remodeling scheme is under way to spruce up this major junction. The square commemorates Christopher Columbus and the discovery of America, which the new arrangement aims to make more coherent by repositioning its key features.

The neo-Gothic column crowned by a figure of Columbus, designed by Jerónimo Suñol and Arturo Mélida in the late 19th century, is set to move from the sidelines to its original location in the middle of the crossroads. On the right, the Teatro Fernán-Gómez Centro de Arte, is a new theater and cultural center used for drama, dance, music and other activities. The large landscaped area behind the theater, known as the **Jardines del Descubrimiento**, commemorates Columbus with three large blocks that represent his sailing ships, each featuring inscriptions and reliefs relating to his voyages. The airport bus terminal is located just under the square.

The southeast corner of the square is taken up by the enormous 19th-century building that houses the **Biblioteca Nacional** at the front and the **Museo Arqueológico Nacional** (see pp. 180–182) at the rear. The book museum on the first floor is not currently open to the public, but there is usually at least one temporary exhibition running at any given time.

The towers on the northwest side, which seem to be joined by a pistachio-colored hat, are the Torres de Jerez, popularly known as the **Torres de Colón.** Built between 1967 and 1976 by Antonio Lamela, they were altered by the same architect in the 1990s. The towers were built from the top down by slotting the stories onto concrete pillars. ■

INSIDER TIP:

There's a rhythm to the city: easy mornings, busy afternoons, and long late dinners in bustling nights. The streets are almost deserted on Saturday mornings.

—JULIE WARD
National Geographic Glimpse contributor

Plaza de Colón
🅰 Map p. 175

Teatro Fernán-Gómez Centro de Arte
✉ Plaza de Colón
☎ 91 480 0300
🕐 Closed Sun. p.m. & Mon.
Ⓜ Metro: Colón, Serrano
www.esmadrid.com/teatrofernangomez

Biblioteca Nacional
✉ Paseo de Recoleto 20–22
☎ 91 580 7805, Exhibitions: 91 580 7894
🕐 Closed Sun. & Sat. p.m.
Ⓜ Metro: Colón, Serrano
www.bne.es

The neoclassical Biblioteca Nacional houses Spain's prestigious literary heritage.

Terrazas

Outdoor cafés, known as *terrazas*, are an integral element of Madrid summers, opening after Easter and closing when the temperature drops to wintry levels in late October. Some provide a shady spot for watching the world go by on a lazy afternoon, while others are more like nightclubs, with throbbing music and a glamorous clientele.

By day or night, El Espejo is one of the popular outdoor cafés on the Paseo de Recoletos.

Terrazas are not a modern phenomenon, however, having been a ubiquitous feature of the city for more than a hundred years. In the 19th century, the Paseo de Recoletos was adorned with gardens and fountains and was such a pleasant place to relax that it became known as Recoletos Beach. A string of kiosks—the precursors of today's cafés—sold refreshments, and people went there to cool down with a lemonade after midday Mass at the San Pascual church or to take a pre-dinner stroll in the evening.

In the 1980s, the terrazas along the Paseo de Recoletos became fashionable, a trend that spread up the Paseo de la Castellana over the years, until the boulevard became a nocturnal promenade stretching for miles. In the 1990s, late-night terrazas moved away from residential areas to bigger spaces where noise was not a problem. Now, some of the hippest places to be seen in the summer are the terrazas flanking the **Príncipe Pío** commercial center near the Río Manzanares, which provides a pleasant, cooling breeze.

The more traditional terrazas offer a range of typical drinks. *Granizado de limón* is crushed ice, sugar, and lemon juice, while *granizado de café* is the same thing with coffee. The thick, creamy liquid that you see some people drinking through a straw is *horchata,* made with *chufas,* which are tubers from the sedge plant and are sometimes called tiger nuts or earth almonds. When crushed with sugar and ice, the chufas acquire a flavor and texture that is unlike anything you are ever likely to have tasted, so give it a try.

The **Paseo del Pintor Rosales,** by the Parque del Oeste (see pp. 202–203) on the western edge of the city, is a good place for a quiet drink with friends, and being just outside the center with views to the mountains means the temperature is a few degrees lower too. This is one of the few places in Madrid where you can still find *leche merengada,* which, if made properly, is a mix of cream, milk, and egg whites, flavored with lemon and cinnamon. You might also come across *blanco y negro,* which is coffee topped with leche merengada, or sometimes just regular vanilla ice cream.

For more of a neighborhood feel, sit at one of the many terrazas in the octagonal **Plaza de Olavide,** which is popular with families who share tapas while the kids and dogs run around the gardens. Perhaps the most traditional terraza of all is Las Vistillas *(Calle Bailén),* with fabulous views of the Palacio Real and the Guadarrama mountains beyond.

INSIDER TIP:

Cafés are great places to hang out, people-watch, and eavesdrop. Locals don't tend to use cafés to study.

—SHOSHANA COHEN
National Geographic contributor

EXPERIENCE: Tasting Spanish Wines

There is a lot more to Spanish wine than Rioja. In fact, there are more than 70 recognized production regions, spread right across the country from Andalucía in the south to Galicia in the north, as well as the Balearic and Canary Islands.

Wine guru Robert Parker is a big fan of the Ribera del Duero and Priorat regions, and his influence has put their wines on the map outside Spain. To help you find your way around Madrid's ever lengthening wine lists, sign up for a tasting session and you'll emerge with enough basic knowledge and curiosity to experiment with greater confidence.

La Carte des Vins *(Calle Postas 26, tel 91 354 6340,* *www.lacartedesvins.com)* This wine store has several branches in Madrid, with the main outlet in a historic building near Plaza Mayor. La Carte des Vins offers a program of wine-tasting courses and individual lessons lasting 90 minutes, some conducted in English.

Lavinia *(Calle José Ortega y Gasset 16, tel 91 426 0604, www.lavinia.es)* If you like wine, head for this vast store, which stocks about 4,500 different varieties. Frequent tasting sessions are held in the restaurant upstairs.

Planeta Vino *(Calle Monte Esquinza 24, tel 91 310 2855, www.planetavino .net)* Planeta Vino is run by American Mary O'Connor, who knows all there is to know about Spanish wine. Take part in one of the enjoyable evening sessions, lasting around three hours, where you try a selection of about eight wines from established and new regions.

Museo Arqueológico Nacional

This is one of Spain's most important museums. It contains archaeological finds but also religious sculptures, ceramics, and architectural fragments. While part of the collection is devoted to ancient civilizations, there are also extensive exhibits that provide a fascinating insight into Spain's history and culture. The museum is undergoing a major overhaul (completion date: 2010), so some sections will be closed and exhibits moved to temporary display areas.

Schoolchildren, frequent visitors to the museum, try their hand at sketching ancient exhibits.

**Museo
Arqueológico
Nacional**

- Map p. 175
- Calle Serrano 13
- 91 577 7912
- Closed Sun. p.m. & Mon.
- $. Free Sat. p.m. & Sun. a.m.
- Metro: Colón, Retiro, Serrano

http://man.mcu.es

The displays begin in the basement with prehistory and the origins of humanity. There are some exceptional pieces in **Rooms 5 and 6,** which deal with the Bronze Age. Look for the copper-and-gold Guadalajara sword, which is a rare example of weaponry from the period (second millennium B.C.), and the bowls from Axtroki in the Basque country,

made of hammered gold with geometric patterns that suggest a cult of sun worship. **Rooms 7–9,** devoted to the Iron Age, contain a beautiful collection of gold Celtic torques (collars) and Celtiberian silver.

Rooms 10–11 deal with the ancient cultures of the Balearic and Canary Islands. While we may now think of these places as holiday resorts, the Balearics were

inhabited as far back as 5000 B.C. The Guanches were definitely living in the Canaries by 2500 B.C. and were probably in the islands a lot earlier than that.

Room 13, a large space in the south wing, is devoted to ancient Egypt and Nubia from 4000 B.C. up to the Roman Conquest. The sarcophagus of Amenemhat (circa 1000 B.C.), from Thebes, is exquisitely decorated over its entire surface with myths related to the afterlife. The exceptional collections of Greek pottery in Rooms 14–16 include a cup painted by Aison, one of the great artists of fifth century B.C., which depicts the exploits of Theseus.

On the first floor, start with the Iberian and Phoenician works in Rooms 19–20 and follow the exhibits clockwise. One of the first things you see is the Pozo Moro monument, a huge structure of carved sandstone blocks that looks as if it belongs in a museum of contemporary art. This is actually a reconstruction of a funerary monument from the end of the sixth century B.C. that was found in the province of Albacete. Also look for the Dama de Galera, a small alabaster Phoenician sculpture from the seventh century B.C. The feminine figure, flanked by two sphinxes, is holding a bowl that was filled with perfume in funeral rituals. Another extraordinary exhibit is the Aliseda Treasure from Cáceres in western Spain. Made by Tartessians in the seventh century B.C., it includes exquisite earrings and bracelets.

Afterward, see the Dama de Baza, a painted, carved figure of a woman also from the fourth

century B.C. The life-size, seated sculpture comes from an Iberian necropolis and has a cavity for ashes. The richly adorned woman, still retaining traces of color, represents the goddess of death, a concept that developed from the Mediterranean tradition of worshipping the Mother God, as represented in Greek mythology by Demeter.

Rooms 21–26 display the Roman collections, which include a mosaic floor from Zaragoza, dating from the second century A.D., that depicts the Triumph of

Dama de Elche

The museum's highlight is the Dama de Elche, the Lady of Elche, a beautiful Iberian sculpture from the fourth century B.C. Found in 1897 in the city of Elche in eastern Spain, this bust of a wealthy woman has a tiara, an elaborate headdress, and impressive coils of hair curling around each side of her face. An indentation at the back was probably intended for the deposit of ashes, and the sculpture is thought to have been a funerary urn.

Bacchus. The rooms contain several bronze tablets engraved with regulations, including the Malacitanian Law, which dates from the first century A.D. and was originally displayed in a public building. A marble seated figure of Empress Livia, originally from Paestum in Italy, is swathed in superbly carved draped clothing.

The outstanding exhibit in **Rooms 27–29,** which are devoted to Visigothic Spain, is the Guarrazar Treasure from the nearby old city of Toledo (seventh century A.D.). It contains votive crowns, crosses, and fragments of various other pieces. The highlight of these is the gold crown of King Recceswinth (r. 649–672), adorned with garnets, pearls, and sapphires.

INSIDER TIP:

Visit the Museo Arqueológico Nacional, housed with the Biblioteca Nacional. It contains many nice Roman antiquities as well as a good dose of Moorish artifacts.

—DEAN SNOW
National Geographic field researcher

Rooms 30 and 31 trace the development of the vast Islamic empire in Spain as well as the emergence of Romanesque art. Exhibits include 11th-century decorative friezes from the Alfajería palace in Zaragoza to the northeast and a 14th-century lamp from the Alhambra palace in Granada, final base of the Moors in Spain. There is in addition a perfectly preserved tenth-century canister from Zamora, finely worked in ivory, silver, and enamel. Fashioned in Córdoba, the cylindrical box is delicately decorated with gazelles, peacocks, pinecones, and roses.

A gilded earthenware urn, which was made in the 14th century at the Cartuja de Jerez de la Frontera, is an excellent example of the work of the Nasrid craftsmen who decorated the exquisite Alhambra. The carvings on an ivory crucifix, donated by King Fernando I and Queen Sancha to the church of San Isidro in León in the 11th century, feature the risen Christ above the crucified figure, which suggests that the craftsman who made the piece was influenced by the art of central Europe.

You enter **Room 32** through a 12th-century decorated arch that came from the monastery of San Pedro de Arlanza in Burgos. The Romanesque displays include a 12th-century polychrome Madonna from Santa Maria de Taull in Catalunya.

Room 33 contains superlative displays of Romanesque, Gothic, and Mudejar art. The 12th-century choir stalls from Santa María de Gradefes in León are a fine example of Mudejar craftsmanship, with vestiges of red and green decoration depicting heraldic lions. Also here is a 14th-century crozier in silver and enamel that belonged to Pope Benedict XIII.

The second floor contains the 16th- to 19th-century collections, as well as extensive displays of coins, but these rooms are frequently closed. Temporary exhibitions are also held on this floor. Outside the entrance, steps lead to an underground space, where there is a replica of the Altamira caves on Spain's north coast, which are covered with fascinating Paleolithic paintings. ∎

Calle Serrano & Around

Most of Madrid's most fashionable shops are located on Calle Serrano and the surrounding Salamanca district. Walking up and down these grand avenues, which are also lined with upscale residences, you feel as though you are in a different city, a world away from the narrow streets of the Old Town. While you could easily spend all day popping into boutiques and drinking coffee at chic cafés, there are a few cultural surprises here that are worth a look.

Calle Serrano gets its name from Francisco Serrano (1810–1885), who held the title of Duke of la Torre and was an influential politician and military man. Along with General Prim, he led the revolution that dethroned Isabel II in 1868.

This area features Spanish designers such as Loewe, Adolfo Domínguez, and Amaya Arzuaga, as well as international names including Armani, Chanel, Prada, and Versace. The most interesting boutiques are at the bottom of Calle Serrano, particularly along Calle Jorge Juan, where well known antique shops can also be found.

Just off Calle Serrano, occupying the block between Calle Ayala

At Adolfo Domínguez, one of Spain's best known designers

Little Luxuries

The apartment blocks in the Salamanca neighborhood were the first in Madrid to have elevators and coal-fired stoves. The city's bourgeoisie had been reluctant to move away from the city center but were eventually tempted by these innovations. The deciding factors were bathrooms with hot running water and toilets that flushed.

Calle Serrano
📍 Map p. 175

Fundación Juan March
✉ Calle Castelló 77
☎ 91 435 4240
🕐 Closed Sun. p.m. & Aug.
Ⓜ Metro: Núñez de Balboa

www.march.es

and Calle Lagasca, is the **Mercado de la Paz** *(tel 91 431 7725)*, one of the best food markets in the city, with fantastic charcuterie and cheese stands. A few minutes' walk farther down, look for **Teatriz** *(tel 91 577 5379)* at Calle Hermosilla 15 on the corner of Calle Claudio Coello. This former theater was transformed by Philippe Starck and Javier

which was created in 1955 by financier March and organizes a prestigious program of exhibitions, concerts, and lectures. Its first-class art collection is divided between this center and the museums of contemporary art in Cuenca and Palma de Mallorca.

One of Madrid's cultural institutions, the **Residencia de Estudiantes** is hidden away off

---

EXPERIENCE: Haute Couture

If you need to justify buying designer clothes on vacation, you might consider that they take up less suitcase room, and weigh less, than bottles of Rioja. Justified or not, garments bought along Calle Serrano are sure to be envied. Noteworthy is the **Centro Comercial ABC Serrano** *(Calle Serrano 61, tel 91 577 5031, www.abcserrano.com)*, a three-story mall filled with upscale designer boutiques. Its name comes from the right-wing newspaper, *ABC*, which once occupied

the buildings. The eighty stores include designers like Zara, Boch, and Minority. There are also salons, restaurants, and wine shops. But this is not the only stop in town; there are innumerable boutiques along and near the wide boulevard Serrano *(Metro: Serrano)*, interesting ones being **Hoss** *(Calle Serrano 18, tel 91 781 0612)*, which is aimed at the younger professionals, and **Javier Simorra** *(Calle Serrano 33, tel 91 576 8699)*, offering funky chic styles for the modern woman.

Residencia de Estudiantes
✉ Calle Pinar 21–23
☎ 91 563 6411
🕐 Closed Sun. p.m.
Ⓜ Metro: Gregorio Marañón, República Argentina

www.residencia .csic.es

Mariscal into a restaurant, bar, and café. It is a good place to take an afternoon break and observe the well-groomed locals.

Only a few of the palaces and mansions from the 19th century still survive, but there is a fine example on the corner of Calle Lagasca and Calle Juan Bravo. Now the Italian Embassy, this neo-baroque structure was originally the **Palacio de Amboage,** built for an aristocratic family between 1914 and 1918 by Joaquín Rojí. Walk around to Calle Velázquez to get a view of the incredible gardens.

A couple of blocks farther east is the **Fundación Juan March,**

the top of Calle Serrano but will become more accessible after a garden is created between the building and the Museo Nacional de Ciencias Naturales (see p. 187). Founded in 1910, the Residencia was originally a liberal teaching center. It soon became a magnet for the great artists, writers, and thinkers of the time. Students over the years included poet Federico García Lorca, painter Salvador Dalí, and film director Luis Buñue, while Maurice Ravel, Igor Stravinsky, Andrés Segovia, and Manuel de Falla all performed there. It now hosts exhibits and other events and has a good café and restaurant, as well. ■

Museo Lázaro Galdiano

The grand home of publisher and businessman José Lázaro Galdiano (1862–1947) houses his impressive collection of Spanish and European paintings, which includes important works by Goya. The extensive exhibits also contain sculpture, jewelry, miniatures, ceramics, enamels, and weaponry. Galdiano and his wife, Paula Florido, were patrons of the arts and played an active role in the cultural life in Madrid in the first half of the 20th century.

The displays are arranged over all four floors of the mansion, which is itself of considerable interest, particularly the *piano nobile* on the second floor. The many notable exhibits include a bronze pitcher from the sixth century B.C. and the late 17th-century cup of Emperor Rudolph II.

A selection of Spanish art ranging from the 15th to the 19th centuries is displayed chronologically on the **first floor.** Early works include "La Virgen de Mosén Sperandeu de Santa Fé" (1438–1439) by Blasco de Grañén and the Castillian "San Jerónimo en su Escritorio" (circa 1480–1490) by the Maestro del Parral. Among the exceptional works from the 16th and 17th centuries is "San Francisco de Asís" (1577–1580) by El Greco.

The most outstanding of the eight Goya paintings are the terrifying "El Aquelarre" and "El Conjuro," which belonged to the Dukes of Osuna. The former depicts a coven of haggard witches casting a spell, while the latter shows the devil as a goat, appearing before women who have killed their children.

The **second floor** is devoted to European art, with Italian, Flemish, Dutch, French, and English paintings. In this rich collection, of particular interest is "El Salvador Adoloscente" (circa 1490–1495), a panel attributed to Giovanni Antonio Boltraffio, a disciple of Da Vinci. The Flemish paintings include "Meditaciones de San Juan Bautista" by Hieronymus Bosch. In the English collection are works by Joshua Reynolds, George Romney, and John Constable. ∎

Medieval stained glass in the Sala de Musica is just one of the many treasures of the Museo Lázaro Galdiano.

Museo Lázaro Galdiano

- Map p. 175
- Calle Serrano 122
- 91 561 6084
- Closed Tues.
- $. Free Wed.
- Metro: Gregorio Marañon, Rubén Darío

www.flg.es

...eo Sorolla

...quín Sorolla (1863–1923), who was born in Valencia, lived in this house from 1911 until his death. He is best known for his languid beach scenes, many of which have been reproduced on greeting cards and posters. Coveted by collectors during his lifetime, his work was exhibited in London in 1908 and in Boston and New York a year later.

Sorolla's studio remains just as he left it in the early 1900s.

Museo Sorolla

- Map p. 175
- Paseo General Martínez 37
- 91 310 1584
- Closed Mon. & daily p.m., except Wed.
- $
- Metro: Iglesia, Gregorio Marañón, Rubén Darío

http://museosorolla .mcu.es

The first three rooms you visit were his **offices** and **studio,** which are decorated and furnished just as they were in Sorolla's day. Some of his best known paintings are displayed in this section, including the sun-dappled "Pink Bathrobe" (1916) and "Strolling Along the Sea Shore" (1909).

Upstairs, the original bedrooms now contain works from his stays in northern Spain. **Room 6** displays some of the paintings he produced between 1912 and 1919 for the Hispanic Society of America in New York. They show people from all the provinces of

Spain in traditional dress.

Back downstairs, a few rooms have been left as they were when the family lived here. Sorolla decorated the **dining room** with an elaborate border of flowers and fruit, featuring portraits of his wife and daughters.

Sorolla also designed the stunning **gardens,** inspired by the Reales Alcazares in Seville and the Alhambra in Granada. Don't miss the Cordoba-style courtyard off the gardens, which is decorated with tiles from Talavera. Rooms around the courtyard contain Spanish ceramics and drawings of scenes from New York. ∎

Museo Nacional de Ciencias Naturales

The National Museum of Natural Science grew from the Royal Natural History Office founded by Carlos III in 1772. The imposing building, completed in 1887, houses both permanent displays and at least two temporary exhibitions at any time.

The museum's displays are divided between two iron-and-glass pavilions either side of a central dome. You start in the **Biology Zone,** on the left as you face the building. **Mediterranean Nature and Civilization** traces the development of landscapes and life-forms in the region. Displays discuss livestock migration and endangered animals such as

INSIDER TIP:

Visit Museo Sorolla, located in the artist's home. Sitting in Sorolla's garden is like stepping into his paintings.

—BARBARA ASCHER
National Geographic Traveler magazine writer

the Iberian lynx and the brown bear. A room devoted to the Mediterranean has models of lobsters, crabs, and a giant squid.

Downstairs, a circular room re-creates the **Royal Natural History Office** and explains the origins of the museum. In the **Ecology Zone,** at the other end of the building, the **History of the Earth and Life** section contains the skeleton of a megatherium, a giant slothlike creature

found in Argentina in 1788, which is believed to be 1.8 million years old. This and other skeletons on display were found during the many Spanish expeditions to South America at the end of the 18th century. The museum also has a life-size reproduction of a diplodocus skeleton that was found in Wyoming and given to Alfonso XIII by Andrew Carnegie.

Upstairs, exhibits cover evolution from primates to modern humans. A section on geology highlights Spain's minerals. ■

Museo Nacional de Ciencias Naturales

Map p. 175
Calle José Gutiérrez Abascal 2
91 411 1328
Closed Mon. & Sun. p.m.
$
Metro: Gregorio Marañón, Nuevos Ministerios

www.mncn.csic.es

Skeletons of dinosaurs and other animals show the size of long-extinct species at the Natural Science Museum.

Nuevos Ministerios to Plaza Castilla

Development of this stage of the Paseo de la Castellana began in the 1920s but really got going after the Civil War. General Franco wanted to create not only a new gateway to the north, but also a space for military parades and political rallies. The No. 27 bus runs the length of this route and is a good way of seeing the various flagship buildings without getting too exhausted.

Nationalist leader José Calvo Sotelo is commemorated in front of the Torres Puerta de Europa.

It is difficult to believe now, but a century ago this was open countryside with a racecourse at the start of the stretch. Now the land is occupied by the massive white granite structure known as **Nuevos Ministerios,** which was begun in the 1930s and houses several government ministries.

The original architect, Secundino Zuazo, had in mind a kind of bureaucratic version of Juan de Herrera's monastery at El Escorial (see pp. 228–231), with the various sections separated by courtyard gardens. An exhibition venue under the white arches specializes in architectural shows.

Beyond the ministries on the left, on the other side of Calle Raimundo Fernández Villaverde, is another huge complex, this one devoted to shopping and business. It is known as **AZCA,** from Asociación Zona Comercial A. Dominated by a massive El Corte Inglés department store, the concrete buildings have not stood the test of time.

The brown high-rise block next to it at Paseo de la Castellana 79–81 is the **Banco Bilbao Vizcaya,** designed by one of Spain's top 20th-century architects, Francisco Javier Sáenz de Oiza, and completed in 1978.

Next up on the left, past AZCA, is the **Torre Picasso** *(Plaza Pablo Ruiz Picasso),* which has 43 stories and stands 515 feet high (157 m), with a white aluminum casing. It was designed in the early 1980s by Minoru Yamasaki—architect of the World Trade Center in New York—in the last years of his life and completed in 1988.

On the corner of Avenida General Perón is the **Palacio de Congresos y Exposiciones** *(Paseo de la Castellana 99, tel 91 337 8101),* a conference and exhibition center built in 1964. A dramatic mosaic by the Catalan artist Joan Miró provides a welcome splash of color in this commercial area.

Across the street is the **Estadio Santiago Bernabéu,** the home of Real Madrid soccer club, which holds a crowd of 72,000. Stadium tours take you to the locker rooms, presidential box, and field.

At the end of this stretch is **Plaza de Castilla,** a junction dominated by the sloping twin towers known officially as the Torres Puerta de Europa but more usually as the **Torres Kio.** The granite, glass, and metal structures were designed by Philip Johnson and John Burgee and completed in 1998. Behind them rise the skyscrapers of the Cuatro Torres complex, the tallest buildings in Madrid at 820 feet (250 m). ■

Nuevos Ministerios to Plaza Castilla

🅰 Map p. 175

🚇 Metro: Cuzco/ Plaza Castilla, Nuevos Ministerios, Santiago Bernabéu

Nuevos Ministerios

✉ Paseo de la Castellana 67

☎ 91 597 5132

🕐 Closed Sun. p.m. & Mon.

🚇 Metro: Nuevos Ministerios

Estadio Santiago Bernabéu

🅰 Map p. 175

✉ Avenida de Concha Espina 1

☎ 91 398 4300. Ticket sales: 90 232 4324

💲 Guided tours: $$$

🚇 Metro: Santiago Bernabéu

www.realmadrid.com

EXPERIENCE: Surf's Up, Madrid Style

Never to be outdone by Barcelona, Madrileños have decided that they, too, deserve a beach. The fact that Madrid is about 220 miles (354 km) from the coast is little deterrent—they will simply create the beach.

And why not? Urban beaches are all the rage nowadays, sprouting up from Paris to Mexico City. The "Madrid Rio" project was revealed in early 2008. The M30, one of Madrid's main traffic arteries, is moving underground. This frees up a huge amount of space along the Río Manzanares—which will be space that city officials are dedicating to the

gloried tradition of leisure.

The project will be completed by 2010 and will contain a large urban beach near El Matadero. In addition to the beach, the Madrid Rio project will include skating rinks, jogging and bike paths, cafés, and playgrounds. All of this will be only a few minutes from the city center, which is more than most beaches can boast.

And don't worry about the murky waters of the Río Manzanares; the city is also investing in new water-cleaning technology.

For more information: *www.gomadrid .com/beach.*

Contemporary Art

Madrid's lively contemporary art scene is finally becoming more organized after three decades of varying fortunes. Most of the city's galleries were established following the death of General Franco in 1975, when severe restrictions on cultural expression were lifted after nearly 40 years of dictatorship.

At the annual ARCO International Contemporary Art Fair. Madrid's contemporary art scene flourishes, with the ARCO art fair topping the list of events and venues.

A Key Figure

One of the key figures in the contemporary art scene is Juana de Aizpuru, who runs galleries in Seville and Madrid and shows painting, sculpture, and photography by leading Spanish and international figures. Her artists include Sol LeWitt, Mike Kelley, Albert Oehlen, and Franz West, as well as Spanish photographers Alberto García Alix and Cristina García Rodero.

Juana de Aizpuru's greatest contribution to the Spanish art scene, however, was setting up ARCO (Parque Ferial Juan Carlos I, tel 91 722 5800), Madrid's contemporary art fair, in 1982. By inviting leading artists, gallerists, and collectors from all over the world, the fair opened up the Spanish art market. In its early

The Writing on the Wall

Madrid's walls bear the marks of spray paint, stencils, and indelible markers—a rich (but illegal) collaboration among countless artists. Graffiti, from the Italian word *graffio* (to scratch), abounds in European metropoli. While street art is not "embraced" by the authorities, per se, it is tolerated more than in the United States. To dismiss it as mere vandalism is shortsighted. From the cave paintings of Lascaux through the political fliers outside the Sorbonne in Paris, anonymous art has a strong bearing on human history.

The world of fine art was introduced to street art in the 1980s, when New York artists like Jean-Michel Basquiat and Keith Haring brought graffiti to the gallery world. Three decades later you are just as likely to see photorealistic murals on the street corners of major cities as vulgar scribbles matted and framed on gallery walls.

In Madrid, artists with monikers like El Muelle, Sex, Done, Glub, and the Pornostars have added an undeniable vibrancy to the art scene for years. The most graffiti is found in the outskirts of the city, along main roads and train tracks. However, it sprouts up just about anywhere. The problem is, unless the street art is sanctioned (this occurs rarely), it is only a matter of time before it is painted over. This brevity is good for the culture, however, because it provides an impetus for constant productivity and reinvention. Many of the pieces are politicized, and their existence provokes discussion over public space, private property, and the braid of creation and destruction.

years, ARCO gained a reputation as a "fun" art fair. While this undoubtedly attracted audiences, it was only when the fair was put on a more professional footing in the 1990s that sales started to increase. It takes place for a week every year in February and is now an essential event for anyone in the European contemporary art world.

Where To Go

The main areas for galleries are Chueca, Chamberí, the lower blocks crossing Calle Claudio Coello in the Salamanca district, and the streets around the Museo Reina Sofía, particularly Calle Doctor Fourquet. The galleries in each area coordinate their opening evenings, which are detailed on leaflets available in the galleries. If your stay coincides with one of these dates, when galleries are open until midnight, it is an entertaining way to see Madrid's art world at play.

In Chueca, one of the most interesting galleries is Moriarty (*Calle Libertad 22, tel 91 531 4365*), which started in 1981 by showing work from artists emerging from Madrid's cultural explosion, a phenomenon that became known as *la movida madrileña*. The gallery still represents key figures from the movement, but shows work by renowned international artists, too.

Soledad Lorenzo, a revered figure in the art world, always has excellent exhibitions at her large space in Chamberí, a few blocks north of Chueca. The gallery (*Calle Orfila 5, tel 91 308 2887*) shows work by Spanish artists of the caliber of Miquel Barceló, José María Sicilia, and Guillermo Pérez Villalta, as well as international artists, including Julian Schnabel.

The area around the Reina Sofía looks set to become a bustling gallery area. The opening of Jean Nouvel's extension to the museum has helped to consolidate the area as Madrid's contemporary art hub, a situation that has been strengthened by the new CaixaForum space nearby, which opened in 2008 (see p. 154).

Plaza de Toros de las Ventas

Las Ventas is the largest bullring in Spain and the second biggest in the world after the one in Mexico City. Dubbed the "Cathedral of Bullfighting," the ring opened in 1934 and holds almost 24,000 spectators. Bullfights are held from March to October, and the spectacular setting is also occasionally used for concerts, opera, and theatrical performances.

Thousands of spectators pour into Las Ventas in the early evening to attend a bullfight.

Designed by José Espeliú, the red-brick structure is a good example of neo-Mudejar architecture, with horseshoe arches and ceramic decoration featuring the coats of arms of all the provinces in Spain. Outside the ring there is a monument to Dr. Alexander Fleming, whose discovery of penicillin saved many bullfighters' lives.

The arena, which has a diameter of 200 feet (60 m), is surrounded by ten sections of seats, divided into stands, boxes, and upper galleries. The ticket prices, which range from $2 to $300, are based on whether the seat is in the sun or the shade and its proximity to the action. The cheapest, therefore, are in the sun in the upper galleries, while the most expensive are in the shade and either in the boxes or in the rows close to the ring. Stand 7, in the sun, is notorious for having the most critical fans, who sing and chant throughout the fight.

The band sits in Box 29 and only plays at the end, when the bull has been killed. The Royal Box is painted white, with intricate arabesque decoration, and has its own elevator and bathroom.

The key figure at a bullfight is the Presidente, who is usually a chief of police and orchestrates proceedings from the presidential box, advised by two experts. If a bullfighter has performed very well, he may be awarded one or two of the bull's ears; for a superlative fight, he receives the tail. The Presidente signals this by waving a white handkerchief. When the crowd thinks the bullfighter deserves an ear, they will shout and wave handkerchiefs. If they are sufficiently vociferous, the Presidente is obliged to bow to their wishes. A bullfighter awarded two ears may be carried by his team through the gateway known as the Puerta Grande,

used only for this purpose.

If you are not attending a bullfight but want to take the guided tour or visit the museum, enter via the **Patio de Caballos** on the east side of the ring. This is where the horses are kept, and there is also a Mexican-style chapel, where the matadors, dressed in their suits of lights, pray before going into the ring. Next to it is a surgery with two operating theaters.

The fascinating **Museo Taurino** contains portraits with information in English that gives the background of important matadors and explains how each one contributed to bullfighting. The museum has a series of engravings by Goya from 1814–1816, based on a letter about the origin and development of bullfighting. Other exhibits include the bloodstained suit of lights worn by the famous bullfighter Manolete, who was gored to death in 1947. ■

Plaza de Toros de las Ventas
- 🗺 Map p. 175
- ✉ Calle Alcalá 237
- ☎ 91 356 2200. Ticket sales: 90 215 0025
- 🕐 Closed Nov.–Feb.
- Ⓜ Metro: Las Ventas

Museo Taurino
- ☎ 91 725 1857
- 🕐 Closed Mon., Sat., & daily p.m.
- 💲 Guided tours: $$

www.las-ventas.com

EXPERIENCE: Burial of the Sardine

On Ash Wednesday mourners gather to bid farewell to a close friend. Some are weeping, some drunk; all are dressed in black. This doesn't appear odd until you get closer to the funeral procession and realize that the deceased is, well, a sardine. A trip to Madrid during Carnaval isn't complete without witnessing the famous Burial of the Sardine.

How it all began, like most Spanish traditions, is wedged somewhere between apocrypha and rumor. Some say that the burial of fish has religious connotations; others believe that the dead sardine is a symbol of their personal sacrifices. But there is a historical basis.

During the reign of King Carlos III a shipment

of sardines arrived in Madrid for Lent. When the containers were opened, it was discovered that the fish were rotting. Indignant, the king ordered them buried and Madrid endured Lent without sardines. We may never know how this event transformed into a festival, but it's been going on for a long time. Goya even

documented the festivities with his "Burial of the Sardine" painting.

To partake of the ritual, be at the Alegre Cofradia de la Sardinai (the Happy Brotherhood of the Sardine) headquarters at Calle Rodrigo de Guevara 4 (in La Latina) around 6 p.m. You'll know you're at the right place by the fish on the door.

More Places to Visit in La Castellana & Salamanca

Museo Casa de la Moneda

The museum at Spain's Royal Mint, which produces coins and stamps, charts the development of the institution from its origins in the 18th century. The displays detail the different kinds of money used over the centuries, and the coin collection includes Greek, Roman, Visigothic, and Moorish examples. Other sections deal with stamps and lottery tickets, and there is a section on tools and machinery. Coin collectors can purchase the latest issues. www.fnmt.es 🅜 Map p. 175 ✉ Calle Doctor Esquerdo 36 ☎ 91 566 6544 🕐 Closed Sat. & Sun. p.m. & Mon. 🚇 Metro: Goya, O'Donnell

Museo de Escultura al Aire Libre de la Castellana

Under the Juan Bravo overpass on the Paseo de la Castellana are several sculptures by leading Spanish artists of the 20th century. The engineers of the overpass worked with artist Eusebio Sempere to make the most of this rather inhospitable outdoor space. But despite its limitations, the space now contains works by such sculptors as Joan Miró, Julio González, Pablo Palazuelo, and Martín Chirino. The highlights are Eduardo Chillida's suspended sculpture "Stranded Mermaid" and Andreu Alfaro's steel "A World for Children." www .munimadrid.es/museoairelibre 🅜 Map p. 175 ✉ Paseo de la Castellana 41 ☎ 91 588 8672 🚇 Metro: Rubén Darío

Museo de la Ciudad

Madrid's development from its origins to the present day is charted in this modern museum. The Museum of the City contains reconstructions of important buildings and models of key places in the city's history, such as the Palacio Real, Plaza de la Villa, Paseo de la Castellana, and the Las Ventas bullring. For the infrastructure aficionado, one floor of the museum is devoted to the running of Madrid, with displays on the city's public transportation, electricity distribution, and sewer and water supply systems. Another floor deals with Madrid's varied and rich history. www.muni madrid.es 🅜 Map p. 175 ✉ Calle Príncipe de Vergara 140 ☎ 91 588 6599 🕐 Closed Sat. & Sun. p.m. & Mon. 🚇 Metro: Cruz del Rayo

Museo Geominero

More than 6,000 fossils and 3,500 minerals are featured in the permanent displays at this museum dedicated to geology and mining. The collections are housed in the Escuela Superior de Ingenieros de Minas, which was designed by Ricardo Velázquez Bosco and is decorated with ceramic friezes, arches, columns, and statues. Ask at the museum's entrance if you can also take a look at the building's magnificent Gothic-style library. www.igme.es 🅜 Map p. 175 ✉ Calle Ríos Rosas ☎ 23 91 349 5759 🕐 Closed p.m. 🚇 Metro: Ríos Rosas

Abstract sculptures by 20th-century artists enliven the space beneath the Juan Bravo flyover.

Spotted with grandiose Franco-era architecture and festooned with leafy parkland tumbling toward the Río Manzanares

Plaza de España & Western Madrid

Suits of armor at the Museo Cerralbo

Plaza de España & Western Madrid

The area west of Plaza de España has a distinctive character, quite different from that of the dense downtown streets. Here you can easily see how Madrid is set higher than the surrounding countryside, with clear views to the Guadarrama Mountains in the northwest. The breeze from the mountains, together with the proximity to the river, cools the air and reduces pollution, making this a popular residential area.

Plaza de España is flanked on two sides by signature skyscrapers that testify to Franco's illusions of grandeur. Back in the 18th century, the hill to the east of the square was earmarked as the site for the new royal palace. The idea never came to fruition, and instead of a palace, a huge barracks, the Cuartel del Conde Duque, was built between 1714 and 1720 on the hill, which is now a cultural center.

Calle de la Princesa leads off Plaza de España toward Argüelles, an area developed in the second half of the 19th century. The stretch between the Argüelles and Moncloa metro stations is lined with shops, which suddenly give way to the huge redbrick complex of the headquarters of the Spanish Air Force. Beyond this is a triumphal arch, the Arco de la Victoria, built to commemorate Franco's victory in the Civil War.

The futuristic Faro de Madrid (Faro observation tower) is located just in front of the Museo de América, one of Madrid's most important museums, which has outstanding collections from the different cultures of Latin America. A short walk away is the Museo del Traje, which is an excellent new museum devoted to all aspects of fashion and clothing over the centuries.

Beyond Plaza de España to the northwest is the leafy oasis of the Parque del Oeste. Now a pleasant place to stroll or picnic, the park has a dark past as the scene of wartime fighting. A cable car links it to the Casa de Campo park across the river, with its zoo and amusement park. ∎

CAMINO ZARZÓN

Zoo Aquarium

0   400 meters
0   400 yards

Casa de Campo

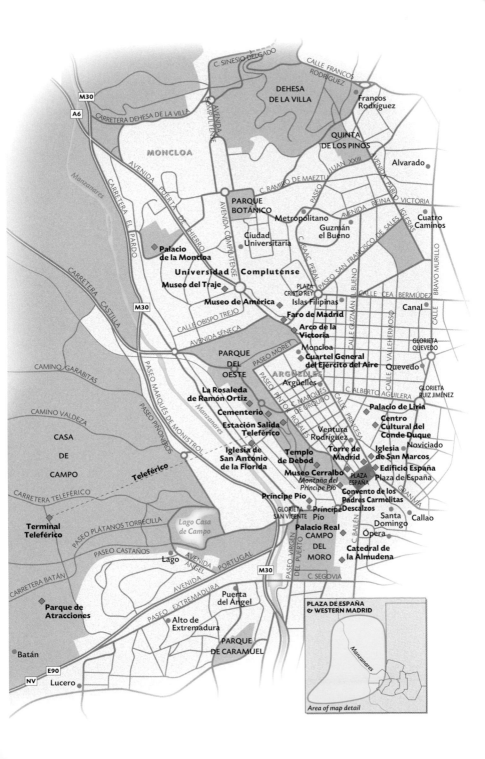

M30
A6
C. SINESIO DELGADO
CALLE FRANCOS RODRIGUEZ
DEHESA DE LA VILLA
Francos Rodriguez
CARRETERA DEHESA DE LA VILLA
QUINTA DE LOS PINOS
MONCLOA
JUAN XXIII
Alvarado
AVENIDA PABLO IGLESIA
C. RAMIRO DE MAEZTU
AVENIDA REINA VICTORIA
PARQUE BOTÁNICO
Metropolitano
Guzmán el Bueno
Cuatro Caminos
Palacio de la Moncloa
Ciudad Universitaria
Universidad Complutense
PASEO SAN FRANCISCO DE SALES
CALLE ISAAC PERAL
BRAVO MURILLO
Museo del Traje
PLAZA CRISTO REY
CALLE CEA BERMÚDEZ
Museo de América
Islas Filipinas
Canal
CARRETERA CASTILLA
Faro de Madrid
CALLE GUZMÁN EL BUENO
M30
Arco de la Victoria
CALLE VALLEHERMOSO
GLORIETA QUEVEDO
CALLE OBISPO TREJO
Moncloa
Quevedo
AVENIDA SÉNECA
PARQUE DEL OESTE
Cuartel General del Ejército del Aire
CAMINO GARABITAS
PASEO MORET
ARGÜELLES
Argüelles
GLORIETA RUIZ JIMÉNEZ
CAMINO VALDEZA
La Rosaleda de Ramón Ortiz
C. ALBERTO AGUILERA
Palacio de Liria
CASA DE CAMPO
Cementerio
Centro Cultural del Conde Duque
Estación Salida Teleférico
Ventura Rodríguez
Noviciado
Teleférico
Iglesia de San Antonio de la Florida
Torre de Madrid
Iglesia de San Marcos
Templo de Debod
CALLE PRINCESA
Museo Cerralbo
Edificio España
Plaza de España
Montaña del Príncipe Pío
PLAZA ESPAÑA
GRAN VÍA
Terminal Teleférico
Príncipe Pío
Convento de los Padres Carmelitas Descalzos
Santa Domingo
Callao
GLORIETA SAN VICENTE
Príncipe Pío
Palacio Real
Ópera
PASEO PLÁTANOS TORRECILLA
Lago Casa de Campo
CAMPO DEL MORO
C. BAILÉN
Catedral de la Almudena
CARRETERA TELEFÉRICO
PASEO CASTAÑOS
Lago
AVENIDA ÁNGEL
AVENIDA PORTUGAL
PASEO VIRGEN DEL PUERTO
M30
C. SEGOVIA
CARRETERA BATÁN
Parque de Atracciones
AVENIDA EXTREMADURA
Puerta del Ángel
Alto de Extremadura
PLAZA DE ESPAÑA & WESTERN MADRID
Batán
E90
NV
Lucero
PARQUE DE CARAMUEL
Manzanares
Area of map detail

Plaza de España

The space now occupied by Plaza de España was known as Leganitos Meadow in the 17th century and features in *Don Quijote* by Cervantes. The site was later occupied by a convent, demolished in 1789, and then by a barracks, demolished in 1908. The current plaza took shape in the mid-20th century, after the victory of General Franco's Nationalists in the Civil War. The imposing square was developed as a symbol of national greatness.

In Plaza de España, Cervantes sits behind his magnificent creations Don Quixote and Sancho Panza.

Plaza de España
- Map p. 197
- Metro: Plaza de España

The top of the square along the Gran Vía is dominated by the massive bulk of the **Edificio España,** one of Madrid's signature buildings. Designed by Joaquín and Julián Otamendi, the tiered structure in brick and limestone with neo-baroque decoration has 25 stories and 32 elevators. When it was completed in 1953, it was the tallest building in Spain at 384 feet (117 m).

The revolutionary building was intended to be a self-contained urban complex, containing offices, apartments, restaurants, stores, a hotel, and a rooftop swimming pool. The building was sold in 2005 and an extensive renovation scheme began two years later.

The **Torre de Madrid,** on the west side of the square, became Madrid's tallest building, and the world's tallest concrete structure, when it was built in the 1950s. The work of the Otamendi brothers, measuring 466 feet (142 m) high with 34 stories, it's called the "Giraffe" by Madrileños owing to its tall, slender shape. It was the tallest building in Madrid for four decades until the construction of the Torre Picasso in 1988 (see p. 189).

In the center of the square, there is a **monument to Miguel de Cervantes,** designed and built between 1925 and 1930 by the architects Rafael Martínez Zapatero and Pedro Muguruza, and sculpted by Lorenzo Coullaut Valera. A stone figure of Cervantes, seated and holding a book,

INSIDER TIP:

During Architecture Week in early October, architecture students offer free guided visits to contemporary and traditional buildings not usually open to the public.

—ANNIE BENNETT
National Geographic author

presides over the monument, with bronze figures of Don Quixote on his horse and Sancho Panza on his donkey in front of the great writer.

The mosaic dome at the bottom of the square belongs to the church of the **Convento de los Padres Carmelitas Descalzos.** Designed in 1916, its facade features neo-medieval decoration. ■

Fundación Arquitectura COAM

✉ Piamonte 23
☎ 91 702 4670

www.fundacioncoam .es/semana_ arquitectura

EXPERIENCE: Day at the Races

For an unusual and fun day out, head to the 1930s-style Zarzuela racecourse on a Sunday morning. Located 5 miles (8 km) west of Madrid, it is easy to reach with a free bus service on race day from the center of the city. The tradition of horse racing dates back to the 19th century, when there were popular racetracks in downtown Madrid, and it is now enjoying a resurgence in popularity after falling out of favor at the end of the 20th century.

Even if you know nothing about horse racing, watching the races is an exhilarating experience, particularly if you have placed a small bet—the minimum is just €1. There are two horse racing seasons.

One runs from March to mid-July, and the other from September to November. The races take place from 11 a.m to 2 p.m.

There is an atmosphere of anticipation as the crowds throng around the paddocks before the races, appraising the horses and their riders, who are often some of the most famous jockeys from Spain and abroad.

Have a beer and a sandwich, place a bet or two, and watch the vociferous Madrileños cheer on their horses. The admission is free at this center of attraction, the **Hipodrómo de la Zarzuela** (*Avenida Padre Huidobro A-6, kilometer 8, tel 91 740 0540, www.hipodromodelazarzuela.es; buses leave from Paseo Moret in Moncloa*).

Museo Cerralbo

The Marquis of Cerralbo, Enrique de Aguilera y Gamboa (1845–1922), was an eccentric maverick who led a rich and varied life. As well as being active in politics, he was an avid archaeologist, traveled widely, and collected art and artifacts from all over the world. His palatial home, which reopens in 2009 after restoration, gives an intriguing insight into how the nobility lived in the late 19th and early 20th centuries.

Museo Cerralbo

- Map p. 197
- Calle Ventura Rodríguez 17
- 91 547 3646 or 91 547 3647
- Closed p.m. & Mon.
- $. Free Wed. & Sun.
- Metro: Plaza de España, Ventura Rodríguez

http://museocerral bo.mcu.es

The Marquis's collections include paintings, armor, clocks, swords, ceramics, and archaeological finds, among other items displayed throughout the mansion. Highlights of the painting collection include "The Ecstasy of St. Francis" by El Greco, as well as works by other 17th-century artists including Titian, Tintoretto, Zurbarán, José de Ribera, and Alonso Cano.

As you walk around the second floor, peek into the **bathroom,** which has an enormous marble tub. Separate bathrooms were a luxurious novelty at the time, as running water had only just become available in Madrid. This floor was where the family lived and contains bedrooms, sitting rooms, and a dining room. Perhaps the most surprising is the **music room,** which is dominated by an enormous lamp made of colored Murano glass in the shape of a gondola.

The grand staircase is decorated with the coat of arms of the Cerralbo family as well as 17th-century tapestries. The third floor was used principally for entertaining, and the rooms are correspondingly grander. The exception is the austere, galleried library, which contains 12,000 books. Exhibits on this floor include the armor worn by the second Marquis of Cerralbo in 1592 defending La Coruña against the English fleet led by Francis Drake. The **ballroom** is the most astounding room in the house, with opulent marble, stucco, and silk decoration.

Don't miss the **basement,** which contains a fascinating collection of photographs and memorabilia related to the family's travels and social life. ■

Frescoes representing dance themes decorate the lavish ballroom in the Museo Cerralbo.

Templo de Debod

When the Aswan Dam was built in Lower Nubia in Egypt in the 1960s, many temples and monuments were in danger of being lost in the floodwaters. The Debod temple was actually underwater, visible only when the dam was opened in the summer and the water level dropped. A team of Spanish archaeologists and engineers helped save the temples of Abu Simbel, and in recognition of their efforts this amazing temple was donated to Spain in 1968.

The ancient Debod temple was brought to Spain from the banks of the Nile.

The construction of the temple began at the beginning of the second century B.C. on the orders of King Adikhalamani of Meroë. Various Ptolemaic pharaohs continued the work, building a series of rooms around the original nucleus. After Egypt was annexed to the Roman Empire, the temple was completed by the emperors Augustus, Tiberius, and possibly Hadrian, who added courtyards, the entrance pathway, and a landing quay on the Nile River.

Dedicated to the gods Amun and Isis, the temple contains a series of chapels, the most interesting of which is dedicated to King Adikhalamani. An audio-visual exhibit re-creates the visit of French archaeologist Jean François Champollion in 1829 to decipher its inscriptions.

The red granite *naos* (inner chamber) was built by Ptolemy XII in 80–51 B.C. and was the most sacred place in the temple. According to tradition, the god Amun was believed to live there, and only priests were allowed to enter. Upstairs, a model shows the original location of Abu Simbel and other temples. ■

Templo de Debod
- Map p. 197
- Parque del Oeste, Paseo del Pintor Rosales
- 91 366 7415
- Closed Sat. p.m., Sun. p.m., & Mon.
- Metro: Plaza de España, Ventura Rodríguez

www.munimadrid .es/templodebod

Madrid's Western Parks

Madrid's two western parks form a substantial green space that stretches for miles toward the Guadarrama Mountains. Separated by the Río Manzanares, they have very different characters. The Parque del Oeste is ideal for walks in the fresh air or a picnic on the grass, as it is a shady space with sandy paths leading through landscaped gardens. The Casa de Campo, while wilder with more scrubland, offers cycling, boating, and swimming in huge outdoor pools.

Reindeer at the Zoo-Aquarium live in a spacious enclosure.

Madrid's Western Parks

🗺 Map p. 197

Parque del Oeste

✉ Avenida del Arco de la Victoria & Paseo del Pintor Rosales

🚇 Metro: Moncloa

Parque del Oeste

One of Ernest Hemingway's favorite spots in Madrid, the Parque del Oeste was designed by landscape gardener Cecilio Rodríguez in 1906. Just three decades later, however, it was virtually destroyed during the Civil War and had to be rebuilt in the 1940s. The sloping L-shaped space stretches from Plaza de España up to the university campus in Moncloa and down to the Río Manzanares in the west.

One of the most beautiful parts of the park is **La Rosaleda de Ramón Ortiz,** a rose garden that hosts a competition for the best blooms each spring.

The southern end, toward Plaza de España, is known as the Montaña del Príncipe Pío and is the highest part of the park, with sweeping views across the city. There used to be a large barracks here, near where the Templo de Debod is now (see p. 201), a stronghold of General Franco's

INSIDER TIP:

For the city's best sunsets, head to Parque del Oeste's Templo de Debod. No matter the time of year, the sun always sets behind this ancient Egyptian temple.

—MATT TAYLOR
National Geographic Channel editor

troops at the start of the Civil War. This area is also where 43 Madrileños were executed by French soldiers on May 3, 1808 (see pp. 204–205). The victims are buried in a small **cemetery** in the center of the park, on Calle Francisco y Jacinto Alcántara. The cemetery opens to the public only on May 2 and 3 each year.

There are several sidewalk cafés by the park on the Paseo del Pintor Rosales. They are pleasant places to stop off for a cool drink or ice cream. Near the cafés is the station for the **Teleférico** cable car *(tel 91 541 7450 or 91 541 1118, $),* which will take you over to the Casa de Campo.

More Parks

The **Casa de Campo** was originally a hunting ground, created by Felipe II in the mid-16th century to link his residence at the Alcázar with the hunting lodge at El Pardo (see p. 232). It became known as the Royal Wood and was extended over the centuries by other monarchs. In the Civil War, Franco's army used this site to attack the city, and trenches still exist in the park.

The recently modernized **Zoo-Aquarium** houses about 6,000 animals on 50 acres (20 ha) of landscaped grounds. The 500 different animal species include gorillas, koalas, and white tigers. The sharks and dolphins are the highlight of the aquarium. Right next to the zoo is the popular **Parque de Atracciones.** This is an amusement park, which includes 40 rides, as well as restaurants and an outdoor arena for summertime concerts. ∎

Casa de Campo
- ✉ Avenida de Portugal
- ☎ 91 479 6002
- 🚇 Metro: Batán, Casa de Campo, Lago. Bus: 33

Zoo-Aquarium
- ✉ Casa de Campo
- ☎ 91 512 3770
- 💲 $$$
- 🚇 Metro: Batán, Casa de Campo. Bus: 33
- www.zoomadrid.com

Parque de Atracciones
- ✉ Casa de Campo
- ☎ 91 463 2900 or 91 463 6433
- 💲 $$$
- 🕐 Closed a.m.
- 🚇 Metro: Batán. Bus: 33, 65
- www.parquedeatracciones.es

Daily Down Time

Visitors to Spain will react to the siesta first with bafflement, then either strong endorsement or frustration. While it is better, biologically speaking, to nap during the day, it also leaves the anxious traveler with several hours of idleness, as most shops and restaurants are shuttered between the hours of 2 p.m. and 5 p.m.

Siestas in one form or another exist in most countries with hot climates, but they are most often associated with Spain. There are several social reasons for the siesta: escaping the heat of the early afternoon, the health benefits of napping, and the fact that family meals occur at this time, in keeping with the dining habits of agrarian societies.

It is worth mentioning that most Spaniards do not use this downtime merely to sleep, choosing instead to eat, relax, or catch up with family and friends. Whatever its local uses, the siesta is a welcome breather for some visitors, and a period of boredom for others.

Patriotic Uprising

May 2 is a public holiday in the Madrid area and marks the start of three weeks of festivities. It is the day when Madrileños celebrate everything that is good about the city, but the events that led to this date of commemoration were anything but happy.

Goya's painting depicting the executions of Madrileños on May 3, 1808, is a haunting image of the brutality of war.

In March 1808, King Carlos IV was out of the country just north of the Pyrenees Mountains in Bayonne, France, with his son Fernando, who wanted his father to abdicate so that he could succeed to the throne. After Manuel Godoy, Carlos's powerful prime minister, was ousted by a popular uprising in Aranjuez (see p. 220) on March 17, the ineffectual Carlos gave in to his son's wishes and Fernando briefly became king.

On March 23, the French army entered Madrid, ostensibly as part of an alliance formed between Carlos IV and Napoleon Bonaparte in order to attack Portugal. Ten thousand soldiers entered the city, with another 20,000 nearby. Fernando was still in Bayonne, where, many Madrileños believed, he was a prisoner. They suspected the entire royal family was planning to flee to France, abandoning them to the Napoleon's troops.

On the morning of May 2, crowds gathered in front of the Palacio Real, as it was rumored that Prince Francisco de Paula, the youngest son of Carlos IV, was leaving Madrid to join his family. As the people became increasingly agitated, French troops started shooting indiscriminately into the crowds, and the situation soon deteriorated into widespread violence.

There were about 8,600 Spanish soldiers in Madrid, most of whom performed ceremonial duties at the Palacio Real and did not have any combat experience. When the trouble began, their commander, Francisco Javier Negrete, ordered his men to remain in their barracks, reasoning that they were underarmed and drastically outnumbered, and therefore unable to resist the French attack. Many managed to escape, however, to fight alongside the citizens of Madrid. A fierce battle took place in the Puerta del Sol, where Madrileños, many of them women, fought against the Mamelukes, a squadron of Egyptian soldiers long renowned for their brutality. The battle was later commemorated by Goya in the painting "The Second of May, 1808, in Madrid: the Charge of the Mamelukes," which is on display in the Prado Museum.

The desperate Madrileños resolved to arm themselves with weapons stored at the Monteleón artillery barracks, located where Plaza Dos de Mayo is now (see p. 107). Two young army captains, Pedro Velarde and Luis Daoíz, took charge of the crowd and armed them with swords. Savage fighting then ensued in the surrounding streets, which led to thousands more French troops being sent to the area to try to gain control of the barracks. Both Velarde and Daoíz died in the battle, in which at least 800 French soldiers were killed.

The French military authorities were incensed at suffering such losses at the hands of a mainly civilian force, and thereby ordered their troops to capture and shoot anyone found on the streets with weapons. These executions were carried out at several locations around the city, but the place that will always be remembered is the Montaña del Príncipe Pío. These shootings, which took place in the early hours of May 3, were depicted by Goya in his seminal painting "The Third of May, 1808, in Madrid: Executions on Príncipe Pío Hill," which is also in the Prado.

Despite their heroic resistance, the Madrileños eventually had to admit defeat. Napoléon installed his brother Joseph as king of Spain, leading to the Spanish War of Independence. The exact number of casualties was never known, but, surprisingly, more French than Spanish died. According to the official figures, about 2,000 French soldiers were killed, but only about 150 Madrileños lost their lives.

The monument built in honor of the citizens of May 2

Ermita de San Antonio de la Florida

This neoclassic church has a rather plain exterior, but often the most unpromising places hold the greatest riches. This is certainly the case here, as the dome is decorated with astonishing frescoes by no less an artist than Francisco de Goya.

Ermita de San Antonio de la Florida

- Map p. 197
- Glorieta de San Antonio de la Florida 5
- 91 542 0722
- Closed Sat p.m., Sun p.m., & Mon.
- Metro: Príncipe Pío

The Greek-cross church, which was designed by Italian architect Filippo Fontana, was completed in 1798. Goya, who was then 52 years old and had become deaf, took only four months to paint the dome. The frescoes depict a miracle said to have been performed by St. Anthony of Padua after his father, Martín de Bulloes, had been accused

of murder. The saint brought the man back from the dead to name the real killer and thereby absolve his father. The scene shows a group of people gathered around a circular railing, using light and color to shape the form of the figures. If you take a look at each of them individually, you will see that they all have very definite and lifelike expressions and features. Some look like rather unsavory characters, while others have kind faces, but above all these are real people, such as you might encounter today.

The church's location so close to the Río Manzanares, together with the perishable paint that Goya used, unfortunately meant that cracks appeared in the walls and the paint gradually deteriorated. In the 1920s, it was decided to try to prevent further damage by building a replica church alongside for everyday parish services. The original building is now also known as the **Museo y Panteón de Goya.** The restoration of the dome frescoes, which did not begin until 1989, was finally completed in 2005, just in time for the popular street festival that takes places every year on the weekend closest to June 13, St. Anthony's day. ∎

Romantic Ritual

On June 13, hundreds of women come to San Antonio de la Florida to take part in a ritual that they hope will improve their romantic prospects for the coming year. The tradition, which was started by seamstresses, involves dropping 13 pins into the font, then putting the palm of your hand on top to see how many stick to it. You do this three times, and the number of pins that stick indicates the number of boyfriends you can expect to come along in the year ahead. Nowadays, women of all ages form a winding line to the font, which is moved to the garden outside the church for the occasion.

Moncloa's Museums

The Moncloa area houses the sprawling campus of the Universidad Complutense, Madrid's main university. Among the facilities are two major museums: one devoted to Spain's former colonies in Latin America and the other to fashion and costume. Also worth visiting is the observation tower known as the Faro de Madrid, which provides panoramic views of the city.

The Museo del Traje displays fashions by leading designers as well as regional costumes.

Museo del Traje

The Museo del Traje, which opened in 2004, has extensive collections of historical costumes and contemporary fashion. The development of clothing is traced from the late 16th century to the present day, with examples of regional costume from all over Spain. One section is devoted to leading Spanish designers from the 20th century, including Mariano Fortuny, Paco Rabanne, and Pertegaz, who designed Letizia Ortiz's dress for her marriage to Crown Prince Felipe in 2004. A room is devoted to Balenciaga, the renowned Basque designer. The textile section includes lace and embroidery, as well as examples of Coptic and Hispano-Muslim designs. The displays are exhibited on a rotating basis to avoid deterioration from excessive exposure to light.

The building, which previously housed the Spanish Museum of Contemporary Art, was designed in the late 1960s by Ángel Díaz Domínguez and Jaime López de Asiaín and won the National Prize

Museo del Traje
- Map p. 197
- Avenida Juan de Herrera 2
- 91 550 4700
- Closed Sun. p.m. & Mon.
- $. Free Sat. p.m. & Sun. a.m.
- Metro: Ciudad Universitaria, Moncloa. Bus: 46, 82, 83, 84, 132, 133

www.museodeltraje.mcu.es

for Architecture. It has a good gift shop, as well as an excellent café and a formal restaurant.

Faro de Madrid

The Faro tower, designed by Salvador Pérez Arroyo in 1992, is 302 feet (92 m) high and is used primarily for telecommunications and traffic supervision. It is also open to visitors, who zoom up to a circular observation deck in a glass elevator. You

the pre-Columbian period to the present day, were either brought to Spain during the centuries of Spanish rule or donated by Latin American governments. The museum is particularly strong on the ancient civilizations of Colombia, Peru, and Mexico.

Although the museum has been open in its current form only since 1994, it has its origins in the 16th century, when Felipe II took steps to found a museum

A sculpture of Aztec goddess Chalchiutlicieis on display in the Museo de América.

Faro de Madrid

- Map p. 197
- Avenida de los Reyes Católicos
- 91 544 8104
- Closed Mon.
- $
- Metro: Moncloa

can see across Madrid with stunning views of the Guadarrama mountains. Information panels on the deck help to identify key buildings around the city.

Museo de América

This museum, which explores the cultures of Spain's former colonies in Latin America, contains unrivaled collections of artworks, ceramics, and weaponry. The exhibits, which range from

for objects brought back from America. In the 18th century, finds from scientific expeditions were added to the collections, which were first exhibited in the Museo Arqueológico Nacional (National Archaeological Museum). Important donations were made to commemorate the fourth centenary of the discovery of America in 1892, including the Quimbayas Treasure from Colombia, one of the highlights of the museum.

INSIDER TIP:

During the festival of San Isidro Labrador in May, Madrileños may walk about wearing traditional local dress. Most will allow you to photograph them.

—TINO SORIANO
National Geographic photographer

The displays are organized in five sections on the second and third floors and are arranged thematically rather than geographically or chronologically. **Area 1** begins with the myths that arose about America in Europe over the centuries, then explains how more accurate information started to come through from Spanish chroniclers and as a result of expeditions. Exhibits include fascinating maps, Amazonian feathered hats, Diquis gold from Costa Rica, and an extraordinary 18th-century feathered cape from Hawaii.

Area 2 covers the geography and landscapes of Latin America then charts how the mix of races and cultures came about from Paleolithic times to the present. Exhibits include letters and logs written by Christopher Columbus.

Area 3 deals with the way different indigenous populations, from tribal communities to complex societies, organized their everyday lives. Ceremonies to mark rites of passage, such as childbirth, puberty, and marriage, are illustrated by feathered headdresses, jewelry, and ornaments. Exhibits include Olmec jades, Incan objects, ceramics from Ecuador, and basketware by Hopi and Chumash

Indians. This section continues on the next floor, where there is a reconstruction of a Maya house.

Some of the most precious pieces in the museum are in **Area 4,** which focuses on religion. There are rooms devoted to funeral rites, fertility symbols, and sacred objects. A highlight is the limestone **Madrid Stele,** which dates from A.D. 600–800 and shows a Maya god. Inscribed with hieroglyphs, the stone originally supported a throne in the palace in Palenque, Mexico. It was found in 1785 by archaeologist Antonio del Río, who was sent to excavate the ruined palace by Carlos III.

Also here is the amazing pre-Columbian **Quimbayas Treasure,** which Colombia would now like to have back in its own country. Discovered in 1819, the 125 objects in the Treasure include crowns, musical instruments, and figures of caciques, mainly in gold and silver. They date from A.D. 500–1000.

The final section, **Area 5,** explores the themes of language and communication. The key exhibit is the **Tro-Cortesian codex,** one of only four Maya manuscripts in the world, thought to date from the 15th century. It comprises 56 pages covered with scenes from Maya life as well as hieroglyphs that link activities such as harvesting and hunting to specific dates. It is packed with religious and magical references.

Also of great interest is the 16th-century **Tudela codex,** which was made at an art school of Franciscan monks in Mexico. Its 125 pages contain paintings by an indigenous artist and texts in Spanish written by a missionary. ■

Museo de América

- Map p. 197
- Avenida de los Reyes Católicos 6
- 91 549 2641 or 91 543 9437
- Closed p.m. & Mon.
- $. Free Sun.
- Metro: Islas Filipinas, Moncloa

www.museodeame rica.mcu.es

More Places to Visit in Plaza de España & Western Madrid

Centro Cultural del Conde Duque

Originally the barracks for the Royal Guard, this massive building was designed by Pedro de Ribera in 1717. It has been extensively restored and refurbished for its current use as a lively exhibition center and concert venue. It also houses the Municipal Museum of Contemporary Art, which has rotating displays of works by artists including Ouka Leele, Ceesepe, and Javier de Juan. www.munimadrid.es/condeduque Map p. 197 ✉ Calle Conde Duque 9–11 ☎ 91 588 5928 or 91 588 5861 🕐 Closed Sun. p.m. & Mon. 🚇 Metro: Noviciado, Plaza de España, San Bernardo, Ventura Rodríguez

Cuartel General del Ejercito del Aire

The vast headquarters of the Spanish Air Force were designed in the 1940s by Luis Gutiérrez Soto, who was advised by Hitler's architect, Albert Speer. With its granite and redbrick facade, slate roofs, and slender spires, it emulates the Habsburg architecture of the 17th century. General Franco wanted to create a style for the architecture of his dictatorship that would link him to Spain's period of greatest splendor, and this building certainly reflects his desire for architectural grandeur. 🗺 Map p. 197 ✉ Calle Romero Robledo 8 ☎ 91 549 0700 🚇 Metro: Moncloa

Iglesia de San Marcos

Designed by Ventura Rodríguez in the mid-18th century, the interior of this elegant church features five overlapping ellipses, a device used to overcome the problem of the narrow building site. It was constructed to commemorate the victory of Felipe V at the Battle of Almansa in 1707. The dome is decorated with frescoes by Luis González Velázquez, and there is a polychrome figure of St. Mark by Juan Pascual de Mena on the altarpiece. 🗺 Map p. 197 ✉ Calle San Leonardo 10 ☎ 91 547 1079 🚇 Metro: Plaza de España, Ventura Rodríguez

The Palacio de Liria was built in the 18th century for the third Duke of Berwick.

Palacio de Liria

The Palacio de Liria, which is the home of the Duchess of Alba, was designed by Ventura Rodríguez and Sabatini in the second half of the 18th century. After being damaged by fire in the Civil War, it was restored by Sir Edwin Lutyens. The palace was built for Jacobo (James) Fitz-James Stuart, the third Duke of Berwick. It contains an impressive art collection, including works by such major painters as Rembrandt, Titian, El Greco, Velázquez, and Goya. Unfortunately, the palace is open to the public only by reservation, and viewing is strictly limited. 🗺 Map p. 197 ✉ Calle de la Princesa 20 ☎ 91 547 5302 🕐 Guided tours Fri. a.m. 🚇 Metro: Ventura Rodríguez

Medieval towns, royal palaces, venerable monasteries, and the incomparable city of Toledo

Excursions

The fairy-tale castle of the Alcázar in Segovia

Excursions

There is a huge variety of places to visit around Madrid, and most of them are easy to reach in an hour or so, whether by public transportation or by car. You can choose from historic sites such as Toledo, El Escorial, Segovia, or Aranjuez for your excursion or go for a more leisurely look around the countryside, with a break for a hearty lunch at a traditional restaurant.

Río Tagus almost encircles the old town of Toledo, protecting it from invaders.

There are good train and bus services in and out of Madrid, but a car is useful if you want to combine several places in one day. For many first-time visitors to Madrid, Toledo is the essential day out. After the largely 19th-century appearance of central Madrid, the wealth of medieval monuments lining the narrow lanes of Toledo is quite a contrast. Also high on most people's lists is the massive 16th-century monastery at El Escorial, which encapsulates the spirit of the Habsburg realm.

Nearer Madrid, the university town of Alcalá de Henares is packed with fascinating monuments and is famous as the birthplace of writer Miguel de Cervantes. After a few days in the hectic, noisy capital, however, you may just feel like driving south of Toledo across the plains of La Mancha to see some of the places mentioned in *Don Quixote*. Or, for an even quieter getaway, you can head up to the hills in the Sierra de Guadarrama for a hike through the pine forests in the pure mountain air. ∎

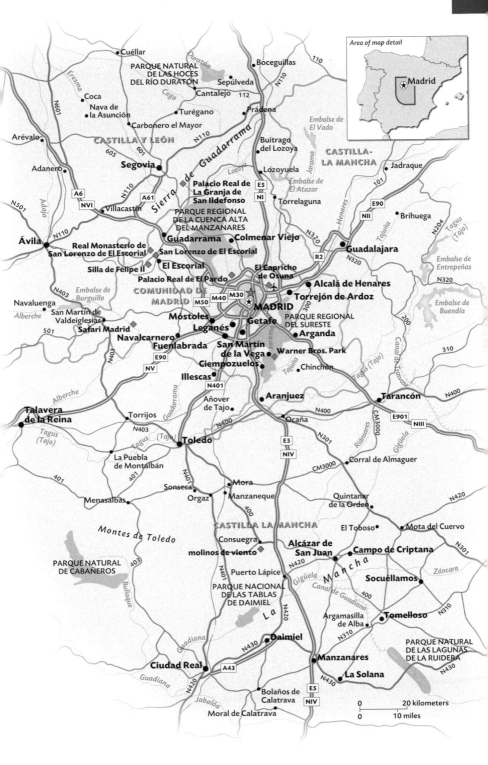

Area of map detail

Madrid

Cuéllar
Boceguillas
110
PARQUE NATURAL
DE LAS HOCES
DEL RÍO DURATÓN
Sepúlveda
N110
Duratón
Cantalejo 112
Coca
Cega
Prádena
Nava de
la Asunción
Turégano
Carbonero el Mayor
N601
Eresma
CASTILLA Y LEÓN
605
Arévalo
N110
601
Segovia
Sierra de Guadarrama
Embalse de
El Vado
Buitrago
del Lozoya
CASTILLA-
LA MANCHA
Jadraque
Adanero
N110
N110
N501
Adaja
Lozoyuela
Lozoya
Embalse de
El Atazar
101
A6
A61
Palacio Real de
La Granja de
San Ildefonso
E5
NI
Torrelaguna
E90
Brihuega
NVI
Villacastín
NII
N204
Ávila
N110
PARQUE REGIONAL
DE LA CUENCA ALTA
DEL MANZANARES
Henares
Tajuña
Tagus
(Tajo)
Real Monasterio de
San Lorenzo de El Escorial
Guadarrama
San Lorenzo de El Escorial
Colmenar Viejo
N320
Guadalajara
Embalse de
Entrepeñas
Silla de Felipe II
El Escorial
R2
N320
N320
Palacio Real de El Pardo
El Capricho
de Osuna
Embalse de
Burguillo
COMUNIDAD DE
MADRID
Alcalá de Henares
Embalse de
Buendía
N403
MADRID
M50 M40 M30
300
Navaluenga
San Martín de
Valdeiglesias
MADRID
Torrejón de Ardoz
Alberche
501
Safari Madrid
Móstoles
Leganés
Getafe
PARQUE REGIONAL
DEL SURESTE
Canal de Estremera
Navalcarnero
San Martín
de la Vega
Arganda
310
N403
Fuenlabrada
E90
Ciempozuelos
Warner Bros. Park
Tajuña
Chinchón
Tajo (Tajo)
200
NV
Illescas
N401
Guadarrama
Añover
de Tajo
Aranjuez
Tarancón
N400
Talavera
de la Reina
Torrijos
N403
Tajo (Tajo)
Ocaña
N400
N301
E901
NIII
Tagus
(Tajo)
CM3000
Toledo
E5
NIV
CM3000
Corral de Almaguer
N400
N420
La Puebla
de Montalbán
Riánsares
Gigüela
401
N401
Sonseca
Mora
Quintanar
de la Orden
Menasalbas
Orgaz
Manzaneque
400
N420
Montes de Toledo
CASTILLA LA MANCHA
El Toboso
Mota del Cuervo
Consuegra
Alcázar de
San Juan
Campo de Criptana
N301
PARQUE NATURAL
DE CABAÑEROS
403
molinos de viento
Mancha
Záncara
Puerto Lápice
Gigüela
Socuéllamos
N401
PARQUE NACIONAL
DE LAS TABLAS
DE DAIMIEL
Canal de Guadiana
400
Bullaque
La
N420
Argamasilla
de Alba
Tomelloso
N310
Daimiel
N430
N310
PARQUE NATURAL
DE LAS LAGUNAS
DE LA RUIDERA
Guadiana
Ciudad Real
A43
Manzanares
N430
Guadiana
N420
N430
La Solana
Jabalón
Bolaños de
Calatrava
E5
NIV
Moral de Calatrava
0   20 kilometers
0   10 miles

Toledo

One of Spain's great historic cities, Toledo is spectacularly situated on a granite hill, almost surrounded by the Río Tagus. Its winding lanes are particularly atmospheric in the evening when the tourist buses have departed, making an overnight stay a rewarding experience if you have time. There is a tremendous amount to see—the entire city center has National Monument status—so plan carefully if you have only one day.

Toledo presents a dramatic profile when twilight falls and the church towers stand out against the backlit sky.

Toledo

- Map p. 213
- 44 miles (71 km) S of Madrid
- By car: via M-40 & A-42. By train: AVE high-speed service, & others, from Atocha station. By bus: Continental Auto from Estación Sur

Inhabited since prehistoric times and settled by the Romans, Toledo became the capital of Visigothic Spain in A.D. 554. When the Moors arrived in 712, they allowed the Christian and Jewish communities to remain in the city and carry on their lives as usual, creating a flourishing trading and cultural center. After Alfonso VI gained control in 1085, Toledo became the capital of the kingdom of Castile and León. The three cultures continued to prosper and played an important role in the development of the Western world, particularly in the fields of astronomy, mathematics, medicine, music, and literature.

The Christian rulers gradually became less tolerant, however, and the Jews began to be persecuted and were eventually expelled in 1492. This was disastrous for the economy, and the situation worsened when Felipe II transferred the court permanently to Madrid in 1561. It was shortly after this, in 1577, that the Greek painter El Greco arrived in Toledo, living through the city's decline until his death in 1614. In the same year, the final Muslim descendants were expelled, which severely affected the manufacturing industry.

The Sights

Standing in the heart of the city, the extraordinary **Catedral** was begun in 1226 and completed in 1493, standing on the site of a sixth-century temple founded by the Visigoths. The intricately carved choir stalls include battle scenes from the conquest of Granada. The altarpiece is a flamboyant Gothic polychrome carving of the life of Christ. In the ambulatory behind the altar is the astounding Transparente (1732), which was designed by Narciso Tomé to allow light to penetrate from the ceiling and consists of marble figures from the Last Supper amid a riot of

INSIDER TIP:

Toledo is famous for
its jewelry, swords,
and winding streets.
But also try the city's
specialty—marzipan
(*mazapán* in Spanish).

—SHOSHANA COHEN
National Geographic contributor

angels and saints. The Treasury
contains a superb 16th-century
monstrance by Enrique del Arfe.
There are several paintings by
El Greco in the **museum,** as well
as works by Titian, Velázquez,
and Goya.

Great Works of Art

West of the Catedral is a cluster
of monuments including the
Iglesia de Santo Tomé *(Plaza del
Conde, tel 925 256 098, $),* which
houses El Greco's masterpiece
"The Burial of the Count of
Orgaz." Nearby is the **Museo
de El Greco** *(Calle Samuel Leví,
tel 925 224 405, closed until 2010
for restoration),* which contains a
good collection of his paintings,
including "View and Map of
Toledo" (circa 1614).

Opposite is the Sinagoga del
Tránsito (Synagogue of the Transit),
which is now the **Museo Sefardí.**
Built in the mid-14th century for
Samuel ha-Leví, who was treasurer
to Pedro el Cruel of Castile, the
interior features bands of Hebrew
calligraphy and a spectacular
cedarwood-coffered ceiling. The
fascinating museum traces the
history and culture of Sephardic
Jews over the centuries.

The Moors built the **Sinagoga
de Santa María la Blanca** *(Calle de
los Reyes Católicos 4, tel 925 227 257,
$)* for Jews in Christian times at the
end of the 12th century. The white
interior looks more like a mosque
than a synagogue, with aisles
divided by horseshoe arches.

A little farther down the road is
the **Monasterio de San Juan de
los Reyes,** built for the Catholic
Monarchs in the late 15th century.
The church was designed by Juan
Guas and combines Gothic,
Mudejar, and Renaissance features.
The cloister has delicate filigree
carvings, with a Mudejar ceiling on
the upper gallery.

An Ancient Beauty

At the top of the hill, east of
the Catedral, stands the massive
Alcázar, which dates from the
11th century but has often been
rebuilt. A Nationalist stronghold
during the Civil War, it was
relentlessly besieged by the
Republicans. When the restoration is completed, the building
will house the Museo de Ejército
(Army Museum), which will be
transferred from Madrid.

Nearby is the busy **Plaza de
Zocodover,** which was a cattle
market under the Arabs before
Juan de Herrera remodeled it
in the 16th century. Just off the
square through an arch is the **Museo de Santa Cruz** *(Calle Cervantes
3, tel 925 221 036),* a beautiful Renaissance structure that Cardinal
Mendoza founded as an orphan-
age in the 16th century. Now a
museum of art and archaeology, it
contains paintings by El Greco and
Goya as well as Roman mosaics,
ceramics, and tapestries. ∎

Visitor Information

- ✉ Puerta de Bisagra
- ☎ 925 220 843
- ✉ Plaza del
  Consistorio 1
- ☎ 925 254 030
- ✉ Zococentro, Calle
  Sillería 14
- ☎ 925 220 300
- www.toledoweb.org
  www.turismocastill
  alamancha.com

Catedral

- ✉ Calle Cardenal
  Cisneros
- ☎ 92 522 2241
- 🕐 Closed Sun. a.m.
- 💲 Museum, chapter
  house, treasury, &
  choir: $$

Museo Sefardí

- ✉ Calle Samuel Leví
- ☎ 92 522 3665
- 🕐 Closed Sun. p.m.
  & Mon.
- 💲 $. Free Sat. p.m. &
  Sun. a.m.
- www.museosefardi
  .net

Monasterio de San
Juan de los Reyes

- ✉ Calle San Juan de
  los Reyes 2
- ☎ 92 522 3802
- 💲 $

Alcázar

- ✉ Cuesta Carlos V 2
- ☎ 92 522 1673
- 🕐 Closed for
  restoration until
  late 2009

A Walk Around Toledo

This walk takes you through steep, high-walled streets, stopping at intriguing churches, convents, and even a mosque. Toledo is full of fascinating corners, so remember to look down side alleys as you walk around, as well as to gaze up at the tiled balconies and into the plant-filled courtyards.

Toledo's Catedral is a superb example of Spanish Gothic architecture.

From **Plaza de Zocodover,** walk down busy Calle Comercio, Toledo's main shopping street. When you reach a crossroad, continue down the hill along Calle del Hombre de Palo, then bear left down Calle Arco del Palacio and walk through the arch to reach the main door of the **Catedral** ❶ (see p. 214).

Walk up the steps to the left of the Palacio **Arzobispal** (Archbishop's Palace) opposite, which lead to the pretty **Plaza del Consistorio.** Make a sharp right and walk up Cuesta del Ordenal. At the top, turn right and immediately left into the narrow Callejón de Jesús María. At the top turn right, where you will see the imposing baroque facade of **San Ildefonso.** Turn left beside the church into Calle de San Román, which leads to the **Iglesia de San Román** ❷; the entrance is around the corner on Calle San Clemente. Originally a Visigoth church, this structure is Mudejar and was built in the

NOT TO BE MISSED:

Catedral • Iglesia de San Román • Convento de Santo Domingo el Antiguo • Mezquita del Cristo de la Luz

12th century. Inside there are Roman columns, Caliphal arches, Romanesque frescoes, and a Plateresque chapel. It now houses a museum of Visigothic culture, the **Museo de los Concilios y de la Cultura Visigoda** *(tel 925 227 872, closed Sun. p.m. & Mon.).*

On leaving the church, continue down Calle de San Román and turn left at the bottom into Plaza de Padilla. Cross the square diagonally to descend the steps, then turn right to skirt the **Convento de Santo Domingo el Antiguo** ❸ (tel 925 222 930, closed Sun. a.m.). This was Toledo's first convent, founded in 1085 by Cistercians, and it is today home to 12 nuns. The church, neoclassic inside, houses the tomb of El Greco and has three of his paintings. Two of these, "St. John the Baptist" and "St. John the Evangelist," are part of the altarpiece; the third, the exceptional "Resurrection of Christ," is on the right. El Greco's tomb is in the crypt, visible through a glass pane in the floor.

Walk down Calle de Santa Leocadia to Plaza Merced, dominated by the grand provincial council building. Turn right up Calle Merced, which becomes a typically narrow, high-sided lane, to Plaza de Capuchinas. Continue up Calle Tendillas and take the first left down Calle Algibes. This brings you to the baroque facade of **Santo Domingo el Real ④**, one of several convents on the square. Walk through the *cobertizo* (covered passageway), turn right up another, and

continue along Calle Santa Clara until you skirt the apse of the 13th-century Mudejar **Iglesia de San Vicente.**

Turn left onto Calle de los Alfileritos, and then take the third lane on your left, Calle del Cristo de la Luz. This brings you to the **Mezquita del Cristo de la Luz ⑤** (tel 92 525 4191, $), a stunning mosque dating from A.D. 999.

Continue through the arch and down the steps. Turn right and immediately left onto Calle Real de Arrabal, which leads to the Gothic-Mudejar **Iglesia Santiago de Arrabal ⑥**, built in the 13th century. Just beyond the church is the **Puerta de Bisagra,** the city's main gate.

⚑	See area map p. 213
▶	Plaza de Zocodover
↔	2.6 miles (4.2 km)
⏱	2 to 3 hours
▶	Puerta de Bisagra

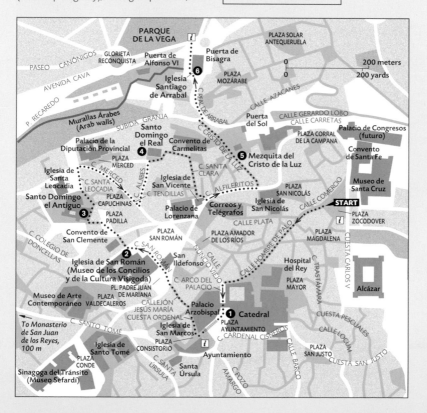

Don Quixote Country

It is four centuries since *El ingenioso hidalgo Don Quijote de la Mancha* (usually known to English-speaking readers as *Don Quixote*) was published in 1605. Written by Miguel de Cervantes (1547–1616), this great novel is set in the vast area south of Toledo, parts of which remain remarkably wild to this day. Don Quixote rides across this landscape with his faithful squire, Sancho Panza, encountering an array of colorful characters along the way.

A newly married couple prepares for a set of wedding photographs at lovely Campo de Criptana.

Don Quixote Country

🗺 Map p. 213

✉ 50–100 miles (80–160 km) S of Madrid

www.donquijotedela mancha2005.com

El Toboso

Visitor Information

✉ Calle Daoiz y Velarde 3

☎ 925 568 226

www.eltoboso.org

Think of Don Quixote, and images of castles, plains, and windmills spring immediately to mind. If you drive southeast from Toledo, you soon pass by a string of castles at Almonacid de Toledo, Mascaraque, Mora, Manzaneque, and the pretty village of Orgaz. Nearby is **Tembleque,** where Sancho Panza worked before joining Don Quixote on his quest to make the world—or at least La Mancha—a better place. Tembleque has a lovely town square, with wooden balconies and granite arcades.

To the east, amid a landscape of lakes and oak forests, is the village of **Villacañas,** founded by the Knights of the Order of St. John in the 13th century. Some inhabitants still live in underground caves. With lakes on either side of the road, you soon come to **Campo de Criptana,** where windmills stretch across the plains. In Don Quixote's illusory world, the windmills became giants who waved their elongated arms to fend off enemies.

Vineyards cover the fields along the road to **El Toboso,**

which was home to the lovely Dulcinea. Her house has been reconstructed in 16th-century style with typical furnishings of the time and is now a museum. Nearby is the **Museo Cervantino**, with many editions of the book. More windmills dot the landscape around **Mota del Cuervo,** on the road to the village of **Belmonte** to the east, which has an imposing 14th-century castle and whitewashed houses.

Perhaps the most impressive windmills are at **Consuegra,** south of Orgaz. The 11 mills, open to visitors, were used to grind wheat for flour. Each *molino* has a name, and the first one, "Bolero," is a tourist center. One of the most interesting is "Sancho," which has its original 16th-century equipment and still operates during the Saffron Rose Festival every October. From "Vista Alegre," near the fortress at the top of the hill, there are panoramic views across

the plains. "Caballero del Verde Gabán" has been turned into a library, with editions of *Don Quixote* in various languages.

Heading south, you arrive at **Puerto Lápice,** a village mentioned several times in the novel and where a medieval atmosphere still prevails. The landscape changes as you cross the wetlands of the **Parque Nacional de las Tablas de Daimiel,** home to many species of aquatic birds.

Continuing south, you reach **Almagro,** a flourishing town in the 16th and 17th centuries. The well-preserved center revolves around its golden age theater, the **Corral de Comedias,** on the main square, where the International Festival of Classical Theater takes place in July. The arcaded **Plaza Mayor** is one of the most spectacular in Spain. With good restaurants, hotels, and shops, Almagro is a good choice for an overnight stop. ■

Casa-Museo de Dulcinea & Museo Cervantino

🖂 Calle Don Quijote 1, El Toboso

☎ 925 197 288

🕘 Closed Sun. p.m. & Mon.

www.eltoboso.org

Consuegra windmills

Visitor Information

🖂 Cerro Calderico

☎ 925 475 731

www.consuegra.es

Parque Nacional de las Tablas de Daimiel

Visitor Information

☎ 926 693 118

www.aytodaimiel.es

Almagro

Visitor Information

🖂 Plaza Mayor 1

☎ 926 860 717

www.ciudad-almagro .com

EXPERIENCE: Into the Country

We may think of Madrid as a major city, but the geographical area it covers includes much of the surrounding countryside, too. By contrast to the urban experience, there is a range of activities you can do in the open air, including spending time on a farm. Information on rural and active tourism is available from the Madrid Region tourist board *(tel 90 210 0007, www.turismomadrid.es).*

There are several environmental education centers that cater to schoolchildren during the week but welcome adults and families on weekends. At **El Molino de Arriba** *(tel 68 943 2188, www.sierran orte.com/ceampusi),* for example, activities

include bird-watching, mushroom gathering, picking wild berries, and looking for medicinal and aromatic plants, with monitors on hand to show you what to do. At the **Albitana farm school** *(tel 91 815 8783, www.albitana.com),* visitors can help out with the grape or olive harvest, learn how to make sausages or bread, or pick fruit and vegetables.

If you would like to explore the countryside on horseback, the **Centro Hípico de Buitrago** *(tel 91 868 1139, www .sierranorte.com/ch-buitrago)* organizes riding treks of varying duration around the hills of the Sierra Norte to suit all levels and ages.

Aranjuez

With a privileged location between the Río Jarama and Río Tagus, this elegant town developed around an 18th-century royal palace. Aranjuez is also renowned for the delicious strawberries and asparagus that grow in the fertile fields alongside the rivers. The extensive gardens around the palace inspired Joaquín Rodrigo to compose the "Concierto de Aranjuez." A visitor train links the various points of interest.

The Palacio Real's Arab Room reflects a warm Moorish style.

Aranjuez
- Map p. 213
- 30 miles (48 km) S of Madrid
- 90 208 8089
- By car: A-4 (direction: Córdoba) to exit 37, then M-305. By train: C-3 from Atocha station. By bus: AISA & SAMAR from Estación Sur

Visitor Information
- Plaza San Antonio 9
- 91 891 0427
- www.aranjuez.com

The **Palacio Real** (*Plaza de Parejas, tel 91 891 1344, closed Mon., $$*) was originally built as a spring and summer residence for Felipe II, but the structure was largely destroyed by fire in 1655. Felipe V asked **Santiago Bonavía** to design and build a new palace, which reflects the French tastes of the Bourbon monarchy. Highlights include the China Room, lined with porcelain tiles made at Madrid's Buen Retiro factory. Also impressive are the Rococo Throne Room and the Arab Room, inspired by the Alhambra in Granada.

The gardens around the palace are open on Mondays when the buildings are closed. The **Jardín del Príncipe** (Prince's Garden) has 371 acres (150 ha) planted with a surprising variety of trees, many of which grew from seeds brought from the Americas.

Beyond the garden is the **Casa del Labrador,** a mansion built for Carlos IV by Isidro González Velázquez in 1804. The most astounding of the lavish rooms is the **Gabinete de Platino,** where the walls are encrusted with gold, platinum, and bronze. Nearby is the **Museo de Falúas Reales,** a museum of leisure boats used by the royal family. ■

Chinchón

There are not many sights in the quaint little town of Chinchón, but people flock here on weekends to enjoy a hearty lunch at one of the restaurants on the porticoed main square, Plaza Mayor. Wooden balconies surround the irregularly shaped medieval space.

The square has been used for bullfights for the past 500 years, but nowadays they take place only during local festivals in July, August, and October. Concerts and theatrical performances are occasionally staged there, too, including a passion play at Easter. Shops around the square sell the local specialties, which include *anís*, a strong aniseed liquor made at several distilleries around the town, as well as chorizo sausage, garlic, and wine.

The hills around the square are a labyrinth of tiny streets lined with grand mansions displaying coats of arms and huge wooden doors. These include the **Casa de la Cadena** (*Calle de la Tahona*), south of the square, where Felipe V stayed in 1706 during the War of Spanish Succession.

Francisco de Goya's brother Camilo was a priest at the 16th-century **Iglesia de la Asunción** (*Calle Arco de Palacio 9*), just north of Plaza Mayor, which has a paint-

INSIDER TIP:

Many taverns have colorful decors. Ask to photograph them and the lively clientele.

—TINO SORIANO
National Geographic photographer

ing attributed to the artist on the altarpiece. Goya used to visit the town regularly, and he liked to paint in the square. The playwright Lope de Vega also used to come here, as his plays were often staged in a theater in the palace of the Counts of Chinchón. The **Teatro de Lope de Vega** now stands on the site, next to Iglesia de la Asunción.

In the 1960s, Orson Welles stayed in town while filming *Chimes at Midnight* and *The Immortal Story*. Chinchón is still a popular location when a director requires a medieval square. It is not unusual to come across a film crew on a weekday morning. ■

Chinchón
- Map p. 213
- 28 miles (45 km) S of Madrid
- By car: A-3 to Puente de Arganda, then M-311, or A-4 to M-404 turnoff. By bus: La Veloz service 337 from outside Conde de Casal metro station (tel 91 409 7602)

Visitor Information
- Plaza Mayor 6
- 91 893 5323
- www.ciudad-chinchon.com

The Politics of Cheese

Boring food is one of the downsides of life under a fascist dictator. When Franco was in power, he outlawed many types of artisan cheese. He tried to collectivize and increase food production and felt the small dairies simply didn't produce enough to justify their existence. Consequently, some dairies went underground, where cheese was made and distributed on the black market by a few brave individuals. But tragically, many artisans disappeared altogether, taking with them a long and varied list of *quesos Españoles*. Luckily, this ended with dairy industry reforms in the late 1980s. Today, artisan cheeses such as Idiazábal, Valdeón, and Majorero are not only great with wine, but also entirely legal.

Alcalá de Henares

Although it is quick and easy to reach from Madrid, Alcalá de Henares gets relatively few visitors. Ugly industrial development on the outskirts means it looks unpromising as you approach, but there is plenty to see once you venture into the center. Its university was founded in 1499, and Miguel de Cervantes was born here in 1547. Leading Golden Age writers studied here in the 17th century, and their plays were performed at a theater that still exists.

Street actors portray a scene from *Don Quixote*.

Alcalá de Henares

- **Map p. 213**
- 21 miles (34 km) E of Madrid
- By car: A-2/N-2 (direction: Zaragoza). By train: C-1, C-2, & C-7A from Atocha station. By bus: Continental Auto service 233 from Avenida de América station (tel 91 356 2307)

Visitor Information

- Callejón Santa María 1
- 91 889 2694

www.alcalaturismo .com

The theater known as the **Corral de Comedias** (*tel 91 877 1950, www.corraldealcala.com*) is located in Plaza de Cervantes, the main square. Dating from 1601, the theater retains its original layout and has recently undergone restoration. It is used for regular performances of classical plays, as well as for concerts.

The main building of the **University** (*Plaza San Diego, tel 91 885 6487*) is the 16th-century Renaissance-style **Colegio de San Ildefonso**. The **Patio Trilingüe** within the university got its name from the schools of Latin, Greek, and Hebrew that were originally located around the courtyard. The **Capilla de San Ildefonso**, completed in 1510, has a magnificent Mudejar coffered ceiling.

Leading off Plaza de Cervantes is the arcaded **Calle Mayor**. It leads to the **Museo Casa Natal de Cervantes** (*Calle Mayor 48, tel 91 889 9654, closed Mon.*), which is a reconstruction of the house where the great writer was born. Farther along Calle Mayor is the late-Gothic **Catedral Magistral** (*Plaza de los Santos Niños, tel 91 888 0930, closed Sat. & Sun., except during services*), built at the beginning of the 16th century. ∎

Ávila

The walled town of Ávila, at an altitude of 3,609 feet (1,100 m), is a World Heritage Site with panoramic views across the plains. It can be cold in winter, but the rest of the year it is a pleasant place to explore on foot. The medieval center is packed with churches and convents, many of them devoted to St. Teresa, the 16th-century mystic who became one of Spain's patron saints. Traditional restaurants in the town serve Iberian black beef from a local breed of cattle.

The walls, built at the end of the 11th century to fend off the Moors, have 88 cylindrical turrets and 9 gateways. At 39 feet (12 m) high and 10 feet (3 m) thick, they are the most substantial walls in the world, showing the importance of the town after the Christian Reconquest. You can walk around them, a distance of 1.5 miles (2.5 km), starting from the Puerta del Alcázar.

The **Catedral** (*Plaza de la Catedral, tel 92 021 1641*), begun in the 12th century, mixes Romanesque and Gothic styles. There are Plateresque carved stalls in the choir and paintings by Pedro Berruguete and Juan de Borgoña. In the ambulatory, don't miss the tomb of Bishop Alonso de Madrigal, nicknamed "El Tostado" ("the toasted one") for his dark complexion. The **museum** (*$*) in the sacristy contains a monstrance (1571) by Juan de Arfe.

The **Convento de Santa Teresa** (*Plaza de la Santa Teresa*) is a 17th-century structure on the site where St. Teresa's house stood. A chapel in the room where she was born contains sculptures by Gregorio Fernández. The saint spent 27 years at the **Monasterio de la Encarnación** (*Paseo de la Encarnación, closed Tues.*), outside the walls, where a museum contains a reproduction of her cell. ∎

Sweet Drink

A favorite beverage of the young, the *calimocho* is a local drink made by mixing equal parts red wine and cola. Sound unappetizing? The calimocho has won over many a critic. A staple of block parties across Spain, it is thought to have originated from those looking for a light alternative to the *cuba libre* (rum and soda). But beware; whatever calimocho lacks in alcohol content, it makes up for in sugar.

Ávila
- Map p. 213
- 70 miles (113 km) NW of Madrid
- By car: A-6 to Villacastín, then N501. By train: From Chamartín or Atocha stations. By bus: Larrea (tel 91 530 4800) from Estación Sur

Visitor Information
- Plaza Pedro Davila
- 92 021 1387
- **www.avilaturismo.com**

Ávila's 11th-century ramparts still surround the city.

Segovia

With its fairy-tale castle, Roman aqueduct, and strategic location on a limestone ridge between two rivers, Segovia is nothing if not dramatic. Despite its wealth of monuments, however, Segovia is not just a tourist town. It has a lively cultural scene, and historic buildings are being assigned new uses as galleries, museums, and schools. No trip would be complete without a meal of roast lamb or suckling pig at one of the town's excellent restaurants.

Segovia's castle, cathedral, and churches are all built from golden sandstone.

Segovia
- Map p. 213
- 53 miles (85 km) NW of Madrid
- By car: A-6 to Guadarrama, then the direct N603, scenic N601, or fastest (toll) AP-61. By train: C-8b from Atocha or Chamartín (local). By bus: La Sepulvedana (tel 91 530 4800) from Paseo de la Florida 11

Before Madrid was made the capital, Segovia was one of the most important places in Castile, as borne out by the town's many Romanesque churches. The Castilian king Alfonso VI installed his court here and Isabella Católica was proclaimed Queen of Castile in the church of San Miguel in 1474. The town declined as Madrid gained in importance, but it enjoyed an 18th-century renaissance when Felipe V built a palace a few miles away at La Granja in the 1720s (see p. 232).

The area was inhabited as far back as 80 B.C., but it came to prominence under the Romans, who built the **aqueduct** at the end of the first century A.D. Made of granite blocks from the Guadarrama mountains, with no binding material to hold them together, it is 95 feet (29 m) high and 2,388 feet (728 m) long, with 166 arches. It was built to bring water from the Río Frío, 12 miles (19 km) away, a function it fulfilled until the 1960s. Following restoration in the 1990s, it can now carry water again, but no longer supplies the town.

From Plaza del Azoguejo, in front of the aqueduct, Calle Cervantes leads up toward Plaza Mayor. On the right you pass the 15th-century **Casa de los Picos,** with a distinctive facade studded with pointed granite stones. The street later becomes Calle Juan Bravo, named after the hero of the Revolt of the Comuneros (1520–1521), when the inhabitants of Castile protested the unfair treatment they were receiving from Carlos V and the nobility. There is a statue of Bravo in **Plaza de San Martín,** next to the church of the same name, which has a Mudejar tower. Nearby is the square 15th-century **Torreón de Lozoya** *(open from 7 p.m.),* which belonged to one of the town's many noble families. Beside the tower is the **Museo de Arte Contemporáneo Esteban Vicente** *(Plaza de las Bellas Artes, tel 92 146 2010, closed Sun. p.m. & Mon.),* which displays work donated by this abstract expressionist painter.

Just off the semiporticoed Plaza Mayor, with its outdoor cafés, rises the vast, late-Gothic **Catedral,** which stands at the highest point of the town. The harmonious, golden sandstone structure was built in the 16th century by Juan Gil de Hontañon and his son Rodrigo. Near the entrance, in the Capilla de la Piedad, there is a polychrome altarpiece (1571) by Juan de Juni. The cloister, by Juan Guas, was moved here from an earlier structure near the Alcázar. The high altar was designed by Francesco Sabatini and was added in the 18th century. As well as Romanesque and Gothic statuary, the museum contains the tomb of the Infante Don Pedro, son of Enrique II, who fell to his death in 1366 from the Alcázar.

The **Alcázar,** on the edge of the ridge, looks like a ship that is about to set sail across the fields of Castile. Originally built by the Trastámara dynasty in the 13th century, the castle was extended by Felipe II, but had to be rebuilt after being largely destroyed by fire in the mid-19th century. With its turrets, spires, parapets, and ramparts, it looks the part of a fantasy castle, and it has featured in numerous movies. The Royal Artillery runs the museum, where weapons and suits of armor are displayed in rooms with beautiful Mudejar ceilings. If you walk up to the top of the tower, you are rewarded with sweeping views. ∎

Nearby Places: Palacio Real de El Pardo

Originally a hunting lodge, this royal palace was embellished and extended by various monarchs over the centuries. The present structure is mostly from the 18th century but with 19th-century decoration. Previously the official residence of General Franco, the Palacio Real de El Pardo is now used by visiting heads of state. There is a good selection of restaurants in the town of El Pardo, most of which specialize in local game.

Visitor Information
- ✉ Plaza Mayor 10
- ☎ 921 460 334
- ✉ Plaza del Azoguejo 1
- ☎ 92 146 6720
- www.segoviaturismo.com

Catedral
- ✉ Calle Marqués del Arco 1
- ☎ 92 146 2205
- $ Cloisters, chapter house, museum: $

Alcázar
- ✉ Plaza de la Reina Victoria Eugenia
- ☎ 92 146 0759
- $ $. Free on Tues. for EU nationals
- www.alcazardesegovia.com

Palacio Real de El Pardo
- ✉ Calle Manuel Alonso, El Pardo
- ☎ 91 376 1500
- $ $
- 🚌 By bus: Intercity line 601 from Calle Princesa
- www.patrimonionacional.es

A Drive Around the Guadarrama Mountains

The Sierra de Guadarrama, northwest of Madrid, is a range of granite mountains that runs between the plains of La Mancha and Castile. This drive takes you through some dramatic landscapes with plenty of places to stop and breathe the mountain air. Roads are good and well marked, but in winter there can be heavy snowfall.

The Cuenca Alta del Manzanares nature reserve is popular with weekend hikers.

NOT TO BE MISSED:

Castillo de Manzanares el Real
• Real Monasterio de Santa
María de El Paular

From central Madrid, head north up Paseo de la Castellana and take the M-607. Just after Colmenar el Viejo, turn onto the M-609, and, after 3 miles (5 km), take the M-608 toward Manzanares el Real. You drive through the Cuenca Alta del Manzanares nature reserve, a good place to stretch your legs.

As you approach **Manzanares el Real ❶,** the village's 15th-century fairy-tale castle *(tel 91 853 0008, closed Mon., $$$)* appears before you. The restored structure was built for the powerful Mendoza family and has cylindrical towers and a gallery with fabulous views. There is also a museum inside that charts the castle's history.

Continue along the M-608, toward Cerceda, then turn onto the M-607 toward Navacerrada. The road starts to climb steadily as you drive past another reservoir on the left. **Navacerrada ❷,** which has a 16th-century church, is popular with weekenders and has several restaurants. Turn right immediately after the vil-

lage onto the M-601 up to the mountain pass of **Puerto de Navacerrada.** At 6,168 feet (1,880 m), this is a ski resort on the border between the Madrid region and Segovia province, which stretches out below you as you reach the top immediately beyond the village. Turn right at the junction here onto the M-604 toward Cotos, with the valley on your left and the steep hillside covered in pine trees to the right.

After 10 minutes you reach **Puerto de Cotos** mountain pass at 6,004 feet (1,830 m), which used to be a ski station but has recently been turned into the Peñalara nature reserve. On the hillside above the café there is an information center where you can pick up a leaflet detailing well-marked walking routes.

Continue along the M-604 toward Rascafría. The road now winds down into the Lozoya Valley, dropping 2,300 feet (700 m). After 20 minutes, just before Rascafría, you reach the **Real Monasterio de Santa María de El Paular** *(tel 91 869 1425, www.monasterioelpaular.com).* Founded in 1390, the monastery is home to a small community of Benedictine monks. The 16th-century church has an altarpiece with Gothic tracery. Part of the monastery has been converted into the upscale **Hotel Santa María de El Paular** *(tel 91 869 1011),* which has two restaurants.

Rascafría ❸, five minutes farther along the

M-604, has a range of restaurants. From the village, take the M-611 toward Miraflores de la Sierra, which is 15 miles (24 km) away over the Puerto de Morcuera pass. After crossing the Río Lozoya, the road climbs again with a series of sharp bends. As you drive over the Puerto de Morcuera pass at 5,892 feet (1,796 m), the plains of Castile open up before you, and the road winds down to **Miraflores de la Sierra ❹**. The village, which is surrounded by oak forests, is a pleasant place for a stroll and a coffee at an outdoor café.

To return to Madrid, follow the signs along the M-611, M-609, and M-607, passing Soto del Real and Colmenar el Viejo. As you approach Madrid, keep in the lane for the M-30, then take the Paseo de la Castellana exit.

ⓜ	See area map p. 213
▶	Madrid
↔	110 miles (177 km)
⏱	1 day, including stops
▶	Madrid

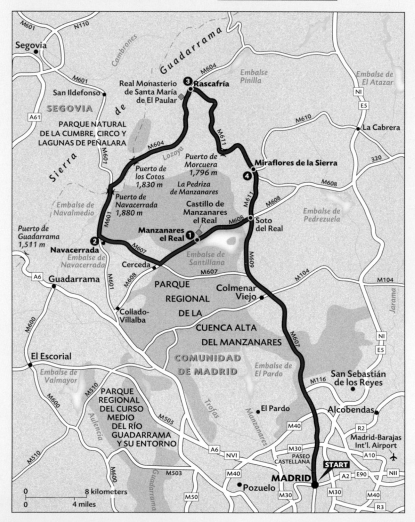

El Escorial

The palace-monastery of San Lorenzo de El Escorial was founded by Felipe II to provide a suitable resting place for his father, Emperor Carlos V, and future Spanish monarchs. The enormous granite structure symbolizes the glory of the Habsburg dynasty, the power of the Spanish Empire, and Felipe's firm commitment to the Catholic faith. The charming small town of San Lorenzo below the monastery has a range of cafés and restaurants.

Bell towers flank the solemn basilica at the heart of El Escorial's complex.

The name commemorates the Spanish victory over the French at the battle of St. Quentin in 1557, which took place on August 10, St. Lawrence's day. The structure has a parallelogram layout, which represents the gridiron on which the saint was burned to death. Built between 1563 and 1584, it was designed by Juan Bautista de Toledo. After Toledo's death in 1567, Juan de Herrera took over the project, which included not only the monastery, but also a palace, college, seminary, and library. The building is 673 feet (205 m) from north to south and 525 feet (160 m) from east to west. There are 2,673 windows, 1,200 doors, and 16 courtyards.

The original Hieronymite monks were forced to leave the monastery following the disentailment of religious property in 1836. A community of Augustinians moved into the monastery in 1885 and now run a school in the building.

Visiting El Escorial

The visit follows a set route, which is well signed with information panels in Spanish and English. You start in the **Sala de San Mauricio,** which contains the El Greco painting "The Martyrdom of St. Maurice and the Theban Legion" (1580–1582). Stairs lead down to the **Museo de Arquitectura,** a museum that charts the development of the building and the ways in which Herrera modified the original plans. Most of El Escorial's superlative art collection is now in the Prado, but the nearby **Museo**

INSIDER TIP:

Where a museum allows photos, don't settle for photographing paintings alone; photograph people looking at paintings.

—TINO SORIANO
National Geographic photographer

de Pintura still contains several Spanish, Flemish, and Italian masterpieces. These include stunning works by Titian, Tintoretto, Paolo Veronese, Rubens, and José de Ribera. Look for the triptych by Michel Coxcie (1499–1592), "The Martyrdom of St. Philip."

Stairs lead to the **Palacio de Felipe II,** where the first rooms were occupied by his daughter, the Infanta Isabel Clara Eugenia. The **Sala de Retratos** contains numerous portraits of Habsburg monarchs. The king's bedchamber, where he died in 1598, is surprisingly austere. Felipe's servants had the bed angled so that Felipe could more easily see the high altar of the church.

Regal grandeur soon returns as you descend to the baroque **Panteón Real,** an octagonal chamber adorned with gilt, red jasper, and black marble. The pantheon contains the tombs of nearly all the Spanish monarchs from Carlos I to Alfonso XIII. There are also nine adjoining chambers containing tombs of princes and princesses.

The vaulted chapter houses, the **Salas Capitulares,** contain still more outstanding paintings by artists such as El Greco, Velázquez, and Titian. Don't miss "Christ Carrying the Cross" as well as "The Crown of Thorns" by Hieronymus Bosch.

The courtyard **Patio de los Evangelistas** is surrounded by a cloister, which is decorated with frescoes on the theme of the Redemption. Situated in the courtyard's center is a small Doric temple.

The magnificent **Basílica** stands at the center of El Escorial, surrounded by 43 side chapels. It is crowned by a dome 302 feet (92 m) high and decorated with stunning frescoes by Lucas Jordán. The **Capilla Mayor,** which is the spiritual core of the entire building, is dominated by an altarpiece in gilded bronze and marble, flanked by sculptures of

San Lorenzo de El Escorial
Map p. 213
30 miles (49 km) NW of Madrid
By car: A-6 to Guadarrama, then M-600. By train: C-8a from Atocha or Chamartín. By bus: Herranz (tel 91 896 9028) service 661 or 664 from Intercambiador de Moncloa station

Visitor Information
Calle Grimaldi 2
91 890 5313
www.sanlorenzoturismo.org

Real Monasterio de San Lorenzo de El Escorial
Map p. 213
Paseo de Juan de Borbón y Battenberg
91 890 5902, 91 890 5903, 91 890 5904
Closed Mon.
$$. Free Wed. for EU nationals
www.patrimonionacional.es/escorial/escorial.htm

The tombs of Spanish monarchs are traditionally kept in the Panteón Real at El Escorial.

Earth in the center of the universe.

In the gardens around the monastery there are two pavilions that Juan de Villanueva designed during the reign of Carlos III. Beware though: Opening times vary during the year, so ask at the monastery if you are interested in seeing the interiors.

Surrounded by magnolia, sequoia, and cedar trees in the Jardínes del Príncipe is the Italianate **Casita del Príncipe,** which has

Carlos I and Felipe II and their families. One of the side chapels contains a monumental marble "Christ" sculpted by Benvenuto Cellini (1500–1571) in 1562.

Above the Patio de los Reyes (Courtyard of the Kings) on the west side of the structure is the barrel-vaulted **Royal Library,** which is 180 feet (55 m) long and contains more than 40,000 books and documents, including the diary of St. Teresa and Greek, Latin, Arab, and Hebrew manuscripts. Look up at the ceiling frescoes, which were painted by Pellegrino Tibaldi and represent Philosophy, Theology, Grammar, Rhetoric, Music, Arithmetic, Geometry, Dialectics, and Astrology. The books are stacked with the spines facing inward and the leaves outward, a technique that allows air to permeate the paper. Among several globes, the most intriguing is the pine **Armillary Sphere,** which was made about 1582 and shows the solar system as it was defined by the Greek astronomer Ptolemy, with the

El Escorial

Main entrance

College with four courtyards

Grand entrance

a neoclassic facade and was built in 1772 for the future Carlos IV. Inside are ornate tapestries, paintings by Lucas Jordán and Corrado Giaquinto, and a room covered with porcelain plaques made at the Buen Retiro factory in Madrid.

More Sights

The town of San Lorenzo holds an elegant 18th-century theater, the **Real Coliseo de Carlos III.**

A 20-minute walk along the Paseo de Carlos III brings you to the **Casita del Infante** (or Casa de Arriba; *Crta. de Robledo de Chavela, tel 91 890 5903, $*), a small hunting lodge that was home to King Juan Carlos when he was a student.

Three miles (5 km) up the hill south of the monastery is the **Silla de Felipe II,** a seat carved from rock where the king watched the building's construction. ■

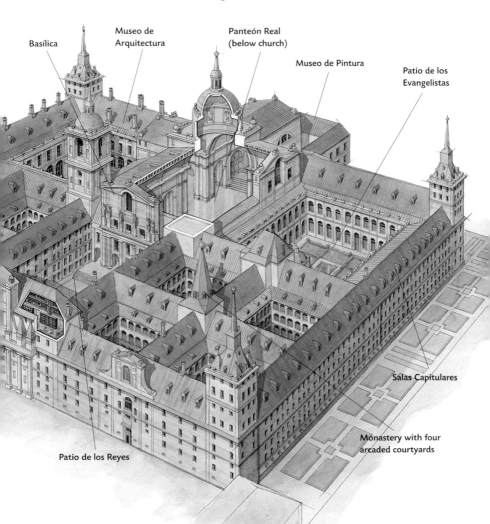

Basílica

Museo de Arquitectura

Panteón Real (below church)

Museo de Pintura

Patio de los Evangelistas

Salas Capitulares

Monastery with four arcaded courtyards

Patio de los Reyes

More Excursions Around Madrid

El Capricho de Osuna

This neoclassical palace and collection of gardens near the Madrid airport were built in the 18th century for the Duke and Duchess of Osuna. The extensive gardens were designed by Jean-Baptiste Mulot, gardener to Marie Antoinette, and include a lilac maze. There are also an artificial lake and river, down which the duchess would boat guests to a Chinese pagoda for lunch. Badly damaged during the Civil War, the complex has been meticulously restored. ⚇ Map p. 213 ✉ Paseo de la Alameda de Osuna, 6 miles (10 km) east of Madrid center ☎ Information from Madrid Tourism Center, tel 91 588 1636 🕐 Closed Mon.–Fri. 🚇 Metro: Canillejas, then Bus: 101, 105, 151

Palacio Real de La Granja de San Ildefonso

This royal palace was built for Felipe V starting in the 1720s and reflects the French tastes of the early Bourbon monarchs. The gardens were designed by René Carlier and contain spectacular fountains. In the village is the **Real Fábrica de Cristales** (Paseo del Pocillo 1, tel 92 101 0700, closed Mon. & Tues.), a glass factory, founded in 1770, where glass-ware is on sale. www.patrimonionacional .es ⚇ Map p. 213 ✉ Plaza de España 17, La Granja de San Ildefonso, 56 miles (90 km) northwest of Madrid ☎ 92 147 0019 🕐 Palace closed Mon. 💲 $$. Free Wed. for EU nationals 🚌 Bus: La Sepulvedana from Paseo de la Florida 11 (tel 91 530 4800).

EXPERIENCE: Visiting Madrid's Vineyards

Madrid is the only European capital with its own wine appellation, known as a Designation of Origin. This official status was awarded in 1990, and there are now more than 40 wineries around Madrid. Many of these wineries welcome visitors, though it is best to call ahead for arranging a time.

Visiting wineries is also a good way to explore the countryside. Wine production is divided among three areas, the largest of which is Arganda, southeast of Madrid, with about half the total production. Navalcarnero, in the southwest, is crossed by the Río Guadarrama. The higher rainfall and proximity to mountains in San Martín to the west provide good conditions for quality wines.

Bodega Jesús Díaz (Calle Convento 38, 28380 Col-menar de Oreja, tel 91 894 3378, www.bodegasjesus diaz.com) This winery was founded in the late 1800s and uses traditional methods of winemaking.

Bodega Ecológica Luis (Carretera de Escalona 5, 28650 Cenicientos, tel 91 460 6053 www. bodegasaavedra.com) This family-run winery in the village of Cenicientos in the San Martín area produces high-quality organic wines that are enjoying great success not only in Spain but in Europe and the United States.

Bodegas Pablo Morate (Avenida del Generalísimo 33-34, 28391 Valdelaguna, tel 91 893 7172, www.boe gasmorate.com) Award-winning wines are produced at this winery, which dates all the way back to 1873. Tasting sessions and meals are available by arrangement, and there is also a wine museum housed in a 15th-century wine cellar.

More information on Madrid wines: Vinos de Madrid Calle Bravo Murillo 101–3, 28020 Madrid, tel 91 534 8511, www .vinosdemadrid.es

Travelwise

A heavy-laden postcard stand

TRAVELWISE

PLANNING YOUR TRIP

When to Go

Madrid is welcoming all year round and, being small for a capital city (population about 3 million), it is compact and easy to explore, even on foot—the best way to get to know it. The most comfortable months as far as temperatures go are April–May and September–October, when Madrid's street life is at its most active.

August is traditionally family vacation month. Many head for the coast, and the smaller and most typical bars, restaurants, and shops tend to close. The museums and monuments do stay open, however, and the Veranos de la Villa (Summers in the City) festival, between June and September, fills the town with concerts, art exhibitions, and theatrical performances, many free of charge.

Climate

Madrid is right in the middle of Spain. On the high *meseta* (plateau) at an altitude of 2,120 feet (646 m) above sea level, it is the highest capital in Europe. It is also the one with the most hours of sunshine. The city gets very hot in midsummer, not cooling down much even at night, and pretty cold and windy in midwinter. The rainiest months are October–December and April–May, so if you come then, bring rainwear. The atmosphere generally is very dry.

Average minimum/maximum temperatures:
Jan. 36.7/49.5°F (2.6/9.7°C)
Apr. 45/63.5°F (7.2/17.5°C)
July 65.1/88.2°F (18.4/31.2°C)
Oct. 50.4/66.2°F (10.2°C/19°C)

Main Events

Madrid has many festivals and fiestas, some national, some city wide, and others barrio based. The key Madrid festival is that of San Isidro, its patron saint, on May 15, a classic *romería* (pilgrimage) involving a religious procession, Mass, offerings to the saint, a picnic, and then music and dancing. Centered around the church of San Isidro, it then shifts to the Pradera (meadow) of San Isidro, and concerts take place in Plaza Mayor and Las Vistillas park. The San Isidro bullfighting festival at Las Ventas offers prestigious bullfights every day for a month.

The Carnaval, in February or early March, celebrates the final days before Lent with a mixture of processions, fancy dress balls, and cultural events. The Baile de Máscaras at the Círculo de Bellas Artes is a 3,000-strong fancy-dress ball on Carnaval Saturday, and Sunday is a wonderful day out for children (disguised as pirates, princesses, or whatever they fancy), ending with live music and theater.

Easter week (Semana Santa) can be in March or April; it fills the town with colorful medieval-style religious processions, and there's an enjoyable combination of ancient ritual and eating and dancing.

From August 6 to 15, Madrid celebrates three of its most thoroughly Madrileño festivals: San Cayetano, San Lorenzo, and the Virgen de la Paloma. The days are dominated by religious processions and the evenings by *verbenas* (outdoor dances). The locals dress in the classic Madrileño outfits: men in corduroy or finely checkered trousers, white shirt, neckerchief, black vest, and flat cap, and women resplendent in long dresses and scarves tied over their hair.

October sees the Festival de Otoño (Autumn Festival), offering music from the classical to the most modern, as well as dance and theater.

What to Take

You should be able to buy most necessities. Spaniards generally tend to dress more formally than North Americans and the British. While casual clothes and footwear are perfectly acceptable during the day, if you are going to a fancy restaurant or out for the evening, it is worth dressing up.

Most North American appliances (such as hair dryers) will require converters (see p. 238).

Bring any essential prescription medication. For other medicines, Spanish pharmacists are knowledgeable and helpful, and they will dispense many drugs that need prescriptions in other countries.

Health

No vaccinations are required. Madrid tap water is safe to drink and remarkably soft and tasty. Plastic 1-liter or 1/3-liter (34 or 10 ounce) bottles of mineral water are widely available. The primary health concerns are sunburn and dehydration. If you are out in the sun for a while, make sure you wear suitable clothing and put sunscreen on. During the hottest parts of the day in the summer, few local people will be out on the street if they can avoid it.

Insurance

Make sure that you have adequate travel and medical coverage for treatment and expenses, including repatriation expenses, and protection in the case of baggage and money loss. Keep all the receipts of your expenses. Report losses or thefts to the police and obtain a signed statement (*una denuncia*) from a police station to help you back up insurance claims.

HOW TO GET TO MADRID

Entry Formalities

U.S. and Canadian citizens may enter Spain and remain there for up to 90 days without a visa. The 90-day limit applies to the EU as a whole, so crossing an EU internal border does not extend it. U.S. and Canadian citizens planning a longer trip should submit visa application forms to their nearest Spanish consulate or embassy well ahead of time. British citizens can enter Spain without a visa for an indefinite period. It is advisable to keep your identity card or passport on you at all times.

By Air

The national carrier, Iberia, has regular direct flights to Madrid from New York, Chicago, and Miami. It also operates in collaboration with American Airlines in the United States from 20 other airports and with British Airways in Canada from Toronto, Montreal, and Vancouver. These flights often involve stopovers. Onward internal flights in Spain bought in conjunction with the international flight are often a very good value. U.S. airlines such as Delta also offer direct flights. Many European carriers, such as Air France, Lufthansa, and British Airways, have regular flights to Madrid as well.

Useful Numbers & Internet Addresses

In Spain

Air Europa, tel 902 401 501
American Airlines, tel 902 115 570
British Airways, tel 902 111 333
Delta Airlines, tel 91 749 6630
Iberia, tel 902 400 500

In the U.S. & Canada

Air Europa, tel 212/921-2381, www.air-europa.com
American Airlines, tel 800/433-7300 (English), 800/633-3711

(Spanish), www.aa.com
British Airways, tel 800/247-9297 (U.S.) or 416/250-0880 (Toronto), www.britishairways.com
Delta Airlines, tel 800/241-4141, www.delta.com
Iberia, tel 800/772-4642 (U.S.) or 800/423-7241 (Canada), www.iberia.com

Arriving from the Airport

International flights to Madrid arrive at Barajas airport, which is 8 miles (13 km) from Madrid city center. A taxi ride to the center will cost roughly €25 to €30 ($30–$36) and take about 30 minutes, depending on the traffic and time of day. Buses run every 10 minutes to Avenida de América (not in central Madrid) from 5:36 a.m. to 11:30 p.m., costing €1($1.20) per passenger. To get into the center, you will still need to take a taxi, a subway train (metro), or a bus. The metro (line 8) runs direct to Nuevos Ministerios station, where you change for the center. This is not advisable with heavy luggage. The special airport ticket costs €2 ($3), or you can get a 10-trip Metrobus ticket for €6.70 ($10), which is also valid on buses, and pay a €1 ($1.50) airport supplement. Punch them in the machine by the driver when you board.

Returning to the airport, Iberia, Air Europa, or Spanair ticket-holders can check in at Nuevos Ministerios metro station instead of Barajas. Some hotels have a direct shuttle to and from the airport.

By Train

Travelers can reach Madrid by train from London via the Eurostar from Waterloo Station, which goes through the Channel Tunnel before reaching Paris and the Gare du Nord. Changing stations, you catch the evening *trenhotel*

(trainhotel) from Paris (Gare d'Austerlitz), on which you can eat, drink, and get a good night's sleep, to arrive at Chamartín station in Madrid the next morning.

GETTING AROUND

By Bus

Madrid has an extensive bus network, run by the Empresa Municipal de Transporte (EMT; *Municipal Transport Company, tel 902 507 850 or 91 406 8810*). All buses are air-conditioned and most have disabled-access facilities. Services operate every day from 6 a.m.–11 p.m., and there are night buses (*búhos*, or "owls"), with 25 different routes, starting from Plaza de la Cibeles, leaving every half-hour on the half-hour between midnight and 3 a.m., and hourly on the hour from 3–6 a.m. Drivers will stop only when hailed in good time from a bus stop or if a passenger inside presses the stop-request button. Dogs are admitted only if they are guide dogs for the blind or small dogs being carried.

By Car

In Madrid, finding a place to park a car can be difficult (slightly easier in August) unless you have access to hotel or other private parking. But it's easy to see the city without a car, except perhaps for exploratory excursions outside town. Circling Madrid are three ring roads, the innermost M-30, the M-40, and the M-50, which provide access to the highways leading out. Outside Madrid, the different road types are: *autopistas* (freeways) and *autovías* (state highways), which are almost all toll-free; *carreteras nacionales* (national roads), marked in red on the maps, old main roads that also carry local traffic; *carreteras comarcales* (local roads), smaller roads marked in yellow; and small country lanes, marked in white.

Driving Information

European Union driver's licenses are valid in Spain. U.S. and Canadian citizens should obtain International Driving Permits, available through the American and the Canadian Automobile Associations (www.aaa.com, www. caa.ca). You must carry ID. It is compulsory to carry in the car two warning triangles, spare light bulbs for the headlamps, fuses, two reflective vests, and a spare tire. It is illegal for the driver to use a cell phone in the car, unless with a hands-free device, or to consume alcoholic drinks. Children under 12 are not allowed to ride in the front seats. The minimum legal age for driving is 18, and, for renting a vehicle, 21. If in your own vehicle, ensure that you have the appropriate insurance, including the green card, available from your insurers.

Breakdown Assistance

Autopistas and autovías have emergency telephones, marked "S.O.S.," at intervals along the roadside. A tow truck will be sent to help you. You are legally obliged to wear a reflective jacket if you leave the vehicle and to carry and use reflective triangles. If you belong to AAA, CAA, or AA, you can get help from RACE, their Spanish equivalent (tel 902 300 505).

Drinking & driving The alcohol limit for drivers is 0.25 milligram of alcohol per liter in a breath test or 0.5 gram of alcohol per liter in a blood test. The fine for exceeding this starts at €600 ($935). If you have had a driving permit for less than two years, the limits are 0.15 milligram and 0.3 gram.

Fines For exceeding the alcohol limit, fines start at €600 ($935); for speeding and seat-belt violations they begin at €300 ($470). Nonresidents of Spain are required to pay fines on the spot or to guarantee payment via a finance company

that the traffic police (Guardia Civil) will put you in contact with. Nonpayment results in your vehicle being immobilized.

Fuel Fuel prices are controlled by the government and are typically slightly cheaper than U.K. prices, but nearly twice those of the U.S. The types of fuel available are: Super (4-star), Normal (3-star), Sin plomo (Unleaded), and Gasoleo (Diesel).

Parking A continuous yellow line on the road or along the pavement means no parking or stopping. A broken yellow line means no parking, or time-limited parking where a sign indicates specified times. Blue lines indicate paid parking. Pay for your ticket at a dispensing machine (marked by a sign of a coin being pushed into a slot) and display it in your car. If your car has been towed away, look for an orange sticker on the pavement that gives details of your car, when it was removed, and the number to call.

Road signs If you are leaving Madrid on a car trip, finding the right road can sometimes be difficult. Signs sometimes appear at the last moment; often do not mention the destination, just the road number; and sometimes use old numbers (e.g. N-4, E-5) instead of the current one (e.g., A-IV). All distances in Spain are indicated in kilometers (1 km = 0.62 mile).

Seat belts Wearing seat belts is compulsory in the front seats, and in the back as well if the car is equipped with them.

Speed limits The speed limits are: autopistas and autovías 75 mph (120 kph); interurban roads either 62 mph (100 kph) or 56 mph (90 kph) as indicated; towns and built-up areas 31 mph (50 kph) or less, as indicated.

Traffic circles Vehicles already in a traffic circle have the right of way over those entering it, unless it is clearly marked otherwise.

What to do in a car accident See p. 240.

Renting a Car

Renting a car in Spain is straightforward and relatively cheap. There are many small companies as well as international ones, including Hertz and Avis.

> **Avis,** tel 902 180 854
> **Europcar,** tel 902 105 030
> **Hertz,** tel 902 402 405

If you are planning a trip out of Madrid, it may make sense to go by public transportation and then rent a car for local travel. Check availability before leaving Madrid.

By Metro

The subway system is the fastest mode of public transportation, running from 6 a.m. to 2 a.m., with rush hour (to be avoided) 7:30–9 a.m. Children under four travel for free. Each line has a distinct color code and two platforms, one in each direction, with the final station indicated. Keep your ticket for inspection until reaching the exit (salida). It gets very hot underground in high summer. Customer service, tel 902 444 403.

By Public Transport

Single tickets on the metro and on buses cost €1($1.50). The ten-journey Metrobús ticket is cheaper at €6.70 ($10) and works on the metro (except suburban line 12) and the bus network. It is on sale at metro stations, authorized newspaper stands, and tobacco shops (estancos, identified by a sign showing a yellow "T" and "tabacos" on a brown background), but not on buses. There is also a Tourist Travel Pass (Abono Transportes Turístico), covering Madrid city (Zona A) and valid for 1, 2, 3, 5, or 7 days. It costs from €4 to €20.40 ($6–$32), with children under 11 at half-price. These can also be bought in municipal tourist offices. There is also a monthly travel pass *(Abono Mensual de Transportes)* for the metro and buses, which costs €27–€42 ($41–$65) or €10.50 ($16) for persons over 64. As in any major city, you should be sensibly security-conscious, especially during rush hours and nighttime.

By Taxi

Downtown Madrid teems with taxis, which are white with a diagonal red stripe on the front doors and the shield of Madrid on the side. If the roof light next to the "taxi" sign shows green, they are available for hire. Taxi stands are indicated by a white "T" on a blue sign. Taxis are not very expensive, and there are no charges for luggage or for dogs, but large dogs (except for guide dogs) will generally not be admitted. Trips to or from a bus or train station carry an extra charge of €2.75 ($4), and those to or from the airport cost an additional €5.25 ($8.50). Payment should be in cash. Private cab companies, charging the same rates, include **Radio-Taxi Asociación Gremial:** tel 91 447 5180 or 91 447 3232; **Radio-Taxi Independiente:** tel 91 405 1213 or 91 405 5500; **Radio Teléfono Taxi / Euro Taxi:** tel 91 547 8200; and **Teletaxi:** tel 91 371 2131, 91 371 3711, or 630 907 990 (cell phone).

By Train

Renfe (Red Nacional de los Ferrocarriles Españoles) is Spain's main rail network, and a good way to explore sights beyond Madrid. The TALGO trains (Tren Articulado Ligero Goicoechea Oriol) and the high-speed AVEs (Alta Velocidad Española) are fast, comfortable, and include well-equipped bars with food. Madrid's main stations are Chamartín and Atocha. The fastest, most modern trains, the AVEs, leave from Atocha. Tickets can be bought from your home

travel agent, from agents in Spain displaying a Renfe sticker, from Renfe offices in central Madrid, in the Corte Inglés department stores, at railway stations, by telephone *(90 224 0202)* or online *(www.renfe.com).* During rush hours and major holidays, trains are likely to be crowded. Arrive to catch your train with plenty of time to spare—trains have been known to depart early.

Return tickets are sold with a 20% discount if the round-trip is within a 60-day period. Children under 13 receive a 40% discount on all tickets. Children under four travel for free if not occupying a seat. InterRail and Eurail passes are valid in Spain. For EU citizens, the InterRail One Country Pass allows 3 to 8 days limitless travel within a one-month period for between 110 and €230 ($173–$362).

The Flexipass, available only to non--pean residents, offers 10 to 15 days' unlimited travel within a two-month period for between €470 and €731 ($742–$1,154); Those under 26 and over 60 pay less. Additional supplements are charged for seat reservations and sleeping accommodation. First class is known as *Preferente* and second class as *Turista.* Check for new offers and discounts.

PRACTICAL ADVICE
Communications
Internet

Most 3-star hotels and better offer their customers Internet access in some form. Madrid is full of cybercafés and Internet centers; here are a few of the more reliable ones.

Workcenter: Calle Alberto Aguilera 1, Calle María Molina 40, and Paseo de la Castellana 149. www.workcenter.es, tel 90 211 5011. Open 24 hours every day. Although not cheap, as well as Internet access, Workcenters

provide a wide range of office services, including mail, photocopying and printing. Cost: €1.95 ($3.10)/30 minutes.
Café Comercial: Glorieta de Bilbao 7, tel 91 521 5655. Metro: Bilbao. Open Mon.–Thurs., 8 a.m.–1 a.m.; Fri. & Sat., 8 a.m.–2 a.m.; Sun. 10 a.m.–1 a.m. Cost: €1 ($1.20)/50 minutes.
Cafetería Zahara: Gran Vía 31, tel 91 521 8424. Metro: Callao. Open 9 a.m.–1 a.m. Coin-operated: about €2 ($2.40)/hour.
Casa de Internet: Calle Luchana 20, tel 91 594 4200. Metro: Bilbao. Open Mon.–Fri., 9 a.m.–12:30 a.m.; Sat. & Sun. 10 a.m.–12:30 a.m. Cost €2.10 ($2.52)/hour.

Post Offices

A letter or postcard weighing less than 20 grams costs €0.31 ($0.50) to send within Spain, €0.60 ($1) within the EU, and €0.78 ($1.20) to North America. To send a registered letter *(carta certificada)* weighing less than 20 grams from a post office *(correos)* costs €2.44 ($4.25) within Spain, €2.84 ($4.45) within the EU, and €3.02 ($4.70) to North America. Stamps can also be bought in *estancos* (closed 2–5 p.m.).

Post offices are open 8:30 a.m.– 8:30 p.m., Mon.–Fri., and 9:30 a.m.–1 p.m. on Sat. A very few (e.g., Paseo Santa María de la Cabeza 42) are open on Sunday from noon until 10 p.m. American Express offices will hold letters (not packages) sent to cardholders. The Palacio de Comunicaciones post office in Plaza de la Cibeles will hold mail addressed to you at "Lista de Correos, Oficina Principal de Madrid, 28070, Spain" for 15 days only, after which it will be returned to sender.

Telephones

All Spanish phone numbers have nine digits. The first two or three digits (91 in the case of Madrid) indicate the province but must always be dialed, even if you are calling from next door. Numbers beginning with 6 are mobile phone numbers and suitably expensive. Toll-free numbers start with 900.

To call Spain from the U.S. To call Spain from the United States, dial 011-34 (international and Spain country codes) and the nine-digit number.

To call from Spain To call from Spain, dial 00 followed by the country code (1 for North America, 44 for the U.K.), then the area code and the telephone number. When calling the U.K., omit the first 0 in the regional code.

Telephone cards To make a call from telephone booths in Spain, you can use coins or (preferably) buy a *tarjeta telefónica* (phone card). Tarjetas telefónicas are sold at post offices and estancos in denominations of €5 to €150.

Operators & directory information For calls within Spain, the operator's number is 1009; for Europe, North Africa, and Turkey, 1008 and for the rest of the world, 1005. For national directory information, dial 11818; for international, 11825.

Conversions

1 kilo = 2.2 pounds
1 liter = 0.2642 U.S. gallon
1 kilometer = 0.62 mile
1 meter = 1.094 yards

Women's clothing

U.S.	8	10	12	14	16	18
Spanish	36	38	40	42	44	46

Men's clothing

U.S.	36	38	40	42	44	46
Spanish	46	48	50	52	54	56

Women's shoes

U.S.	6-6.5	7-7.5	8-8.5	9-9.5
Spanish	38	39	40-41	42

Men's shoes

U.S.	8	8.5	9.5	10.5	11.5	12
Spanish	41	42	43	44	45	46

Discount Card

The Madrid Card gives you free admission to 43 of Madrid's main museums, including the Prado, the Reina Sofía, and the Thyssen-Bornemisza; unlimited trips on the three Madrid Visión sightseeing bus routes; free access to the Descubre Madrid (Discover Madrid) guided walking tours; free admission to the Madrid Parque de Atracciones (Amusement Park), the Zoo-Aquarium, the Teleférico (cable car), the Faunia nature park, and IMAX Madrid with its ultra-large and modern movie screens; and discounts to some shops, restaurants and stores.

The card costs €42 ($66) for 24 hours, €55 ($86) for 48 hours, and €68 ($107) for 72 hours, with discounts if bought online. It is available from municipal tourist offices, major railway stations, travel agencies, and selected hotels. Children's cards were introduced in 2006. Tel 902 088 908, www .madridcard.com.

Electricity

The standard electricity voltage in Spain is 220V, 50 Hz, not 110V as in North America. Most electrical equipment will need a transformer, except for some laptops that have conversion features. Cheaper appliances, such as hair dryers or razors, may be worth buying in Spain. Most U.K. 240V appliances will work fine.

Etiquette & Local Customs

The Spanish siesta is not a myth, although it is often spent eating and talking rather than sleeping. Many shops shut from 1:30–4:30 p.m. or 2–5 p.m. It is unusual to start lunch, often the day's main meal, before 2 p.m. and it often lasts until 5 p.m., or even longer on Sunday. The evening meal starts at any time

between 9:30 p.m. and 11 p.m. If you eat earlier, it will be easier to get a table.

Holidays

Spain has national, regional, and local holidays, and Madrid has even more at barrio level. The Spanish national holidays are: January 1 (El Año Nuevo, New Year's Day), January 6 (El Día de los Reyes Magos, Ephiphany), Maundy Thursday and Good Friday, May 1 (May Day or Labor Day), July 25 (Santiago Apóstol, St. James the Apostle), August 15 (Asunción de la Virgen, Assumption of the Virgin), October 12 (Día de la Hispanidad, Spanish National Day), November 1 (Todos los Santos, All Saints), December 6 (Constitution Day), December 8 (Immaculate Conception), and December 25 (Día de Navidad, Christmas Day).

The Madrid-wide festivals are: May 2 (Madrid Day), May 15 (San Isidro, patron saint of Madrid), September 9 (Santa María de la Cabeza or La Melonera, the melon lady), and November 9 (La Almudena, Madrid's patroness). Madrid keeps functioning during these *días festivos* (holidays), their main effect (apart from the celebrations) being that national and local government buildings tend to close. If the holiday falls on Sunday, it is usually moved to Monday; if it falls on Tuesday or Thursday, it creates *un puente* (a bridge), resulting in the intervening Monday or Friday becoming a holiday too.

Media

Newspapers

The three most popular daily newspapers are *El País, El Mundo,* and *ABC.* The left-leaning *El País* has the most in-depth international coverage. English-language newspapers are widely available in the more central parts of Madrid, particularly on the Gran

Vía. The most common North American paper is the *International Herald Tribune,* and most British national newspapers are on same-day sale.

Radio

The airwaves are full of national radio stations. The state-run Radio Nacional de España (RNE) has four stations covering classical and traditional music, pop music, news and current affairs, and sports. These are generally better than the local stations. The Voice of America is broadcast on shortwave, but moves around according to the time of day: Try 9700, 15205, and 15255 MHz. The same applies to the BBC World Service: Try 1323, 6195, 9410, 12095, 15565, and 17640.

Television

Spanish television has good news and sports coverage but otherwise tends to be a mess of soap operas, celebrity gossip, and quiz and game shows. The TV will often be on in bars and even in restaurants.

There are two state-run national channels, TVE1 and TVE2, and two national independents, Antena 3 and Tele 5, plus a local channel, Tele-Madrid. Hundreds of satellite channels are available in many bars and hotels, including English-language channels such as CNN, Fox News, BBC World Service, and Sky News.

Money Matters

Spain's currency is the euro, which comes in coins of 1, 2, 5, 10, 20, and 50 cents *(céntimos)* and of €1 and €2. Notes are available in 5, 10, 20, 50, 100, 200, and 500 euros. Many smaller businesses will not accept large bills, fearing counterfeits.

Try to arrive in Spain with some cash in euros; otherwise change some money at your arrival point. Take a combination of traveler's checks and credit or debit cards to get cash from the plentiful ATMs; most add a small charge for use. Major credit cards are widely accepted. Traveler's checks are a secure way to hold money and can be changed in banks (better exchange rates) and money-changing centers (longer opening hours).

Opening Times

Banks are open from 8:30 a.m. to 2 or 2:30 p.m. (Mon.–Fri.) and from 8:30 a.m. to 1 p.m. on Saturdays. There are branches of Caja Madrid in Atocha and Chamartín stations, at the Puerta del Sol, and in Barajas airport that are open from 8:15 a.m. to 7:45 p.m. (Mon.–Fri.) and from 10:15 a.m.–2:30 p.m. on Saturdays.

Most museums, apart from the Reina Sofía and a few others, are closed on Mondays (For museums open on Monday, see p. 97.)

Store opening times in Madrid vary: Large department stores, and shops in the Gran Vía and Sol areas, open at 9:30 or 10 a.m. and close at 10 p.m. Otherwise, shops and pharmacies open at 9:30 or 10 a.m., shut at 1:30 or 2 p.m., re-open at 4:30 or 5 p.m., and close for the night at 8 or 8:30 p.m. Although most shops close on Sundays, stores in the Puerta del Sol area are open, and many central shops are open on the first Sunday of the month and on every Sunday during Christmas and the month of August.

Restaurants usually open about midday, close about 5 p.m., reopen at about 7 p.m., and often serve food until after midnight. Cafés open at 7 a.m., many bars at 8 a.m., and they tend to stay open all day, closing late. In the evening, bars often don't liven up until 11 p.m. Music bars usually close at 3 a.m. and discotheques at 7 a.m.

Places of Worship

When visiting churches in Spain, remember that most are still places of worship. You are not required to dress formally, but be aware of where you are and act accordingly.

Rest Rooms

Public toilets are rare outside the most tourist-oriented areas. But in Spain you are never very far from a bar or café and it would be unusual if you were not allowed to use the toilet. Carry toilet paper with you, as this is often in short supply.

Time Differences

Madrid is generally six hours ahead of Eastern Standard Time in the U.S., but can vary by one or two hours owing to either country's conversion and back to daylight savings time. The Internet can tell you the current time difference. Madrid is one hour ahead of the U.K.

Tipping

Service is already included in all restaurant bills, so you do not have to tip if you do not want to. However, Spanish service workers are generally poorly paid and a tip for good service would be a helpful thank-you gesture.

The Spanish often leave their small change when paying for drinks and tip about 5% in restaurants. Tip porters €1-2, and give cab drivers small change or up to €2 for an airport trip.

Travelers with Disabilities

Spain has only recently catered to the needs of people with disabilities. Newer buildings are more accessible than older ones, but problems may persist. Check with hotels and restaurants before booking. Advice is available from: **Disabled Peoples' International (DPI)** 748 Broadway, Winnipeg, MB R3G 0X3, Canada, tel 204/287-8010, email dpi@dpi.org, www.dpi.org

European Disability Forum Rue du Commerce 39-41, B-1000 Brussels, Belgium, tel 32 2 282 4600, email info@edf-feph.org, www.edf-feph.org

Mobility International U.S.A. P.O. Box 10767, Eugene, Oregon, 97440, tel 541/343-1284, email info@miusa.org, www.miusa.org

RADAR (Royal Association for Disability & Rehabilitation) 12 City Forum, 250 City Rd., London EC1V 8AF, U.K., tel 020 7250 3222, email radar@radar.org.uk, www.radar.org.uk

EMERGENCIES
Embassies in Spain
United States, Calle Serrano 75, tel 91 587 2240, emergencies 91 587 2200. Metro: Rubén Dario, Núñez de Balboa. www.embusa.es
Canada, Calle Núñez de Balboa 35, tel 91 423 3250. Metro: Velázquez. www.canada-es.org
United Kingdom, Calle Fernando El Santo 16, tel 91 700 8200. Metro: Alonso Martínez.
Consulate: Paseo de Recoletos 7-9, tel 91 524 970, emergencies 606 987 626, Metro: Colón. www.ukinspain.com.

Spanish Embassies
United States, 2375 Pennsylvania Ave., N.W., Washington, D.C. 20037, tel 202/452-0100, www.spainemb.org. Consulates in nine other cities.
Canada, 74 Stanley Ave., Ottawa, Ontario K1M 1P4, tel 613/747-2252, www.embaspain.ca. Consulates in eight other cities.
United Kingdom, 39 Chesham Pl., London SW1X 8SB, tel 020 7235 5555.
Consulate: 20 Draycott Pl., London, SW3 2RZ, tel 020 7589 8989, www.conspalon.org. Consulates also in Manchester and Edinburgh.

Emergency Phone Numbers
The central emergency number

for police, fire, and ambulance services is 112. If you have been the victim of a crime and want to report it to the police, at least to put it on the record, there is a 24-hour phone line, 902 102 112, where English speakers are available. You will be told which police station (comisaría de policía) to go to, to sign the official police report and to collect a copy of it.

Police
Spain has three distinct police forces. The Policía Municipal (or Local) is controlled by the local town hall and deals with minor matters like traffic infringements. The Policía Nacional is the main crime-fighting force in the cities. The Guardia Civil tends to operate in the countryside and on the highways, and it controls the borders and prisons.

Loss of Credit Cards
American Express España, tel 902 375 637 (24 hours)
Diners Club Español, tel 901 101 011 (24 hours)
Mastercard, tel 900 971 231 (24 hours)
VISA International, tel 900 991 124 (24 hours)

What To Do in a Car Accident
The Guardia Civil operates special units to deal quickly with serious accidents. If your car has ended up where it might cause more accidents, mark its position as accurately as possible before moving it to the safest place nearby. Put on your reflective jacket(s). Set up reflective triangles, one in front of and one behind the car, at 165 feet (50 m) distance. If it is more than a minor accident, telephone 112 and wait for the police. If it is a minor accident with no injuries, but involving another vehicle, there is no need to call the police

if both parties agree about what occurred and who was responsible and reach a settlement. If you cannot agree, phone the police and get the name(s), address(es), car registration(s), and license number(s) of the other driver(s) involved and their insurance details. If there are witnesses, take their contact details. If you need repairs, call from an SOS emergency phone or call RACE on 902 300 505 (service available only to members of AAA, CAA, and AA). If the car is rented, phone the rental company.

Health
Make sure you have health insurance coverage for Spain, often not covered by standard American policies. Check whether your insurance covers an air-ambulance home should this prove necessary. EU citizens should carry a European Health Insurance Card (EHIC) issued in their home country, available in the U.K. from a post office or online from www.dh.gov.uk/travellers. This entitles the bearer only to state-provided medical care, so private health insurance may still be a sensible precaution. If it is an emergency, ring 112 and ask for an ambulance (ambulancia), or if near a hospital, head for urgencias, the emergency room. The U.S. Embassy maintains a list of English-speaking physicians in the Madrid area.

The International Association for Medical Assistance to Travelers (IAMAT, www.iamat.org) is a nonprofit organization that anyone can join free of charge. Members receive a directory of English-speaking IAMAT doctors on call 24 hours a day, and they are entitled to services at a set rate.

IAMAT United States: 162 Military Rd., Suite 279, Niagara Falls, NY 14304-1745, tel 716/754-4883

IAMAT Canada: 1287 St. Clair Ave. W., Suite 1, Toronto, Ontario M6E 1B8, tel 416/652-0137.

Hotels & Restaurants

From converted 17th-century palaces to cutting-edge modern hotels, from bullfighters' taverns to nouvelle-cuisine restaurants, Madrid is well prepared to welcome visitors. Although prices have gone up since the days when everything in Spain was unusually cheap, there has been a parallel improvement in quality and services provided.

Hotels

Some hotels offer *media pensión* (breakfast and dinner included) or *pensión completa* (lunch as well) at good prices, so ask when reserving or on arrival. Justly famous for its late-running nightlife, Madrid can be noisy in the town center, so if you are a light sleeper, it is worth asking for the quietest room available; bear in mind that you may lose the good view.

Stars: Hotels in Madrid are graded with a star system of one to five, five being top of the range. The distinction is based on a mix of aesthetic and practical factors, such as the provision of heating and air-conditioning, the quality of bathroom facilities, and the size of the rooms. Any hotel with two or more stars should have an en suite bathroom; if three or more, with a bath and a shower. The cheaper *hostales* and *pensiones* have a separate system of one to three stars.

NOTE 7% I.V.A. (Value Added Tax) is added to the quoted prices. Breakfast is usually not included in the quote. Most double rooms have twin beds; if you want a double bed, ask for a *cama de matrimonio*. The new smoking law prohibits smoking in certain areas. In high season, reserve well in advance. You may be asked for a deposit or credit card and I.D./passport number.

Credit Cards: Many hotels accept all major cards—but it's best to check whether they accept yours. Abbreviations used in this guide are: AE (American Express), DC (Diners Club), MC (Mastercard), and V (Visa).

Restaurants

Madrid offers a wonderful array of food from all over Spain, as people from all over Spain have come to Madrid over time, bringing their dishes with them. Enormous quantities of fresh fish and seafood are also trucked into the capital every evening from the coast. If you want to see the menu, ask for *la carta*. If you ask for the *menú,* you will be told about the *menú del día,* usually offered only for lunch. This is a well-priced three-course set meal, where you can choose between limited options. In more expensive restaurants, the equivalent is the *menú degustación,* an avalanche of small portions. Many of the most authentic restaurants close in August.

Tapas Bars, Bars, & Cafés:

A regular Madrid bar is not a *bar de copas,* which is a drinking establishment, but a center of social life from early in the morning until whenever. According to legend, tapas started life as slices of ham or cheese placed on top of glasses of wine to stop the flies or dust getting in, *tapar* meaning "to cover." Once a free snack provided with every alcoholic drink ordered, now they have a price tag, but they are a wonderful way to try small portions of the food available. If you want a bigger portion, ask for a *ración* (plateful). The norm when *tapeando* (eating tapas) is to have one or two, then change bars and start again. Typical Madrid tapas are *boquerones en vinagre* (fresh anchovies in

salt and vinegar), *albóndigas* (meatballs), *callos* (tripe), *croquetas* (croquettes), and *tortilla de patatas* (Spanish potato omelette), but there are many more. The fact that the Spanish eat something every time they have a drink makes public drunkenness rare. Many tapas bars also have restaurants—if the tapas convince you, have a full sit-down meal.

Organization

Hotels, restaurants, and tapas bars have been listed by price, then in alphabetical order, within each neighborhood chapter division. For bars and cafés, see p. 261.

L=Lunch   D=Dinner

■ PLAZA MAYOR & OLD TOWN

Hotels

▦ **HOTEL REYES CATÓLICOS**
$$ ★★★
CALLE ÁNGEL 18
TEL 91 365 8600
FAX 91 365 9867
www.hotelreyescatolicos.com
Near the Basílica de San Francisco el Grande, this hotel is one of the few in the Austrias quarter and is a good base for visiting the city. It has large, well-equipped, and well-maintained rooms.
ⓘ 38 🅿 🚇 Puerta de Toledo
🚭 🌡 🈂 All major cards

▦ **PETIT PALACE POSADA DEL PEINE**
$$ ★★★★
CALLE POSTAS 17
TEL 91 523 8151

FAX 91 523 2993
www.hthoteles.com
The very central Posada del Peine started life as an inn near the edge of Madrid in 1610. It is now the oldest surviving hotel in Spain. Next to Plaza Mayor and the Puerta del Sol, it has been recently renovated and boasts highly modern facilities, making it one of the best hotels in Madrid.
🛏 69 🚇 Sol 🅂 ⬛ ◼ All major cards

🏨 WESTERN CORTEZO
$$ ★★★
CALLE DOCTOR CORTEZO 3
TEL 91 369 0101
FAX 91 369 3774
www.hotelcortezo.com
Close to Plaza Mayor and the Puerta del Sol, this comfortable, simple hotel was last renovated in 1997 and is pleasantly modern. Many rooms have sitting areas with a desk and armchair. The public spaces match the guest rooms in freshness.
🛏 85 🅿 🚇 Tirso de Molina 🅂 ◼ ◼ All major cards

Restaurants

🍴 CASA LUCIO
$$$$
CALLE CAVA BAJA 35
TEL 91 365 3252
They make very simple dishes but with high-quality ingredients. Try the *huevos estrellados* (fried eggs mixed with potatoes), Madrid-style stewed tripe (*callos a la madrileña*), and the rice pudding (*arroz con leche*). Fine jabugo ham. Very *castellano* (Castilian).
🍴 120 🕐 Closed Sat. L & Aug. 🚇 La Latina 🅂 ◼ All major cards

🍴 EL LANDÓ
$$$$
PLAZA DE GABRIEL MIRÓ 8
TEL 91 366 7681
Simplicity at its most sophisticated. Have some legendary

jamón ibérico (Iberian ham) with *pan con tomate* (bread with crushed tomato) to prepare your taste buds. The restaurant uses excellent raw materials, deliciously prepared: *cocido madrileño, huevos estrellados*, lentils, stews, fish, meats, homemade cakes, and desserts, with very good wine. Reserve in advance.
🍴 65 🕐 Closed Sun. & Aug. 🚇 La Latina 🅿 ◼ ◼ All major cards

🍴 BOTÍN
$$$
CALLE CUCHILLEROS 17
TEL 91 366 4217
Reputed to be the world's oldest restaurant, and, according to Hemingway, the best, Botín was founded in 1725. Recommended are the traditional roast suckling pig (*cochinillo asado*), roast lamb (*cordero asado*), gazpacho, and *almejas marineras* (clams).
🍴 260 🚇 Sol 🅂 ◼ All major cards

🍴 CASA CIRÍACO
$$
CALLE MAYOR 24
TEL 91 548 0620
This very Madrileño restaurant first opened in 1917 and is still much frequented by high society. It has excellent home cooking: try *alubias* (kidney beans) *de La Granja, gambas al ajillo* (garlic shrimp), or their famed *pepitoria de gallina* (hen fricassée). *Cocido madrileño* (typical Madrid stew with meat, chickpeas, and sausage) is available only on Tuesdays. Advisable to reserve.
🍴 65 🕐 Closed Wed. & Aug. 🚇 Sol 🅂 ◼ All major cards

🍴 CASA PACO
$$
PLAZA PUERTA CERRADA 11
TEL 91 366 3166
Typically Madrileño, child-friendly, and popular with bullfighters. Specializes in roast

meat sold by weight, which turned the likes of Orson Welles into faithful customers. Also try their *cocido, callos, sopa de ajo* (garlic soup), and *pisto manchego* (La Mancha vegetable hash).
🍴 100 🕐 Closed Sun. & Aug. 🚇 Sol 🅂 ◼ DC, MC, V

🍴 LA CAMARILLA
$$
CALLE CAVA BAJA 21
TEL 91 354 0207
A traditional old Madrileño restaurant with a menu that changes with the seasons. Try *risotto de champiñón* (mushroom risotto), *cigalas* (crayfish), or *rollito de ternera con gratén de pato* (beef roll with duck au gratin), if available. Excellent *menú del día* at lunchtime for 11 euros.
🍴 60 🕐 Closed Mon. 🚇 La Latina 🅂 ◼ All major cards

🍴 LA CHATA
$$
CALLE CAVA BAJA 24
TEL 91 366 1458
This restaurant, decorated in classical bullfighting style,

offers good traditional Spanish cooking such as roast suckling pig, *rabo de toro* (bull's tail), *chopitos* (whole baby squid), *gambas al pulpo* (shrimp with octopus), and *bacalao a la Chata* (cod cooked to their secret recipe).

🛏 250 🕐 Closed Tues. & Wed. L 🚇 La Latina 🆑 🆂 All major cards

🍽 TABERNA ARTE DIVINO
$$

PLAZA DE LA PROVINCIA 3
TEL 91 364 2706

A very good restaurant, in a 17th-century building, dedicated to creative cooking and fine wine. Try their *bellota* ham, *foie* (liver pâté) with apple and wild mushrooms, *cecina a las cinco especies* (five-spiced cured meat), or *lasaña de verdura* (vegetable lasagna). You should reserve in advance.

🍴 40 🕐 Closed Tues.–Sat. L, Sun. D, Mon., & Aug. 🚇 Sol 🆑 🆂 All major cards

Tapas Bars

CASA DANI
CALLE CALATRAVA 11
TEL 91 365 2621

Beautiful old-style bar, also known as Vinos 11, friendly, and chatty. Try the well-priced *longaniza picante* (spicy pork sausage), *chicharrones* (pork cracklings), jamón, the excellent *queso manchego*, and whatever other tapas they are currently offering.

🕐 Closed Mon. L & Sun, 🚇 La Latina

CASA LUCAS
CALLE CAVA BAJA 30
TEL 91 365 0804

Small bar with very good wine and inventive tapas. Try *revuelto de morcilla y tomate dulce* (scrambled eggs with blood pudding and sweet tomato), *solomillo de cerdo con cebolla confitada* (pork sirloin with onion confit), or *tataki de bonito con puré de manzana* (bonito tataki

with apple purée).

🕐 Closed Wed. L 🚇 La Latina

CERVECERÍA MONJE
CALLE ARENAL 21
TEL 91 548 3598

The amiable Monje family serves a lovely seafood tapa with your drink, tempting you to order raciones—*ostras* (oysters), *gambas*, *percebes* (gooseneck barnacles), *berberechos* (cockles), or *mollejas de cordero* (lamb sweetbreads), to name a few. The freshest produce and good prices.

🕐 Closed Tues. 🚇 Ópera

EL ALMENDRO
CALLE EL ALMENDRO 13
TEL 91 365 4252

A bell rings out to call you to the kitchen hatch to pick up your freshly made food. This bar is almost always packed—let the bell ring for *pringá* (pork, sausage, and chickpea stew), *jamón*, *porra antequerana* (salmorejo Antequera-style), or *roscas* (sweet pastries).

🚇 La Latina

EL BONANNO
PLAZA DEL HUMILLADERO 4
TEL 91 366 6886

Excellent, atmospheric bar, slighty pricy, and popular with the flamenco world. Good place to visit on Sunday morning on your way to the Rastro. Try their *paté de pato* (duck pâté), *cecina* (cured meat), and *boquerones en vinagre* (fresh anchovies in vinegar).

🚇 La Latina

LA ESCONDÍA
PLAZA DE PUERTA CERRADA 6
TEL 91 365 3419

Just by Plaza Mayor, this very Madrileño little bar is a good place to have a *caña* (draft beer) and a tapa in the La Latina quarter. Try the *torta del Casar* (a strong, creamy sheep's cheese), some *morcón* (sausage made with chorizo and pork loin), *mojama* (salted

tuna), or their jamón.

🚇 La Latina, Tirso de Molina

LAMIAK
CALLE CAVA BAJA 42
TEL 91 365 5212

This friendly Basque tapas bar, with a restaurant downstairs, offers inventive tapas such as *bocados de rabo de toro* (bull's tail snacks), *bacalao ajoarriero* (salt cod with peppers), *kokotxas* (cod or hake cheeks), *chipirones en su tinta* (squid cooked in their own ink), or *codorniz en salsa de chocolate* (quail in chocolate sauce).

🕐 Closed Mon. & Sun. D 🚇 La Latina

LA SALAMANDRA
CALLE ALFONSO VI 6
TEL 91 366 0515

Well-chosen wines by the glass or by the bottle. Their delicious seasonal dishes, on the pricey side, include *magret de pato* (duck breast), *torta de queso* (cheesecake), *solomillo de bellota* (pork loin), and an inventive *revueltos* (scrambled egg dishes).

🕐 Closed Sun. D 🚇 La Latina

ENE
CALLE NUNCIO 19
TEL 91 366 2591

The gourmet tapas attract a glamorous crowd to this stylish, minimalist space. The changing menu might include spinach ravioli with squash sauce, swordfish carpaccio or cod croquettes. There is also a restaurant and cocktail bar, and Ene is particularly popular for Sunday brunch.

🕐 Closed Sun. D. 🚇 La Latina

LA TORRE DEL ORO
PLAZA MAYOR 26
TEL 91 366 5016

A favorite bar of bullfighters since 1940 and full of memorabilia. It specializes in paella, fried fish, and sausages.

🚇 Sol

SANLÚCAR

CALLE SAN ISIDRO LABRADOR 14

TEL 91 354 0052

Open since 2002, this friendly Andalusían bar is already famed for its manzanilla sherry and tapas such as *tortillitas de camarones* (baby shrimp pancakes), bellota ham, *langostinos* (king prawns), and *salmorejo* (cold vegetable soup).

🕒 Closed Sun. D & Mon.

🚇 La Latina

■ PALACIO REAL & AROUND

Hotels

SOMETHING SPECIAL

🏨 CASA DE MADRID

$$$$ ★★★★★

CALLE ARRIETA 2

TEL 91 559 5791

FAX 91 540 1100

www.casademadrid.com

This discreet and luxurious seven-room hotel is one of Madrid's best-kept secrets. In a beautiful 18th-century building in the old city, facing the Teatro Real opera house, it feels like the noble family home that it was until 2003. Spacious rooms and excellent service.

ℹ️ 8 🅿️ 🚇 Ópera ⬆️

🃏 All major cards

🏨 LAS MENINAS

$$$ ★★★★

CALLE CAMPOMANES 7

TEL 91 541 2805

FAX 91 541 2806

www.hotelmeninas.com

With elegant decor in soothing gray tones in a remodeled 19th-century building near the Teatro Real, Las Meninas is a good choice for opera lovers but also convenient for major sights. Top-floor rooms are particularly stylish. Breakfast is included with online bookings.

ℹ️ 37 🚇 Opera 📶 🈂️ ⬆️

🃏 All major cards.

🏨 CARLOS V

$$ ★★★

CALLE MAESTRO VICTORIA 5

TEL 91 531 4100

FAX 91 531 3761

www.hotelcarlosv.com

On a pedestrian-friendly street by the Puerta del Sol, this amiable family-run hotel has an unusual art nouveau entrance. Rooms are large and elegantly decorated—ask for one with a balcony. The top-floor rooms have terraces. There is shuttle service to airport. Breakfast included. Cafeteria.

ℹ️ 67 🅿️ 🚇 Sol 🈂️

🃏 All major cards

🏨 HOTEL ÓPERA

$$ ★★★

CUESTA DE SANTO DOMINGO 2

TEL 91 541 2800

FAX 91 541 6923

www.hotelopera.com

Near the opera house, this hotel has comfortable rooms with large windows, some with balconies. Customer service is friendly. Non-smoking rooms available. The hotel restaurant, *El Café de la Ópera ($$$$, Calle Arrueta 6, tel 91 542 6382)*, is well-regarded, serving Spanish and international food while regaling you with opera and *zarzuela* (Spanish light opera) music. Sometimes waiters—opera singers between jobs—join in.

ℹ️ 79 🚇 Ópera 📶 🈂️

🃏 All major cards

🏨 MARIO

$$ ★★

CALLE CAMPOMANES 4

TEL 91 548 8548

FAX 91 559 1288

www.room-matehotels.com

Chic and well-equipped but reasonably priced, the Mario features designs by Tomás Alía and Philippe Starck. Rooms have plenty of natural light and staff are friendly and helpful.

ℹ️ 54 🚇 Ópera 📶 🈂️

🃏 All major cards

🏨 PETIT PALACE ARENAL

$$ ★★★

CALLE ARENAL 16

TEL 91 564 4355

FAX 91 564 0854

www.hthoteles.com

In a restored 19th-century palace near the Puerta del Sol, this hotel has large rooms, friendly customer service, beautiful decor, and good bed-and-breakfast deals. One floor is kept for non-smokers. Technologically well equipped.

ℹ️ 64 🚇 Ópera 📶 🈂️

🃏 All major cards

Restaurants

🍴 ALGARABÍA

$$$

CALLE UNIÓN 8

TEL 91 542 4131

Delicious food from the Rioja region, with a seasonally changing menu including traditional dishes such as pork fillet with caramelized onions or tempura asparagus. For dessert, don't miss the black chocolate pizza. There are only 11 tables, so be sure to book.

🪑 34. 🚇 Opera 🃏 All major cards

🍴 ENTRE SUSPIRO Y SUSPIRO

$$$

CALLE CAÑOS DEL PERAL 3

TEL 91 542 0644

Good Mexican food in a lovely old palace. Excellent *cebiche* (raw fish or seafood in lemon juice). The corn quesadillas filled with *cuitlacoche* (corn mushrooms) and jalapeño chilis are very tasty, as is the *ensalada mandinga* (shrimp, mango, onion, and coriander salad). Good margaritas and tequilas.

🪑 65 🅿️ 🕒 Closed Sat. L & Sun. 🚇 Santo Domingo, Ópera 🈂️ 🃏 All major cards

---

🍴 EL PATO MUDO
$$
CALLE COSTANILLA DE
LOS ÁNGELES 8
TEL 91 559 4840
In the middle of the *casco viejo* (old quarter), good traditional Mediterranean cooking, especially paellas and rice dishes with duck, fish, or vegetables. Cozy, bohemian atmosphere. Call ahead on weekends.
🔲 55 🕐 Closed Sun. 🚇 Santo Domingo, Ópera 🅿️ 🅰️ All major cards

🍴 LA BOLA
$
CALLE BOLA 5
TEL 91 547 6930
Founded in 1870, this excellent corner restaurant serves typical Madrid food and is something of a shrine to *cocido madrileño*. The *caldo* (stock) is served as a soup and, as a stew, you get the delicious *garbanzos* (chickpeas), chorizo, *morcilla* (blood pudding), chicken, pork and ham, cabbage, leeks and potatoes, all cooked up over oak embers. Other specialties include *callos a la madrileña* (tripe Madrid-style) and roast lamb, and for dessert *buñuelos de manzana* (apple fritters).
🔲 100 🅿️ 🕐 Closed Sun. D 🚇 Santo Domingo 🅿️

Tapas Bars

ANCIANO REY
DE LOS VINOS
CALLE BAILÉN 19
TEL 91 559 5332
A delightful century-old bar, with beautiful tiles, serving very good wines and sherries. With each drink they offer a savory biscuit or a tapa of *cabrales* (strong Asturian cheese) or *anchoa con tomate* (anchovy with tomato). Try *escabeche* (soused fish), *pavías de bacalao* (fried salt cod in saffron batter), or *albóndigas*. A specialty is *torrijas*, milky bread fried in batter with

honey or sugar and wine.
🕐 Closed Tue. 🚇 Ópera

CAFÉ DE ORIENTE
PLAZA DE ORIENTE
TEL 91 541 3974 OR 91 547 1564
On top of the ruins of the 17th-century San Gil convent (whose vaulted ceilings still survive), the café offers imaginative cooking and good draft beer. Its excellent tapas include *mero confitado en aceite de almendras con brandada de arenque ahumado* (slow-cooked sea bass in almond oil with strips of smoked herring). If you want a full sit-down meal, book in advance.
🚇 Ópera

SOMETHING SPECIAL

TABERNA DEL
ALABARDERO
CALLE FELIPE V 4 & 6
TEL 91 547 2577
With a French Basque flavor and offering a modern take on traditional dishes, this restaurant serves tapas in its bar. Try the *bacalao con tomate* (cod with tomato) or *con pisto* (vegetable hash), the *chipirones en su tinta* (baby squid in their own ink), or the house specialty, *chistorra*, a tasty Basque sausage.
🚇 Ópera

■ DOWNTOWN MADRID

Hotels

🏨 QUO PUERTA DEL SOL
$$$ ★★★★
CALLE SEVILLA 4
TEL 91 532 9049
FAX 91 531 2834
www.hotelesquo.com
This hotel opened in a very central early 20th-century building in 2003. The interior is very cleanly designed, sharp, and modern. Good views from the rooms on the main street and little noise through the double-

glazed windows. Friendly and helpful staff.
ℹ️ 62 🚇 Sevilla 🅰️ 🅰️ 🅰️ 🅰️ All major cards

🏨 HOTEL INFANTAS
🍴 $$ ★★★★
CALLE INFANTAS 29
TEL 91 521 2828
FAX 91 521 6688
www.lussohoteles.com
In the trendy Chueca area near the Gran Vía, you can walk almost everywhere from the Infantas. With a chic restaurant on the ground floor which is popular with non-guests and reasonable rates, this is an attractive option if you want to combine sightseeing with nightlife.
ℹ️ 40 🚇 Banco de España 🅰️ 🅰️ 🅰️ 🅰️ All major cards

SOMETHING SPECIAL

🏨 HOTEL DE LAS LETRAS
🍴 $$ ★★★★
GRAN VÍA 11
TEL 91 523 7980
FAX 91 523 7981
www.hoteldelasletras.com
The 1917 neoclassical exterior encloses an avant-garde interior with a literary theme. It has a library, and the corridors are lined with interesting quotations. The bar on its summer roof terrace has excellent views of Madrid. Very modern, well equipped, and with good service. It has a successful new restaurant, DL's *(Calle Caballero de Gracia 11, tel 91 523 7850, $$),* whose chef, Ernesto Hinojal, offers an original cosmopolitan take on traditional dishes like cocido madrileño. Standouts include *brocheta de chipirón* (baby squid kebab), the carpaccios, the sushi, and *taco de atún a la plancha* (grilled tuna bites).
ℹ️ 107 🚇 Gran Vía, Sevilla 🅰️ 🅰️ 🅰️ 🅰️ All major cards

🏨 LIABENY

$$ ★★★★

CALLE SALUD 3
TEL 91 531 9000
FAX 91 532 7421
www.liabeny.es

Large and modern, the hotel is
two minutes from the Puerta
del Sol and Gran Vía. It has
marble bathrooms and all the
facilities expected of a four-star
hotel. Helpful and courteous
staff. Easy parking.

🛏 220 🅿 🚇 Sol, Gran Vía
🛗 🚭 🚱 🛒 All major cards

🏨 OSCAR

🍴 **$$ ★★★**

PLAZA VÁZQUEZ DE MELIA 12
TEL 91 701 1173
FAX 91 521 6196
www.room-matehotels.com

In the heart of buzzing
Chueca, with stunning avant-
garde design and a trendy bar
and restaurant, the Oscar is
unsurprisingly a favorite of
the fashion and media crowd.
Great facilities for the price.
The latest of the growing
Room Mate group, it opened
in 2008.

🛏 75 🚇 Chueca 🛗 🚭 🛒
🛒 All major cards

🏨 PETIT PALACE DUCAL

$$ ★★★

CALLE HORTALEZA 3
TEL 91 521 1043
FAX 91 521 5064
www.hthoteles.com

In a recently refurbished
19th-century palace just off
the Gran Vía, this hotel is now
modern, high-tech, and a good
base for exploring the city.

🛏 58 🚇 Gran Vía 🚭 🛗
🛒 All major cards

🏨 REGINA

$$ ★★★

CALLE ALCALÁ 19
TEL 91 521 4725
FAX 91 522 4088
www.hotelreginamadrid.com

This centrally located hotel
is comfortable, clean, and
recently renovated. Spacious

rooms for the tired sightseer.
No restaurant. Breakfast
included in the rate.

🛏 180 🅿 🚇 Sevilla 🛗 🛒
🛒 All major cards

🏨 VINCCI CENTRUM

$$ ★★★★

CALLE CEDACEROS 4
TEL 91 360 4720
FAX 91 522 4515
www.vinccihoteles.com

Opened in March 2004, this
centrally located hotel (very
close to the three main art
museums) is stylish, modern,
and well equipped, and the
staff multilingual and friendly.
Some of the more expensive
(superior) rooms have balco-
nies with lovely views of the
Madrid skyline.

🛏 87 🚇 Sevilla 🛒 🛗 🛒
🛒 All major cards

Restaurants

🍴 LA TERRAZA DEL CASINO

$$$$$

CALLE ALCALÁ 15
TEL 91 532 1275

This Casino de Madrid
restaurant has grand dining
rooms and a beautiful sum-
mer terrace. Its chef, Paco
Roncero, a creative disciple
of the Catalan genius Ferrán
Adriá, has already achieved his
first Michelin star. Imagina-
tive modern Mediterranean
cuisine—try anything, as the
textures, aromas, and flavors
are wonderful. Famous dishes
include *tortilla en tres pisos*
(three-story omelette), served
in a glass.

🪑 65 🅿 🕐 Closed Sat. L, Sun.,
Aug., & Easter week 🚇 Sevilla
🛒 🛒 All major cards

🍴 LA CASTAFIORE

$$$$

CALLE MARQUÉS DE
MONASTERIO 5
TEL 91 310 6651 OR 91 319 4221

Named after the co-star of
several Tintin adventures, this

PRICES

HOTELS

An indication of the cost of
double room in the high sea-
son is given by $ signs.

$$$$$	Over $240
$$$$	$160–$240
$$$	$110–$160
$$	$70–1$10
$	Under $70

RESTAURANTS

An indication of the cost of
three-course meal without
drinks is given by $ signs.

$$$$$	Over $65
$$$$	$50–$65
$$$	$30–$50
$$	$20–$30
$	Under $20

---

restaurant has waiters who are
opera singers between jobs.
They will sing for your supper
(not at lunchtime) and end
the evening with an ensemble
performance, so don't go for
a quiet conversational dinner.
The food is Mediterranean
with a Basque touch. Try
merluza rellena de langostinos
(hake filled with king prawns),
*lubina a la espalda con patatas
panaderas tosca* (grilled sea bass
with roast breaded potatoes),
or *solomillo de buey con salsa de
boletus* (ox sirloin with boletus
sauce). Reserve in advance.

🪑 125 🕐 Closed Sat. L & Sun.
🚇 Recoletos, Colón 🛒 🅿
🛒 All major cards

SOMETHING SPECIAL

🍴 LHARDY

$$$$

CARRERA DE SAN JERÓNIMO 8
TEL 91 521 3385

Established in 1839, this place
is legendary. Upstairs is the
restaurant, ornate in its original Isabelline style and famed
for its *cocido madrileño*,
its seasonal game, and its
excellent fish—try the *lubina al
horno* (baked sea bass). Reserve

🏨 Hotel 🍴 Restaurant 🛏 No. of Guest Rooms 🪑 No. of Seats 🚇 Metro 🅿 Parking 🕐 Closed 🛗 Elevator

in advance. Downstairs is a very fancy stand-up snack bar, serving delicious croquettes, *hojaldres* (light, flaky pastries), tapas, and, famously, a stupendous consommé poured into porcelain cups from silver samovars. If you fancy a dash of *jerez* (sherry) in it, don't hesitate to ask.

🍴 130 🕐 Closed Sun. D & Aug. 🚇 Sol, Sevilla ❄️ 💳 All major cards

🍴 LA TASQUITA DE ENFRENTE
$$$$
CALLE BALLESTA 6
TEL 91 532 5449
Just off the Gran Vía, this small restaurant is one of the best in Madrid. Run by chef Juanjo López, expect traditional Spanish dishes with a creative twist, made with top-quality produce sourced from all over the country. Particularly good seafood. Booking essential.

🍴 20 🚇 Gran Vía ❄️ 💳 All major cards

🍴 ERROTA-ZAR
$$$
CALLE JOVELLANOS 3
1ST FLOOR
TEL 91 531 2564
This restaurant offers excellent traditional Basque cooking, an impressive wine list, and a large selection of cigars (*puros*). Try *boletus al horno* (roast boletus mushrooms), *kokotxas de merluza en aceite* (hake cheeks in olive oil), and the delicious homemade sheep's-milk yogurt (*cuajada*). You should reserve in advance.

🍴 142 🕐 Closed Sun. & Aug. 🚇 Banco de España, Sevilla ❄️ 💳 All major cards

🍴 EL MENTIDERO DE LA VILLA
$$$
CALLE SANTO TOMÉ 6
TEL 91 308 1285
In this modern Spanish restaurant, decorated with

wooden fairground horses and a trompe l'oeil ceiling, chef José Ynglada is nothing if not imaginative. Try his *crujiente de morcilla sobre salsa de miel y gengibre* (crunchy blood pudding in honey and ginger sauce) or the *pularda rellena de foie con salsa de boletus y trufas* (hen stuffed with pâté in boletus and truffle sauce). Disabled access. Reserve in advance.

🍴 50 🅿️ 🕐 Closed Sat. L, Sun., & Aug. 🚇 Chueca, Colón ❄️ 💳 All major cards

🍴 BOCAÍTO
$$
CALLE LIBERTAD 4
TEL 91 532 1219
This friendly restaurant offers Andalucían cooking with an occasional Madrileño touch. The fish menu varies with today's catch. Delicious on toast: *berberechos* (cockles), *gambas* (shrimp), and *trigueros* (wild asparagus). Regular stewed dishes: on Wednesday, *judiones de la granja con almejas* (huge fresh beans with clams); on Thursday, *cocido madrileño;* and on Friday, *potaje castellano* (vegetable and pulse stew from Castilla). Good tapas.

🍴 80 🕐 Closed Sat. L, Sun., & Aug. 🚇 Chueca ❄️ 💳 All major cards

🍴 LA PAELLA DE LA REINA
$$
CALLE LA REINA 39
TEL 91 531 1885 OR 91 531 6014
This Valencian restaurant specializes in paellas and rice dishes, as its name suggests—*paella de bogavante* or *de marisco* or *de la casa* or *valenciana* (lobster or seafood or house or Valencian paella); *arroz a'banda* or *negro* or *caldoso con bogavante* (rice in fish broth, or with shrimp and cuttlefish and its ink, or soupy with lobster). Fine desserts and good wines. Reserve in advance.

🍴 70 🚇 Banco de España ❄️ 💳 All major cards

🍴 ZARA
$
CALLE INFANTAS 5
TEL 91 532 2074
The friendliest Cuban restaurant in Madrid, serving delicious *ropa vieja* (literally, "old clothes," but here a meat stew). Delicious *tortilla de plátano* (banana omelette), *yuca frita* (fried cassava), and *picadillo de ternera con arroz y plátano* (minced beef with rice and banana). Famous daiquiris. Small, with no reservations, so go early.

🍴 45 🕐 Closed Sat., Sun., & Aug. 🚇 Chueca, Gran Vía

Tapas Bars

BODEGAS LA ARDOSA
CALLE COLÓN 13
TEL 91 521 4979
This friendly bar has been selling drinks (including Irish beers and vermouth on tap) and tapas since 1892. Their *salmorejo* (a thick, cold soup, similar to gazpacho, but with ham and egg and without peppers and cucumber) is historic. Try *cecina de León* (cured beef), *fabes con calamares* (Asturian beans with squid), or their varied *croquetas*.

🚇 Tribunal

CASA LABRA
CALLE TETÚAN 12
TEL 91 531 0081
Here since 1860, this bar is famous as the 1879 birthplace of the Spanish Socialist Workers' Party. It specializes in croquetas and in *bacalao* (cod), of which the freshly fried *tajadas* (slices) are particularly tasty.

🚇 Callao

LA COSA NOSTRA
CALLE DE LA CRUZ 3
TEL 91 521 2153
This bar's name refers to its decorative theme, not to its regular customers. Very central, it offers straightforward and rapidly served food, based on

crepes dulces or *saladas* (sweet or savory pancakes) and *empanadas*.

🚇 Sevilla

LA CRUZ BLANCA
CALLE DE LA CRUZ 11
TEL 91 521 0770

Owned by the brewery, this establishment sells very good Cruzcampo draft beer and good *raciones* of *pulpo a la gallega* (octopus Galician-style), *chopitos* (baby squid), and *sepia* (cuttlefish), as well as other seafood and good cheese and ham.

🕐 Closed Mon. 🚇 Sevilla

TABERNA DE ÁNGEL SIERRA
CALLE GRAVINA 11
TEL 91 531 0126

A very typical 1917-vintage Madrid bar with a beautiful facade. Excellent draft beer and very good vermouth on tap, with fine tapas including *anchoas* (anchovies) and wonderful *escabeches*.

🚇 Chueca

■ AROUND PLAZA DE SANTA ANA

Hotels

🏨 ME MADRID
$$$$ ★★★★
PLAZA DE SANTA ANA 14
TEL 91 701 6000
FAX 91 522 0307
www.mebymelia.com

Overlooking the Plaza de Santa Ana, the historic old Grand Hotel Reina Victoria has been transformed into a calm and discreetly high-tech temple of contemporary cool, while retaining its traditional beauty. The rooftop bar has beautiful views over the city, and it turns into something of a hotspot come evening. Inside, there are plenty of good places to hang out. Friendly and efficient 24-hour service.

ℹ️ 192 🅿️ 🚇 Sol 🛗 ♿ 🍽️
🚇 All major cards

🏨 INGLÈS
$$ ★★★
CALLE ECHEGARAY 8
TEL 91 429 6551
FAX 91 420 2423
www.ingleshotel.com

Opened in 1886, this hotel—where Virginia Woolf and other writers and artists used to stay—has few frills, but it is well situated near Plaza de Santa Ana and very close to iconic bars like Viva Madrid and Los Gabrieles. Clean, friendly, and well-priced.

ℹ️ 58 🅿️ 🛗 🚇 All major cards

🏨 MIAU
$ ★★★
CALLE DEL PRÍNCIPE 26
TEL 91 369 7120
FAX 91 429 3068
www.hotelmiau.com

Welcoming family-run hotel, behind a beautiful 18th-century facade, on Plaza de Santa Ana. Some of the rooms have small balconies overlooking the square. Reasonably priced and close to public parking facilities.

ℹ️ 20 🚇 Antón Martín, Sevilla 🛗 ♿ 🚇 All major cards

Restaurants

🍴 EL RINCÓN DE ESTEBAN
$$$
CALLE SANTA CATALINA 3
TEL 91 429 9289

Cozy and elegant, much frequented by politicians, this restaurant's specialties include *manda huevos* (fried eggs, thin-cut potato fries, shavings of *jamón ibérico*, and baby eels), *merluza con almejas* (hake with clams), and *perdiz estofada a la toledana* (Toledo-style partridge stew). In May and December, it opens on Sundays for lunch.

🪑 60 🅿️ 🕐 Closed Sun. & Aug. 🚇 Sevilla ♿ 🚇 All major cards

🍴 PRADA A TOPE
$$
CALLE PRÍNCIPE 11
TEL 91 429 5921

Delicious reasonably priced food from the León village of El Bierzo. Good tapas at the bar. Try their local specialty, *botillo* (chickpeas, cabbage, potatoes, and pork ribs), chorizo cooked in wine, or their famous *codillos* (pig's trotters), served with chorizo, potatoes cooked in theirskins, cabbage, and refriedvegetables.

🪑 45 🕐 Closed Sun. D & Mon. 🚇 Sevilla, Sol ♿ 🚇 DC, MC, V

🍴 ZERAIN
$$
CALLE QUEVEDO 3
TEL 91 429 7909

This friendly country-style Basque restaurant specializes in cider (hence the large barrels). Its grilled fresh fish and meat is delicious. Also try their *tortilla de bacalao* (cod omelette), *alubias de Tolosa* (Tolosa kidney beans), or their more elaborate fish dishes.

🪑 140 🕐 Closed Sun. & Aug. ♿ 🚇 All major cards

🍴 ¡CUANDO SALÍ DE CUBA!
$
CALLE TERNERA 4
TEL 91 522 9318

This friendly Cuban joint was one of Hemingway's favorite *tabernas* in Madrid. It offers unpretentious Cuban food and a well-priced lunch menu as well as good daiquiris and mojitos. Live Cuban music, 10:30 p.m.–2 a.m., Wed.–Sat.

🪑 40 🕐 Closed Sun. 🚇 Callao, Santo Domingo ♿ 🚇 DC, MC, V

🍴 LA BIOTIKA
$
CALLE AMOR DE DIOS 3
TEL 91 429 0780

A warm and cozy macrobiotic vegetarian hangout that makes

🏨 Hotel   🍴 Restaurant   ℹ️ No. of Guest Rooms   🪑 No. of Seats   🚇 Metro   🅿️ Parking   🕐 Closed   🛗 Elevator

delicious salads and homemade soups as well as tofu-based dishes. Near Plaza de Santa Ana.

🔢 25 🕐 Closed Sun. D 🚇 Antón Martín ⛔ Not accepted

🍴 LA VACA VERÓNICA
$

CALLE MORATÍN 38
TEL 91 429 7827

A small, informal, romantic Argentine restaurant, quiet and beautifully decorated. Delicious beef, as you would expect, cooked over hot stones, but also other meats and fresh fish, as well as a wide selection of salads. Try the homemade pastas, the one with *carabinero* (large grilled red shrimp) being legendary. There are also some impressive chocolate desserts. Reserve in advance.

🔢 60 🕐 Closed Sat. L 🚇 Antón Martín 🅿️ ⛔ All major cards

Tapas Bars

CASA ALBERTO
CALLE HUERTAS 18
TEL 91 429 9356

This bar and restaurant, dating from 1827, is much loved by bullfighters and aficionados. It is famous for its *rabo de toro estofado* (stewed bull's tail). Vermouth on tap, delicious with a good tapa. Try the *callos, jamón ibérico, albóndigas* (meatballs), or *croquetas.*

🕐 Closed Mon., Sun. D, & Aug. 🚇 Antón Martín

CERVECERÍA ALEMANA
PLAZA DE SANTA ANA 6
TEL 91 429 7033

A lovely bar, open since 1904 and right in Plaza de Santa Ana. Happily, it is little changed since the days when Hemingway used to drink here, normally by the window. Tapas include good salads, *surtido de ahumados* (selection of smoked fish), *esparragos y palmitos* (asparagus and palm hearts), and *ensalada*

de tomate con queso de cabra (tomato salad with goat's cheese).

🕐 Closed Tues. 🚇 Sevilla

LA AGUJA
CALLE AVE MARÍA 25

If you fancy listening to rock, blues, and jazz while you eat tapas and you're up for a bit of a party, then this is your place. Try the *tortilla de patatas al curry* (curried potato omelette), *croquetas de espinaca* (spinach croquettes), or *tostas de lacón con albahaca* (pork shoulder with fresh basil on toast) as you swallow your draft beer.

🚇 Lavapiés

LA TABERNA DE ANTONIO SÁNCHEZ
CALLE MESÓN DE PAREDES 13
TEL 91 539 7826

Named in the early 19th century after the original owner's son, who died in the bullring, the taberna still retains its connections with the bullfighting world. The food is suitably Madrileño: *caracoles guisados* (stewed snails), *acelgas con almejas* (Swiss chard with clams), *tortilla San Isidro* (cod omelette), and *huevos estrellados.* Try the *torrijas*—milk-soaked bread fried in batter and sweetened with honey or sugar and wine.

🕐 Closed Sun. D 🚇 Tirso de Molina

TABERNA LA DOLORES
PLAZA DE JESÚS 4
TEL 91 429 2243

Founded in 1908, this is one of the best known old-style bars in Madrid, with its lovely tile facade. Delicious *boquerones* (fresh anchovies), *empanadas,* and good draft beer.

🚇 Sevilla, Antón Martín

LA TRUCHA
CALLE MANUEL FERNÁNDEZ Y GONZÁLEZ 3
TEL 91 429 5833

This is a very Andalusian bar, both in decor and in tapas, and

hence the accent on frying. Try the *pescaíto frito* (small whole fried fish), the *berenjenas fritas* (fried sliced eggplant), the *alcachofas fritas* (fried artichoke), and the *verbena de ahumados* (smoked fish selection). Summer terrace.

🚇 Sevilla, Sol

LA VENENCIA
CALLE ECHEGARAY 7
TEL 91 429 7313

Famous for its wines and sherries, along with excellent tapas such as *mojama* (salted tuna), *lomo embuchado* (pork loin sausage), *encurtidos* (pickles), and very good *anchoas* (anchovies). A hang-out for wine experts, so avoid asking for a glass of soda—or risk being surrounded by raised eyebrows.

🚇 Sevilla

◼ PASEO DEL PRADO

Hotels

🏨 PALACE
🍴 $$$$$ ★★★★★
PLAZA DE LAS CORTES 7
TEL 91 360 8000 OR 888/625-5144 (U.S. OR CANADA)
FAX 91 360 8100
www.palacemadrid.com

Inaugurated by King Alfonso XIII in 1912, the Palace has sumptuous public spaces with period furniture, chandeliers, and tapestries. The enormous stained-glass cupola in one of the salons is impressively beautiful. Rooms are small, but interior furnishings and bathrooms are first-class. The bar is a favorite haunt of politicians, actors, and writers.

ℹ️ 465 🅿️ 🔄 ❄️ 🛡️ ⛔ All major cards

🏨 RITZ
🍴 $$$$$ ★★★★★
PLAZA DE LA LEALTAD 5
TEL 91 701 6767
FAX 91 701 6776
www.ritz.es

Built in 1910 for King Alfonso

XIII, who realized that there was no hotel in Madrid grand enough for the guests invited to his wedding to Queen Victoria's granddaughter. The hotel is full of beautiful antiques and chandeliers, and it is surrounded by gardens.

🛈 167 🅿 ⊟ 📶 🎛 �e All major cards

SOMETHING SPECIAL

🏨 VILLA REAL
🍴 $$$$ ★★★★★
PLAZA DE LAS CORTES 10
TEL 91 420 3767
FAX 91 420 2547
www.derbyhotels.es
A modern hotel in an ideal location, built to blend in with older surroundings. Decor is the French style. It boasts wonderful modern and antique sculptures, paintings, and other art, including a collection of third-century Roman mosaics. Guest rooms have sitting areas with mahogany furniture and bathrooms with Carrara marble. Suites have balconies and saunas.

🛈 120 🅿 ⊟ 📶
�e All major cards

🏨 HOTEL MORA
$ ★★
PASEO DEL PRADO 32
TEL 91 420 1569
FAX 91 420 0564
www.hotelmora.com
Close to Atocha railway station, the major museums, and parks, this friendly five-story hotel is well priced and recently refurbished. Rooms on the upper stories are quieter. Good bar.

🛈 62 🚇 Atocha ⊟ 📶 �e All major cards

Restaurants

🍴 ALBOROQUE
$$$$$
CALLE ATOCHA 34
TEL 902 203025
One of Madrid's top restaurants, run by award-winning

chef Andrés Madrigal. A beautiful 19th-century palace has been turned into a gourmet center, with an exhibition space and also a less formal restaurant. Madrigal's unique style of cooking is sometimes described as Mediterranean fusion, owing to such dishes as partridge dim sum. A real experience.

🍴 60 🕐 Closed Sat. L & Sun. 🚇 Antón Martín 📶 �e All major cards

🍴 BALZAC
$$$$
CALLE MORETO 7
TEL 91 420 0177
Balzac's chef, Andrés Madrigal, is inventive, and a master of aromas. His dishes are constantly evolving, so trying the *menú degustación* may be a sensible decision on the first visit. Madrigal is famous for his seafood. Reserve in advance.

🍴 70 🕐 Closed Sat L, Sun., & second half Aug. 📶 �e All major cards

🍴 PARADÍS RF CASA DE AMÉRICA
$$$
PALACIO DE LINARES
PASEO DE RECOLETOS 2
TEL 91 575 4540
Cutting-edge Catalan and Mediterranean cuisine under the guidance of famed chef Ramón Freixa, in a modern minimalist setting inside the Palacio de Linares. The restaurant is noted for its rice and codfish dishes and inventive use of the freshest seasonal raw materials. Good wine selection. Try also the sister restaurant inside the Thyssen-Bornemisza museum.

🍴 60 🅿 🕐 Closed Sat. L & Sun. 🚇 Banco de España 📶 �e All major cards

🍴 AROLA MADRID
$$
REINA SOFÍA MUSEUM
ALLE ARGUMOSA 43

PRICES

HOTELS

An indication of the cost of double room in the high season is given by $ signs.
$$$$$	Over $240
$$$$	$160–$240
$$$	$110–$160
$$	$70–1$10
$	Under $70

RESTAURANTS

An indication of the cost of three-course meal without drinks is given by $ signs.
$$$$$	Over $65
$$$$	$50–$65
$$$	$30–$50
$$	$20–$30
$	Under $20

TEL 91 467 0202
Inside the brand-new Nouvel-designed wing of the Museo Reina Sofía and looking onto the beautiful enclosed plaza, this very modern restaurant is most informal of top chef Sergi Arola's restaurants in Madrid. Try the *pastel de bacalao con naranja y cebolleta* (codfish pie with orange and spring onion) before moving on to the *espuma de chocolate blanco* (white chocolate foam).

🍴 104 🅿 🕐 Closed Mon. (from 9 p.m.) & Tues. 🚇 Atocha 📶 �e All major cards

🍴 IBOO CIBELES
$
CALLE ALCALÁ 55
TEL 91 781 1555
This is one branch of a very original chain invented by the successful young chef Mario Sandoval; it has high-class Mediterranean food, fast-food-style, at popular prices. Delicious salads, fish and meat dishes, and desserts in a modern and sophisticated setting. Open all day. Other branches at Calle Sor Ángela de la Cruz 17 (*Metro: Cuzco*) and at Calle Génova 4 (*Metro:*

Alonso Martínez).
🛏 120 🚇 Banco de España
📷 📋 All major cards

■ **PARQUE DEL RETIRO & AROUND**

Hotels

🏨 **AC PALACIO DEL RETIRO**
$$$$$ *****
CALLE ALFONSO XII 14
TEL 91 523 7460
FAX 34 91 523 7461
www.ac-hotels.com
In an early 20th-century palace, restored and converted into a hotel in late 2004, this impressive but cozy hotel has excellent facilities and a good combination of traditional and modern design. With lovely views of the Parque del Retiro, it is perfectly situated for visiting the major museums.
🚪 50 🅿 🚇 Retiro 📷 ⬛
📋 📺 📋 All major cards

🏨 **HOTEL WELLINGTON**
🍴 **$$$$$** *****
CALLE VELÁZQUEZ 8
TEL 91 575 4400
FAX 91 576 4164
www.hotel-wellington.com
A lovely, traditional hotel, with beautiful views of the Parque del Retiro. Popular with bullfighters, who dress here before leaving for the bullfight. Well furnished and decorated, it has a lovely garden with a swimming pool. Its associated modern Basque restaurant, Goizeko Wellington *(Calle Villanueva 34, tel 91 577 0138, $$$$, closed Sat. D, July, & Aug., all major cards)* is very good, with a mix of traditional dishes like *kokotxa de merluza* (hake cheeks) and original ones like *ensalada de ostras con granizado de gin tonic* (oyster salad topped by gin tonic slush).
🚪 300 🅿 🚇 Retiro 📷 ⬛
📋 🏊 📋 All major cards

🏨 **HOSPES MADRID**
$$$$ *****
PLAZA INDEPENDENCIA 1
TEL 91 432 2911
www.fuenso.com
Overlooking the Parque del Retiro and close to the major museums and shops of the Salamanca district, the Hospes has a fantastic location, but is also a beautiful hotel decorated in soothing tones with a renowned restaurant and a great spa. The best rooms are duplex with beamed ceilings.
🚪 41 🅿 🚇 Retiro 📷 ⬛
📋 All major cards

Restaurants

🍴 **HORCHER**
$$$$$
CALLE ALFONSO XII 6
TEL 91 522 0731
Set up in 1943 by a Berlin restaurateur escaping the war, this elegant establishment now also serves more international cooking, specializing in seasonal wild game dishes, such as wild boar *(jabalí)*, venison *(venado, ciervo)*, and duck *(pato)*. It also has good fish and desserts. Dress formally. Reserve in advance.
🛏 70 🅿 🕐 Closed Sat. L, Sun., & Aug. 🚇 Retiro 📷
📋 All major cards

🍴 **CASA RAFA**
$$$$
CALLE NARVÁEZ 68
TEL 91 573 1087
Said by many to serve the best seafood in Madrid—but the meat dishes are also good. The chef is extremely rigorous in selecting his raw materials, mainly from the Cantabrian coast. Delicious *gambas a la plancha* (grilled shrimp), *percebes* (gooseneck barnacles), *rodaballo* (turbot), *centolla* (spider crab), *salpicón de marisco* (seafood salad), and delicious stews like *langostinos con verduras en fideuá* (king prawns and vegetables in

noodles). Mouth-watering. Reserve in advance.
🛏 80 🅿 🕐 Closed Mon. D
🚇 Ibiza 📷 📋 All major cards

🍴 **VIRIDIANA**
$$$$
CALLE JUAN DE MENA 14
TEL 91 523 4478
Named after Buñuel's 1961 film masterpiece, this is one of the very best restaurants in Madrid. It is led by the creative chef Abraham García, who is also a writer, a film buff, and a lover of bullfighting and horse racing, as the decor reflects. He serves the freshest seasonal foods, free-range or wild meat and fish, with glorious taste and aroma. Try absolutely anything. The wine list is highly rated also. Reserve in advance.
🛏 60 🅿 🕐 Closed Sun.
🚇 Banco de España, Retiro
📷 📋 All major cards

🍴 **LA GAMELLA**
$$$
CALLE ALFONSO XII 4
TEL 91 532 4509
Begun in 1988 by an American owner and looking onto the Parque del Retiro, La Gamella serves excellent, delicate, and imaginative Spanish and American dishes. Try the *steak tártar al Jack Daniel's, magret de pato en salsa agridulce de frutas rojas* (duck breast in sweet-and-sour red-fruit sauce), or just go for a top-quality hamburger. Welcoming and relaxing. Reserve in advance.
🛏 48 🕐 Closed Sat. L, Sun., & first half Aug. 🚇 Retiro 📷
📋 All major cards

🍴 **CASA DOMINGO 1920**
$$
CALLE ALCALÁ 99
TEL 91 431 1895
This friendly family restaurant, serving typical Madrileño food since 1920 in an art nouveau setting, is a historical monument. Try the *gallina en*

📷 Nonsmoking 📋 Air-conditioning 🏊 Indoor Pool 🏊 Outdoor Pool 📺 Health Club 📋 Credit Cards

pepitoria (hen fricassée), *pastel de cabracho* (scorpion-fish pie), *estofado de rabo de toro* (bull's tail stew), or their famous *callos* (tripe). On the dessert front, their crêpes suzettes are, appropriately, legendary. Reserve in advance.
🛏 150 🅿 🚇 Retiro 💲 ♿ All major cards

🍴 CASA PELLO
$
CALLE DOCTOR CASTELO 2
TEL 91 574 0103
A small and friendly family restaurant offering fine local fare, well priced. Don't miss their *cocido madrileño*, *pimientos rellenos de bacalao con gambas* (peppers stuffed with cod and shrimp), and *croquetas de espinacas y roquefort* (spinach and Roquefort croquettes). Reserve in advance.
🪑 35 🕐 Closed Sun. 🚇 Ibiza ♿ All major cards

Tapas Bars

LA ANTIGUA
CALLE O'DONNELL 12
TEL 91 576 4198
Have a *caña* (glass of draft beer) and a good traditional *tapa* or *ración* at the bar. This regular joint fills up at lunchtime because of the tasty food and very good prices.
🚇 Príncipe de Vergara, Retiro

LUCHARNA
CALLE MENORCA 9
TEL 91 573 2243
Friendly family atmosphere with a good selection of wine and tapas. Choose one of the many clear soups on offer or try their *gallega* (Galician) specialties such as *empanada de zamburiñas* (scallop pastries) or, from elsewhere, their *bacalao ajoarriero* (salt cod with peppers) or *ensalada de ventresca con pimientos del piquillo* (tuna belly meat with red peppers).
🕐 Closed Sun. 🚇 Ibiza

LA TABERNA DE BUENDI
CALLE DOCTOR CASTELO 15
TEL 91 578 2737
This fine, friendly, and typically Madrileño bar is like an extension of your own home but with more people and less work. Good Spanish wine selection. Try their *jamón iberico*, *boquerones en vinagre* or canapés on toast—like *cabeza de jabalí con brie fundido* (boar's head with melted Brie) and *bacalao ahumado* (smoked cod).
🚇 Ibiza

TABERNA DEL PUERTO
CALLE FERNÁN GONZÁLEZ 50
TEL 91 504 6699
Excellent Andalucían cooking: Concentrate on fish and seafood, often in batter, fast-fried, crunchy on the outside and mouth-watering on the inside. The sister restaurant is at Calle Diego de León 58 *(tel 91 309 2887, Metro: Diego de León)*. Try the *salmonetes frescos* (fresh red mullet), *acedía* (plaice), *calamares en fritura* (frittered squid), *boquerones fritos* (fried fresh anchovies), or *chirlas guisadas* (stewed clams).
🅿 🕐 Closed Sun. D 🚇 Ibiza

◼ LA CASTELLANA & SALAMANCA

Hotels

🏨 ADLER
🍴 $$$$$ *****
CALLE VELÁZQUEZ 33
TEL 91 426 3220
FAX 91 426 3221
www.lesein.es/adler
Opened in 2001 in a completely rehabilitated 1884 palace in the Salamanca barrio, this hotel is well equipped and well furnished, welcoming and cozy. The service is friendly and attentive. It has a haute-cuisine restaurant, with a very good wine list.
ℹ 45 🛏 55 🅿 🚇 Velázquez 💲 💲 ♿ All major cards

🏨 VILLA MAGNA
🍴 $$$$$ *****
PASEO CASTELLANA 22
TEL 91 587 1234
FAX 91 431 2286
www.madrid.park.hyatt.com
This hotel's modern facade contrasts with the Carlos IV-style interiors. Rooms are decorated with plants in the bathrooms. The hotel also has two fine restaurants: The walnut-paneled **Berceo** specializes in fish, and **Tse-Yang** serves the highest quality Chinese cuisine in the capital. The hotel is surrounded by wonderful gardens and has a terrace to dine on in summer.
ℹ 182 🅿 🚇 Rubén Darío 🛗 💲 🐕 ♿ All major cards

SOMETHING SPECIAL
🏨 PUERTA DE AMÉRICA
🍴 $$$$ *****
AVENIDA DE AMÉRICA 41
TEL 91 744 5400
FAX 91 744 5401
www.hotelpuertamerica.com
A spectacular hotel, opened in 2005, with each of its 12 floors designed by a different cutting-edge architect (including Jean Nouvel, Zaha Hadid, Norman Foster, and Arata Isozaki). Impressively well designed and well equipped. Outside the center, but quieter for it. Its restaurant, **Lagrimas Negras** *($$$$, tel 91 744 5400)*, is led by the up-and-coming chef José Luis Estevan. It offers such imaginative food as *cangrejo de caparazón blando* (soft-shelled crab), fried to be both crunchy and juicy, and *tórtolas asadas* (roast turtle doves).
ℹ 342 🅿 🚇 Cartagena 🛗 💲 🐕 ♿ All major cards

SOMETHING SPECIAL
🏨 SANTO MAURO
🍴 $$$$ *****
CALLE ZURBANO 36
TEL 91 319 6900

FAX 91 308 5477
www.ac-hotels.com
Built in neoclassical style by
the Duke of Santo Mauro in
1894, this palace has interiors
by Josep Joanpere, combining
the original cornices and Italian
marble fireplaces with contemporary furniture and textiles.
No two rooms are the same.
In the basement is a pool with
columns and vaulted ceilings.
Its restaurant, **Santo Mauro**
(closed Aug.), occupies the old
library. Try the *ensalada tem-
plada de vieiras* (warm scallop
salad), *rodaballo salvaje asado
con crujiente de verduras y salsa
de lima y gengibre* (roast wild
turbot with crunchy vegetables
and lime and ginger sauce), or
*lomo de cordero presalé asado con
ensalada crujiente especiada de
verduras* (roast lamb loin with
crunchy spicy vegetable salad).
There is a beautiful garden for
summer dining.

🚪 51 🛏 56 🅿 🚇 Gregorio
Marañon 🔄 🚭 ❄ 🔧 🌾 All
major cards

🏨 **VINCCI SOMA**
🍴 $$$ ★★★★
CALLE GOYA 79
TEL 91 435 7545
FAX 91 431 0943
www.vinccihoteles.com
Revamped in 2007, this fash-
ionable boutique-style hotel is
in the heart of the Salamanca
quarter. Removed from Ma-
drid's nightlife, it is peaceful
and comfortable, with atten-
tive service. The restaurant
offers fresh Mediterranean
food with a hint of Japanese
influence and a creative, often
changing menu.

🚪 167 🅿 🚇 Goya, Velázquez
🔄 🚭 🔧 🌾 All major cards

🏨 **GALIANO**
$$ ★★★
CALLE ALCALÁ GALIANO 6
TEL 91 319 2000
FAX 91 319 9914
www.hotelgaliano.com
Originally a convent, this beau-

tiful little palace now houses
a noble family's private home
as well as the hotel. It is nicely
quiet for a place so central.
With Chueca on one side and
Salamanca on the other, it is
well placed for exploring.

🚪 29 🅿 🚇 Colón 🔄 🚭
🌾 AE, MC, V

Restaurants

SOMETHING SPECIAL

🍴 **LA BROCHE**
$$$$$
CALLE MIGUEL ANGEL 29
TEL 91 399 3437
Part of the group of restaurants overseen by Sergi Arola,
new superchef Angel Palacios
now in charge. Standards are
as high as ever in this elegant,
minimalist restaurant, where
the changing menu might
include such surprising concoctions as a langoustine carpaccio with blood sausage and
pork. There are only 40 seats,
so book well in advance.

🛏 40 🅿 🕐 Closed Sat L, Sun,
Mon L and August. 🚇 Gregorio
Marañon 🚭 🌾 All major cards

🍴 **JOCKEY**
$$$$$
CALLE AMADOR DE LOS RÍOS 6
TEL 91 319 2435
Ranked among the top restaurants in Spain, Jockey has an
elegant, old-fashioned, British-
influenced decor of wood
paneling and racing prints.
Start with the house aperitif,
Gin Jockey. Specialties include
*langostinos crudos al caviar
con crema fresca* (thinly sliced
raw king prawns with caviar
and fresh cream), *tuétano con
patatas, foie gras, y salsa de
champagne* (squash with potatoes, foie gras, and champagne
sauce), *mollejas* (sweetbreads),
and *faisán a las uvas con vino de
Oporto* (pheasant with grapes
in port). Excellent wines and
ports. Dress up and reserve
well in advance.

🛏 100 🅿 🕐 Closed Aug.
🚇 Colón 🚭 🌾 All majorcards

SOMETHING SPECIAL

🍴 **SANTCELONI**
$$$$$
HOTEL HESPERIA
PASEO DE LA CASTELLANA 57
TEL 91 210 8840
In the Hotel Hesperia, the
Madrid wing of the celebrated
chef Santi Santamaría's Barcelona base has already earned
two Michelin stars. The cooking is supervised by his disciple
Óscar Velazco. Fresh, seasonal,
and innovative, without ever
losing touch with tradition. Try
the *mero marinado con puré de
manzana ahumado* (marinated
sea bass with smoked apple
purée), *terrina de pularda y
foie gras con trufas* (terrine of
fattened hen and foie gras
with truffles), *jarrete de ternera
blanca con puré de patata* (white
beef hock with potato purée),
or *espardeñas con mollejas de
cordero* (sea cucumber with
lamb sweetbread). Legendary.
Reserve well in advance.

🛏 45 🕐 Closed Sat. L, Sun., &
Aug. 🅿 🚇 Gregorio Marañon
🚭 🌾 All major cards

🍴 **ZALACAÍN**
$$$$$
CALLE ÁLVAREZ DE BAENA 4
TEL 91 561 4840
The restaurant that introduced nouvelle cuisine to
Spain is still one of its top
kitchens. The much-admired
Basque chef Benjamín Urdaín,
recently awarded his second
Michelin star, offers a mixture
of Zalacaín classics along with
new fruits of his creativity.
Always fresh and seasonal.
Try the *manitas de cerdo rellenas
de cordero* (pig's trotters stuffed
with lamb), *ostras en salsa verde*
(oysters in green sauce), the
potato soufflé with anything,
or the *tartar de bonito con
beluga y pimienta verde* (bonito
tartar with Beluga caviar and

fresh pepper). Dress up and reserve well in advance.

🍴 120 🅿 🕓 Closed Sat. L, Sun., Aug., & Easter week 🚇 Gregorio Marañón 🚈 🗝 All major cards

🍴 EL AMPARO
$$$$

CALLE PUIGCERDÁ 8
TEL 91 431 6456

This charming Basque restaurant led by Carlos Posadas offers a creative take on that culture's traditional cuisine. Stand out dishes include *foie caliente a la sartén con crujiente de calabaza dulce y salsa perigord* (goose liver heated in the skillet with crunchy sweet squash and Périgord sauce), *cigalas salteadas con ravioli de queso y romero* (sautéed Dublin Bay shrimp with cheese and rosemary ravioli), and *lechona confitada con puré de manzana y membrillo* (honeyed suckling pig with apple purée and quince jelly). The hot chocolate soufflé is exquisite. Excellent wine cellar. Reserve in advance.

🍴 65 🅿 🕓 Closed Sat. L. & Sun. 🚇 Serrano 🚈 🗝 All major cards

🍴 EL BODEGÓN
$$$$

CALLE PINAR 15
TEL 91 562 8844

Traditional Basque cooking with a Catalan element and original touches, headed by chef José Machado. Formal, but friendly. Try the *menú degustación* to explore, or start with *potaje de lentejas y perdiz* (lentils and partridge soup), vichyssoise, or any of the fish soups, and then move on to *lomo de salmonete en caldo gelatinoso de hinojo* (red mullet in jellied fennel stock), *pichón con ciruelas* (pigeon with plums), or the classic filet mignon à la béarnaise. Dress up and reserve in advance.

🍴 60 🅿 🕓 Closed Sat. L, Sun., & Aug. 🚇 Gregorio Marañón 🚈 🗝 All major cards

🍴 LOS CLARINES
$$$

CALLE BOCÁNGEL 2
TEL 91 356 9859

Very Madrid, very close to Las Ventas bullring, and very bullfight-aficionado. Its menu stays on track, from *rabo de toro* (bull's tail) to *estofado de toro* (bull stew). Also good fish, such as *merluza a la cosquera* (hake in shellfish sauce). During the Feria de San Isidro, from mid–May to early June, it stays open all day, every day, except during the bullfights (roughly 7–9 p.m.).

🍴 70 🕓 Closed Mon. except during San Isidro 🚇 Ventas 🗝 All major cards

🍴 PRÍNCIPE DE VIANA
$$$

CALLE MANUEL DE FALLA 5
TEL 91 457 1549

One of the best loved restaurants in the city, with Basque-Navarrese cuisine. Try these specialties: *menestra de verduras de Tudela* (asparagus stewed with other vegetables), *bacalao ajoarriero con langosta* (cod with peppers and lobster), or *merluza en salsa verde* (hake in parsley, garlic, and olive oil sauce). The ham croquettes are famous. Reservations essential.

🍴 80 🅿 🕓 Closed Sat. L & Sun. 🚇 Santiago Bernabéu 🚈 🗝 All major cards

🍴 DONDE LEO
$$

CALLE PEDRO HEREDIA 22
TEL 91 356 6561

One of the favorite restaurants of the bullfighting fraternity, this very Madrileño restaurant is presided over by the Virgen de la Paloma and portraits of bullfighters. Stand-out dishes are: *rabo de toro con caracoles* (bull's tail with snails) as well as the croquetas.

🍴 75 🕓 Closed Mon. except during San Isidro 🚇 Ventas 🚈 🗝 All major cards

🍴 LA CASUCA
$$

CALLE AGUSTÍN DE FOXÁ 16–18
TEL 91 314 5696

La Casuca offers a great opportunity to try classic Cantabrian cooking and more, all in the hands of Antonio Hoyas. The stews and roasts are excellent. Try typical northern dishes like *cocido montañés* (stew of kidney beans, blood sausage, cabbage, pork, chorizo, cabbage, and pig's ears), *rabas* (fried squid), *marmitako de bonito* (bonito stew), or *brandada de bacalao con vinagreta de pulpo* (cod strips with octopus vinaigrette). Reserve in advance.

🍴 90 🅿 🕓 Closed Sun. D 🚇 Plaza de Castilla, Chamartín 🚈 🗝 All major cards

🍴 LA TABERNA DE BUENAVENTURA
$$

CALLE HERMOSILLA 69
TEL 91 575 8365

Popular old-style Madrid restaurant offering high-quality local dishes, including a famed *cocido madrileño*, *callos*

a la madrileña (Madrid-style tripe), and fresh fish dishes. A *cupletista* (cabaret singer) livens things up on Saturday nights. Reserve in advance.
🔚 96 🕐 Closed Mon., Sun. D, & Aug. 🚇 Goya 🅿️
🅾️ DC, MC, V

Tapas Bars

FINOS Y FINAS
CALLE ESPARTINAS 6
TEL 91 575 9069
This is a popular bar (and small restaurant) with inventive, high-quality tapas. Try the *pimientos de piquillo rellenos de níscalos y jamón ibérico* (red peppers filled with wild mushroom and ham), *tartaletas de calamares, or de pollo en pepitoria* (squid or fricasséed chicken pies), or the *croquetas*.
🕐 Closed Sun. D, Aug. 🚇 Velázquez, Príncipe de Vergara

EL RINCÓN DE JAÉN
CALLE DR. GÓMEZ ULLA 6
TEL 91 355 4011
DON RAMÓN DE LA CRUZ 88
TEL 91 401 6334
These friendly and generous bars/restaurants are said by some to have the best Andalusían food in Madrid. Delicious fried fish, seafood, sausages, and salads.
🚇 Manuel Becerra

O'CRUCEIRO
CALLE NUÑEZ DE BALBOA 29
TEL 91 577 8447 OR 91 577 7302
This *gallego* restaurant offers first-rate seafood in its bar: *vieiras* (scallops), *percebes* (gooseneck barnacles), *ostras* (oysters), *navajas* (razor shells), and *langostinos*. Excellent empanadas of vieira and of *bacalao con pasas* (cod with raisins), as well as *pulpo a la gallega* (Galician-style octopus).
🅿️ 🕐 Closed Sun. D 🚇 Goya

LA TABERNA DEL BUEY
CALLE GENERAL PARDIÑAS 7
TEL 91 578 1154

This is a popular tapas bar, which offers delicious Swiss cheese, *ahumados* (smoked fish), *gulas* (baby eels), *pimientos de piquillo rellenos de bacalao* (red peppers stuffed with cod), with perfect *patatas paja* (fine-cut crunchy fried potatoes) and fine canapés.
🚇 Velázquez

PLAZA DE ESPAÑA & WESTERN MADRID

Hotels

HUSA PRINCESA
$$$$ ★★★★★
CALLE PRINCESA 40
TEL 91 542 2100
FAX 91 542 3501
www.hotelhusaprincesa.com
Spacious, modern hotel, completely redone in 2001, on the edge of the historic center and not far from the parks. The outdoor terrace is open from May to October. Facilities for the disabled.
🛈 275 🅿️ 🚇 Argüelles 🅾️
🅾️🅾️🅾️🅾️ All major cards

EL COLOSO
$$ ★★★★
CALLE LEGANITOS 13
TEL 91 548 7640
FAX 91 547 4968
www.hotelelcoloso.com
Comfortable hotel, close to the center and well equipped. Attentive service. Good deals in the low season.
🛈 132 🅿️ 🚇 Plaza de España, Santo Domingo 🅾️🅾️🅾️ All major cards

T3 TIROL
$$ ★★★
CALLE MARQUÉS DE URQUIJO 4
TEL 91 548 1900
FAX 91 541 3958
www.hotel-tirol.com
Recently renovated, a comfortable, modern hotel with good facilities. It is outside the

center, but very close to the metro station. Up-to-half-price offers available at times.
🛈 98 🚇 Argüelles 🅾️🅾️
🅾️ All major cards

Restaurants

SOMETHING SPECIAL

🍽 CLUB ALLARD
$$$$
CALLE FERRAZ 2
TEL 91 559 0939
In a beautiful art deco building, this used to be a private politicians' and bankers' club, but it is now a wonderful restaurant led by chef Diego Guerrero, who has worked with some of the finest Basque and Catalan chefs. Try starters such as terrine of goose liver with a honey vinaigrette or *huevos con pan y panceta sobre crema ligera de patata* (eggs with bread and belly pork over lightly creamed potato). Good meat courses include *coquelet de Bresse confitado en grasa de pato con jugo de uvas* (young Bresse chicken confit in duck fat with grape juice) and *cochinillo confitado con canela y comino* (suckling pig confit with cinnamon and cumin). The menu keeps developing, but the fish section changes every day according to which wild fish are brought in. Excellent wine list. Dress up and reserve in advance.
🔚 70 🅿️ 🕐 Closed Sun., Sat L, & Mon. D 🚇 Plaza de España 🅾️ 🅾️ All major cards

🍽 LAS CUATRO ESTACIONES
$$$$
CALLE GENERAL IBÁÑEZ ÍBERO 5
TEL 91 553 6305
Classic yet modern French-influenced Mediterranean food in a quiet setting. The fresh, seasonal menu includes *gazpacho con bogavante* (cold tomato-based soup with

lobster), *foie caliente a las uvas* (goose liver cooked with grapes), and *verduras a la plancha* (grilled vegetables). Their callos a la madrileña are famed, as are their steak tartare and their potato soufflé. Excellent wine list.

🍴 130 🕐 Closed Sat. L, Sun., Aug., & Easter week 🚇 Gúzman el Bueno 🅿 🚭 ♿ All major cards

🍴 BOKADO
$$$
AVENIDA JUAN DE HERRERA 2
TEL 91 549 0041
This fine restaurant in the Museo del Traje (Clothing and Costume Museum) also has a lovely terrace by the Moncloa gardens. Take your choice of two *menus degustación,* or try the terrine of foie gras with crème fraîche and canteloupe, *rape negro en salsa de almejas* (black monkfish in clam sauce), or *ravioli de changurro con jugo de carabinero con verduritas fritas* (crab ravioli with shrimp juice and fried vegetables). A children's menu is available.

🍴 90 🅿 🕐 Closed Mon. & Sun. 🚇 Ciudad Universitaria 🚭 ♿ DC, MC, V

🍴 LAS BATUECAS
$$
AVENIDA REINA VICTORIA 17
TEL 91 554 04 52
There is good, traditional food in this restaurant, which is unchanged in 50 years. Try their famed *tortilla con callos* (omelette with tripe sauce), *puerros gratinados* (leeks au gratin), croquetas, *berenjenas rebosadas* (sliced and battered eggplant), or *cordero asado* (roast lamb). Reserve in advance.

🍴 60 🕐 Closed Mon.–Wed. D, Thurs.–Fri. L, Sat. D, Sun., & Aug. 🚇 Cuatro Caminos 🚭 ♿ Not accepted

🍴 SAL GORDA
$$
CALLE BEATRIZ DE BOBADILLA 9
TEL 91 553 9506
A cozy, traditional, and reasonably priced restaurant. Recommended dishes include *bacalao ajoarriero* (cod in garlic, pepper, and tomato sauce), *lomo de buey* (ox fillet), or *pencas de acelgas rellenas de jamón* (ham-filled Swiss chard). Reserve in advance.

🍴 65 🕐 Closed Sun. & Aug. 🚇 Guzmán el Bueno 🚭 ♿ All major cards

🍴 CON DOS FOGONES
$
CALLE SAN BERNARDINO 9
TEL 91 559 6326
Fusion cuisine in this small, country-style, but modern restaurant, designed for both vegetarians and carnivores. Try the *hamburguesa de merluza* (hake burger) with tomato sauce, squash tempura, soy sauce, and honey, or the *bacalao confitado con pisto de hongos y crema de ajos* (cod confit with wild mushroom hash and garlic cream). Very reasonable prices. Reserve for dinner.

🍴 45 🚇 Plaza de España 🚭 ♿ All major cards

Tapas Bars

CUENLLAS WINE BAR
CALLE FERRAZ 5
TEL 91 542 5621
A gem in a tapas-rich street, this bar offers excellent tapas and canapés and has a restaurant as well. Try *soldaditos de Pavía en fritura ligera a la madrileña* (cod fritters Madrid-style), Beluga caviar, or *cecina con aceite de oliva* (cured meat with olive oil). A treat.

🕐 Closed Sun. 🚇 Ventura Rodríguez

ENTREVINOS
CALLE FERRAZ 36
TEL 91 548 3114

There are wonderful wines, tapas, and raciones in this good-looking bar/restaurant. Try its meat or fish carpaccios, *cecina artesana* (cured meat prepared on the premises), the excellent *jamón ibérico de bellota* (ham from acorn-fed pigs), or the cheese board.

🕐 Closed Sun. & Aug.
🚇 Ventura Rodríguez, Plaza de España

PRADA A TOPE
CUESTA DE SAN VICENTE 32
TEL 91 547 8020
Like its twin in the Santa Ana barrio, this bar and restaurant offers food from the village of El Bierzo in León. Try the *botillo* (chickpeas, cabbage, potatoes, and pork ribs), *codillos* (pig's trotters), or the *morcilla* (blood pudding).

🚇 Plaza de España

TABERNA LOS PORCHES
PASEO PINTOR ROSALES 2
TEL 91 542 4900
With lovely views of the park and the ancient Templo de Debod, this taberna has a friendly family atmosphere. Good *ahumados* (smoked fish), *morcilla de Burgos* (Burgos blood pudding), and *tostas* (servings on toast). Crowded on weekends.

🕐 Closed Mon. 🚇 Ventura Rodríguez

Shopping in Madrid

Shopping in Madrid can transport you across centuries within a few steps. Old, established, family-run shops selling shawls and mantillas and convents selling sweets and pastries made by unseen nuns reflect Madrid's old traditions. On the other hand, boutiques offering clothes by some of Europe's most imaginative, ground-breaking designers represent the extraordinary creative explosion that followed Franco's death in 1975—a burst of artistic development that continues to this day.

Central Madrid has three main shopping areas. The first centers around the Puerta del Sol, including the pedestrian-only street Preciados that connects Plaza de Callao to the Gran Vía. At Sol's southern end, it stretches from Plaza Mayor to Plaza de Canalejas. The area includes department stores, fashion chains, and modern stores selling everything from clothes, shoes, jewelry, and crafts to books and music. There are many tourist outlets, but you will also find typically Madrileño shops, some generations old.

The second area is in the exclusive Salamanca quarter, a chic district with the nickname La Milla de Oro (Golden Mile). It concentrates around streets Serrano, Castelló, Claudio Coello, Goya, Velázquez, Jorge Juan, Núñez de Balboa, and Ortega y Gasset. The area houses the international haute couture establishments and classy design houses, which—while not cheap—are better-priced here than abroad.

Close by is the third area, centered around Madrid's gay quarter Chueca, as well as on Fuencarral, where fashion tends to be younger, and hipper, by the newest designers. In Chueca, wander down Hortaleza, Almirante, Argensola, Augusto Figueroa, and their side streets. On Fuencarral, which also has a good mix of other stores, dive into the Mercado Fuencarral, with its 60 up-to-the-minute shops.

Opening Times

See p. 239.

Payment

Supermarkets, chain stores, and many (but not all) smaller stores accept credit cards backed by an I.D., which you should carry with you. Check the signs on the door as you go in, and, if in doubt, check with an assistant (¿Aceptan tarjetas de crédito? "Do you accept credit cards?").

Returns

If you have any complaints about a purchase, return it as soon as possible with the receipt (el recibo) as proof of purchase. Items bought on sale, however, are usually nonrefundable.

Exports

A 16% purchase tax, known as IVA, is included in the price of most retail goods; for books it is 4%. Non-EU citizens are entitled to claim back the IVA element if they have spent 90.16 euros ($108.19) or more in one store and will be removing the goods from the EU within three months. Ask the shop for an invoice (una factura) showing the price, the IVA paid for each item and identifying the vendor and the purchaser (you must show your passport/I.D.). When leaving Spain, you must have the invoice stamped by customs (aduana). Either mail it back to the vendor, who will mail you the refund, or take the invoice to the nearest Banco Exterior branch (there's one at Barajas airport), where you will get your refund, if the relevant shop has an arrangement with them.

Typical Madrileño Stores

Belloso
Calle Mayor 23
tel 91 366 4258
Metro: Sol
Making and selling religious artifacts—vestments, images, chalices, figures—since 1893.

Capas Seseña
Calle Cruz 23
tel 91 531 6840, Metro: Sol
Beautiful capes sold to high society—from the Spanish royal family to Hillary Clinton—for more than a century.

Casa de Diego
Puerta del Sol 12
tel 91 522 6643, Metro: Sol
Calle Mesoneros Romanos 4
Metro: Callao
Classic silver-handled walking sticks, umbrellas, sunshades, castanets, ornamental combs, shawls, and fans since 1858.

Casa Hernanz
Calle Toledo 18
tel 91 366 5450, Metro: Sol, Ópera
Wonderful range of handmade espadrilles in shop dating back to the 1840s.

Casa Jiménez
Calle Preciados 42
tel 91 548 0526, Metro: Sol
Gorgeous embroidered shawls and lace mantillas, as well as fans and combs; the store also rents formal clothes.

Casa Yustas
Plaza Mayor 30
tel 91 366 5084, Metro: Sol, Ópera
Founded in 1894, Casa Yustas sells hats ranging from boinas (berets), through patent-leather Guardia Civil tricorne headgear, to elegant men's and women's styles.

El Caballo Cojo
Calle Segovia
tel 91 366 4390, Metro: Sol, Ópera

An old-fashioned store with beautiful ceramics, particularly from the 17th and 18th centuries, and handicrafts and furniture.

El Convento de las Carboneras
Plaza Conde de Miranda 3
tel 91 548 3701, Metro: Sol
The convent shop sells delicious sweets and pastries made by a closed order of Hieronymite nuns.

El Flamenco Vive
Calle Conde de Lemos 7
tel 91 547 3917, Metro: Ópera
For flamenco aficionados, everything from guitars, castañuelas, and drum chests to dresses or waistcoats and trousers.

Filatelia Arias
Plaza Mayor 28
tel 91 366 4499, Metro: Sol
A beautiful store for collectors of stamps and old or ancient coins—including Greek and Roman ones.

La Favorita
Plaza Mayor 25
tel 91 366 5877, Metro: Sol
Selling hats since 1894.

La Pajarita
Calle Villanueva 14
tel 91 435 7454, Metro: Recoletos
Quality candies and chocolates. The specialty: *pajaritas* (little birds) of chocolate.

La Violeta
Plaza de Canalejas 6
tel 91 522 5522, Metro: Sevilla
A Madrileña candy store since 1915, named after its famous violet-shaped and -colored delights.

Maravillas Trajes Regionales
Calle Sal 3
tel 91 366 5248, Metro: Sol
Spanish regional costumes, flamenco outfits, shawls, and fancy dress clothes.

Books
Booksellers
Calle Fernández de la Hoz 40
Tel 91 442 7959
A large selection of books in English.

Casa del Libro
Gran Vía 29
tel 91 524 1900

Metro: Gran Vía
Calle Maestro Victoria 3
tel 91 521 4898,
Metro: Callao, Sol
Large, comprehensive stores, with limited English section.

J&J
Calle Espíritu Santo 47
tel 91 521 8576,
Metro: Noviciado
Bookstore (and café/bar) with plenty of secondhand books in English, run by an American woman and her Spanish husband. They don't close for lunch.

Libros Madrid
Calle Campomanes 5
tel 91 547 8736, Metro: Ópera
The largest seller of antique and secondhand books in Madrid.

Clothing
High-fashion
Spanish designers
Adolfo Domínguez
Calle Serrano 18
tel 91 577 8280
Calle Serrano 96
tel 91 576 7053, Metro: Serrano
Classic but relaxed, well-made clothes for men and women, as well as unusual bags and shoes.

Ágatha Ruiz de la Prada
Calle Serrano 27
tel 91 319 0501, Metro: Serrano
Madrid-born designer who came to fame in the 1980s *movida;* colorful and imaginative men's and women's fashions.

Amaya Arzuaga
Calle Lagasca 50
tel 91 426 2815, Metro: Velázquez
Bold, sensual design for men and women. She also sells wine from her father's bodega.

Ángel Schlesser
Calle Claudio Coello 46
tel 91 435 4869
Calle Don Ramón de la Cruz 2
tel 91 575 5574 , Metro: Serrano
Restrained, timeless, chic urban daywear and spectacular evening wear for women.

Antonio Miró
Calle Lagasca 65
tel 91 426 0225, Metro:

Velázquez
Often inspired by painters, his style is colorful, bold, and innovative. For men and women.

The Deli Room
Calle Santa Bárbara 4
tel 91 521 1983, Metro: Tribunal
Here the designers are all Spanish and all young. It's an excellent and funky place to get a glimpse of the future of Spanish fashion. Mainly for women.

Elena Benarroch
Calle Lagasca 88
tel 91 435 5144, Metro: Núñez de Balboa
Best known for her coats and leather clothes, Elena Benarroch also stocks designer labels. For men and women.

El Jardín de Serrano
Calle Goya 6–8
tel 91 577 0012, Metro: Serrano
This is a luxurious 23-store shopping center packed with pricy designer labels.

Hoss Homeless
Calle Serrano 16
tel 91 781 0612
(also at Tetuán 19 and Fuencarral 16)
Hip and Spanish. Here are young women designing for women.

Javier Larraínzar
Calle Castelló 16
tel 91 577 8835, Metro: Príncipe de Vergara, Velázquez
A reinvented classicism and elegance for women, with the focus on evening wear and suits made to order.

Jesús del Pozo
Calle Almirante 9
tel 91 531 3646, Metro: Chueca, Colón
Classic and beautiful Spanish style for women from a leading young designer, much frequented by young actresses.

Kina Fernández
Calle Claudio Coello 75
tel 91 426 2420, Metro: Serrano, Núñez de Balboa
Ultra-feminine urban style, beautifully cut and structured.

La Compañía Multihispana

Calle Hortaleza 30
tel 91 532 3833, Metro: Gran Vía
Women's clothes from their own
collection and from designers like
Sybilla and Hoss Homeless. Fashionable but well priced.

Loreak Mendian
Calle Argensola 5
tel 91 319 4716, Metro: Alonso
Martínez
Cutting-edge men's fashion from
a Basque designer.

Mercado Fuencarral
Calle Fuencarral 45
tel 91 521 4152, Metro: Tribunal
A 60-store shopping center in an
old market building, with young
designers focused on the hip
crowd with clothes, shoes, jewelry, and accessories.

Paco Casado
Calle Castelló 6
tel 91 431 0150, Metro: Avenida
de América
Well-established and popular,
noted for his showy and glamorous women's wear.

Pedro del Hierro
Calle Serrano 24 and 63
tel 91 575 6906, Metro: Serrano
Sophisticated and simple clean
lines for men and women from
this creative Madrileño.

Pedro Morago
Calle Almirante 20
tel 91 521 6628
Metro: Colón
Hip designer for men and women:
colorful, daring, and classic.

Purificación García
Calle Serrano 28
tel 91 577 8370, Metro: Serrano,
Colón
Elegant, well made, and discreet
clothes for women by this well-
known designer.

Roberto Verino
Calle Claudio Coello 27
tel 91 577 7381
Calle Serrano 33, Metro: Serrano
Famous for his elegant but simple
and comfortable clothes for men
and women.

Supreme
Calle Martín de los Heros 24
tel 91 541 0042, Metro: Ventura

Rodríguez Young, feisty, with up-
and-coming labels for men and
women.

Sybilla
Callejón Jorge Juan 12
tel 91 578 1322, Metro: Serrano
Spain's most original designer
for clothes, shoes, and household
items. Jocomomola, her younger
line, is sold in the shop next door.

Victorio y Lucchino
Calle Lagasca 75
tel 91 431 8786, Metro: Núñez
de Balboa
These famous designers from
Seville make theatrical, well-
made, flamenco-inspired clothes
for women and have now moved
into menswear.

Other Clothing

Algarabía
Calle Ayala 74
tel 91 575 6291, Metro: Goya
Women's fashion from well-
known designers at low prices.

Ararat
Calle Almirante 10/11
tel 91 531 8156, Metro: Recoletos
Sophisticated suits and cosmopol-
itan party clothes for women.

Cristina Guisado
Calle Doctor Fourquet 1
tel 91 528 8788, Metro: Lavapiés
New and secondhand 1960s and
'70s clothes plus accessories.
Imaginative and well priced.

Escuela de Divinos
Calle Zurbarán 16
tel 91 308 2816, Metro: Rubén
Dario
Spanish designer clothes at
reduced prices.

Lefties
Calle Carretas 10
tel 91 531 2188, Metro: Sol
End-of-line fashions, many from
Zara, at very low prices.

Mango
Calle Fuencarral 70
tel 91 523 0412, Metro:Tribunal
In most shopping areas,
you'll find a branch of this
good-quality and inventive wom-
en's fashion chain.

Restaurante Cambalache

Calle San Lorenzo 5
tel 91 310 0701
Despite the name, secondhand
clothes with high quality and low
prices, plus accessories.

Zara
Gran Vía 34
tel 91 521 1283, Metro: Gran Vía
Excellent chain store for good
well-priced women's and children's clothes, and menswear.
There are Zara stores in most
shopping barrios.

Crafts

Adamá
Avenida Felipe II 24
tel 91 435 9988, Metro: Goya
Top contemporary Spanish
ceramics.

Antigua Casa Talavera
Calle Isabel la Católica
tel 91 547 3417, Metro: Santo
Domingo
Excellent ceramics shop, selling
yellow and blue Talavera pottery
and fine work from Manises in
Valencia.

Cántaro
Calle Flor Baja 8
tel 91 547 9514, Metro: Santo
Domingo
Beautiful handmade pottery.

Vinçon
Calle Castelló 18
Tel 91 578 0520, Metro: Velázquez
Great for unusual gifts by top
Spanish designers, including toys,
household goods and stationery.

El Arco
Plaza Mayor 9
tel 91 365 2680, Metro: Sol
Contemporary Spanish handicrafts, pottery, jewelry, glass,
and leatherware.

La Tierra
Calle Almirante 28
tel 91 521 2134, Metro: Chueca
Beautiful arts and crafts shop,
offering from terra-cotta ceramics
and sevillano tiles to the more
traditional kitchenware.

Mercado Puerta de Toledo
Ronda de Toledo 1
tel 91 366 7200,
Metro: Puerta de Toledo

Once a 19th-century fish market, now a modern shopping center. Good for antique, craft, and design stores.

Department Store

El Corte Inglés
Calle Serrano 47
tel 91 432 5490, Metro: Serrano
(Also at Preciados 1, 2, 3, & 9; Princesa 41, 47, & 56; Goya 76 & 85; Plaza de Callao; and elsewhere)
This is the top department store chain in Spain, covering what seems to be everything and doing it well. Good toy section, bargains, and food.

Food, Wine & Spirits

La Oleoteca
Calle Juan Ramón Jiménez 37
tel 91 359 1803
Wonderful olive oil from all over Spain. More easily transportable are the wooden cooking and salad utensils.

Lavinia
Calle José Ortega y Gasset 16
tel 91 426 0604, Metro: Núñez de Balboa
Huge wine (and spirits) store, stocking 4,500 wines and staffed by multilingual experts.

Mariano Aguado
Calle Echegaray 19
tel 91 429 6088
Over 150 years of selling wine and spirits, underneath an eye-catching painted ceiling.

Mercado de la Paz
Calle Ayala 28
tel 91 435 0743, Metro: Velázquez
In this beautiful market, the stars are the cheeses and prepared meats, but all the food is good quality. Built by Gustave Eiffel in the 19th century, it became a market only in 1943.

Mercado de Maravillas
Calle Bravo Murillo 122
tel 91 534 8429, Metro: Alvarado, Cuatro Caminos
The biggest traditional market in Madrid, with the largest offering of fresh fish in town and all the

bustle and spectacle of a good market—plus a famous sculpture by Luis Muguruza.

Leather & Shoes

Acosta
Calle Hermosilla 36
tel 91 710 3026, Metro: Velázquez
A long-established shoemaker, producing high-quality, comfortable, and expensive shoes.

Camper
Calle Preciados 2
tel 902 364 598, Metro: Callao
(Also at Ayala 13, Princesa 75, Gran Vía 54, and Serrano 24)
A very stylish chain with original and well-made footwear, cheaper in Spain than abroad.

Guantes Luque
Calle Espoz y Mina 3
tel 91 522 3287, Metro: Sol
This glove shop, more than 100 years old, has even more gloves than years, but persevere and you will find some fitting beauties.

Loewe
Calle Serrano 26 for women
tel 91 577 6056
Calle Serrano 34 for men
tel 91 426 3584, Metro: Serrano, Gran Vía 8
Top-class leather purses, belts, and clothes.

Nere Denda
Calle Castelló 38
tel 91 435 9723, Metro: Velázquez
Purses, shoes, and other leather goods by young designers.

Piamonte
Calle Marqués de Monasterio 5
tel 91 522 4580, Metro: Chueca, Recoletos
Calle Villanueva 16
tel 91 435 3747, Metro: Serrano
Very modern and colorful Spanish designer shoes, bags, and belts; the Villanueva shop is cheaper, as it sells remainders.

Street Markets

El Rastro
Calle Ribera de Curtidores/Plaza de Carrasco
tel 91 588 2900 (Madrid Tourist Office)

Open every Sun. 7 a.m.–2 p.m.
Metro: La Latina
One of the world's finest flea markets, selling everything from antiques to leather goods to junk. Lively and noisy, with plenty of cafés for breaks. Payments in cash. Watch out for pickpockets, and don't forget to bargain.

Feria del Libro
Cuesta de Claudio Moyano
Metro: Atocha
By the Jardín Botánico and the Parque de Retiro. Rare and unusual books, all year round.

Mercado de Monedas y Sellos
Plaza Mayor
Metro: Sol
Every Sunday morning, the beautiful old square is lined with stalls selling antique coins and stamps.

Toys

Bazar Mila
Gran Vía 33
tel 91 531 8728, Metro: Gran Vía
An old-style toy store for the younger (pre-computer games) child.

Gepetto
Calle Diego de León 47
tel 91 563 4507, Metro: Diego de León
Puppets and handmade wooden toys of every kind. Expensive, but unique and exquisite. **Sanatorio de muñecos**

Entertainment

Madrid is packed with bars, cafés, and things to do in the evenings. Madrileños tend to stay up very late, often until sunrise, and really know how to enjoy themselves. The weekly *Guía del Ocio* is an excellent guide to what is going on. You can also pick up information on entertainment and events from tourist information centers, often in English.

For tickets for the theater, cinema, concerts, bullfights, and football all over Spain, phone or reserve online (commission added) at:
Caixa Catalunya tel 902 101 212, www.telentrada.com
El Corte Inglés tel 902 400 222, www.elcorteingles.es/entradas
Entradas.com tel 902 488 488, www.entradas.com
Localidades Galicia Plaza del Carmen 1, tel 91 531 9131 & 91 531 2732, www.eol.es/lgalicia
ServiCaixa tel 902 332 211, www.serviticket.es

Bars

Midnight Rose
Hotel ME Madrid, Plaza Santa Ana 14
Tel 91 701 6000
Stylish bar frequented by fashion and film crowd; good for pre-dinner cocktails.
Casa Pueblo
Calle León 3
tel 91 429 0515, Metro: Sevilla
Designer meets bohemian with a jazz background. Closed Mon.
Barrio Alto
Calle Humilladero 16, Metro: Latina
Friendly bar hidden away down a sidestreet, with great music, cocktails, and snacks.
Museo Chicote
Gran Vía 12
tel 91 532 6737, Metro: Gran Vía
An award-winning classic cocktail bar, associated with writers and stars such as Hemingway and Elizabeth Taylor, but always up-to-date. Closed Sun.
Viva Madrid
Calle Manuel Fernández González 7
tel 91 429 3640, Metro: Sevilla
A beautifully tiled bar with bull-

fighting connections. Tapas during the day, drinking and talking at night.

Bullfighting

Plaza de Toros Monumental de las Ventas
Calle de Alcalá 237
tel 91 356 2200 , Metro: Ventas
Spain's biggest bullring, open mid-March to Oct. The most important corridas, in the Feria de San Isidro, are daily from mid-May to early June. Buy in advance; the best seats are in the shade *(sombra)*. You can buy tickets from the bullring or authorized ticket agencies.

Cafés & Chocolaterías

Madrid is full of cafés—these are a few of the best. There are fewer chocolaterías, which are dedicated to hot chocolate and *churros* (sweet fritters).
Café Central
Plaza del Ángel 10
tel 91 369 4143, Metro: Antón Martín
Unusual café, often with live music, mainly jazz. A haunt of the intelligentsia.
Café Comercial
Glorieta de Bilbao 7
tel 91 521 5655, Metro: Bilbao
Traditional old-style café, as charming and talkative as a century ago.
Café de Barbieri
Calle Ave María 45
tel 91 527 3658, Metro: Lavapiés
Quiet but lively, this very traditional café looks onto Plaza de Lavapiés. Films show in the evening (small fee), usually in the original language.
Café del Espejo

Paseo de Recoletos 33
tel 91 308 2347, Metro: Colón
Beautiful and elegant, with a magnificent shaded summer terrace and lovely coffee.
Café del Círculo de Bellas Artes (La Pecera)
Calle Marqués de Casa Riera 2
tel 91 521 6942, Metro: Banco de España
Beautiful and quiet; good for chatting or reading.
Café de Oriente
Plaza de Oriente 2
tel 91 547 1564, Metro: Ópera
On the ruins of an old convent, with lovely views of the royal palace. Elegant and old-fashioned. Serves breakfast, snacks, and tapas and has a restaurant.
Café Español
Calle del Príncipe 25
tel 91 420 1755, Metro: Sevilla
The café of the Teatro Español. Daily classical music concerts on the upper level and magic shows every Thurs. Closed Mon.
Café Gijón
Paseo de Recoletos 21
tel 91 521 5425, Metro: Banco de España, Colón
Traditional meeting point for poets and writers, also serving a good lunch.
Café Libertad 8
Calle Libertad 8
tel 91 532 1150, Metro: Chueca, Banco de España
A traditional haunt of the anti-Franco opposition, now hosting theatrical shows, storytelling, and live music (usually acoustic). Open late.
Chocolatería San Ginés
Pasadizo San Ginés 5
tel 91 365 6546, Metro: Sol
Open Mon.–Tues. 6 p.m.–7 a.m.,

Wed.–Sun. 10 a.m.–7 a.m.
Open all night, every night: a
chocolate paradise for the sleep-
less, with excellent churros.
Café Panini
Calle Campomanes 11
Tel 91 547 3404
American-run café near the Royal
Palace, with tasty sandwiches and
homemade cakes.

Children's Activities
Faunia
$$$$
www.faunia.es
Avenida de las Comunidades 28
tel 91 301 6210, Metro: Valde-
bernardo
A cross between a zoo and a
theme park, re-creating the
world's different ecosystems.
Enjoyable and educational.
Museo de Cera (Wax Museum)
$$$
www.museoceramadrid.com
Paseo de Recoletos 41
tel 91 319 2649, Metro: Colón
Closed 2:30–4:30 p.m. Mon.–Fri.
From Frankenstein to Bart Simp-
son, including a multimedia his-
tory of Spain.
Parque de Atracciones
$$$$
www.parquedeatracciones.es
Casa de Campo
tel 91 463 2900, Metro: Batán
Open daily May–mid-September,
& otherwise mainly on weekends.
Huge amusement park, with roller
coasters, train rides, boat trips,
puppet theaters. Plenty of cafés
and restaurants.
Parque del Retiro
Plaza de la Independencia
Metro: Retiro, Ibiza, Menéndez
Pelayo
A lovely park to visit with
children for a walk, the swings, or
a boat trip on the lake. The park is
specially nice on weekends, when
there are puppet shows, mimes,
and jugglers.
Planetario (Planetarium)
$
www.planetmad.es
Avenida del Planetario 16 Parque

Tierno Galván
tel 91 467 3461, Metro: Méndez
Álvaro, Closed Mon., open Tues.–
Fri. 5–7:45 p.m., Sat.–Sun. 11
a.m.–1:45 p.m., 5–8:45 p.m.
Magical eclipses and journeys
through outer space.
Safari Madrid
$$$
Finca El Rincón, Aldea del Fresno
tel 91 862 2376, Open daily 10:30
a.m.–6:30 p.m. (winter) & 9:30
p.m. (summer) Take highway A-5
or N-5 to Navalcarnero, exit at
km 32, and head for Aldea del
Fresno. Best to visit this beautiful
nature reserve by car to see the
wild animals in a natural setting.
The reserve also has birds of prey
and insect and reptile houses.

Cinema
These central cinemas show
films in their original language
(*versión original*).
Alphaville Calle Martín de los
Heros 14, tel 91 559 383, Metro:
Plaza de España.
Cine Doré (Filmoteca Nacional)
Calle Santa Isabel 3, tel 91 369
1125, Metro: Antón Martín.
Pequeño Cinestudio Calle Magal-
lanes 1, tel 91 447 2920, Metro:
Quevedo.
Princesa Calle Princesa 3,
tel 91 559 9774, metro: Plaza
de España.
Renoir Cuatro Caminos Calle
Raimundo Fernández Villaverde
10, tel 91 541 4100, metro: Cuatro
Caminos.
Renoir Plaza de España Calle
Martín de los Heros, tel 91 541
4100, metro: Plaza de España.
Renoir Retiro Calle Narváez 42,
tel 91 541 4100, metro: Ibiza.
Verdi Calle Bravo Murillo 28, tel
91 447 3930, metro: Quevedo.
Yelmo Cineplex Ideal Calle Doc-
tor Cortezo 6, tel 902 220 922,
Metro: Tirso de Molina.

Discoteques
El Sol
Calle Jardines 3

tel 91 532 6490, Metro: Sol
A classic disco since the 1980s
movida, but now with the hippest DJs: everything from acid
jazz, hip-hop, Brit, and funk to
whatever's happening. Closed
Sun. & Mon.
Joy Madrid
Calle Arenal 11
tel 91 366 3733, Metro: Sol
Very successful and stylish, with
the accent on techno and house,
packed with people from the
movie, fashion, sports, and TV
worlds. Open 11:30 p.m.–
6 a.m. every day.
Kapital
Calle Atocha 125
tel 91 420 2906, Metro: Atocha
Huge disco with seven floors and
a roof terrace, each floor offering different vibes: house music,
funk, R&B, Spanish and Latin,
live shows, or karaoke. Closed
Mon.–Wed.

Flamenco
Café de Chinitas
Calle Torija 7
tel 91 559 5135, Metro: Santo
Domingo, Good, traditional, and
authentic flamenco from 9:30
p.m.; all the greats have played
here. Food (not cheap) and drink
served. Closed Sun.
Candela
Calle del Olmo 2
tel 91 467 3382, Metro: Antón
Martín, This is a cult bar where
flamenco professionals and enthu-
siasts meet. Sessions are held
almost daily; one or more unan-
nounced artists may start singing,
dancing, or playing. Authentic.
Cardamomo
Calle Echegaray 15
tel 91 369 0757, Metro: Sevilla
New, young flamenco in a bar-like
setting, with interesting programming. At the Cardamomo sessions
every Wednesday evening, recognized flamenco artists mix their
art with jazz and pop.
Corral de la Morería
Calle Morería 17
tel 91 365 8446, Metro: Ópera

Open since 1956 and once frequented by Frank Sinatra and Ava Gardner. From 9:30 p.m.

La Soleá
Calle Cava Baja 34
tel 91 365 5264 , Metro: La Latina
A classic Madrileño Gypsy joint, sometimes enlivened by the unforeseen intervention of artists moved to join in. Entrance fee includes a drink.

Taberna Casa Patas
Calle Cañizares 10
tel 91 369 0496, Metro: Antón Martín
Top flamenco singers, dancers, and guitarists perform here. Reservations needed. Try the bull meat. Closed Sun.

Opera & Classical Music
Auditorio Nacional de Música
Calle Príncipe de Vergara 146 tel 91 337 0140, Metro: Cruz de Rayo
Classical music.

Teatro Monumental
Calle Atocha 65
tel 91 429 8119, Metro: Antón Martín
Classical music is the norm here but occasional one-off concerts such as flamenco.

Teatro Real
Plaza de Oriente
tel 91 516 0606, Metro: Ópera
The grandest theater in Madrid for opera and ballet.

Teatro de la Zarzuela
Calle Jovellanos 4
tel 91 524 5400, Metro: Banco de España, Sevilla Devoted to zarzuela, the Spanish light opera genre.

Pop, Rock, & Jazz
Berlín Cabaret
Calle Costanilla de San Pedro 11
tel 91 366 2034, Metro: La Latina
Lovely old 1930s-style cabaret joint, recently renovated. Shows during the week as late as 1:30 a.m. On weekends, it becomes a regular bar. No cover. Closed Sun.

El Berlin Jazz Café
Calle Jacometrezo 4
Tel 91 521 5752, Metro: Callao

Live traditional and modern jazz right in the center of town. Closed Sun and Mon.

Clamores
Calle Alburquerque 14
tel 91 445 7938, Metro: Bilbao
Originally a jazz club, now also fusion, flamenco, Latin, and ethnic music. Concerts generally start at 10 p.m. Post-concert jam sessions until 3 a.m. on Fri. & Sat.

Galileo Galilei
Calle Galileo 100
tel 91 534 7557, Metro: Islas Filipinas
A stage mainly for stand-ups and singer-songwriters, but also for poetry readings and other cultural and arts events.

Honky Tonk
Calle Covarrubias 24
tel 91 445 6886, Metro: Alonso Martínez
A classical rock and pop venue, going since the 1980s, all week. Also has a restaurant.

La Boca del Lobo
Calle Echegaray 11
tel 91 429 7013, Metro: Sevilla
Music, film shows, and theater. Music is varied: rock, Spanish, ethnic, reggae. Gigs start at 10:30 or 11 p.m. Closed Sun.–Tues.

La Sala
Avenida Nuestra Señora de Fátima 42
tel 91 525 5444, Metro: Carabanche
This is a big two-story place offering modern Spanish and international music.

Oba Oba
Calle Jacometrezo 4
Metro: Callao
Brazilian joint with live weekend concerts, often with Brazilian artists, and lively all week.

Populart
Calle Huertas 2
tel 91 429 8407, Metro: Antón Martín
Live jazz from 11 p.m. Free entry.

Siroco
Calle San Dimas 3
tel 91 593 3070, Metro: San Bernardo
Small, with two floors, one with

concerts, and one with quiet music. Closed Sun.–Wed.

Theater
A good place to catch Madrid-style theater is at Madrid's Theater Festival, running from late October to the end of November, featuring all forms of theater, including dance.

Cuarta Pared
Calle Ercilla 17
tel 91 517 2317, Metro: Embajadores
Contemporary theater. Children's programming on Sundays.

El Canto de la Cabra
Calle San Gregorio 8
tel 91 310 4222, Metro: Chueca
Popular, modern, and experimental theater.

Teatro Abadía
Calle Fernández de los Ríos 42
tel 91 448 1627, Metro: Quevedo
A mix of classical and modern theater, dance, and musicals.

Teatro Alfil
Calle del Pez 10
tel 91 521 4541, Metro: Noviciado
A popular venue for stand-up comics, mainly Spanish.

Teatro Calderón
Calle Atocha 18
tel 91 429 5890, Metro: Tirso de Molina
The biggest theater in Madrid, with more than 2,000 seats. Big musical productions.

Teatro de Bellas Artes
Calle Marqués de Casa Riera 2
tel 91 532 4437, Metro: Banco de España
Classical theater.

Teatro Pavón
Calle Embajadores 9 (Plaza de Cascorro)
tel 91 528 2819, Metro: La Latina
A beautifully restored *modernista* theater, currently housing the Compañía Nacional de Teatro Clásico while that company waits for restoration work to be finished on the Teatro de la Comedia in 2009-2010.

LANGUAGE GUIDE

Useful Words & Phrases

excuse me *perdón*
hello *hola*
good-bye *adios*
please *por favor*
thank you *gracias*
you're welcome *de nada*
good morning *buenos días*
good afternoon/evening *buenas tardes*
good night *buenas noches*
today *hoy*
yesterday *ayer*
tomorrow *mañana*
now *ahora*
later *más tarde*
this morning *esta mañana*
this afternoon/this evening *esta tarde*
Do you speak English? *¿Habla inglés?*
I am American *Yo soy norteamericano/a*
I don't understand *No entiendo*
where is...? *dónde está ...?*
I don't know *No sé*
at what time? *¿A qué hora?*
when? *¿Cuándo?*
Do you have...? *¿Tiene...?*
a single room *una habitación individual*
a double room (double bed) *una habitación doble (con cama de matrimonio)*
for one night *para una noche*
I need a doctor/dentist *Necesito un médico/dentista*
Can you help me? *¿Me puede ayudar?*
hospital *hospital*
police station *comisaría de policía*
I'd like *Me gustaría*
How much is it? *¿Cuánto es?*
Do you accept credit cards? *¿Aceptan tarjetas de crédito?*
cheap *barato*
expensive *caro*
post office *correos*
visitor information center *oficina de turismo*
open *abierto*
closed *cerrado*
every day *todos los días*

MENU READER

desayuno breakfast
almuerzo/la comida lunch
cena dinner
me gustaría pedir I'd like to order
¿Está incluido el servicio? Is service included?
carta menu
menú del día fixed-priced three-course meal including a drink
a la carta Ordering anything other than menú del día
carta de vinos wine list
la cuenta the check
cubiertos knives and forks
a la parrilla grilled
a la plancha grilled on a hotplate
ahumado smoked
crudo raw
estofado stew
el pan bread
frito fried
horno oven
empanada savory pastry
ración portion, helping
tapa small snack taken with a drink
tortilla Spanish omelette made with potatoes

Beverages & Condiments

un agua mineral mineral water
    sin gas still
    con gas sparkling
el azúcar sugar
un café americano large black coffee
un café con leche large white coffee
un café descafeinado decaffeinated coffee
un café solo short black coffee/espresso
una cerveza beer
la leche milk
la sal salt
un té tea
un vino blanco white wine
un vino tinto red wine
un zumo de naranja orange juice

Meat & Poultry

callos tripe
cerdo pork
chorizo spicy sausage
conejo rabbit
cordero lamb
jamón ham
lomo loin (usually of pork)
pato duck
pavo turkey
perdiz partridge
pollo chicken
salchicha sausage
ternera beef

Seafood

almejas clams
atún tuna
calamares squid
camarones shrimp
cangrejo crab
chipirones small squid
gambas shrimp
langosta lobster
lenguado sole
lubina sea bass
mejillones mussels
merluza hake
ostra oyster
pescadilla whiting
rape monkfish
vieira scallop

Vegetables

alcachofa artichoke
arroz rice
berenjena eggplant
calabacín zucchini
cebolla onion
champiñones mushrooms
col cabbage
espárragos asparagus
espinacas spinach
guisantes peas
habas broad beans
judías beans
lechuga lettuce
patatas fritas fried potatoes
pepino cucumber
puerro leek
seta wild mushroom
zanahoria carrot

Fruit

albaricoque apricot
cereza cherry
ciruela plum
frambuesa raspberry
fresa strawberry
limón lemon
mandarina tangerine
manzana apple
melocotón peach
naranja orange
sandía watermelon
uva grape

265

INDEX

Boldface indicates illustrations
CAPS indicates thematic categories.

A

Accidents 240
Agrotourism 219
Airports 235
Aizpuru, Juana de 190
Alcalá de Henares 11, 212, 222, **222**
Alcázar, Segovia **211,** 225
Alcázar, Toledo 215
Almagro 219
Almodóvar, Pedro 50, 100–101
Apartment rentals 95
Aranjuez 220, **220**
Architecture 36–39
ARCO 190–191
Arts 36–43, 46–50, 190–191
Ateneo de Madrid **116,** 117
Atocha train station 100, 171
Ávila 223, **223**
AZCA 189

B

Banco Bilbao Vizcaya Argentaria 94, 176
Banco de España 144
Banco Español de Crédito 94
Banks 239
Barrio de las Letras 110
    map 115
    walk 114–115
Bars **64,** 64–65, 106, 113, 241, 261
Basílica, El Escorial 229–230
Basílica de San Francisco el Grande 66, **66**
Basílica Pontificia de San Miguel 58
Beaches 189
Biblioteca Nacional 177, **177**
Bocadillo 119
Bolsa de Comercio 139
Bosch, Hieronymus 127
Bullfights 16, 17, **44,** 44–45, 192–193, 261
Buses 10, 235, 236–237

C

Café Comercial 119
Café Gijón 119, 176
Cafés **118,** 118–119, 178–179, 241, 261–262
CaixaForum 97, 124, 159, **159**
Calimocho 223
Calle Alcalá **89,** 90, 94–95
Calle Cava Baja 61
Calle Cervantes 116–117
Calle Prado 117
Calle Serrano 183–184
Campo de Criptana 218, **218**
Campo del Moro 77
Capilla de San Isidro **62,** 63
Capilla del Obispo 63
Car rentals 10, 236, 240

Carnaval 193, 234
Casa Alberto 65, 115
Casa de América 145
Casa de Campo 196, 202, 203
Casa de Cisneros 58
Casa de Correos 92–93
Casa de la Panadería 55
Casa de la Villa **57,** 57–58
Casa de las Siete Chimeneas 102
Casa del Labrador, Aranjuez 220
Casa Labra 65
Casa-Museo de Lope de Vega 115, 116–117
Casino de Madrid 94
Catedral, Ávila 223
Catedral, Segovia 225
Catedral, Toledo 214–215, 216, **216**
Centro Cultural Blanquerna 108
Centro Cultural del Conde Duque 196, 210
Cervantes, Miguel de 43, 65, 222
    Don Quixote Country 218–219
    monument **12, 198,** 199
Cervecería Alemana 113
Chapel of Our Lady of Bethlehem 113
Cheese 221
Children's activities 262
Chinchón 221
Chocolaterías 82–83, 261–262
Chueca district 91, 102, 106–107, 191
CHURCHES
    Basílica, El Escorial 229–230
    Basílica de San Francisco el Grande 66, **66**
    Basílica Pontificia de San Miguel 58
    Capilla de San Isidro **62,** 63
    Capilla del Obispo 63
    Catedral, Ávila 223
    Catedral, Segovia 225
    Catedral, Toledo 214–215, 216, **216**
    Chapel of Our Lady of Bethlehem 113
    Convento de las Carboneras 58
    Convento de Santa Teresa, Ávila 223
    Convento de Santo Domingo el Antiguo, Toledo 216–217
    Ermita de San Antonio de la Florida 206
    Iglesia Arzobispal Castrense 59
    Iglesia de Jesús de Medinaceli 16–17, 122
    Iglesia de las Calatravas 95
    Iglesia de las Salesas Reales 102–103, 107
    Iglesia de San Andrés 63
    Iglesia de San Cayetano 121
    Iglesia de San Ginés 88
    Iglesia de San Isidro el Real **37,** 59, 67, **67**
    Iglesia de San José 108
    Iglesia de San Marcos 210
    Iglesia de San Nicolás de los

Servitas 58–59
    Iglesia de San Pascual 176
    Iglesia de San Pedro el Viejo 60, 63
    Iglesia de San Sebastián 113
    Iglesia de Santa Cruz 68
    Iglesia de Santiago 88, **88**
    Nuestra Señora de la Almudena **2–3,** 71, **78,** 78–79
    Real Basílica de Nuestra Señora de Atocha 171–172
    Real Oratorio del Caballero de Gracia 99
    San Antonio de los Alemanes 105, **105**
    suggested dress 239
Churros 82–83
Cinema
    see Movies
Cines Capitol 99
Círculo de Bellas Artes 95, 100
Civil War 33, 134
Climate 234
Clothing
    shopping 258–259
    sizes 238
    suggestions 234, 239
Cocido madrileño 65
Coffee 55
Columbus, Christopher **26,** 27, 177
Congreso de los Diputados 138
Consuegra 219
Contemporary art 190–191
Convento de las Carboneras 58
Convento de las Trinitarias Descalzas 115, 117
Convento de San Plácido 108
Convento de Santa Teresa, Ávila 223
Convento de Santo Domingo el Antiguo, Toledo 216–217
Cooking lessons 141
Corral de Comedias, Alcalá de Henares 222
Corral del Príncipe 112
Crafts 259–260
Credit cards 240, 241
Cuartel General del Ejercito del Aire 210
Cuesta de Claudio Moyano 170
Customs, local 238

D

Dama de Elche (sculpture) 181
Dance 262–263
    ballet **46–47**
    classes 56
    flamenco 46–48, 56, **56,** 262–263
Disabilities, travelers with 240
Discoteques 262
Don Quixote Country **218,** 218–219
Downtown Madrid 89–108
    Banco Bilbao Vizcaya Argentaria 94, 176
    Banco Español de Crédito 94
    Calle Alcalá **89,** 90, 94–95

ILLUSTRATIONS CREDITS

X Tiffany Parisi
Parisi@gwu.edu
Viascio.blogspot.com
772-215-7415